Teaching Reading
Foundations and Strategies

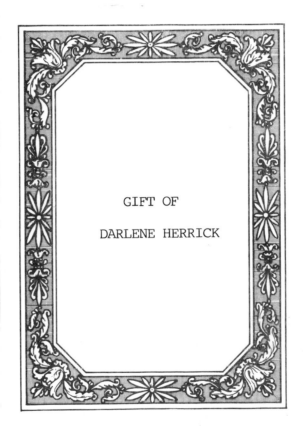

GIFT OF

DARLENE HERRICK

CONTRIBUTORS

Pose Lamb, Purdue University
Emerald Dechant, Fort Hays State College
James L. Laffey, James Madison University
Raymond Morgan, Old Dominion University
Yetta Goodman, University of Arizona
Carolyn Burke, Indiana University
Peggy Ransom, Ball State University
Ronald W. Mitchell, International Reading Association
Bjorn Karlsen, Sonoma State University
Alden J. Moe, Purdue University
Dale D. Johnson, University of Wisconsin
Lloyd Ollila, University of Victoria
Richard Arnold, Purdue University
John Miller, Wichita State University
Frank J. Guszak, University of Texas at Austin
James V. Hoffman, University of Texas at Austin
Carl Smith, Indiana University
Sharon L. Smith, Indiana University
Darryl Strickler, Indiana University
William Eller, State University of New York at Buffalo

Teaching Reading

Foundations and Strategies
Second Edition

Pose Lamb

Richard Arnold

Purdue University

Wadsworth Publishing Company

Belmont, California

A division of Wadsworth, Inc.

Education Editor: Joan Garbutt
Production Editor: Dick Palmer
Copy Editor: Michael Vizzolini

Printed in the United States of America

1 2 3 4 5 6 7 8 9 10—84 83 82 81 80

Library of Congress Cataloging in Publication Data

Main entry under title:

Teaching reading.

    Earlier ed. (c1976) published under title: Reading.
    Includes bibliographies and index.
    1. Reading.   I. Lamb, Pose.   II. Arnold, Richard,
1929–   III. Reading.
LB1050.R4117   1980   372.4'1   80-12519
ISBN 0-534-00847-X

Contents

4 **Language and Psycholinguistic Bases   79**
Yetta Goodman, University of Arizona
Carolyn Burke, Indiana University

PART TWO: STRATEGIES   105

5 **Curriculum and Objectives   107**
Peggy Ransom, Ball State University
Ronald W. Mitchell, International Reading Association

6 **Assessment and Diagnosis of Reading Abilities   133**
Bjorn Karlsen, Sonoma State University

7 | **Current Approaches, Part One   171**
Alden J. Moe, Purdue University
Dale D. Johnson, University of Wisconsin

8 | **Current Approaches, Part Two   205**
Dale D. Johnson, University of Wisconsin
Alden J. Moe, Purdue University

9 | **Preparing the Child   237**
Lloyd Ollila, University of Victoria

13 | **Attitudes and Interests   375**
Darryl Strickler, Indiana University
William Eller, State University of New York at Buffalo

Preface

Scholars agree that progress in understanding and teaching reading will occur only when knowledge from many disciplines is gathered and synthesized. Experts in such disciplines as psychology, linguistics, sociology, and psychometrics are bringing new perspectives to an understanding of the reading process, and teachers of reading are adapting these insights in developing new methods and materials for instruction. It is no longer possible for one person to develop a high level of expertise in all the fields related to reading; thus the editors have asked several authors with demonstrated competencies in specific reading disciplines to contribute chapters to this revised text. The result is *Teaching Reading: Foundations and Strategies,* a text that combines extensive syntheses of information that is basic to reading with discussions of different methods of reading instruction. *Teaching Reading* is intended as an aid for all who are interested in methods of teaching reading—prospective teachers as well as in-service teachers.

In a book of this type you can expect to find differences in position and emphasis among the contributors. We consider this to be a strength rather than a weakness, since you will be challenged to compare, contrast, and synthesize the various points of view. We believe that every teacher of reading must develop an understanding of the reading process and the principles of reading instruction. In addition, teachers should remain flexible about the needs and capacities of individual pupils. The variety of viewpoints presented here will encourage you to formulate your own theory of reading and help you select appropriate methods and materials for a variety of classroom situations.

The book has been organized to help you attain this goal. Part One, Foundations, is devoted to a discussion of the physical, psychological, sociocultural, and psycholinguistic bases of reading. Included are discussions of:

1. The basic elements of the reading process.
2. The language problems of blacks, Mexican-Americans, American Indians, Puerto Ricans, Appalachians, Cubans, and other minorities, and reading programs designed especially for these groups.
3. The use of diagnostic tools in reading assessment.

The authors of these chapters present the rationale that determines what approach the teacher uses with the pupil. Contrary to some currently popular beliefs, we are convinced that this knowledge is as important as a knowledge of techniques, materials, and direct experience with children.

Part Two, Strategies, is devoted to discussion of reading instruction, including:

1   The organization of a reading curriculum, including both long-term and short-term learning objectives within the context of the school program.
2   Self-actualization and the problems of teacher expectations.
3   The use of teaching assistants and other aides in the classroom.
4   Various approaches to teaching reading, including basal reader approaches, the language-experience approach, individualized instruction, linguistic approaches, programmed materials, computer-assisted instruction, and others.
5   An analysis of the reasons readers prefer certain materials, and suggestions for stimulating interest in reading.
6   A discussion of the various skills required for successful reading of "content area" materials.

Part Two provides the extensive treatment of methods and materials that teachers need to develop a sound, flexible reading curriculum. Thus the organization of this book reflects the two parallel dimensions, the "why" and the "how" of reading.

Each chapter begins with a preview, followed by objectives, which you may use as a self-check to be sure you have understood the main points of the chapter. The reference list at the end of each chapter provides documentation for the text and serves as a guide for further reading. In the second edition references have been updated, and material has been added from several new authors.

For their helpful suggestions in preparing the text, we would like to thank the reviewers of the second edition: Mary Anne Hall, Georgia State University; William G. Herrold, University of North Florida; Bette H. Roberts, Central State University, Edmond, Oklahoma.

Pose Lamb
Richard Arnold

FOUNDATIONS

PREVIEW

Some educators believe that a discussion of reading at the theoretical level is unnecessary, and in the past, many texts on reading instruction omitted such discussions. However, the author of this chapter, Pose Lamb, believes that without a theoretical orientation and a philosophical foundation, a teacher will be directionless and confused in applying principles of reading instruction. In addition, teachers are being asked to justify their instructional practices, so they need to know why they selected the methods and materials they are using.

In this chapter Lamb shows that the teacher's definition of reading will have a significant impact on teaching strategies. She presents several different theoretical viewpoints and their implications for methods of teaching reading. She highlights the theoretical positions by contrasting two divergent viewpoints: one held by some psycholinguists, and the other held by those with strong beliefs in a skills-centered approach to reading. These positions and the resulting implications for reading methods are further discussed in other chapters in the book. You should be aware of the sharp differences in definitions represented, and we hope you will profit from understanding this divergence. While Lamb emphasizes that each position can be justified, she does not suggest that an effective reading program will operate from diverse and sometimes discordant theoretical bases. The best reading program is one in which teachers work together and arrive at some consensus about the process and the instructional implications of a particular view of that process. This chapter provides a framework within which rational decision making in reading programs can occur.

1

Definitions and Beliefs

Pose Lamb, Purdue University

OBJECTIVES

After you have read this chapter, you should be able to:

1. **State two major implications which result from one's definition of reading.**

2. **Select teacher's guides for two current sets of reading materials which reflect contrasting definitions of reading; state the definitions upon which the materials appear to be based.**

3. **Identify two specific teaching techniques which are characteristic of each contrasting definition. Use suggestions from the teacher's guides that accompany the materials chosen for Objective 2.**

4. **Write your own definition of the reading process, and list specific components of the definitions discussed in the chapter.**

What does the term *reading* mean to you? It can be defined in many ways. One reads the expression on another's face. The weather, changes in foliage, and the behavior of birds and squirrels are read for signs of seasonal change. A mother very quickly learns to read her infant's cries, to distinguish a cry of pain from a cry of hunger. So, too, does an infant learn to read a mother's behavior for signals indicating satisfaction, displeasure, or affection. Clocks, calendars, road maps, and wordless picture books are read. In its broadest sense, then, reading can be viewed as a process of discrimination and interpretation, whether or not printed or even oral codes are involved.

While classroom teachers are aware of these facets of the reading process, their central concern is with the printed page, and their goal is helping the learner deal with print with increasing effectiveness, efficiency, and pleasure.

Reading the expression on a person's face and reading a paragraph from a book are processes which have certain common elements. Both involve perception, memory, cognition, and comprehension. The observer must find relationships between the immediate sensory input and previous experience. These relationships, which will be based at least in part on attitude or affect, are ordered, rearranged, and expanded, and some preconceptions may be discarded.

A major difference between reading the expression on a face and reading print is that in the case of print, the code to be cracked is linguistic: words are involved. Printed words are arranged according to certain conventions. In American English, one reads from *left* to *right,* from the *top* of the page to the *bottom,* and from the *front* of a book to the *back.* Furthermore, these words represent, to some degree, the sounds of our language.

A definition of reading that focuses on language—specifically, written language—as the medium of communication is a narrower definition of the term; but it is still by no means specific enough for the classroom teacher, or anyone else seriously concerned about the reading process. Even within this narrower, linguistically oriented context, there is controversy concerning the nature of this process. Although the task is difficult and complex, no teacher should avoid the responsibility of searching for a reasonably satisfactory and practical, although tentative, definition of reading. A definition of reading will give focus and structure to the teaching-learning process.

Two terms frequently used for purposes of contrast in describing the basic components of the reading process are *decoding* and *meaning.* The term *decoding* usually refers to the techniques that a reader uses to relate the printed words on a page to the language sounds these represent. A clear grasp of the relationships between sounds and symbols, operating at an efficient, even automatic level, is obviously essential to the reading process. Decoding skills are not sufficient in themselves, however. Understanding *meaning*—the concepts the words represent—is also necessary. Meaning can be viewed as operating on several levels, from literal comprehension to interpreting, reacting to, and evaluating what has been decoded.

The relationship between these two major components of the reading process has definite instructional implications. If reading is viewed primarily as a decoding process, the reading lesson will be far different from one in which the emphasis is on meaning and comprehension. Different materials will be used, and the questions asked and the tasks required of pupils will also be different. The materials used by a teacher who emphasizes decoding will be prepared and selected with primary concern for the basic word recognition skills pupils develop as they learn to read. Such skills will be presented in a carefully arranged sequence, which the teacher is directed to follow, varying only the rate of presentation while maintaining that sequence in order to avoid gaps in the child's array of reading competencies. In contrast, when meaning and comprehension strategies receive more emphasis, work on decoding skills is supplemented or even replaced by materials designed to cause children to *think about and react to* what they have read. In classrooms where meaning and comprehension are emphasized, experience charts, trade books, newspapers, and appropriate periodicals become basic teaching tools and learning resources.

Most of the questions asked of pupils in the "decoding emphasis" class have answers which are clearly correct or incorrect: the word is *pit,* or *pet,* or *pot.* It is the *pattern* represented—in this case vowel substitution in the consonant-vowel-consonant pattern—rather than word meaning which is stressed. In the classroom where understanding, interpreting, and evaluating receive primary emphasis, the questions asked may not have right or wrong answers. After reading Ezra Jack Keats's *The Snowy Day,* a child might be asked: "Why did Peter put the snowball in his pocket? Do you think he ever knew what happened to it? Do you think he is likely to do something like that again?" In other words, questions are designed to stimulate children's thinking.

It is obviously a gross oversimplification to cite only two extreme viewpoints of the nature of reading and to note the results of operating at one of these two extremes. Ruddell (1974) identifies five types of reading programs, each operating from a slightly different definition of the reading process:

> During the last decade a wide variety of reading-language programs has been developed, and teachers have used these programs in organizational plans ranging from totally individualized efforts to instruction of large numbers of youngsters. These programs can be roughly characterized . . . in the following ways:
>
> 1. Programs emphasizing control of grapheme-phoneme correspondence and letter-sound patterns for decoding and encoding.
> 2. Programs emphasizing language structure (relational meaning) designed to enhance reading-listening comprehension and oral and written expression.
> 3. Programs emphasizing conceptual (lexical meaning), interpretative (semantic interpretation), and problem-solving abilities (cognitive strategies basic to reading-listening comprehension and oral and written expression).
> 4. Programs emphasizing reading-language interests and attitudes (affective mobilizers).
> 5. Programs attempting to integrate the previous components in a systematic manner.[1]

Clearly, few reading programs are limited strictly to either decoding or comprehension skills. Most programs consist of strategies designed to develop both kinds of skills, as well as encourage positive attitudes toward reading. Nevertheless, by observing the materials and methods most frequently and consistently used by a reading teacher, we can gather significant evidence regarding the teacher's operational (if not theoretical) definition of reading. We now *know* that the *teacher* is the key to an effective reading program; and knowledge of the theoretical base combined with a definition of the process being taught, and learned, is a vital part of effective teaching.

MATURATION AND THE READING PROCESS: CHANGING EMPHASES

The teacher concerned with beginning reading instruction will almost certainly place more emphasis upon decoding or relating speech to print than will the teacher of older children. It seems logical to assume that most nine- to twelve-

---

[1] From Robert B. Ruddell, *Reading–Language Instruction: Innovative Practices,* 1974, pp. 116–117. By permission of Prentice–Hall, Inc., Englewood Cliffs, New Jersey.

year-old children have broken the code. They have some concept of letter-sound relationships. The teachers of children in upper elementary and junior high school can and should place more emphasis on interpreting, reacting to, and determining author purpose in what is read. However, the teacher of older children must not ignore those who still need help in basic word analysis skills, just as teachers of young children must not force their pupils to remain at the decoding stage any longer than is necessary.

As Gibson and Levin note, the *qualitative* differences as a reader matures are of tremendous significance to the classroom teacher.

> We can make more firm generalizations about the skilled reading process which have the status of principles and as such tell us where the novice is heading and what we should look for in his behavior to see if he is getting there. The first thing to emphasize is that reading is an adaptive process. It is active and flexible, the processing strategies changing to meet the demands of the text and the purpose of the reader.
>
> A second major principle is that trend toward increasing economy in the adult reader. This trend breaks down into two important sub-principles. One is that the reader will direct his attention to processing textural material in the most economical way he can.
>
> The second sub-principle states that adaptive reading is character-ized by continual reduction of information (Gibson and Levin, 1975, pp. 481–482).

While the emphasis a teacher places on the various facets of the reading process will vary with the maturity of the student, neither decoding nor com-prehension should be emphasized to the exclusion of the other. Both decod-ing and comprehension are of concern to teachers at all levels, although the emphasis will change as the reader matures. However, the fact that a teacher's understanding of the reading process changes with reference to the maturity of the pupils being taught should not be an excuse for devoting less attention to the teaching of reading with older children. Very few adults have reached full maturity in the reading process; most could profit by further developing flexibility in rate, selective retention of major points, and those skills loosely, but significantly, categorized as critical reading skills.

Briefly, then, the writer believes that teachers must work toward a defini-tion of reading that is consistent with their beliefs about children and youth, is consonant with their understanding of how children acquire language, and is a definition based on comprehension of the intimate relationship between thought, language, and that use of language we call reading.

Working toward a practical, rational definition of reading is important because a teacher's concept of reading strongly influences the teaching mate-rials selected and the manner in which these will be used. Smith, Otto and Hansen have said it very well:

> If teachers are to formulate classroom practices that reflect the best knowl-edge that we have about how reading occurs and is taught, then they must understand the emerging theories and must participate actively in the dialogue and debate that occurs as different theories collide.

A teachers' careful understanding of theory is also required by the need for order and system in pedagogy. Although teaching is an art and learning only a partially understood mystery, theory provides the important patterns for an artist's decision (Smith, Otto, and Hansen, 1978, pp. 17–18).

VARIOUS WAYS OF VIEWING THE READING PROCESS

One's definition of reading should not remain static. An effective teacher is constantly growing, stretching, and learning in this area as in other areas. Furthermore, an alert teacher will quickly discover that authors who write textbooks on reading or articles for journals do *not* agree on what reading is, or what facets of the reading process should be emphasized at various levels of a child's development. Edmund B. Huey wrote in 1908 that:

> . . . to completely analyze what we do when we read would indeed be the acme of a psychologist's achievements, for it would describe very many of the most intricate workings of the human mind as well as unravel the tangled story of the most remarkable specific performance that civilization has learned in all its history (p. 6).

Although the process is indeed difficult to analyze—even to fully comprehend—the search for a definition of the reading process is *very* important. It results in growth on the part of the teacher and a more effective program for children.

For purposes of sharp contrast, the definitions of reading provided by Russell Stauffer (1969) and Leonard Bloomfield (1961) might be examined. According to Clarence Barnhart, Bloomfield believed that "Reading involves nothing more than the correlation of a sound image with its corresponding visual image, that is, the spelling" (Bloomfield and Barnhart, *Let's Read,* jacket cover).

Russell Stauffer is in almost complete disagreement with Bloomfield. He writes in *Directing Reading Maturity as a Cognitive Process:*

> . . . reading is a mental process requiring accurate word recognition, ability to call to mind particular meanings, and ability to shift or reassociate meanings—until the constructs or concepts presented are clearly grasped, critically evaluated, accepted and applied or rejected. This means that knowledge gained through reading can increase understanding and, in turn, influence social and personal adjustment, enrich experience, and stimulate thinking (p. 16).

Stauffer includes the *uses* of reading in his definition; Bloomfield does not.

Arthur Heilman (1977) notes that reading is a complicated process, and difficult to define, like ". . . love, salvation, democracy and intelligence" (p. 6). However, he proposes the following general definition: "Reading is interacting with language that has been coded into print. The uncontrolled variable is the degree of interaction that is posited" (p. 5). It is interesting to note that he believes that "In some cases, reading may involve getting the meaning. This is likely to occur only occasionally . . ." (p. 5).

Harris and Sipay (1979) attach much more significance to meaning. They write: "Reading may be defined as the attaining of meaning as a result of the interplay between perceptions of graphic symbols that represent language, and the memory traces of the reader's past verbal and non-verbal experiences" (p. 27).

If getting the author's meaning, insofar as this is possible, is *not* central to the reading process, one might well ask, "Why bother?"

George and Evelyn Spache (1977) write:

> A process that we stress throughout the student's entire school career obviously cannot be a simple act. Reading changes from what is primarily considered word recognition, through development of sight and meaning vocabulary and several methods of word attack, through different types and degrees of comprehension, to a mature act involving most of the higher mental processes. Because of its complexity and the many stages of development, it is apparent that one definition will not suffice. For these reasons we will describe or define reading in a variety of ways (p. 4).

They suggest eight different viewpoints of the reading process:

1   Reading as Skill Development: "The reader directs his attention to the printed word with his mind intent on meaning. He reacts to each word with a group of mental associations regarding the word form, its meaning and its sound. With the aid of these associations, he discriminates this word from all others . . ." (p. 4). It is possible that these various skills might be separated for purposes of isolated drill, to the potential detriment of the child's reading achievement. This view of reading has some clear and significant limitations.

2   Reading as a Visual Act: "Reading is first of all a visual act and it cannot be taught soundly if the functions of the eye are not understood" (p. 7). While such an understanding may be valuable, one wonders if it is reasonable to expect classroom teachers to also be vision specialists.

3   Reading as a Perceptual Act: It involves ". . . the stimulus of the printed word, the processes of recognizing this word and attributing meaning to it, based upon the reader's experiences" (p. 12). It is important for classroom teachers to recognize that the perception of the same stimulus will elicit different responses in different pupils. A picture of an ocean elicits one response from a child who lives on the Atlantic shore, another from the child raised on or near a desert. Perceptions of words, phrases and sentences will also vary.

4   Reading and Language: Here the Spaches discuss the influence on reading achievement of variant dialects and learning to read when English is a second language. They conclude, as most writers do on this topic, that the problem is not the dialect or language, but teachers' attitudes toward pupils who are "different." Hopefully, these attitudes are gradually changing.

5 Reading as a Reflection of Cultural Background: "Reading differs in its purposes, breadth and quality among societies as well as among social classes within societies" (pp. 19–20). According to the Spaches, some of the influencing factors on the quality and quantity of reading are education, cultural interests, income level, family stability, and vocational adjustment.

6 Reading as a psycholinguistic process: ". . . the reader uses the graphic cues of letters, the semantic cues of word meanings, and the syntactic cues of word order to obtain the message of the selection" (p. 24).

7 Reading as Information Processing: "Reading is conceived of as a visual scanning directed by the child's general information store (or long-term memory, as it is called) and the information derived from the material being read (which is temporarily stored in short-term memory). According to this concept of reading, new material is assimilated into past experiences of related nature . . ." (p. 27).

8 Reading as Associational Learning: ". . . reading is not a single stage process of simply looking at a word and pronouncing it. First there are the properties of the stimulus of letters and words. The child must discriminate among these stimuli and gradually acquire responses. These associations must be reinforced by a number of means . . ." (p. 30). The Spaches note that this view of reading ". . . does not encompass all facets of the reading process but rather is pertinent largely to word recognition" (p. 30).

Kenneth Goodman emphasizes the role of language in the reading process. In *Reading: A Psycholinguistic Guessing Game,* Goodman writes:

> Reading is a selective process. It involves partial use of available minimal language cues selected from perceptual input on the basis of the reader's expectation. As this partial information is processed, tentative decisions are made to be confirmed, rejected, or refined as reading progresses. More simply stated, reading is a psycholinguistic guessing game. It involves an interaction between thought and language. Efficient reading does not result from precise perception and identification of all elements, but from skill in selecting the fewest, most productive cues necessary to produce guesses which are right the first time. The ability to anticipate that which has not been seen, of course, is vital in reading, just as the ability to anticipate what has not yet been heard is vital in listening (p. 260).

Theodore Clymer (1967), the senior author of a major publisher's basal reading series, approaches a definition of reading by citing four major "aspects" of the reading process. The reader's first task, he says, is decoding the author's message. The reader's next task is understanding the author's message. Unless the reader has been involved in both the decoding and understanding processes, reading has not occurred.

The third aspect of reading, according to Clymer, is interpretation and critical evaluation of the author's message into one's own behavior. One might question whether the evaluative and incorporative stages are always present. Does one invariably evaluate the accuracy of the printed directions on a dress pattern, a recipe, or an interstate highway sign? It is probably true that some visually-processed information is accepted rather uncritically. One might also question the extent to which a reader's behavior changes as a result of evaluating material already read. Try to recall the last book you read which profoundly, or even minimally, changed your beliefs or overt behavior. If such change occurs, it is probably both gradual and cumulative. Few readers incorporate even an author's direct messages into their behavior. It seems a bit naive to assume that voters' decisions are greatly influenced by newspaper editorials, or that everyone who reads the Surgeon General's warning on a pack of cigarettes stops smoking.

Thus, while decoding and understanding appear to be fundamental to the reading process, evaluation and incorporation may occur less commonly. The fact that readers too seldom evaluate or incorporate material which has been read may well represent a serious indictment of reading instruction designed for older children and adolescents. As has been noted before, reading instruction should not be concluded when pupils have acquired basic word analysis and comprehension skills. In a more recent publication (1968) Clymer writes:

> Most educators with special interest in reading assign relatively broad goals or outcomes to reading instruction. The implied principle seems to be that, if reading instruction can make an important contribution to an outcome, even if it is not necessarily a unique contribution, the outcome is a legitimate objective of the reading program. This view places a broad range of outcomes within the province of the reading program.
>
> What are the outcomes or goals which are customarily assigned to reading and how much agreement on these goals does the literature reveal? The answer to this question is not easily obtained. While the following statements may be oversimplified, it seems that four relatively separate but major outcomes of the reading program can be listed. . . . The four outcomes might be listed as: (a) decoding, which corresponds to . . . "word perception"; (b) grasping the author's meaning . . . "literal interpretation"; (c) testing and recombining the author's message with the understanding and background of the reader; (d) application of ideas and values to decisions and actions and extension of author's ideas to new settings.
>
> These outcomes differ greatly in their complexity, with decoding the least complex application and extension the most complex. The characteristic of complexity seems to bear a direct relationship to the agreement in the literature that the outcome is a legitimate concern of the reading program. The less complex the outcome, the more general is the agreement in the literature on its inclusion as an objective for reading. The broad goals are often excluded from the reading program by some specialists such as linguists, psychologists, and others.
>
> The lack of definite information on all factors should not obscure one fact of enormous importance to teachers and educators: Our definition of reading and the outcomes we hold for the reading program have immediate and important implications for how we teach reading and what we

teach in it. There is no question more important to ask than: "What is reading?" (pp. 27–29).

IMPLICATIONS FOR THE TEACHER

What difference does all of this make? Should the teacher be advised just to teach, without a clear-cut definition of reading, but following certain commonly accepted principles and practices, such as individualized instruction, a flexible program, and continuous diagnosis? This is, of course, much easier than struggling to develop a rational, theoretically sound, yet practical definition. But can the issue be avoided so easily? One's beliefs do make a difference. If a teacher operates primarily from a decoding framework, then learning is viewed in narrow terms. Specific facets of cognitive development may be neglected while others are stressed, and the affective domain may be de-emphasized or even ignored.

If, on the other hand, the teacher operates basically from a "meaning" framework, the child may never develop the fundamental word recognition skills he needs for independence in reading. Maturity in reading clearly involves the ability to relate printed words to speech and to the concepts represented by speech.

You'll recall the definition of reading provided by Goodman in a 1970 publication; he has more recently defined reading as follows:

> Reading is a receptive language process. It is a psycholinguistic process in that it starts with a linguistic surface representation encoded by a writer and ends with meaning which the reader constructs. There is thus an essential interaction between language and thought in reading. The writer encodes thought as language and the reader decodes language as thought (Goodman, 1978, pp. 19–20).

Goodman, whose miscue analysis work is discussed in some detail in Chapter Four, believes that oral reading provides the most useful, and valid, data on the nature of the reading process. Researchers and classroom teachers learn a great deal about the reading process, and a child's place in this process, by listening to the oral reading of new material, and noting the strengths and weaknesses this reading reveals. The data gathered can be used diagnostically and form the basis for the instructional program. Obviously, reading programs would not be identical; therefore the teacher must be a careful listener and observer and possess the organizational skills and competence necessary to make such an individualized program really effective.

Psycholinguists tend to favor an analytic *whole-word* approach to word recognition and view a hierarchy of skills, as listed in most basal readers, as unnecessary, without an empirical base and inappropriate when applied to individual readers. In his recent book, *Developmental Reading: A Psycholinguistic Perspective,* Daniel Hittleman writes: "Of the three traditional word recognition categories, two, phonics and structural analysis are of questionable value as they are usually taught. . . . Normal reading does not involve decoding. We do not understand words on the basis of their sounds, rather we attend to the meaning of the spelling patterns of the words" (Hittleman, 1978, p. 293). Some children do, in fact, learn to read without proceeding through every step specified in some of the competency based reading programs. It is possible that drill in sound–symbol relationship may be more important for some children than for others.

Although there probably is not a *method* of teaching reading which is espoused by psycholinguists, they have been identified with the language-experience approach for the initial stages of reading instruction. In this approach—which is discussed in detail in Chapter Eight—the major instructional materials are created by children themselves, and skills are taught as the teacher sees the opportunity, and need, to teach them. For older pupils, an individualized reading program is consistent with psycholinguists' views. Children select their own reading materials, usually library or trade books rather than basal readers. This approach is also discussed in some detail in Chapter Eight.

Cooper and Petrosky (1976) have noted a psycholinguistic base for the Neurological Impress Method of teaching reading, in which all sensory systems are coordinated in responding to print. That is, oral reading by the teacher and pupil, in unison, is supported by visual kinesthetic tactile feedback. The combination of oral and visual responses to print impresses a few psycholinguists, apparently, as being a more holistic and naturalistic way of learning to read. Unfortunately, the results of the First Grade Studies—and most studies recently conducted (Lamb, 1978)—do not give clear positive support to this, or any other method of organizing for reading instruction.

La Berge and Samuels (1976) view reading very differently; theirs has been termed an information processing view; the Spaches, you'll recall, viewed it as an example of associational learning. At the first stage, the reader selects relevant distinctive features.

> The rate of learning to select the appropriate features of a pattern may be quite slow the first time a child is given letters to discriminate. However, after a child has experienced several discrimination tasks, he may develop strategies of visual search which permit him to move through this first stage of perceptual learning at an increasingly rapid rate (p. 554).

In Samuel's view, efficient reading has the characteristic of speed so rapid as to be termed automatic. At stage two *unit codes* are formed from the discriminated features. Not only are letters processed this way, but so are spelling patterns and words. With practice, this process also becomes automatic. Samuels claims that automaticity in discriminating elements of the phonological system occurs in a similar fashion. The unitizing can take place in either the visual or the phonological system.

> . . . for the experienced reader, the particular location used is optional. If he is reading easy material at a fast pace, he may select as visual units words or even word groups; if he is reading difficult material at a slow pace, he may select spelling patterns and unitize these into word units at the phonological level (pp. 561–562).

What about meaning? According to La Berge and Samuels, another system, the semantic system, is elicited by the connection between the other two systems. The child's previous experience with speaking and listening is helpful in developing this system to the level of automaticity. In their view, practice is essential in developing automaticity whether the unit is visual (a letter or letters of the alphabet), phonological (sounding spelling patterns), or semantic (adding new meanings to words).

A teacher who is expected to use one or several basals from the adopted series must make a decision regarding the extent to which the explicit instructions in the guide will be followed. These suggestions are frequently based upon concepts of the reading process which assume a hierarchy of skills, each of which is considered essential to effective and proficient reading. If a teacher's definition of the reading process does *not* include the concept of such a hierarchy, or if the hierarchy is different, the basal will assume a different role, and so will the other materials children read. These materials are sometimes termed "supplementary." The teacher must decide how important letter recognition is, and whether or not every phonics generalization stressed in the primary level basal is essential (or even useful). Are there essential reading and prereading skills? If so, how many? What is the appropriate role of drill? If automaticity, at least in responding to phonological, graphemic and syntactic patterns, is desirable, can this goal be achieved without conveying the impression that meaning is less important? The decision to use a basal reader, and even more significantly, the decision to follow rather carefully the scope and skills sequence developed by the authors and publishers of the series implies the acceptance of some fundamental beliefs about the reading process: a definition of reading.

If the language experience approach is selected, or an individualized reading program emphasizing trade or library books (rather than basals) is utilized, a definition of reading is also clearly implied. Some questions can be (need to be) raised about this definition as well. Would most children learn to read, without much instruction, as easily as they learn to talk? Is reading, in fact, a natural extension of speaking and listening? Is it reasonable to expect a teacher, who is responsible for many, many very different pupils, to know the skills, even somewhat limited in number and not sequentially ordered, which each child needs and correctly assess the appropriate time and strategy for teaching these skills?

If reading comprehension is important, does one wait until a solid foundation of word recognition skills has been established before teaching the important elements of understanding and responding to print? If "reading is thinking" can reading comprehension, in fact, be *taught* at all? Perhaps the best one can hope for is the arrangement of a facilitative climate for thinking about what one is reading and has read.

Whether the issue is as broad as the use of a basal reader or trade books, or as specific as the size of the decoding unit to be dealt with (letter, graphemic pattern, word, phrase or sentence), it will be resolved largely on the basis of one's view of the reading process and one's definition of reading. It is the professional obligation of each teacher to develop a sound definition based on the best data available, then subject this definition to continuous scrutiny and use the definition in making the important decisions about materials and teaching strategies every teacher must make. The fact that viewpoints of the reading process conflict, that we don't have definitive answers to the questions raised in this section of the chapter, and that one's views are almost certain to change with new knowledge and experience, should not deter a teacher who wants to be an effective teacher of reading.

SUMMARY

The process of answering the question "What is reading?" is more than an intellectual exercise. One's beliefs about reading and the way one conceives of the reading process strongly influence the methods and materials one uses in teaching. It follows that a teacher's definition of reading will influence the type of reader a pupil becomes. It is not an accident that over-analytic readers— readers who isolate sounds, apply unnatural pitch and stress patterns, and have difficulty blending sounds into something resembling natural speech— consistently come from the same teachers' classrooms. Children have been taught to read this way. Children from other classrooms may consistently demonstrate positive attitudes toward reading but have inadequate decoding or word recognition skills. These conditions are also the result of learning. Furthermore, although we currently know little about the relationship, one's learning style probably has some impact upon whether psycholinguistic or more highly structured approaches will be more effective. Teaching style is another factor which probably should be considered.

As teachers learn more about the complex process of reading, their definition of reading should change. Such growth occurs as one studies the reading process, as one learns more about language and the development of the cognitive processes, and as one studies and learns more about children.

It seems clear that reading is not the same at all stages of development. Reading for a six-year-old is not quite the same process as it is for a ten- or a sixteen-year-old. One's definition should account for this.

It may appear to the reader that the theoretical positions and the definitions discussed in this chapter are unduly complex and difficult to interpret. The process of reacting to these positions and evaluating them, should result in more thoughtful, objective teaching and rational answers to the questions raised.

REFERENCES

Bloomfield, L., and Barnhart, C. *Let's Read: A Linguistic Approach.* Detroit: Wayne State University Press, 1961.

Chall, J., *Learning to Read: The Great Debate.* New York: McGraw-Hill, 1967.

Clymer, T., "What is 'Reading'?" *Elementary School Notes, Language Arts Issue.* Boston: Ginn, 1967.

Clymer, T., "What is 'Reading'?: Some Current Concepts." In *Innovation and Change in Reading Instruction.* 67th Yearbook of the National Society for the Study of Education, edited by Helen M. Robinson. Chicago:

University of Chicago Press, 1968, pp. 27–29.

Cooper, C.R. and Petrosky, A.R., "A Psycholinguistic View of the Fluent Reading Process," *Journal of Reading* 20:184–207 December 1976.

Davis, F.B., ed., *The Literature of Research in Reading with Emphasis on Models.* New Brunswick, N.J.: Rutgers Graduate School of Education, 1971.

Dechant, E.V., *Improving the Teaching of Reading.* Englewood Cliffs, N.J.: Prentice-Hall, 1970.

Fries, C.C., *Linguistics and Reading.* New

York: Holt, Rinehart and Winston, 1962.

Gephart, W.J., *Application of the Convergence Technique to Basic Studies of the Reading Process.* Bloomington, Ind.: Phi Delta Kappa, 1970.

Gibson, E.J. and Levin, H., *The Psychology of Reading,* Cambridge, Mass.: The MIT Press, 1975.

Goodman, K. S., "Reading: A Psycholinguistic Guessing Game," in *Theoretical Models and Processes of Reading,* edited by H. Singer and R.B. Ruddell, Newark, Del.: International Reading Association, 1970.

Goodman, K.S., "The Reading Process" in *Sixth Western Symposium on Learning: Language and Reading,* Sandra Wiley and J.C. Towner, eds. Bellingham: Western Washington State College, 1975.

Harris, A.J., and Sipay, E.R., *How to Teach Reading,* New York: Longman, 1979.

Heilman, A.W., *Principles and Practices of Teaching Reading,* Fourth Edition, Columbus, Ohio: Charles E. Merrill, 1977.

Hittleman, D., *Developmental Reading: A Psycholinguistic Perspective,* Chicago: Rand McNally, 1978.

Huey, E.B., *The Psychology and Pedagogy of Reading,* New York: Macmillan, 1908.

Keats, E.J., *The Snowy Day,* New York: Viking Press, 1962.

La Berge, D., and Samuels, S.J., "Toward a Theory of Automatic Information Processing and Reading" in *Theoretical Models and Processes of Reading,* Second edition, Newark, Del.: International Reading Association, 1976.

Lamb, P.M., *Is There a Data Base to Support the Language Experience Approach?* Unpublished paper presented to IRA Preconvention Institute, Houston, Texas, 1978.

Robeck, M.D., and Wilson, J.A.R., *Psychology of Reading: Foundations of Instruction,* New York: John Wiley, 1974.

Ruddell, R., *Reading-Language Instruction,* Englewood Cliffs, N.J.: Prentice–Hall, 1974.

Ruddell, R.B., and Bacon, H.G., "The Nature of Reading: Language and Meaning" in *Language and Learning to Read: What Teachers Should Know About Language,* edited by R.E. Hodges and E.H. Rudorf, Boston: Houghton Mifflin, 1972.

Singer, H., and Ruddell, R., eds., *Theoretical Models and Processes of Reading,* Second edition, Newark, Del.: International Reading Association, 1976.

Smith, R.J., W. Otto, and L. Hansen, *The School Reading Program,* Boston: Houghton Mifflin Company, 1978.

Spache, G.D., and Spache, E., *Reading in the Elementary School,* Fourth edition, Boston: Allyn and Bacon, 1977.

Stauffer, R.G., *Directing Reading Maturity as a Cognitive Process,* New York: Harper and Row, 1969.

Wier, E., *The Loner,* New York: David McKay, 1963.

PREVIEW

In this chapter Emerald Dechant continues and expands the discussion of theories and models of reading initiated in Chapter One. His focus is primarily upon the psychological contributions to a theory of reading, and he discusses several of the most important models. This discussion is prefaced by comments on the physiology of reading, the sign system, language structures, and the psychology of cognition. Dechant places theories of reading within a comprehensive theory of child development.

Dechant's treatment of the psychological bases of reading represents a new synthesis of some recent contributions of cognitive psychology and psycholinguistics. This chapter reflects many of the viewpoints regarding the interdisciplinary convergence on the reading process today.

2

Psychological Bases

Emerald Dechant, Fort Hays State College

OBJECTIVES

After you have read this chapter, you should be able to:

1. **Describe the theories of the reading process discussed by the author.**
2. **Describe the relationship between cognition and perception, as these relate to reading.**
3. **Compare and contrast the cue systems in reading.**
4. **Compare and contrast two of the models of the reading process discussed in the chapter.**
5. **List and discuss the most significant physiological limitations which can inhibit success in reading.**

Reading is an exceedingly complex process and specialized skill. It is a type of human behavior that should be studied and analyzed by psychologists, but perhaps because it is a form of behavior that is not directly observable, it has not been given the attention by learning theorists that it deserves. For this reason, Kingston (1968) feels that at present a systematic, well-formulated psychology of reading does not exist and that what is available is inadequately structured to be of much value to the classroom teacher.

Psychology has nonetheless had a profound effect on such concepts as readiness, developmental reading, practice, sensation, and evaluation of student progress, and on our understanding of perception, cognition, and learning.

Kingston (1968) keynotes the purpose of this chapter. He notes that a major contribution of psychology to reading is to provide the impetus needed to develop a more adequate theory of reading. We are on the verge of some significant movement in this direction.

Reading is a *language* and *communication process*. It is the process of putting the reader in contact with the ideas of the writer as expressed through the symbols of written language. The nature of the reading process will become clearer as this chapter develops. Here let us comment briefly upon three aspects: the sign system in reading, the decoding process, and the role that language structures play in decoding. Our reason for doing so is that reading always involves a sign system—the words or symbols on the printed page; it involves decoding—association of meaning with the symbols; and it involves language structures—a syntax that mediates between the surface structure and meaning.

The Sign System

Reading is a sensory process. The reader must learn to identify and learn to respond to graphic symbols. Reading is a *word-identification* process, and one aspect of the beginning reader's problem is to discover the critical differences between letters and words. He needs to learn the distinctive features of written language. These distinctive features—the visual configuration of the letters—form the raw material of reading (Smith, 1971, p. 4).

For many years, reading research has focused on the skills required for developing quick recognition responses to our alphabetic writing. Research was designed to develop the child's ability to see the significant contrastive features of the separate letters (Cooper, 1965). Research therefore emphasized feature analysis of the written symbols, or the *surface structure* of the language. The reading teacher spent most of his time and energy teaching children to identify letters and words.

Within the space of this chapter, it is impossible even to sample the thousands of studies on the sensory aspects of reading or the many methods of letter and word identification. We can, however, examine the major findings of this research. Studies indicate that eye-movement patterns reflect the maturity that the reader has attained. The poor reader makes extra fixations and regressions while reading a line of print. The studies also clearly indicate that successful methods of word identification generally combine the best of both *surface structure* analysis (letter, sound, or syllable identification) and *deep structure* analysis (identification from context). The beginning reader has to rely on feature analysis much more than the fluent reader because of an inability to make full use of the context information, both syntactic and semantic (Smith, 1971, p. 221). The beginning reader must deduce meaning primarily from surface structure analysis rather than deep structure analysis.

The Importance of Decoding

Theorists and practitioners have been quick to point out that reading is much more than simply recognizing the graphic symbols. It is even more than pronouncing the words on the printed page, or matching the written code with the spoken code. This is *recoding,* but it is not *decoding. Decoding* occurs only when the reader *associates* meaning with the written symbol (Goodman, 1971) and *understands* the meaning that the writer intended. A team of experts, under the sponsorship of the United States Office of Education, has therefore tentatively defined reading as "a term used to refer to an interaction by which meaning *encoded* in visual stimuli by an author becomes meaning in the mind of the reader."

Reading of graphic symbols consists of two processes: the visual process involved in bringing the stimuli to the brain and the mental process involved in interpreting the stimuli after they get to the brain. When the light rays from the printed page hit the retinal cells of the eyes, signals are sent along the optic nerve to the visual centers of the brain. Before this can be called reading, however, the reader must bring *meaning* to the graphic symbol. The critical element in reading often is not what is on the page, but rather what the graphic symbols signify to the reader. So reading might be described as the process of giving the significance intended by the writer to the graphic symbols by relating them to one's own fund of experiences (Dechant, 1970, p. 19).

Reading is thus a *perceptual process* as well as a *conceptual process*. The reader interprets what is read by associating it with past experience. Reading is a process of forming tentative judgments and interpretations, and verifying, correcting, and confirming guesses.

Reading for comprehension is something more than reading for word identification. Smith (1971, p. 4) suggests that it is possible to read for comprehension without actually identifying individual words. He adds (1971, p. 222) that the decoding that the skilled reader performs is not to transform visual symbols into sound, but to transform the visual representation into meaning.

The Importance of
Language Structures

Recently, descriptions of the reading process have broadened to focus on language structures. Birkley (1970), for example, defines reading as "the recognition and perception of language structures as wholes in order to comprehend both the *surface* and *deep meanings* which these structures communicate." This definition will be dealt with in detail later in the chapter; here we will point out only its main emphasis.

The advocates of Birkley's view generally agree on what reading is not. They do not perceive reading as a precise process, consisting of exact, detailed, sequential perception and identification of letters, words, and spelling patterns. They emphasize, rather, the conceptual nature of the reading process—specifically, how meaning is acquired and conveyed through the *deep structures* of language.

Goodman (1967) notes that reading is a selective process, involving partial use of available minimal language clues (graphic, semantic, and syntactic) selected from perceptual input on the basis of the reader's expectation. The reader processes this partial information and confirms, rejects, or refines tentative decisions as reading progresses. Goodman points out that a common misconception is that graphic input is precisely and sequentially recoded as phonological input and then decoded bit by bit. He notes that readers utilize all three kinds of information—graphic, semantic, and syntactic—simultaneously. *Certainly without the graphic input there would be no reading, but the reader uses syntactic and semantic information as well.*

Smith (1971) points out that a fluent reader depends more on cues contained in context than on feature analysis. The reader operates at a *deep structure* level and predicts while reading, sampling the *surface structure* as predictions are tested. When predictions are not confirmed, the reader returns to feature analysis.

Smith (1971, p. 44) does not see reading as a matter of decoding printed symbols into sounds and then extracting meaning from the sounds. He suggests that the fluent reader generally is unable to do this because fluent reading is accomplished too fast for the translation into sound to occur. The decoding that the reader does transforms the graphic symbols directly into meaning. *Decoding is effected through syntax;* syntax mediates between the visual surface structure and meaning (Smith, 1971, p. 222).

Wardhaugh (1969) suggests that a reader discovers meaning by using the visual clues of spelling, knowledge of probabilities of letter and word occurrence, knowledge of context, and syntactic and semantic competence to give a meaningful interpretation to the text. He notes that the reader does not process visual signals just to convert these signals into some kind of covert speech. This conversion is merely the beginning of the process; semantic and syntactic processing are also necessary. In support of his view he points out that one cannot read a foreign language by simply being able to vocalize the print.

THE PSYCHOLOGY OF COGNITION

Because reading obviously requires the association of *meaning* with graphic input, a psychology of reading concerns itself with the nature of perception, cognition, and thinking. It also concerns itself with the role that language plays in thought. Language is a system of responses by which individuals communicate with each other (inter-individual communication). Language is also a system of responses that facilitates thinking and cognition (intra-individual communication).

The Role of Language in Thinking

The close relationship between language and thought has always been acknowledged. The Greek word *logos,* for example, is the symbol for both reason and speech. Kant wrote: "To think is to speak to oneself." Watson (1920) referred to thought as "subvocal use of language." DeLaguna (1929) notes that "If an animal cannot express its thoughts in language, that is because it has no thoughts to express; for thoughts which are not formulated are something less than thoughts." Langer (1948, p. 103) writes: "In language we have the free, accomplished use of symbolism, the record of articulate conceptual thinking; without language there seems to be nothing like explicit thought whatever." Laurita (1973) notes that speech is not merely a by-product of thinking but is also a means of thought.

Implicit speech seems to accompany thinking as well as much reading. Jacobsen (1932) suggests that when a person is imagining an object, the muscles controlling the eyes contract as though it were actually being looked at. When the person imagines performing a muscular act, a contraction occurs in the muscle fibers that would normally be involved in that act. When the person thinks, the muscles of the tongue or upper lip vibrate as if the words were being spoken.

Edfelt (1960), studying the electromyographic records of university students and adults, found that all these people engaged in silent speech while reading. Good readers engaged in less silent speech than poor readers, and the more difficult the material, the more silent speech occurred. This, of course, does not mean that reading without silent speech is impossible. It simply means that in these experiments silent speech was always present. Beginning readers may depend almost totally upon speech; more fluent readers probably depend on it less.

There is little doubt that a certain amount of vocal behavior and lip and tongue movement accompany many thought processes and most reading. Experiments show that students preparing for an examination actually become hoarse after four hours of intensive study. Hebb (1958, pp. 59–60) suggests that some verbal behavior may play a vital role in problem solving. Intensive thought is much more than a simple brain function. He adds (1958, p. 60), however, that sentence construction shows that thought and speech are not entirely the same process. Thought processes run well ahead of our articulations. Van Riper and Butler (1955, p. 100) note that "just as there is an eye-voice span in oral reading, so, too, there is a similar scanning process preceding utterance. Our minds keep looking ahead of our mouths, scanning our memory drums for the words which will be needed." We know that aphasics, although unable to speak, do think and do learn to read. However, it is much more difficult for them to do so.

Even though the evidence shows a close relationship between thought and language and between implicit speech and reading, it is not always necessary to go through the auditory-vocal counterparts of the printed symbol to proceed from graphic symbol to meaning. A beginning reader often uses this technique, although it may be of very little use once reading becomes fluent.

The Psychology of Cognition

Later in this chapter we shall examine the cognitive model in detail. Here we will comment on only one aspect of it: namely, that *perception and cognition always go beyond the information given*.

Since the words on the printed page cannot provide meaning by themselves, the reader must be perceiving something beyond what is seen. The reader must be—and is—using information that is not present to the senses. The reader does not see the object, person, or experience of which the author writes. And yet, while reading, meaning is attributed to the word. Reaction to the printed word is determined by the experiences with the objects or events which the symbol represents. This is what is meant by perception (Hebb, 1958). Perception is a consciousness of the experiences evoked by a symbol.

The cognitive theorist emphasizes that both the external stimulus and the central cerebral process (cognition) determine behavior. There simply is not sufficient information in the external stimulus alone to explain the response of the perceiver. The central cerebral processes bring in past learning experiences which are not present in the immediate stimulus at all. Individuals perceive the world in terms of "what they are" as much as "what it is." William James (1890, p. 103) pointed out years ago that "Whilst part of what we perceive comes through our senses from the object before us, another part always comes . . . out of our head."

Horn (1937) points out that the writer does not really convey ideas to the reader; he merely stimulates the reader to construct them from personal experience. And, the reader who brings the most to the printed page gains the most. Chall (1947) gave an information test on the subject of tuberculosis to about one hundred sixth and eighth graders. She then had them read a selection on tuberculosis and gave them a test on the selection. Those children who already knew the most about tuberculosis also made the best comprehension scores on the reading selection. Chall noted that we read in order to gain experience, and yet it is also true that we get more out of reading if we have more experience.

Emerging from cognitive research is a picture of man as an active and selective information-gatherer who both gains and creates knowledge. The brain is constantly processing information, and incoming information is continually being tested, reformulated, and acted upon in the light of prior experience.

We have further evidence that the learner, the perceiver, or reader interprets incoming data on the basis of rules already stored in the brain (Smith, 1971, p. 81).

Identification and Association

Bruner (1957) notes that readers can recognize words when certain letters are deleted or can recognize missing numbers in a sequence. In the sequence 3, 9, 12, _____, for example, a reader will see that the numbers are multiples of three and realize that the missing number is 15. In the sentence, "George _____ was our first president," the word *Washington* is readily filled in.

Similar examples occur in grammar (Osgood, 1957, p. 87). A singular subject calls for a verb ending in *s* (Jack sits); a time element calls for an appropriate tense (*Today,* I *am* king); a dependent clause calls for an independent clause (If you see him, call me); and the order of words itself is set (The boy sat on the log—the log sat on the boy). Changing the order usually alters the meaning.

Bruner (1957, p. 44) believes that, in situations like the above, the *perceiver learns certain formal schemata that are used to order the probabilistic relationships between the data.* In support of his assumption, Bruner (1957, p. 47) refers to a study by William Hull. Hull found that in learning to spell, the good spellers learned a general "coding system" which permitted them to reconstruct the sequence of letters. Similarly, Bruner notes that while the poor spellers learned words by rote, the good spellers learned a set of rules based on the transitional probabilities that characterize letter sequences in English.

The letters in the language are used in a way that permits us to reconstruct them from what we know about the surrounding letters. The letters follow one another in a predictable order. Some sequences never occur in English; others occur frequently. The letter *q,* for example, is invariably followed by *u*. The chances are rather good that the letter *p* completes the word *com act*—the probability of occurrence of *p* is greater than that of any other letter. Readers often infer missing words or letters from the context.

In the same way, grammatical forms are inferred. The three-year-old is using the context or the transitional probabilities that characterize the English language when using regular endings such as *selled, runned,* or *mans* for the irregular *sold, ran,* or *men,* and so does the first grader who reads *come* as /kōm/. Although linguists still have not adequately constructed the rules of grammar, the child of three and a half knows them (Dechant, 1970, p. 147). Children learn language in a rapid, smooth, and predictable sequence (Ervin and Miller, 1963; Kean and Yamamoto, 1965), indicating that they are equipped biologically both *to use* and *to learn* language (Smith, 1971, p. 49).

Language learning appears to be largely instinctive—a part of our biological inheritance. Any child can learn any of the world's languages because he spontaneously emits the sounds of all languages (Emans, 1973). The acquisition strategy is the same for all babies everywhere in the world (Gunderson, 1973). The child is born ready to speak a language—namely, the babytalk of childhood—which is gradually modified to approximate parental language. It appears to be a systematic trying out of alternative rules, constantly testing them against adult language.

Piaget's work has contributed additional evidence to support the view that basic language skills are innate. He has shown that very little language learning is attributable to imitation. Children's utterances simply do not approximate those of the adults around them. They gradually change their constructions to conform to adult language, but they do this by starting with a language of their own, not by starting from nothing (Smith, 1971, p. 51). Furthermore, the sequence in which they learn language is orderly and systematic and is closely related to physical and motor aspects of development.

The Cue Systems in Reading

It is clear from what we have said so far that many different factors can cue meaning (Smith, Goodman, and Meredith, 1970), factors both outside and inside the reader. Cues inside the reader are basically experience and the innate rules of language; cues outside the reader are cue systems within words, cue systems in the flow of language, and cue systems that are external both to the reader and to the language.

Even though the reader does not necessarily use all the cue systems when reading, instruction in reading must not ignore any of these systems. Reading is message reconstruction, and for the most part comprehension of meaning consists of using all the cues available.

The various cue systems that operate in reading to cue meaning are the following (Smith, Goodman, and Meredith, 1970):

1 Cue systems within words
  a Letter–sound relationships (grapheme-phoneme correspondences)
  b Shape (word configuration or physiognomy)
  c Known little words in new words or comparison of new words to known words

    d Affixes, prefixes, and suffixes
    e Recurrent spelling patterns, phonograms
    f Diacritical marking systems, color coding
    g Legibility factors

2 Cue systems in the flow of language
    a Patterns of word order or function order (subject, predicate)
    b Inflectional endings (*ed, s, es, ing*)
    c Function words (articles, auxiliary verbs, prepositions, conjunctions)
    d Intonation patterns (pitch, stress, juncture)
    e Verbal or grammatical context in which the word or words are placed
    f Redundancy cues (In the sentence, "The boys eat their lunches," there are at least four cues that the subject is plural.)
    g Grammatical and syntactical patterns
    h Punctuation marks

3 Cues external to the reader and to language
    a Pictures, art activities, dramatization, tracing, etc.
    b Prompting (telling the child what the word is)
    c Concrete objects

4 Cues within the reader
    a Language facility (especially innate rules of language)
    b Dialect differences (cultural factors)
    c Physiology (biological–neurological and maturational factors)
    d Learned responses to graphic cues or the perceptual skill of the learner
    e Experiential and socioeconomic background of the learner
    f Intellectual and conceptual development of the learner
    g Physical, social, and emotional factors

The last category (cues within the reader) leads us to a discussion of the developmental process.

THE DEVELOPMENTAL PROCESS

A psychology of reading must be concerned with child development. Reading cannot be completely understood until the perceptual, cognitive, and developmental aspects of living and learning in general are understood.

    A great deal of research has been done on maturational and environmental learning influences. Psychologists have studied intelligence, physical development, sensory development, auditory and visual discrimination, psychomotor abilities, personality, social-emotional adjustment, socioeconomic status, and neurological functioning. In general, we have found that the human system can be programmed in three ways: structurally (genetically and through hereditary endowment); environmentally (by the environment with which it interacts); and by learning processes (Blake, 1970, p. 94). The basic assumption underlying all this research is that reading is a learned process and that learning to read, like all learning, is interrelated with the learner's total growth and development.

There are both biological and environmental determinants of readiness for and achievement in reading. Growth and development are a variable and so is achievement in reading. There is for each child a most teachable moment for learning to read and for the learning of every subsequent reading skill. The teachable moment depends on many developmental factors, especially on those identified above.

The obvious inference we can make from the research is that without adequate maturation children cannot learn to read and without experiences they have nothing from which to learn. The teacher must not, however, overemphasize either maturation or experience. Placing too much emphasis on maturation may lead to useless postponing of what could be learned; on the other hand, too much emphasis on experience may lead to futile attempts at teaching something for which children are not ready. How close the pupils come to attaining their potential, however, depends upon their experiences and the uses they make of them.

Bruner (1962) adds a slightly different dimension when he observes that readiness for learning depends more on our ability to translate ideas into the language and concepts at the age level being taught than on maturation.

Piaget and Cognitive Development

To illustrate how developmental factors relate to reading achievement, let us examine one concept, cognitive development, and restrict the discussion to one psychologist, Piaget, who has probably done the most impressive work in the field of cognitive development. Piaget's model is particularly significant because it supports the linguists' scientific approach to an explanation of the reading process.

Piaget's hypothesis (Avdul, 1974; Piaget, 1969, 1961, 1957, 1952; Inhelder, 1963; Inhelder and Piaget, 1958) is that cognitive development, and by extension the concrete operation of cognition including language development, is "an integrated process of successive equilibrations of cognitive structures, each structure . . . deriving logically and inevitably from the preceding one" (Flavell, 1963). Piaget, positing four interrelated stages of cognitive development, perceived the process of development as structured sequentially. Organisms develop and evolve in a patterned fashion. The process of change is neither cyclic nor linear; it is spiral. In a linear order it is possible to jump over one stage and still get to the next one. According to Piaget, each stage integrates the preceding stage and prepares the way for the following one (Jennings, 1967).

Development is therefore a series of different stages of complex behaviors related in a continuous progression (Svoboda, 1973). The stages are *lawful* in that they are invariant in their developmental sequence from sensorimotor to formal operations; and they are *hierarchical* in that each successive stage is dependent upon prior development and integration of each preceding stage (Laurita, 1973).

Piaget focused his research on cognition, that one function which distinguishes behavior as human. Like other developmental functions, cognition was perceived as developing in a logical, dialectically patterned process. Piaget sees the individual as learning about patterns, growing in knowledge, and building in the mind structures of thought which the Gestaltists believe are innately acquired (Emans, 1973). He suggests that children at different ages have different ways of thinking about the world. The child is perceived as a constructor who acts on the world, not as passive reactor to the environment (Gardner, 1973).

Piaget suggests that mental acts reflect *structives,* or coherent systems of actions that evolve at certain points in a child's development (Gardner, 1973). His cognitive theory starts from the central postulate that motor action is the source from which mental operations emerge (Tuddenham, 1966). Intelligence is born of action; the organism must act to acquire the knowledge that it needs to function in the world.

A second central postulate, as indicated earlier, is that intellectual operations, which are acquired by interaction between the organism and the environment, are acquired in a lawful sequence. Piaget's intent has been more to elucidate the sequence of stages rather than to establish exact age norms for the stages of development.

Sensorimotor Period In the first stage, the *Sensorimotor Period* (from birth to age two), children adapt to their environment and manifest their intelligence through sensorimotor action rather than through symbolic means. This stage carries the child from inborn reflexes to acquired behavior patterns, from a body-centered or self-centered world to an object-centered one. The child's mental activity during this stage consists of establishing relationships between sensory experiences and action by physically manipulating the world. The child's sensorimotor actions on objects and interaction with the environment thus result in knowledge of the perceptual invariants of the environment. The objects perceived tend to remain within even when not in view. If the appropriate linguistic forms are associated with these perceptual invariants, children begin to use these linguistic forms to identify objects and to represent their actions on them. At about twelve months a child can say two words.

Preoperational Period The *Preoperational Period,* from approximately ages two to seven, covers the important period when rapid growth of language occurs. During the *pre-conceptual period* (ages two to four) the child rapidly learns to represent objects and the world by symbolic means such as language and mental images. For example, 50 percent of children age two can identify common objects such as a cup or the parts of the body of a doll. At this age the child can normally repeat two numbers. However, the child tends to orient activities on the basis of appearances. A child is easily misled by what is seen. To a child language is not something apart from objects and experience. The name of the thing inheres in the thing itself. A chair is called a chair; a rocker is something else entirely (Raven and Salzer, 1971). Every event is new. At age four children can repeat a nine- to ten-word sentence and name a variety of objects.

In the latter part of stage two (ages four to seven) the *intuitive period,* children move from nearly total dependence on sensation and perception to the initial stages of logical thought. They can now group objects into classes by noting similarities and differences, but still pay attention to one aspect of an object to the neglect of other aspects. This tendency is termed *centration*. They can form the concept of "fruit," relating "orange" and "apple." They have intuitively learned and use the grammar of the language spoken in their environment. All the parts of speech are used and this vocabulary is transformed into a variety of utterances. They have a vocabulary of from 2,500 to 7,500 words, have learned the physical relationships of time and space, and have some idea of causality. Their causal reasoning, however, is dependent upon perceptions and therefore is often in error because attention is centered on irrelevant or insufficient attributes. For example, they conclude that a narrow, tall glass contains more liquid than a wide, short glass, even though they have seen the same amount of liquid poured from one glass into the other.

Piaget feels that a mental age of four is all that is required to manage reading skills (Furth, 1970), and in fact most children begin learning to read during this period. By age seven, the child is capable of producing simple, active, declarative sentences and can apply inflectional rules. However, the child during this period will still experience difficulty (1) with sounds that occur in the middle or final position of a word; (2) with certain consonant sounds; and (3) with such clusters of consonants as *lfth* (twelfth). The child is gradually consolidating language structures and is just beginning to comprehend the passive construction. A child will seldom use the passive in spontaneous speech (Palermo and Molfese, 1972).

Concrete Operational Period   Beginning about age seven, the *Concrete Operational Period,* children develop the capability of carrying out logical operations. They can classify according to one or more criteria, they can order in a series, and they can number. Because children have developed the logical structure of groups, they can organize cognitive activities much better. They develop some concept of linear measure and weights about age nine. They are less dependent upon their own perceptions and motor actions and show a capacity for reasoning. They can internalize actions that represent physical objects and relationships. For example, a child can use imagination to mentally reverse actions such as breaking a candy bar in half and then mentally putting the parts together. Children also can now make transformations. They will notice that, in pouring liquid from a short glass into a tall glass, nothing is added and nothing has been taken away. They can also transform and manipulate sentences. Such operations suggest that in this period thought and language are freed from dependence upon sensation and perception, but the child's mental activity is still tied to concrete or physical situations or experiences.

Formal Operational Period   During the *Formal Operational Period* (ages about eleven to fifteen) children attain the fourth and mature stage of mental development. They can imagine possible and hypothetical relationships, can intellectually manipulate the purely hypothetical, and can think in terms of formal propositions. They can deal with abstract relationships instead of just with things. Whereas the concrete operational child reasons only from directly observed data, an older counterpart is freed from dependence on directly experienced events and begins to deal with conditional, suppositional, and hypothetical statements and propositions.

Although the sequence of these stages of cognitive development is the same for everyone, not all children pass through the stages of intellectual growth exactly in the same way or exactly at the same rate. As children acquire more experience, their concepts broaden, become clearer, and are hierarchically organized. Concepts are also less egocentric and take on conventional significance. Children pass from a sensorimotor stage, to a preoperational stage, to a concrete operational stage, to a formal operational stage in their own way. As the concepts of individuals become consistent with the concepts of their culture, they can and do communicate more effectively and efficiently.

Children whose experience is more limited, who have less verbal interchange with adults, or who are asked to deal with content that is unfamiliar to them are less likely to attain the *information, linguistic forms,* and *syntax* for organizing and communicating new experiences. Their understanding will not go much deeper than the making of a few verbal associations. Because of some gaps in the materials, in their experience, or in their thinking, they often cannot communicate effectively in certain content areas, even though they have the requisite mental capabilities.

Palermo and Molfese (1972) note that the research data in fact indicate a steady development of linguistic ability from age five to adolescence, with the ages of five to eight and ten to thirteen being special transitional points in which significant development occurs. These are precisely the periods in cognitive development that are reported by Piaget to be transition points from preoperational to concrete to formal operational (between ten and thirteen). It is during these periods that we note large increases in grammatical constructions and high error rates on some constructions.

Because cognition precedes expression in language, and because numerous studies have shown that cognitive development is closely related to reading achievement, it becomes increasingly clear that a theory of language development must be articulated within the larger context of a theory of cognitive development.

THE PHYSIOLOGY OF READING

Reading is a physical act, requiring the reader to respond to graphic symbols. Certain physiological factors may prohibit the reader from making the appropriate response:

1   The reader must first *see* and *identify* the words before taking meaning to them. A reader may be inhibited from doing this by inadequate vision; lack of single vision or clear vision, lack of visual coordination or muscular imbalance, restrictions of the visual-information processing system, or tunnel vision.

Tunnel vision occurs because the amount of information that can be picked up in a single glance is limited. There is a limitation on the rate at which information can be processed from a *sensory store* (immediate memory), or from the number of distinctive features required to identify four or five unrelated letters three or four times every second. The *output* from a single fixation may be four or five letters, two unrelated words, or four or five words in a meaningful sequence (Smith, 1971, p. 218).

The simple fact is that the more difficulty a reader experiences with reading, the more the reader must rely on feature analysis. The reader is forced to analyze all the constituents of the surface structure to be able to apply syntactic skills (Smith, 1971, p. 222).

2   The reader must have adequate auditory acuity, auditory discrimination, auditory blending, and auditory comprehension. Inhibitory factors are intensity deafness and tone deafness (as from a conductive hearing loss stemming from a punctured eardrum or a malfunction of the three small bones in the middle ear, or from a nerve loss resulting from an impairment of the auditory nerve). Intensity deafness and tone deafness cause difficulty with sounds represented by *f, v, s, sh, zh, th, t, d, b, p, k,* and *g.* The pupil will have difficulty with phonics and with oral reading.

3   The reader must have adequate neural functioning. Inhibitory factors are brain damage, inadequate development of the brain, lack of (or crossed) cerebral dominance, or lack of neurological organization generally.

Most physiological deficits make it difficult to read fluently and at an appropriate rate. Rate is important apart from its economy because it helps the pupil to comprehend by discovering the syntactic rules.

THEORETICAL MODELS OF READING

Following the lead of Williams (1973), we categorize theoretical models of reading instruction as follows:

1   Taxonomic Models
2   Psychometric Models
3   Psychological Models
   a Behavioral
   b Cognitive
4   Information Processing Models
5   Linguistic Models
   a Early Formulations
   b Transformational–Generative Grammar

Taxonomic Models

Taxonomic (classification) models identify the basic skills needed for successful reading. Gray (1950, 1960) gives a purely descriptive model. He describes reading as consisting of four skills: word perception, comprehension, reaction, and assimilation.

Psychometric Models

The statistically-determined models of Holmes (1965) and Singer (1969), constructed by the use of substrata analysis, are designed to determine the combination of hierarchically-organized subsystems that form a working system for attaining speed and power of reading. Models have been developed for college, high school, and elementary levels. The four systems, accounting for 89 percent of the variance in power of reading, are word recognition, word meaning, morphemic analysis, and reasoning in context. Three subtests (reasoning in context, auditory vocabulary–word meaning, and phrase perception discrimination) accounted for 77 percent of the variance in speed of reading.

The model suggests that silent reading ability is divisible into two major interrelated components, speed and power of reading. In changing from speed to power of reading, the reader reorganizes his sets of systems (and subsystems) from emphasizing the visuo-motor perceptual system to one stressing morphemic and word recognition systems.

Psychological Models

Behavioral Learning theories are proper content for a psychology of reading because learning to read is representative of learning in general. Learning theorists have sought to discover and specify the experimental variables that control and determine behavioral changes that occur with practice, experience, or perception, and furthermore they have tried to formulate the functional interrelationships or laws that hold between these variables.

All theorists agree that the observable response is a function of the physical and social world and the condition of the organism. Furthermore, as we observe response, we note changes in response and infer that these are accompanied by certain internal changes. These internal changes or hypothetical learning factors in turn affect present performance. Theorists agree that the character of these internal events is partly determined by the impinging stimulus and partly by various organic states and past experience; they disagree, however, in their conceptions of these hypothetical learning factors.

Learning theories can be divided into Stimulus–Response Theories and Field Theories:

Smith (1971, p. 71) notes that learning to read cannot be explained if only one of the theories of learning is adopted.

The behavioral model holds that all learning is habit formation, a connection between a stimulus and a response. The connection is referred to as an S–R bond. The S–R theorist is focused on the response or the observable action; the learner learns an action or a response. The S–R theorists assert their predilection for conditioning, which to them is the clearest and most simple instance of a response to a stimulus. Learning is defined as the acquisition of new behavior patterns or the changing of behavior either by strengthening or weakening of old patterns as a result of practice or training.

The best contemporary exponent of behaviorism is B. F. Skinner. In Skinnerian terminology, all behavior can be understood, predicted, and controlled in terms of *habits* established or shaped by a process of successive

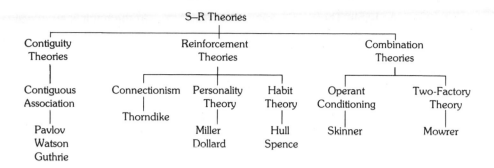

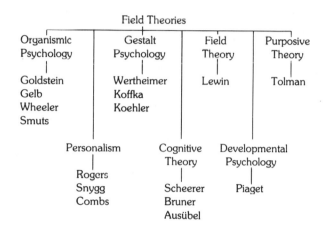

Figure 2.1
Learning Theories

approximation by the reinforcement of a response in the presence of a particular stimulus.

Reinforcement determines whether conditioning in fact takes place. A particular S–R bond will be established only if the organism is reinforced in a particular way while responding in the presence of a stimulus.

The type of conditioning in Skinner's experiments is called *operant conditioning* in contrast to *classical conditioning*. In this type of conditioning, the reinforcement occurs after the behavior that is to be conditioned. For Skinner, the behavior had first to be emitted before reinforcement could occur.

The process of setting up the type of behavior that it is desired to reinforce is known as *shaping*. Shaping of behavior does not wait until the learner's response is exactly correct. Operating learning may be quite gradual. At first, it may be necessary to reinforce gross approximations to the final response. Behavior is thus molded into shape by a process of successive approximation. It is through shaping that the very fine discriminations required in reading are produced. Through a process of *chaining*, elaborate sequences of behavior—like those required in reading—are built up.

The behaviorist view explains *why* learning takes place (by reinforcement), and once the habit is established, we find that habits have their own momentum. The very exercise of the habit (reading) reinforces and consolidates the habit. The simple opportunity to engage in the habit is an effective reinforcer (Smith, 1971, pp. 61–66).

Cognitive   Recently, there has been a resurgence of interest in the psychology of cognition, in thinking, and in cognitive styles. Psychologists dealing with this aspect of psychology are grouped into the neobehaviorists (Hebb, Staats), cognitive theorists (Bruner, Ausübel), and the developmentalists (Piaget, Vygotsky).

In *Improving the Teaching of Reading* (Dechant, 1970, pp. 365–374), the author discussed cognitive functioning in detail as the process of moving from percept through perceptual schematism, contextual perception, and perception of differences, to concept and categorization. The course of development of thinking is described as moving from the concrete toward the more decentralized, analytical, and abstract.

The cognitive model, representing as it does the second significant explanation of learning, perceives the learner as a consumer of information (Smith, 1971, pp. 68–79). The cognitive theorists do not believe that language skills can be explained as habits established by the conditioning of S–R bonds. Rather they point out that the reader extracts meaning from what is read on the basis of the visual information (the surface structure of the language) and also on the basis of all the deep structure of language, knowledge, and experiences contained within the brain (Smith, 1971, p. 69). Language and what is read cannot be comprehended unless the reader (listener) makes this critical, active contribution. Therefore, one of the principal tenets of the cognitive theorist is that perception is a constructive process, adding something to the stimulus aspects. Cognition is defined as the integrative activity of the brain, overriding reflex response behavior and freeing behavior from sense dominance (Hebb, 1974). Cognition is the central brain process that determines the reader's particular reaction to graphic symbols.

The cognitive theorist speaks of restructuring perceptions or relationships. The pupil is taught a system of attacking new words, and uses this system to make an insightful response to a new word. A pupil does not have to be conditioned to come up with the correct response. The reaction to a word (perception of meaning) is an indication that the learner has organized experiences in a specific way. The response is a sign that perceptual organization or learning has occurred.

The cognitive theorists emphasize cognitive processes, purposive behavior, and the organizational nature of the learning process. They are interested more in what the child *knows* and *understands* than in what the child *does*. They believe strongly that learning is guided by intervening mental processes which are labelled cognition, thought, or perception. Cognition organizes the incoming sensory data into a meaningful pattern. To the cognitive psychologist, what is interesting is the unobservable manner in which information is acquired and organized by the brain (Smith, 1971, p. 60).

Smith (1971, pp. 68–80) rejects the behaviorist view because:

1   There is no simple correspondence between sound (writing) and meaning.

2 Skill in language production and comprehension cannot have developed through the establishment of S–R bonds because practically all the sentences we speak or read are novel ones.

3 Perception is a constructive process, adding something to the stimulus aspects. A reader extracts meaning on the basis of the visual information (the surface structure of the language) and of the deep structure of the language and the knowledge in the brain. The reader makes decisions on the basis of two kinds of evidence: *current information* received from the environment by a receptor system and the *stored* information that is available in memory. Writing cannot be comprehended unless the reader makes this critical, active contribution. Our fund of knowledge about the world is given a variety of technical names (cognitive schemata, cognitive structures, cognitive maps).

4 Since sentence meaning cannot be determined on a sequential word-by-word basis, information from several printed words has to be held in short-term memory. The load on short-term memory is reduced by "chunking" information into larger units—by storing words rather than letters, or meanings rather than words (Smith, 1971, pp. 78–79).

The cognitive theorist postulates an internal store of information, and distinguishes three stages of memory function:

1 A *sensory store* (or a *visual image*) or *immediate memory* in which the raw material of perception is briefly stored, perhaps for a quarter of a second or more. Information received decays rapidly as new information is taken in.

2 A *short-term memory* in which the information is held while it is being processed. The information is much less than in the sensory store, perhaps no more than four or five items and generally is retained for only a few seconds. A person wanting to make a telephone call often finds that he looks up the number but in the midst of the dialing, forgets it, and has to look it up again. How much is retained depends on *how* it is formed, either single letters, single words, or a related set of words. The learner can also commit the information to long-term memory by repeating the information to himself.

3 A *long-term memory* in which information may be stored permanently.

That a short-term memory and a long-term memory do in fact exist is shown by neural injury. A neural injury often obliterates long-term memory but leaves intact events learned within a fifteen-minute time span prior to the injury. Conversely, electrical stimulation of a surgically exposed brain while a person is awake can cause the individual to remember experiences long thought forgotten. The same thing can happen during hypnosis.

Yanoff (1972) separates the cognitive process into four major functions:

1 *Input* (sensory-motor)
   a The stimulation of the sense organs.
   b Reception and discrimination of the stimulus.

    c Stimulus-redefinition—the passing of accurate messages to the brain.

Cognition begins with appropriate perception, and perception begins with a sensory stimulation.

2 *Integration*

    a Neural excitement—the brain receives electrical impulses, the redefined stimulus, and acts upon it.

    b Imprinting templates—if the incoming data are congruent with previous experiences, or fit previously formed templates, they are assimilated. When *new* templates are formed, the process is termed *accommodation*. Accommodation is a restructuring of concepts that enables the person to assimilate formerly discrepant events (Suchman, 1969). The brain is thus perceived as an information-processing system. A template allows one to record an idea or experience. Templates form the structure of the brain. As data bombard the brain, it either *recalls* previously-formed templates, *connects* previously-formed templates, or *develops* new templates. Templates allow the brain to test and evaluate all incoming data. This makes the brain different from the computer, which can only store data. The brain actually decides which sensations the perceiver will attend to. The creative individual is one who takes existing templates and restructures them. Seeing is only input; visualization combines input and integration.

    c Neural redefinition—the ideas or templates from the brain are redefined as electrical impulses.

3 *Output*

The electrical impulses are carried to the neuromuscular system where they are redefined and exhibited as:

    a Communication—any form of language-based interaction.

    b Product—the construction of an idea.

    c Performance—an exhibition of an ability such as singing a song or giving a speech.

Output is the only measure that we have of cognition, and unfortunately it can never fully represent what has occurred in the integrative process: concepts are lost because we cannot express them; muscular incoordination can keep us from drawing what we have visualized.

4 *Feedback*

    a Reward.

    b Reinforcement.

    c Self-evaluation of the information.

Feedback is the recycling of a person's thinking. The effect of the output is fed back into the system as input. When a person sings, hearing is the feedback, and singing is adjusted according to what is heard. Feedback fixes the template. Reward and reinforcement are feedback that strengthen the tendency for a particular response to follow a specific stimulus. The major feedback agent is the person's self-evaluation of the information—it permits constantly tested information.

Information Processing Models

One of the best descriptions of reading as information processing is offered by Smith (1971, pp. 12–27).

A key principle in the psychology of reading is that reading is a communications process, and the purpose of all communication is the sharing of meanings. Reading takes place only when the reader shares the ideas that the writer intends to convey. Writing has no purpose without a reader. The graphic symbol must carry the burden of meaning between the communicator and the receiver of the communication. For this reason a knowledge of theories of communication and information and signal detection theory are relevant to a study of the psychology of reading. The terminology of communication theory is especially useful in describing a theory of reading. Two points stand out:

1 Reading is an active process—the reader must make an active contribution to the information-seeking process. In fact, the information acquired by a receiver is much more than is actually present in the physical representation of that information in the form of graphic symbols.
2 All information acquisition in reading, from the identification of individual letters or words to the comprehension of a passage, is a reduction of uncertainty.

Terms from communication theory that have special significance in understanding reading are: *communication channel, limited channel capacity, noise, information,* and *redundancy.*

Communication Channel   The writer (transmitter) and the reader (receiver) are two ends of a *communication channel* along which information flows. As a message passes through the communication channel, it takes on a variety of forms. At each part of the communication process, it is possible that the message will be changed in some way.

Limited Channel Capacity   Just as in a communication system, there also is a *limited channel capacity* in the communication system of the reader. There is a limit to the speed at which the eye can travel over a passage of text making information-gathering fixations and to the amount of information that can be acquired in a single fixation.

Noise   A message or communication may be confused or made less clear by extraneous signals called *noise*. Because all communication channels have limited capacities, noise may overload the system and prevent the transmission of informative signals. In reading, noise may be a type face that is difficult to read, poor illumination, or distraction of the reader's attention. Smith (1971, p. 16) notes that because of noise, reading is intrinsically more difficult for the beginning reader than for the experienced reader. Everything is much "noisier" for the beginner. Anything that one lacks the skill or knowledge to understand automatically becomes noise.

Information   *Information* is defined as a reduction of uncertainty. In reading, information exists when the reader can reduce the number of alternative possibilities and can discriminate a given letter from the other twenty-five possibilities. If he can eliminate all alternatives except one, then the amount of information transmitted is equal to the amount of uncertainty that existed.

Redundancy   *Redundancy* exists whenever information is duplicated by more than one source—that is, whenever alternatives can be eliminated in more than one way. Presenting a word both visually and orally is a form of redundancy that helps the learner. In reading, it is immediately apparent that the larger the context, the greater the redundancy. And the more redundancy there is, the less visual information the skilled reader requires (Smith, 1971, p. 23).

The application of redundancy to reading, of course, suggests that the skilled reader does not need a fixed amount of information to identify a word or to ascertain the meaning. The amount of information needed depends on the difficulty of the passage, the reader's skill, and the reader's decision-making criteria. Does the reader demand absolute certainty before venturing a guess? Is the reader willing to take a chance? Setting criteria too high for word identification may mean difficulty identifying a word quickly enough to comprehend it. The beginning reader may not venture a guess for fear of being wrong and so become a very inefficient reader. Generally, readers establish relatively low criteria for words that are common in their experience and require more information if the word is one that appears infrequently (Smith, 1971, p. 26).

Linguistic Models

Early Formations   The early linguistic models were developed by Bloomfield, Fries, and Lefevre. In general, Bloomfield (1942) emphasized that beginning reading should present only regular correspondences between orthography and speech. Fries (1963) stressed letter-sound relationships. Lefevre stressed syntactical cues, both intra-word (such as inflections) and inter-word (such as sentence structure). Lefevre (1964, p. 68) noted that "grasp of meaning is integrally linked to grasp of structure—intonation gives the unifying configuration." Genuine reading proficiency is described as the ability to read language structure. The best reader is aware of the stresses, elongations of words, changes of pitch, intonation, and rhythms of the sentences that are being read. If a reader reads a sentence the way the writer would like it to have been said, true communication of meaning may be possible. Fries and Bloomfield concentrated on letters, sounds, and words as the prime units in reading; Lefevre makes the sentences the key unit in reading.

Bloomfield and Fries define reading as the act of turning the stimulus of graphic shape on a surface back into speech (Edwards, 1966). Bloomfield differentiated between the *act of reading* (recognition of grapheme-phoneme correspondences) and the *goal of reading* (comprehension).

The central thesis of the Bloomfield-Barnhart (1961) method is that there is an inseparable relationship between the graphic symbols and the sounds for which the letters are conventional signs, and that converting letters to meaning requires from the beginning a concentration upon letter and sound to bring about an automatic association between them as rapidly as possible. Bloomfield's system is a linguistic system of teaching reading which separates the problem of the study of word-form from the study of word-meaning. He notes that children come to school knowing how to speak the English language, but they do not know how to read the form of words.

Lefevre, whose emphasis is different from Bloomfield's, adapted linguistic ideas to teaching reading. He suggests an analytical method of teaching reading emphasizing language patterns. He emphasizes that meaning comes only through grasping the language structure of a sentence. Meaning therefore depends on the intonation, the word and sentence order, the grammatical inflections, and certain key function words. Intonation, or the pauses and stresses in oral language, are represented (1) by capital letters, periods, semicolons, and question marks, (2) by the order of the words, (3) by grammatical inflections signaling tense, number, and possession, and (4) by such function words as *the, when, nevertheless,* or *because.* Only by reading structures can the reader attain full meaning. Or, to put it another way, unless the reader correctly translates the printed text into the intonation pattern of the writer, the meaning intended may be missed.

Bloomfield felt that initial teaching of reading for meaning is incorrect, and that meaning will come quite naturally as the student learns the alphabetic code. Lefevre is critical of Bloomfield's approach, criticizing him for confining himself largely to phonemic analysis and for neglecting intonation and syntax.

The early linguists focused primarily on the problems of beginning reading and more specifically on the problems of word recognition (Chall, 1969). Both Bloomfield and Fries subscribed to the primacy of the spoken word over the written word, with the written form being essentially a representation of the spoken form. Reading is thus basically described by Bloomfield and Fries as decoding printed symbols into sound and then extracting meaning from sound. Smith (1971, pp. 44–45) rejects this view because:

1   Fluent reading is accomplished too fast for the translation into sound to occur.
2   It does not follow that reading must go through sound: deaf people do learn to read.
3   Writing is not necessarily speech written down; it might be meaning written down.

Transformational–Generative Grammar   The theorists in this group (Chomsky, 1957, 1968, 1970; Goodman, 1966, 1970) reject the notion that reading is simply sequential word recognition. Reading is perceived as a psycholinguistic process, *only superficially different* from the comprehension of speech. The beginning reader is thought to use abstract rules about language structure to arrive at comprehension. They emphasize the linguistic competence of the reader while the structuralists (Bloomfield and Fries, for example) emphasize *what* the reader must learn (Weber, 1970).

This approach emphasizes that all languages and hence all sentences have a *surface structure* and a *deep structure.* Sounds or written words are the surface representation of a message; meaning, syntactic and semantic interpretation are the deep level. The deep structure gives the meaning of the sentence; the surface structure gives the form (Jacobs and Rosenbaum, 1968).

The first fact that strikes the student of language is that there is no simple correspondence between the surface structure of language (phonology) and meaning (Smith, 1971, p. 29). There are aspects of meaning which are not in the written word.

The transformational-generative grammar model suggests that grammar—the rules of syntax—is a set of rules by which sense is made out of language, or by which words are arranged into sentences. *Grammar is the link between sound and meaning.*

Chomsky hypothesized that human beings have an innate rational ability to generate the underlying rules or syntax of their language after having been sufficiently exposed to it. The rules are identified as deep structures which are transformed to surface structures while being given phonological and semantic flesh (Vogel, 1974). Children, even at an early age, appear to be rule-producing learners. They can construct sentences they have never heard but which are nevertheless well-formed in terms of general rules. They can produce novel sentences.

Language consists of phonemes, words, and utterances. *Phonemes,* of which there are about forty-six in English, are not single sounds; they are rather collections of sounds. They are a class of closely related sounds constituting the smallest unit of speech that will distinguish one utterance from another (Smith, 1971, p. 31). They are perhaps better described as a network of differences between sounds (Hockett, 1958, p. 24). A *grapheme* (the counterpart of the phoneme) is a letter or a group of letters constituting the smallest unit of writing that will distinguish one word from another.

Language thus is a continuum of sound classified into a limited number of permitted single sounds called phonemes that join in a limited number of permitted combinations (Jolly, 1972).

A *morpheme* is the smallest linguistic unit in our language that has meaning. The unit has lexical meaning if it has a meaning of its own (as do, for example, prefixes and suffixes), and it has relational meaning if it has a grammatical meaning. For example, in the sentence, "She insists on it," the *in* in *insists* has lexical meaning. It has meaning wherever it occurs; the *s* at the end of the word has no meaning of itself. It has meaning only to the extent that it makes the verb a third person singular. It is said to have relational meaning. The *s* may also take on a relational meaning when it changes a noun from the singular to the plural or when it denotes the possessive case.

Words are the smallest meaningful linguistic units that can stand alone in a sentence. The study of how words are constructed is called *morphology.* An *utterance* is a series of words spoken at one time. The manner in which words are grouped into utterances is called *syntax.* And syntax and morphology compose the *grammar* of a language. Grammar has only one basic function: to make our utterances clearer. It is an aid to the expression and interpretation of meaning. Figure 2.2 illustrates the relationships existing among the various factors.

Morphology, for example, allows us to introduce minute changes into a word to bring out a special meaning. The various uses of *s* given above are examples of this. Syntax permits us to group words to suggest certain nuances of meaning. For example, the same words might be grouped in two ways to suggest two meanings: "The weak girl is playing a game of tennis," or "The girl is playing a weak game of tennis"; "The boy sat in a chair with a broken arm," or "The boy with a broken arm sat in a chair"; "The lion in the cage roared at the man," or "The lion roared at the man in the cage." The formal distinction between *runs* as a verb and *runs* as a noun ("He *runs* home"; "There were six *runs* on the bank") is syntactic (Ives, 1964). The reader must first recognize the distinction in arrangement before the distinction in meaning can be perceived. An adjective can become a noun by syntax: "The *best* is not good enough for him." To read the word *lead,* the reader must know whether it is a noun or a verb (Reed, 1965).

Punctuation in writing and pauses in speech are not so much an aid to writing and speaking as they are to reading and listening. The writer knows what the sentences mean; he does not need punctuation aids to get the meaning.

In addition to phonemes, morphemes, and words, there are certain characteristics about the utterance that add to and develop meaning. The loudness of the voice changes or certain words are stressed more than others. We give a heavy, medium, light, or weak stress. The pitch is either low, normal, high, or extra high. High pitch is often associated with heavier stress. In speaking, utterances are combined by what are termed *plus junctures;* they are ended by *terminal junctures.* The plus junctures separate words; the terminal junctures are usually accompanied by falls or rises in pitch, and differentiate one phrase unit from another or one type of sentence from another. The declarative sentence has a slight drop in pitch at the end. Phrasing depends on the placement of the junctures.

Words do not give meaning to sentences; rather, words receive their meaning from the sentence or the verbal context of which they are a part. The pupil who has become a word reader has fallen into the error of not reading the phrase or sentence unit that gives meaning to the word. The word must be looked upon merely as *one* element in a series of elements that constitute a

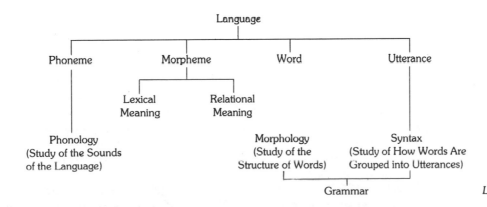

Figure 2.2
Language Structure.

sentence. The sentence circumscribes the word, giving it the distinct meaning intended by the speaker or writer.

Grammatical transformations are special ways of converting the deep structure of a sentence into a variety of surface representations; transformational rules, conversely, permit the reader to move from the surface structure to the deep structure or meaning. Transformational grammar is nothing more than "a finite set of rules that generates an infinite number of grammatical sentences of a language . . ." (Jacobs and Rosenbaum, 1968). The role of syntax, to mediate between visual surface structure and meaning, is precisely the function that generative-transformational grammarians attribute to it (Smith, 1971, p. 222).

RECENT RESEARCH

The position of Smith and others of the psycholinguistic school is supported by recent research and by the observations of other reading specialists. Denner (1970) found that problem readers (grades three to four) and children expected to be poor readers (grade one) performed more poorly than normal children on tasks requiring representational and syntactic competence.

MacNamara (1972), producing evidence from syntax, lexicon, and phonology, concluded that infants learn their language by determining the meaning that a speaker intends to convey to them and then working out the relationships between meaning and language. The child uses meaning as a clue to language rather than language as a clue to meaning. He notes that children's thinking is more advanced than their language.

Walcutt, Lamport, and McCracken (1974, pp. 41–42), noting that syntax concerns itself with meaning-bearing patterns, point out that "The word *dogs* can be easily understood on a surface level as two morphemes that express a recognized relationship among certain animals. But consider the differences among 'Dogs make good pets,' 'It's a dog's life,' and 'He's gone to the dogs,' all of which employ the same two morphemes. Meaning comes to us through syntax by intonation, patterns, word form changes, and the use of structure and function words."

Steiner, Wiener, and Cromer (1971) found that poor readers fail to extract contextual clues essential for word identification, and they fail to utilize such cues in identification even when they are presented with them. "They seem to be identifying words as if the words were unrelated items unaffected by syntactical or contextual relationships."

Bever and Bower (1966) report that the best readers among able college students do not read sentences in linear fashion, but in terms of their deep syntactic structure.

Hittelman (1973) suggests that the cloze procedure, which involves the deletion of every *n*th word in a selection and the evaluation of the success a reader has in supplying the deleted word, may measure only an entity within the surface features of the reading. These measurements may be only partly representative of those factors which determine readability.

Weber (1967) found that an analysis of errors on the syntactic and semantic level suggests that even early readers can successfully make use of preceding verbal context. It is apparent that they do not depend solely on graphic representation to make a response.

Burke and Goodman (1970), using Goodman's Taxonomy of Cues and Miscues in Reading, analyzed the reading of a boy named Daniel and concluded that there was little relationship between the miscues and comprehension. Some miscues simply did not result in changed meaning, and they were usually corrected if they did. Miscues tended to be corrected when the resulting syntax was unacceptable.

Vogel (1974) found that dyslexic children with reading comprehension difficulties are deficient in oral syntax.

SUMMARY

We have progressed in our understanding of the reading process and may well be on the threshold of an adequate theory of reading.

The theoretical model that the author began developing in the first edition of *Psychology in Teaching Reading* (and which he leans toward today) is basically a psycholinguistic model, but it is surely eclectic in that it has some elements of the taxonomic model, the psychometric model, the psychological models (both behavioral and cognitive), the information processing model, and the linguistic models (both the early formulations and the transformational-generative grammar models).

There probably is no pure model. Every model seems to have many elements in common with other models. Singer (1969) notes that probably a series of models is necessary to explain and predict reading performance. We agree with the observations of Williams (1973) that there is a growing rapprochement among theorists toward a view of reading as both a complex cognitive skill aimed at obtaining information and a complex language system.

The psycholinguistic approach, especially in the formulation given by Smith (1971), has perhaps the most to offer in reading instruction. It suggests that reading involves a basic knowledge of language as well as the utilization of complex active perceptual and cognitive strategies of information selection and processing. Reading is an active cognitive skill. It is not merely a simple associative learning process; it is not a passive process "with the graphic input cueing directly and automatically the already learned and therefore instantly meaningful speech code."

Reading requires a sign system in which messages are formulated (the graphic system). Reading thus is a sensory process, requiring discriminative visual responses to graphic symbols. It is a process by which a person reconstructs a message encoded graphically by a writer (Goodman, 1970). Encoding is the process of translating thought messages into written symbols. The reader goes from the written language, visually perceived, to a reconstruction of the message encoded in the written language by the writer. Comprehension occurs when the reconstruction agrees with the writer's intended message.

Language has a surface structure (the sounds and written representations of language) and a deep structure (which gives meaning) (Smith and Goodman, 1971). The basic requirement for reading is for the learner to be able to deal efficiently with both the surface and the deep structure.

Reading is both a perceptual process and a conceptual process. Meaning is supplied as the reader processes the symbolic system by relating it to experiences and conceptual structures. Reading is not a process of combining individual letters into words and strings of words into sentences from which meanings spring automatically. Rather, the evidence suggests that, for the fluent reader, the deep-level process of identifying meaning either precedes or makes unnecessary the process of identifying individual words (Smith and Goodman, 1971).

The fluent reader can go directly to meaning by using syntactic and semantic redundancy. Words around a given word (the context) are used to identify the word. The beginning reader must put letters together to form words; the skilled reader only rarely does this. The fluent reader decodes not from visual symbols into sound, but from visual symbols to meaning. The reader predicts his way through a passage of text.

The two levels of language (surface and deep structure) are related in a complex way through the rules of grammar (Smith and Goodman, 1971). Grammar is the link between sound and meaning. The rules of syntax determine how the particular visual-semantic associations should be interpreted for a cognitive organization (Smith, 1971, p. 216). Children learn these rules rapidly between the ages of eighteen months and four years (Smith, 1971). The pattern of development of these rules is so systematic and invariant that it is believed that children have an innate predisposition for discovering the rules of language (Smith and Goodman, 1971).

Because the acquisition of language and reading skills occurs in predictable stages of development, the reading teacher needs to develop a theory of reading within a theory of the total process of child development.

REFERENCES

Avdul, Richard. "Piaget Was a Quarterback." *Teacher* 91 (April 1974): 10–12.

Bever, Thomas, and Bower, Thomas. "How to Read Without Listening." Ithaca: Cornell University, 1966.

Birkley, Marilyn. "Effecting Reading Improvement in the Classroom through Teacher Self-Improvement Programs." *Journal of Reading* 14 (November 1970): 94–100.

Blake, James Neal. *Speech Education Activities for Children.* Springfield: Charles C. Thomas, 1970.

Bloomfield, L. "Linguistics and Reading." *Elementary English Review* 19 (1942): 125–130, 183–186.

Bloomfield, L., and Barnhart, Clarence L. *Let's Read: A Linguistic Approach.* Detroit: Wayne State University Press, 1961.

Bruner, Jerome S. "Going Beyond the Information Given." *Contemporary Approaches to Cognition.* Cambridge, Mass.: Harvard University Press, 1957.

Bruner, Jerome S. *On Knowing.* Cambridge, Mass.: Harvard University Press, 1962.

Burke, Carolyn L., and Goodman, Kenneth S. "When a Child Reads: A Psycholinguistic Analysis." *Elementary English* (January 1970).

Carroll, John B. *Language and Thought.* Englewood Cliffs, N.J.: Prentice Hall, 1964.

Carroll, John B. "The Nature of the Reading Process." In *Theoretical Models and Processes of Reading,* edited by Harry Singer and R. B. Ruddell. Newark, Del.: International Reading Association, 1970, pp. 292–303.

Chall, Jeanne S. "The Influence of Previous Knowledge on Reading Ability." Ohio State

University, *Educational Research Bulletin* 26 (December 1947): 225–230.

Chall, Jeanne S. "Research in Linguistics and Reading Instruction: For Further Research and Practice." In *Reading and Realism,* edited by J. Allen Figurel. Volume 13, International Reading Association Conference Proceedings, 1969, pp. 560–571.

Chomsky, Noam. *Syntactic Structures.* The Hague: Mouton, 1957.

Chomsky, Noam. *Language and Mind.* New York: Harcourt Brace and World, 1968.

Chomsky, Noam. "Phonology and Reading." In *Basic Studies in Reading,* edited by Harry Levin and Joanna P. Williams. New York: Basic Books, 1970.

Cooper, Bernice. "Contributions of Linguistics in Teaching Reading." *Education* 85 (May 1965): 529–532.

Dechant, Emerald. *Improving the Teaching of Reading.* Englewood Cliffs, N.J.: Prentice-Hall, 1970.

DeLaguna, Grace. "Perception and Language." *Human Biology* 1 (1929): 555–558.

Denner, Bruce. "Representational and Syntactic Competence of Problem Readers." *Child Development* 41 (1970): 881–887.

Edfelt, Ake W. *Silent Speech and Silent Reading.* Stockholm: Almquist and Wiksell, 1959; Chicago: University of Chicago Press, 1960.

Edwards, Thomas J. "Teaching Reading: A Critique." In *The Disabled Reader,* edited by John Money. Baltimore: Johns Hopkins Press, 1966, pp. 349–362.

Emans, Robert. "Oral Language and Learning to Read." *Elementary English* 50 (September 1973): 929–934.

Ervin, Susan M., and Miller, Wick R. "Language Development." *Child Psychology.* Chicago: University of Chicago Press, 1963.

Flavell, J. H. *The Developmental Psychology of Jean Piaget.* Princeton: D. Van Nostrand, 1963.

Fries, C. C. *Linguistics and Reading.* New York: Holt, Rinehart and Winston, 1963.

Furth, Haus G. *Piaget for Teachers.* Englewood Cliffs, N.J.: Prentice-Hall, 1970.

Gardner, Howard. "France and the Modern Mind." *Psychology Today,* June 1973, p. 59.

Goodman, Kenneth S. "Comprehension-Centered Reading." *Claremont*

Reading Conference Yearbook 34 (1970): 125–135.

Goodman, Kenneth S. "Decoding—From Code to What?" *Journal of Reading* 14 (April 1971): 455–462, 498.

Goodman, Kenneth S. "A Psycholinguistic View of Reading Comprehension." In *New Frontiers in College-Adult Reading,* edited by George B. Schick and Merrill M. May. Milwaukee: National Reading Conference, 1966, pp. 188–196.

Goodman, Kenneth S. "Reading: A Psycholinguistic Guessing Game." *Journal of the Reading Specialist* 4 (May 1967): 126–135.

Gray, W. S. "Growth in Understanding of Reading and Its Development Among Youth." *Keeping Reading Programs Abreast of the Times,* Supplementary Educational Monographs, No. 72. Chicago: University of Chicago Press, 1950, pp. 8–13.

Gray, W. S. "Reading and Physiology and Psychology of Reading." In *Encyclopedia of Education Research,* edited by C. W. Marris. New York: Macmillan, 1960, pp. 1086–1088.

Gunderson, Doris V. "New Developments in the Teaching of Reading." *Elementary English* 50 (January 1973): 17–21, 148.

Hansen, Halvor P. "Language Acquisition and Development in the Child: A Teacher-Child Verbal Interaction." *Elementary English* 51 (February 1974): 276–285, 290.

Hebb, D. O. *A Textbook of Psychology.* Philadelphia: W. B. Saunders, 1958.

Hebb, D. O. "What Psychology Is About." *American Psychologist* 29 (February 1974): 71–79.

Herrick, Judson. *The Evolution of Human Nature.* Austin, Tex.: University of Texas Press, 1956.

Hittelman, Daniel R. "Seeking a Psycholinguistic Definition of Readability." *The Reading Teacher* 26 (May 1973): 783–789.

Hockett, Charles F. *A Course in Modern Linguistics.* New York: Macmillan, 1958.

Holmes, Jack A. "Basic Assumptions Underlying the Substrata-Factor Theory." *Reading Research Quarterly* 1 (1965): 5–28.

Horn, Ernest. *Methods of Instruction in the Social Studies.* New York: Charles Scribner's Sons, 1937.

Inhelder, Bärbel. "Criteria of the Stages of Mental Development." In *Psychological Studies of Human Development,* edited by R.

Kuhlen and G. J. Thompson. 2nd ed. New York: Appleton-Century-Crofts, 1963, pp. 28–48.

Inhelder, Bärbel, and Piaget, Jean. *The Growth of Logical Thinking from Childhood to Adolescence.* New York: Basic Books, 1958.

Ives, Sumner. "Some Notes on Syntax and Meaning." *The Reading Teacher* 18 (December 1964): 179–183, 222.

Jacobs, Roderick A., and Rosenbaum, Peter S. *English Transformational Grammar.* Waltham, Mass.: Blaisdell Publishing Co., 1968.

Jacobsen, Edmund. "Electrophysiology of Mental Activities." *American Journal of Psychology* 44 (October 1932): 677–694.

James, William. *Principles of Psychology.* New York: Holt, Rinehart and Winston, 1890.

Jennings, F. "Jean Piaget: Notes on Learning." *Saturday Review,* May 20, 1967.

Jolly, Allison. *The Evolution of Primate Behavior.* New York: Macmillan, 1972.

Kean, John M., and Yamamoto, Kaoru. "Grammar Signals and Assignment of Words to Parts of Speech Among Young Children: An Exploration." *Journal of Verbal Learning and Verbal Behavior* 4 (August 1965): 323–326.

Kingston, Albert J., "The Psychology of Reading." *Forging Ahead in Reading.* IRA Conference Proceedings, International Reading Association, 1968, pp. 425–432.

Langer, Susanne K. *Philosophy in a New Key.* New York: Mentor Books, New American Library, 1948. Originally published by the Harvard University Press.

Langman, Muriel Potter. "The Reading Process: A Descriptive, Interdisciplinary Approach." *Genetic Psychology Monographs* 62 (August 1960): 1–40.

Laurita, Raymond E. "Bringing Order to the Teaching of Reading and Writing." *Education* 93 (February/March 1973): 254–261.

Lefevre, C. *Linguistics and the Teaching of Reading.* New York: McGraw-Hill, 1964.

MacNamara, John. "Cognitive Basis of Language Learning in Infants." *Psychological Review* 79 (January 1972): 1–13.

Miller, G. A. "Psycholinguistics." *Encounter* 23 (July 1964): 29–37.

Miller, G. A. "Some Preliminaries to Psycholinguistics." *American Psychologist* 20 (January 1965): 15–20.

Osgood, Charles E. "A Behavioristic Analysis of Perception and Language as Cognitive Phenomena." *Contemporary Approaches to Cognition.* Cambridge, Mass.: Harvard University Press, 1957.

Palermo, David S., and Molfese, Dennis L. "Language Acquisition from Age Five Onward." *Psychological Bulletin* 78 (December 1972): 409–428.

Piaget, Jean. "The Genetic Approach to the Psychology of Thought." *Journal of Educational Psychology* 52 (1961): 271–276.

Piaget, Jean. *Logic and Psychology.* New York: Basic Books, 1957.

Piaget, Jean. *The Mechanisms of Perception.* New York: Basic Books, 1969.

Piaget, Jean. *The Origins of Intelligence in Children.* New York: International Universities Press, 1952.

Raven, Ronald J., and Salzer, Richard T. "Piaget and Reading Instruction." *Reading Teacher* (April 1971).

Reed, David W. "A Theory of Language, Speech and Writing." *Elementary English* 42 (December 1965): 845–851.

Robinson, H. M. "The Major Aspects of Reading." In *Reading: Seventy-Five Years of Progress,* edited by H. S. Robinson. Chicago: University of Chicago Press, 1966, pp. 22–32.

Singer, Harry. "Theoretical Models of Reading." *Journal of Communication* 19 (June 1969): 134–156.

Smith, E. Brooks; Goodman, Kenneth S.; and Meredith, Robert. *Language and Thinking in the Elementary School.* New York: Holt, Rinehart and Winston, 1970.

Smith, Frank. *Understanding Reading: A Psycholinguistic Analysis of Reading and Learning to Read.* New York: Holt, Rinehart and Winston, 1971.

Smith, Frank, and Goodman, Kenneth S. "On the Psycholinguistic Method of Teaching Reading." *Elementary School Journal* 71 (January 1971): 177–181.

Smith, Henry P., and Dechant, Emerald. *Psychology in Teaching Reading.* Englewood Cliffs, N.J.: Prentice-Hall, 1961.

Steiner, Rollin; Wiener, Morton; and Cromer, Ward. "Comprehension Training and Identification for Poor and Good Readers." *Journal of Educational Psychology* 62 (December 1971): 506–513.

Suchman, J. Richard. "The Child and the Inquiry Process." *Intellectual Development: Another Look.* Washington, D.C.: Association for Supervision and Curriculum Development, 1969.

Svoboda, Cyril P. "Sources and Characteristics of Piaget's Stage Concept of Development: A Historical Perspective." *Journal of Education* (1973): 28–39.

Tuddenham, Read D. "Jean Piaget and the World of the Child." *American Psychologist* 21 (1966): 207–217.

Van Riper, Charles, and Butler, Katharine G. *Speech in the Elementary Classroom.* New York: Harper and Row, 1955.

Vogel, Susan A. "Syntactic Abilities in Normal and Dyslexic Children." *Journal of Learning Disabilities* 7 (February 1974): 103–109.

Walcutt, Charles C.; Lamport, Joan; and McCracken, Glen. *Teaching Reading.* New York: Macmillan, 1974.

Wardhaugh, Ronald. "Reading: A New Perspective." In *Reading: A Linguistic Perspective,* by R. Wardhaugh. New York: Harcourt Brace Jovanovich, 1969.

Watson, J. B. "Is Thinking Merely the Action of Language Mechanism?" *British Journal of Psychology* 11 (October 1920): 87–104.

PREVIEW

In this chapter Laffey and Morgan treat a difficult and sensitive topic with a great deal of concern and objectivity. The issues surrounding the education of culturally different pupils arouse strong emotions; few people, for example, are apathetic about busing as a means of compensating for de facto *segregation. Unfortunately, the attention given to the educational interests of blacks, American Indians, Mexican Americans, and other minorities has not, to date, significantly narrowed the problems these pupils are experiencing.*

After reading this chapter you should be more sensitive to the special educational problems of culturally different pupils and more knowledgeable about alternative, appropriate solutions.

Laffey and Morgan effectively treat the issues related to sex bias in books, both text and trade. They also present current data and informed opinion concerning sex differences in reading achievement. Television has long been regarded as competitive with reading. In this chapter it is discussed in terms of its supportive and reinforcement possibilities as a resource in teaching reading.

3

Sociocultural Bases

James L. Laffey, James Madison University
Raymond Morgan, Old Dominion University

OBJECTIVES

After you have read this chapter, you should be able to:

1. **State a definition of "culture" which shows your familiarity with several different ways of looking at that concept.**

2. **Specify the regional, ethnic, and racial groups who comprise the vast majority of the "culturally different" in American society today.**

3. **List the most significant effects that "cultural differences" have on school achievement in general and specifically on reading achievement.**

4. **List the positive characteristics of most "culturally different" pupils.**

5. **Review and evaluate the authors' list of characteristics of the successful teacher of the "culturally different" pupil.**

6. **Discuss the impact of television on children's reading, from both a positive and negative perspective.**

7. **Cite the most recent evidence regarding sex differences in reading achievement.**

8. **Be aware of the signs of sex bias and racial bias in basal reading materials and trade books for children.**

For at least the past twenty years there has been a national educational effort to provide more effective reading-language programs for the "culturally different." Educators, politicians, students, and the public in general have come in contact with terms like "culturally different" or "culturally disadvantaged" time and again and have interpreted them according to various individual conceptions and misconceptions. Most people interpret "culturally disadvantaged" to mean lacking a cultural background. Others broaden the definition by using "educationally deprived," underprivileged," "lower class," "lower socioeconomic group," and "disadvantaged" as synonyms for "culturally disadvantaged" or "culturally different" (Riessman, 1962, p. 1).

Whatever its definition, "culturally different" is something that middle-class America is definitely glad that it is not. The term conjures up thoughts that are incompatible with the America of the affluent society. Social theorist Michael Harrington has described another America which, although containing forty to fifty million citizens, is an invisible land. This America belongs to the poor, to the "unskilled workers, the migrant farm workers . . . the minorities," who "are pessimistic and defeated" because "they are victimized by mental suffering to a degree unknown in Suburbia" (Harrington, 1962, p. 10). Middle-class America, the dominant class in American society, consciously and unconsciously views its own culture and institutions as positive and those of the lower class as negative. Consequently, any culture other than the dominant one is in danger of losing its identity and becoming a non-culture, while its members are viewed as "culturally deprived," here meaning without a culture.

DEFINITIONS OF CULTURE

Can a people be "culturally deprived"—that is, without a culture? Most anthropologists say "no," for reasons that lie in their definitions of the word "culture." Bronislaw Malinowski, for example, defines culture as

> . . . the integral whole consisting of implements and consumers' goods, of constitutional charters for the various social groupings, of human ideas and crafts, beliefs and customs (1944, p. 36).

Frank Riessman defines culture as "the traditions, values, and mores of a specific group, many of which have a long history" (1962, p. 6). His definition of culture includes a people's institutions, structures, and methods of organization.

One of the broader definitions of culture is that of Sophie Elam. She views culture as

> . . . primarily a learning which is begun at birth and which provides the base for living. It permeates all behavior, from the simple fundamentals of eating and dressing and talking to the more complex and involved patterns of communication, use of symbols, and the development of a value system. Culture is also considered to be a determinant of the way one perceives oneself and others. It involves the totality of living from the biological to the social and intellectual. And the greatest complexity of the adjustment lies largely in the social sphere (Elam, 1966, pp. 296–297).

According to the above definitions, culture involves certain activities in which human beings consistently engage in order to cope with the world around them. No human being therefore, no matter how poor or from what background, is deprived of a culture.

Who then are the "culturally different"? They are those who do not participate in the life of middle-class America—who do not share the benefits of the
affluent society—who are among the 31 percent of the nation's population
who are ill-clothed, ill-fed, poorly housed, and poorly educated (Riessman,
1962, p. 3). The culturally different are those who are caught in a cycle of
despair. Their desire to achieve economic success is thwarted because the
access to the means of success is less available to them (Hyman, 1962, p.
427). They find themselves in a cycle of low paying jobs, low income housing,
and school failure.

The culture of those caught in this cycle is sometimes equated with their
environment. Culture and environment, however, are not the same. Culture
is an attempt to cope with one's environment. Often the coping techniques
are ineffective because of the various physical, psychological, educational,
and economic problems related to poverty. Other times, they are effective.
Protest movements are examples of effective coping, as are trade unions,
storefront churches, neighborhood clubs, and large extended families (Riessman, 1962, p. 6). It is important that middle America recognize the struggles
and successes of these people in combatting their difficult environment. To
see only their ineffectiveness and failures, is to see them one-sidedly.

In the late nineteenth and early twentieth centuries, many of the disadvantaged were found among the ranks of the "hyphenated" Americans,
the immigrants who came from Europe and settled primarily in urban areas.
These were the city tenement-dwellers who spoke little or no English, who
worked at unskilled jobs, who were for the most part uneducated, and who
were poor. Gradually, however, these immigrants made their way into the
dominant American culture, probably because many of their customs—
parental dominance, child obedience, and the passing on of paternal occupations—were similar to those they found in this country (Glazer, 1974, p. 56).
Also, the immigrants were of the same race as the dominant group. Their
children grew up speaking two languages, and their children's children grew
up with the language and cultural patterns of the dominant group. After the

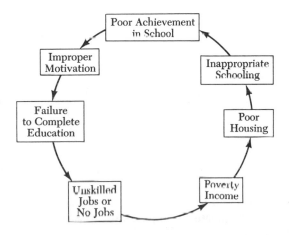

Figure 3.1
Poverty Cycle of Despair.

third generation, most perceptible evidence of their ethnic origins had disappeared. Along with it went their distinction as a minority group.

Today, the American "disadvantaged" are primarily the blacks of the urban North and rural South, the Mexican Americans of Texas and California, the American Indians, the Puerto Ricans of New York City, and the poor white inhabitants of Appalachia. These people are objects of prejudice and discrimination because their race, nationality, customs, religion, or language differ from those of the dominant group, which is white, American, Protestant, English-speaking, and middle class.

If Americans are to realize the dream of a pluralistic society, these groups must receive schooling which does not perpetuate racial prejudice or undesirable beliefs and attitudes. Teachers—who are, for the most part, members of the middle class—have often dealt with students from other cultures according to middle-class ideas and consequently have prevented the schools from meeting their needs. It is hoped that the events of the 1960s have effected change in this area. By teaching creativity, decision making, and flexibility, teachers must help all pupils build strong self-concepts and pride in their heritage, and prepare them to act effectively socially, economically, and politically.

SOCIOCULTURAL CHARACTERISTICS

Before attempting to structure reading programs for the "culturally different," we should take a closer look at the groups which have been lumped together under that banner. For our puposes here we shall consider the sociocultural characteristics of the blacks, Mexican Americans, Puerto Ricans, Indians, and poor whites of Appalachia.

Blacks

Between 40 and 50 million Americans live in poverty. We can understand the seriousness of this situation in relation to black Americans only by comparing the number of blacks who live in poverty with the total number of Americans who live in poverty (Johnson, 1970). Of the 22 million blacks in the United States, the number with a yearly income below $4,000 is approximately 13 to 15 million, or 60 to 70 percent of the total black population. Only 26 percent of white families live below this figure (Johnson, 1970, p. 45). It is clear from these statistics that black Americans have largely been excluded from participation in the dominant American culture.

The roots of discrimination against blacks in America go deep—back to their entrance into the colonies as slaves in 1619. It is difficult for a people who for nearly 250 years have been treated as property to suddenly acquire a sense of identity and self-importance. One's self-concept is formed in relation to the rest of society. If the society, as seen on television or in advertisements, is happy, clean, wholesome, well-clothed, and well-fed, as well as white, it becomes obvious to many blacks that they are not able to meet the standards of the society. And so they become submerged more and more in the life of the ghetto or isolated in the rural areas. Many blacks, of course, do participate in the dominant white culture. Yet remnants of discrimination and prejudice persist, and a sense of separation remains. An examination of recent black literature, music, and art shows a preoccupation with themes of alienation, struggle, and the search for an authentic black identity.

The black family finds itself under a great deal of duress when trying to socialize children into the dominant American society. In *Black Families in White America* Andrew Billingsley indicates that the historical development of the black family in the United States, the caste-like qualities of the American stratification system (an informal social system that designates the social pecking order, and which relegates all blacks to inferior status), and economic systems which keep most blacks in the lower economic classes force the black family to teach its children not only how to be human but also how to be black in the white society. This training must also separate blackness and badness, for there is a strong tendency to equate the two (Billingsley, 1968, pp. 28–29). The result is that blacks develop fear and hatred toward the dominant group, and these emotions find their outlets either in explosions such as Watts, Detroit, and Newark or in self-destruction through addiction to drugs and alcohol.

Since the black family has so often been unable to provide for itself because of white discrimination and the unskilled nature of its labor, it has had to turn to government agencies for financial assistance. Unfortunately, assistance has too often depended on the absence of the male head from the family. To some degree, this may account for the fact that 25 percent of black families are headed by women (Johnson, 1970, p. 51). Historically, it has been easier for black women to be employed than black men. The result is that the women tend to be economically independent of the men, and so the family gravitates around the mother.

In 1964, 29 percent of the black male population was unemployed at one time or another (Johnson, p. 53). The income security which the white male takes for granted is denied the black male. Not only is the black father frequently removed from his position as head of the family, as breadwinner, he also experiences the breakdown of his own self-concept. The breakdown of the family has a tremendous effect upon black children as well. Boys do not have effective male models, and girls learn from their mothers that a black man "ain't no good" (Johnson, 1970, p. 55). Those blacks living in the ghettos of big cities see not only the breakdown of their families but also the breakdown of the human spirit through disease, hunger, crime, and inadequate housing. The educational implications of this situation, particularly for reading, will be discussed later in this chapter.

Mexican Americans

Individuals of Spanish origin in the territories encompassing the present states of Arizona, California, Colorado, New Mexico, and Texas were first extended citizenship in 1848 as a result of the Mexican-American War. Ever since, people of the United States have rather consistently overlooked Mexican Americans as a group to be assimilated into American society. Only recently, since the decade of the sixties, has the plight of Mexican Americans been brought to public attention.

Although Mexican Americans are basically a rural people, a majority of them have migrated to urban areas in order to be present where jobs are available. Research has shown that 80 percent of Mexican Americans live in urban communities. And of that 80 percent a large portion (87 percent) live in urban poverty ghettos in the southwestern United States (Rodriguez, 1969, p. 35).

The *barrios,* Spanish enclaves in the cities, have been pockets of social and residential shelter for Mexican Americans. There Spanish tradition, with its emphasis on the patriarchal structure of the family, is preserved. The father is the authority figure. He provides a strong male model for the sons to emulate and is expected to represent the family with honor at all times. The mother's role is that of homemaker. She cares for the children, cleans, cooks, and sews. She is expected to show her husband absolute respect. She represents the soul of the family, and for this she is loved and honored. Included within the family structure are relatives such as grandparents, aunts, uncles, cousins, and godparents. These individuals contribute to the close-knit nature of the family by being responsible to and for one another.

The *barrios,* while providing shelter from the outside world, also contain within their walls all the miseries of ghetto life. Children are exposed to poverty, squalor, and disease. They are also witness to the dissolution of the strong family life which is their protection. If the father is unable to find employment, he can no longer provide the image of strength which Spanish tradition insists upon. When the mother seeks employment outside the home in order to provide for the family needs, she steps into a male role. Conflict is likely to ensue as a result of either or both events.

Mexican Americans have been objects of both economic and educational discrimination in the United States. Economically, they have been exploited in agriculture. American growers have hired smuggled-in Mexican nationals, who will work for very low wages, in preference to Mexican Americans, thus denying employment opportunities to resident workers.

Educationally, public schools have discriminated arbitrarily against Mexican Americans. For example, the Spanish language as a medium for teaching was banned by section 288 of the Texas Penal Code (Martinez, 1970, p. 280). Inferior buildings and equipment have been used in schools with high Mexican-American populations. Teachers have not been properly trained to deal with Mexican-American children. As a result, the median level of education among Mexican Americans is very low—approximately 8.6 years. In Texas, almost 80 percent of students who have Spanish surnames drop out before finishing high school (Rodriguez, 1969, p. 35). In California almost 74 percent of Mexican-American students do not finish high school. Later in this chapter, we will relate these statistics specifically to reading and literature.

Puerto Ricans

Puerto Ricans are another group of Hispanic origin which has sought entrance into life in the United States. They have settled for the most part in New York City. The 1961 census showed that 613,000 Puerto Ricans live in the city. Glazer and Moynihan have described two migratory patterns typical of Puerto Rican families with children. The first is for the father to migrate alone, stay with friends or relatives when he arrives on the mainland, find a job and living quarters for his wife and children, and then bring over his family. The second pattern involves migration of the mother with the children. The father does not accompany them either because he has deserted the mother or because she "has decided to leave home and go to New York, where jobs are plentiful, where the government is reputed to be 'for women and the children' and where relief is plentiful" (Glazer and Moynihan, 1963, pp. 122–123).

Puerto Rican culture is similar to Mexican American in that boys are raised to exhibit "machismo" or manliness, girls to be mothers, and individuals to be aware of self-pride and dignity. Nevertheless, it is different from Mexican-American culture in two ways:

1. Puerto Rican culture is weak in its ties to Spain, to the folk arts, and to the Catholic Church. The Church, so often the transmitter of culture, was not strong in Puerto Rico because it was viewed as the institution of the rich and because there were too few clergy. Spanish tradition was also weakened by Spain's neglect of Puerto Rico as a colony and by the fact that Puerto Ricans have been citizens of the United States since the turn of the century and have been influenced by American thoughts and ideas.

2. Families of Spanish origin tend to be strong in structure. Not so with the Puerto Rican family. More than a quarter of Puerto Rican marriages are consensual or common-law, with the result that children of these marriages are "illegitimate." Concubinage and male unfaithfulness further weaken the structure. Add to these factors crowded living conditions, unemployment, underemployment, and family members' various stages of entrance in the United States, and we can see how family stability is threatened (Glazer and Moynihan, pp. 88–89).

Acculturation provides educational problems for the Puerto Rican child. Puerto Rican parents would like their children to be well educated, and often hope they will be professionals. School, however, proves to be a frustrating experience to the child, and so educational hopes are often unrealized. Language presents a formidable barrier. In New York City at one time nearly 56,000 children in elementary school could neither speak nor understand English. Most of these children were Spanish-speaking (Glazer and Moynihan, p. 127). Another problem faced by both the Puerto Rican family and school personnel is the difference in opinion concerning the role of the school. Puerto Rican parents fear that the school views itself as a surrogate family, and they frequently consider classroom methods much too informal. These attitudes in combination with the language barrier constitute formidable obstacles which Puerto Rican youngsters and their teachers must overcome if they are to achieve success (Johnson, 1970, pp. 82–83).

American Indians

American Indians are a proud people whose cultural heritage is almost completely different from the dominant white culture. During the colonial period of American history and the period during which Indian tribes were controlled by treaties, the Indian population was decimated and the few people who remained were gradually driven from their land. During the reservation period from 1887 to 1914, the Indian lands were systematically reduced from 138 million acres to 47 million acres. Another phase in the period saw forced assimilation during which, among other things, Indian children were taken from their tribes, placed in boarding schools, and forbidden to use Indian language or practice Indian customs (Marden and Meyer, 1968, p. 363). No attempt was made to adapt the curriculum to the students.

There have been many attempts to deal with the Indian problem since the reservation period. The Indian Reorganization Act in 1934 brought about changes by improving the Indian economic situation, by increasing tribal self-government, and by improving the welfare of the Indians on the whole. The Relocation program of the 1950s was unsuccessful because so many of the Indians who had left the tribal lands to move to industrial centers returned, having found only poor employment and abysmal housing. The Udall Plan of 1966 provided for bringing the Indians into decision making policies and for upgrading their educational system (Marden and Meyer, 367–371).

Today, the condition of America's nearly 500,000 Indians is still appalling. The Indians are considered one of the poorest of America's minority groups. Their average income has been estimated at approximately $1,500. Unemployment figures range from 40 to 45 percent, with the Sioux reaching a high of 75 percent. Because of their poverty, Indian children usually come from overcrowded, unattractive homes where privacy, food, and clothing are insufficient (Narang, 1974, pp. 190–191).

The experiences as well as the concepts of the Indian child are limited when measured by the white culture which dominates the schools. The schools have not been successful institutions for the Indians for several reasons: (1) Indian culture does not make room for individualism as it is understood in white society. Since Indians operate in a network of formalized relationships, the individual is important only as a member of the group. (2) Interpersonal relationships stress cooperation rather than competition. (3) Men and women, boys and girls have traditional roles to play; any attempt to violate the arrangement is taboo.

So American culture, with its emphasis on individualism, competition, and, to a certain degree, equality of the sexes, runs completely counter to Indian traditions. If the schools are to be successful, teachers and other school personnel must work with the Indian child in his cultural setting (Kluckhohn, 1962, pp. 339–340). Education must be presented as means of contributing to Indian society as a whole, not as a means of making money for individuals or of individual assimilation. Only in this manner will the Indians be able to enter American society as a vibrant, viable community.

Appalachians

The term Appalachia often suggests poverty, and rightly so. For many years Appalachia has been an economic problem area. Appalachians, those nearly 10 million people who live in the mountain areas of northern Alabama, Georgia, North and South Carolina, Tennessee, Kentucky, Virginia, West Virginia (and portions of Pennsylvania, western Maryland and southern New York), have suffered terribly during times of national economic distress and have been unable to benefit from national periods of prosperity. The decline in the area's principal economic activities, especially agriculture and coal mining, is responsible for their almost continuous state of poverty. The employment level in Appalachia's coal mines has declined drastically, according to an analysis of the region done by the Maryland Department of Economic Development. From 1950 to 1959, 60 percent of the mineworkers left their jobs, as did 25 percent of agricultural workers. This decline in employment corresponds to the decline in the region's population. Approximately one and a half million persons, many between the ages of eighteen and forty-four, emigrated from 1950 to 1959 (Maryland Department of Economic Development, 1960, p. 5). These emigrants were some of the region's most productive laborers.

Living standards in Appalachia are low in both rural and urban areas. One out of every three families lives on $3,000 or less per year (Crow, 1966, p. 20). At least one worker in six is jobless or is employed only part time. Houses are small and poorly constructed, and in some rural counties only about 2 percent of them have such ordinary conveniences as running water, a bathtub, and a private toilet (Ford, 1962, p. 17). Health standards are low too. Death rates from influenza and pneumonia, tuberculosis, parasitic diseases, and cardiovascular renal diseases are higher in Appalachia than they are in the rest of the nation. The mortality rate from diseases of early childhood also exceeds that of the nation as a whole (Ford, p. 220).

The Appalachian region has been a somewhat mysterious place to the rest of America for a long time. Sometimes it has been depicted as the home of a group of people who speak a language reminiscent of Elizabethan English, sing traditional English ballads, play dulcimers, and spin their own yarn. At other times Appalachia has been pictured as the home of happy hillbillies who take joy in their white lightning and home folks' company. And at still other times, the stereotype of the Hatfields and McCoys has dominated the scene.

The people of Appalachia, descendants of peasants and yeomen from England, Ireland, and Scotland, are a proud, hardy, and clannish group. Families are close-knit and strong. The father is head of the family and the main authority figure. The mother, while providing warmth and love for the children, is always mindful of the wishes of her husband. In a description of the Appalachian women a century ago, Harry Caudill embodies the virtues and sufferings which are still so typical of the upcountry womenfolk:

> In their world the man was a tyrant who ruled his house with medieval unconcern for his wife's feelings or opinions. She rarely sat down to eat a meal with him, it being her duty to "wait on" him. When a stranger was present she stayed discreetly out of sight. As a girl she saw her brothers and father "laid away," the victims of feuds, quarrels, logging accidents or disease. Her girlhood was spent in graceless toil and crowned by an early marriage. Wasted by a quarter-century of child bearing, she saw a row of graves dug for her children. Often she survived as a widow to fend for the remainder of her brood. She could rarely influence the impetuous decisions of her husband and sons, and, never far from the family graveyard, mourned through long years the results of their efforts (1962, p. 80).

It is from this tradition that the modern Appalachian woman emerges. She is still hardy, still resilient, and, though modern trends and employment in industry have made her less so, still subservient to her husband. Although she may not provide the main income for the family, she is in many ways the motivator of the children, encouraging their education and being held responsible for their failures.

Families are large. Child rearing practices are on the whole permissive and, although children are responsible for certain chores and duties in the home, they are permitted to roam the hills more or less freely (Giffin, 1972, p. 181). The closeness among kin that results from the extended family system tends to make the mountain people suspicious of outsiders. They often refuse help from organizations or from individuals other than relatives.

How does this isolated background affect the education of Appalachian children? In a survey conducted by Ford to determine the educational aspirations of Appalachians for their children, three out of four said they would like to have a son complete college, and two out of three expressed the same wish for a daughter. Less than 1 percent felt satisfied with merely a high school education for their children. Almost all said they would like to help finance part of their children's college education. This rather surprising revelation indicates that the mountain people realize the importance of formal education in today's industrialized society (Ford, 1962, p. 17).

In contrast to these aspirations are the stark realities of the educational level of the inhabitants of Appalachia. The proportion of adults twenty-five and over whose schooling stopped before the completion of eighth grade is approximately 75 percent in rural areas. In non-rural areas in Appalachia the number reaches approximately two-thirds (Giffin, 1972, p. 182). Related to the dropout problem is retardation—school achievement which is considerably below grade level expectations. In 1930 there were thirteen counties in the Appalachian region in which 55 percent or more of the fourth grade pupils were older than they should have been for their grade (Ford, 1962, p. 189). Today, retardation is not as serious a problem as it was in the past. Nevertheless, better school facilities, staff, and programs are needed to narrow the gap between potential achievement and performance. The Appalachian people tend to be content with school systems as they are. Since school boards in the states concerned have no power to set a tax levy within prescribed legal limits, to support a budget, or to call for a referendum on a slashed budget proposal, the amount of money spent per pupil is lower than in other areas. Indeed, it is approximately 50 percent lower than in the rest of the nation. Federal assistance is vital if the schools are to provide an adequate education.

Education is hampered not only by poverty but by the very attitudes of the children. The strong individualism and freedom of movement which are typical of their background prevent them from easily accepting the authority and confinement of school. Their protests often take the form of sullenness, which makes the teaching of anything, including reading, very difficult.

SECOND-GENERATION
AMERICANS

Another culturally different group which has not been studied extensively is the second-generation immigrant Americans who came from foreign language speaking homes. There have not been any large-scale descriptive studies which have attempted to identify some basic cultural characteristics of these students. Possibly, this could be because these students came from very divergent backgrounds.

Morgan (1978) in a brief descriptive study of three graduate students found that the two German students felt there were some very direct, hostile and unkind discriminatory practices exercised by their classmates during their middle school years (Grades 5–8). The Hungarian student on the other hand felt there was no overt discrimination exerted against him.

It is interesting to note all three students felt that two kinds of additional education would have helped. They believed that the teachers needed more education in order to acquire, hopefully, a more sensitive attitude and insight to the cultural differences of their students. They also expressed a need for more exposure to English language experiences which would benefit them.

It appears that educators need to be more sensitive to the educational and cultural needs of students who are second generation Americans. Furthermore, teachers need to be aware of the possible discriminatory practices of the peer group. Some cultural education activities should be directed toward the peer groups of second-generation American students so that these students are not penalized or discriminated against by their classmates.

COMMON CHARACTERISTICS OF CULTURALLY DIFFERENT GROUPS

The following generalizations can be made about those *not* participating in the dominant American culture:

1   The culturally different are isolated by religion, race, ethnic origin, or geography from the American scene. With the exception of the Appalachians, they are not WASPs—White Anglo-Saxon Protestants.

2   The culturally different, for the most part, belong to the lowest economic groups because they cannot qualify—or have been prevented from qualifying—for the high-paying jobs.

3   The culturally different are prone to sickness and disease because of a lack of nutritious food, well-balanced diets, health care, and adequate housing.

4   The parents of culturally different children are frequently bitter and discouraged, more used to defeat than success. They did poorly in school and as a result do not provide an example of success in education for their children.

5   Culturally different children often come from crowded, noisy homes where there is a marked lack of privacy. In order to survive in such an environment, they tend to psychologically shut out many stimuli.

6   The language used in the home of the culturally different child is generally unlike that which is encountered in the school. It has been estimated that the comprehension vocabulary of the disadvantaged child in the beginning years of school is between one third and one half that of the middle-class child.

7   Culturally different children often present a discipline problem to the school because school activities do not sustain their attention, be-

cause their parents are unable or unavailable to control them, or because their sense of individualism prevents them from conforming to the middle-class standards of the school.

In spite of these disadvantages, the lifestyle of the culturally different is not totally negative; it also incorporates many strengths. Riessman drew up a balance sheet and listed the following assets (Riessman, 1962, p. 48):

1 Cooperativeness and mutual aid which mark the extended family.
2 Avoidance of strain that accompanies competitiveness and individualism.
3 Equalitarianism, informality, and warm humor.
4 Freedom from self blame and parental overprotection.
5 Children's enjoyment of each other's company, with a lessened sibling rivalry.
6 Security found in the extended family and in a traditional outlook.

In short, we must realize that those aspects in the lifestyle of the culturally different which appear negative to the dominant American culture are not the result of any genetic inferiority but simply the result of a life of poverty. And there are few problems which the alleviation of poverty would not cure.

The Language Factor

One of the major problems facing culturally different children as they enter the middle-class environment of the school is that their language does not match that which they encounter in the classroom.[1] They may have come from a home where English is not a native language, as is the case with Mexican American, Puerto Rican, and American Indian children, or where so-called standard English is not spoken, as in the homes of many blacks and Appalachian white children.

The language of children from such backgrounds often stigmatizes them socially. As indicated by Robert DiPietro, the price for such individualism in speech has been high in the United States. People who do not speak English or who speak "non-standard" English have been trapped at the bottom of the economy by being excluded from participation in the full life of the standard English speaking majority. If they are urban, they are ensnared in the ghettos; if rural, they are caught in a subsistence environment (DiPietro, 1973, p. 37).

Bilingual Education

For years children in American schools who spoke a language other than English were not only forced to communicate in English, they were also expected to perform as well as speakers of English. The result was often frustration and failure. The early 1960s saw a new trend in bilingual education. In October 1964, the federal government recognized officially that there

---

[1] Language is discussed in greater detail in Chapter Four, "Language and Psycholinguistic Bases."

were thousands of school children "in the Southwest, on the Atlantic coast and in New England, on American Indian reservations, and in the Trust Territories; in Puerto Rico, Alaska, Texas, Arizona, New Mexico, California, Colorado, Hawaii, New York, New Jersey, Vermont, Maine, Louisiana and Florida—whose mother tongue was other than English and who needed specialized instruction in English if they were fully to understand or participate in the American cultural, social, and economic way of life" (Alatis, 1973, p. 44). Several educational acts—most recently the Bilingual Education Act —have provided instruction for children in American schools who come from homes where English is not the dominant language.

The benefits of bilingual education (meaning the education of students in several subjects in two languages) are many. The school's respect for the individual student's language and culture enhances their self-image and motivates them to academic material. When the subject matter is presented in their mother tongue, students learn it more easily, and their resistance to learning the second language is not as great. Most students perform better academically in the second language (Modiano, 1969, p. 93).

There are several standard practices for teaching bilingual and bidialectal children. Virginia Allen French has identified them as follows:

1 Contrastive analysis of the target language (or dialect) with the students' home language (or dialect).
2 Acceptance of the target language and students' language as equally valid systems of communication.
3 Emphasis on grammatical structure of the target language, not on vocabulary.
4 Presentation of the linguistic system of the target language in small steps, each issuing from the last.
5 Measurement of success in the target language in terms of oral fluency, not recitation of rules and definitions (Alatis, 1973, pp. 50–51).

As we can see, the emphasis here is upon recognizing that one language is not "better" than another, upon building an understanding of the structure of the target language, and upon the formation of habits in oral fluency.

Teachers working with children who do not speak English often treat these children the same as those who speak a non-standard dialect. James Alatis has indicated, however, that non-standard dialect speakers tend to have motivational, sociological, and psychological problems, while children who speak other languages are more likely to have cultural and linguistic problems (Alatis, p. 51). Techniques used to teach both types of children include mimicry, repetition, and substitution. Problems arise, however, when non-standard dialect speakers are constantly drilled in these areas. Teachers must remember that it is repetitious and boring to a child who already knows English to repeat constantly such phrases as "This is a red ball" or "This is a book" (Bailey, 1973, p. 107).

What can be done to help teachers deal with the problems of bilingual and bidialectal students? The answer lies in the reeducation of teachers and the preparation of new teachers in language arts programs which are geared away from traditional methods and toward the current demand for equal educational opportunities. Drills and exercises should include many opportunities for experimentation with language and for language play. Finally, funds must be provided for school systems to hire the teachers who are creative, imaginative, and professionally equipped to deal with bilingual and bidialectal children, so that these children can succeed in the schools and ultimately in the dominant society (Bailey, pp. 108–114).

READING PROGRAMS FOR CULTURALLY DIFFERENT STUDENTS

Existing reading programs for culturally different students vary widely in rationale, size, and scope. In fact there are very few common characteristics other than that the majority of such reading programs work toward preventing educational deficits and remediating existing reading problems. These programs are preventive in that they attempt to bridge cultural, language, educational, and reading gaps in the early school period. They are remedial in that there is a sustained effort to hold off the more serious educational and reading deficits that occur at later school periods and to correct problems wherever they occur.

Many of the reading programs designed for culturally different students are based on traditional approaches to teaching reading. We will review one of these traditional approaches here, along with one other program. This is not an in-depth analysis of all reading approaches and programs available, but only an introduction to two of the materials, approaches, and programs which have been designed and used with the culturally different. More detailed discussions and analyses are available elsewhere in this text and in some of the references cited in the various bibliographies at the end of each chapter (see, for example, *Approaches to Beginning Reading* by R. C. Aukerman).

The Distar Reading and Language Program   This instructional system is designed to help students acquire basic concepts and skills in reading and language. According to the authors of the program, these basic skills will enable students to succeed in school. The target population of the Distar Program is the "disadvantaged" (Kim, Berger, and Kratochvil, 1972). While its authors indicate that the program was designed for the culturally disadvantaged (that is, culturally different), they fail to indicate which specific group— the poor black and white of the inner-city ghettoes, children born to poverty in Appalachia, or American Indians. However, no single reading and language program could be effective with all the diverse student populations often incorporated under the descriptive but general term "culturally different."

The Distar Level I instructional program initiates the student into the program with a concentrated series of lessons on the language of instruction. Later, students are introduced to the concept that each letter of the alphabet is associated with a specific sound. An interesting aspect of this program is that it teaches the student to associate the appropriate sound with the appropriate letter, but it does not teach letter names. After learning a certain number of sounds, the student is taught to blend sounds. There is a great deal of emphasis placed on successful blending of sounds. This later enables the student to pronounce whole words.

The teacher's manual for each lesson contains the entire dialogue for that lesson, along with pictures, questions, and stories. The dialogue is presented in a step-by-step sequence difficult to deviate from. The guidelines for use of the program suggest that the teacher work with small groups of children at a time (between five and ten students).

Although this program has many advantages to offer an inexperienced teacher, it also has some disadvantages. To determine both the strengths and weaknesses of the Distar Program, students in a graduate seminar at Madison College studied the program intensively during the summer of 1974. The seminar participants included experienced teachers who had used the program, reading and language arts supervisors, and a number of reading specialists. The result of the study was the following list of the *strengths* and *weaknesses* of the Distar Reading and Language Program:

Strengths
1 The program has a positive approach to teaching which includes constant positive reinforcement as part of the program.
2 The nature of the reading and language input in the program is multi-sensory (that is, tactile, auditory, visual).
3 There is an intensive teacher training component.
4 The reading skills are introduced in a sequential order. The teacher uses already learned skills to introduce new skills. (This is not unique to Distar.)
5 The program appears to enhance the student's self-concept and interest students in independent reading. (This is accomplished in most successful programs.)
6 The program has built-in curriculum evaluation. The students are evaluated on the basis of the skills taught in the program. (This is also true of many basal programs.)
7 The program was designed for a target population—the disadvantaged.
8 The program uses a directed teaching method which can be highly useful for an inexperienced teacher.

Weaknesses
1 There is some difficulty in maintaining a high level of teacher interest in the program due to the overly prescriptive directions in the teacher's manual. Teacher boredom becomes a factor in successfully implementing the program.
2 There is the problem of curriculum consistency in the case where students are transferred to a new school and reading program. This is particularly true of some of the artificial alphabet characters. It is true also in the instances where teaching practices could be dramatically different from the highly teacher-directed learning in the Distar Program.
3 The highly structured nature of the curriculum does not allow for either student or teacher spontaneity.
4 Even a well-qualified teacher is not encouraged to develop alternative learning activities during the reading-language lessons.

5   The curriculum is not a child-centered curriculum but a teacher-centered-curriculum.

6   The heavy emphasis on the decoding skills appears to result in the decoding skills becoming an end in themselves rather than a means to an end—that is, the students seem to decode for the sake of decoding, rather than using decoding as a means to understanding the printed language.

The Distar Reading and Language Instructional System is based on methods developed at the University of Illinois with "culturally disadvantaged" students from large inner-city ghetto environments. Reports of its effectiveness have been made by the publisher of the program (S.R.A., 1971), but further objective evaluations need to be undertaken. An instructional system designed and developed for one culturally different group will not necessarily be effective with other culturally different groups. There are important differences of some educational consequence between cultural groups who are generally referred to as "culturally disadvantaged"; and such differences should certainly be taken into consideration when instructional systems are developed.

Overall, the various phonic-linguistic reading programs now available play a crucial role in instructional programs for the culturally different. They are often highly effective in developing decoding skills among the culturally different groups. The stress on the decoding skills is consistent with the recommendations Jeanne Chall made following her extensive study of instructional methods in reading (Chall, 1967). However, Chall recommends a decoding emphasis only as a beginning reading method—"a method to start the child on" (Chall, p. 307).

Language Experience Approaches

For years teachers have known that children learn to read quite successfully when their own language is used as a basis for reading instruction. This principle is particularly important in teaching culturally diverse pupils, whose dialect is not standard English, and whose experiences are not those of typical middle-class children. This approach to the teaching of reading views learning to read as a part of language development (Spache, 1973). It stresses the close relationship between listening, speaking, reading, and writing. One scholar (R. Van Allen, 1961) has described the language experience approach from the point of view of the student:

> What I can think about,
>   I can talk about.
> What I can say, I can write.
> What I can write, I can read.
> I can read what I write and
>   what other people can write
>   for me to read.

This approach to the teaching of reading brings together all aspects of the communication process into a unified curriculum, using children's language as the instructional program. This strategy capitalizes on the oral language facility of children, which in turn motivates children by showing them that what they talk about is important enough to write about, and later on, to read about. When they read what they have written, children recognize that the content of reading is what they think about and later express.

Usually instruction in the language experience curriculum begins a few days after the students enter school. From the very first day, students are encouraged to express their ideas through such activities as "show and tell." The teacher often records group stories on language experience charts. These stories are then used as instructional reading materials through which the teacher begins teaching words, phrases, selected word perception skills, and some comprehension skills. Later, the teacher puts the children into smaller groups and continues the development of experience stories. At some point, individual children are encouraged to share their ideas so that individual stories can be recorded. These individually recorded experience stories usually motivate students to write their own stories. This natural extension of the language curriculum continues until students are engaged in a wide range of language activities and related art activities.

The language experience approach can be adapted to fit a variety of student needs. Many classroom teachers either use this approach exclusively or integrate it with other teaching approaches. It can be used to provide beginning culturally different readers with materials which match their dialect and/or experiences. These are the steps to follow when using the language experience approach:

1   Have discussions with students about an experience they have had or one that you shared with them. (You can also use a picture, film, filmstrip, record, tape cassette, or any stimulating object as a basis for a discussion.)

2   Record (in manuscript writing for primary grade students) the story or experience. Let the students see you preparing their story.

3   As you write the story do as little editing as possible. If the student speaks in a dialect, record the story in the dialect, using *standard* English spellings, however, since these are what the student will encounter in print.

4   When the story is finished, read it aloud to the student. Then have the student read it back to you.

5   At first, keep the stories short—two or three sentences for young students and a paragraph or two for older students.

6   Older students can type their own stories. Allow the students to illustrate any part of their stories. With young children, it is often appropriate to begin with a self-portrait, for example, and record a story about the picture.

7   Ask the students to choose some words they would like to learn.

8   Print the words (and word phrases) on 3″ × 5″ cards to be used for sight word and vocabulary activities.

9   Language experience stories can be used to teach sight words, word analysis skills, readiness skills, and comprehension and vocabulary skills.

10 A skills checklist can be used to identify the skills the student needs, as well as to keep a record of the skills taught.

11 The teacher can have the students color or paint the best illustrations in their stories. Then the stories can be bound or laminated and used as instructional materials for other students.

Most teachers who have used the language experience approach have found it to be an invaluable teaching tool. It is excellent for culturally different students, since it uses oral language for instruction (Hall, 1972). It not only pays attention to the language of the culturally and linguistically different, but it can also extend these students' language and communications skills by correlating writing, reading, and listening activities in a single simplified curriculum.

THE SUCCESSFUL TEACHER OF THE CULTURALLY DIFFERENT

One of the keys to success in reading instruction with culturally different students is the teacher. In fact the teacher's knowledge and skill are often much more critical than the reading programs used (Harris, Serwer, 1966). Some of the teaching qualities which contribute to success are listed below. Successful reading teachers of the culturally different student are:

1 Knowledgeable about the nature of reading and its role in the life of the individual. The teacher's definition of reading will determine how that teacher teaches reading. A teacher with a broad, comprehensive definition will conduct a program in reading that is broad and comprehensive in nature.
2 Either well-informed about the cultural group they are teaching or willing to study the culture and its impact on individuals.
3 Able to identify the different learning styles of individuals within cultural groups. Since it is not possible for textbook publishers to publish textbook materials for all cultural groups and subcultural groups, it is quite essential that the teacher of culturally different groups be capable of using different ways to adapt instructional materials and/or teaching approaches.
5 Aware of the fundamental importance of language facility in learning to read and consequently able to incorporate all aspects of the language-communication process in the instructional program in reading.
6 Aware of their beliefs and expectations and their impact on children's learning. It has been found that teachers who believe and expect children in their classrooms to achieve in reading do in fact influence positively their students' achievement in reading (Rosenthal, 1973).
7 Well organized and presents well-organized lessons to their students.
8 Persons who sincerely care about the students they teach. This can also be said in an old fashioned way—they *love* the children they teach and are a loving person. This quality is all too often ignored in today's teaching world. To begin to consider the importance of loving in teaching, see Jesse Stuart, *To Teach, To Love*.

9   Cognizant of the role of the student's self-concept in learning to read, and as a result enhances the student's self-concept through positive reinforcement on every possible occasion.

In summary we have discussed some aspects of the culture of poverty and have taken a fairly close look at the inhabitants of the ghetto slums, *barrios,* Indian reservations, and hills of Appalachia. We have noted that, as compared with the children of the middle class, children from these backgrounds are at a definite disadvantage in the milieu of the school culture. Because disadvantaged children have not been provided with readiness skills before entering school, they find it difficult to perform the tasks required of them, particularly in the language arts. Many researchers emphasize that the schools must meet the psychosocial and psychophysical needs of the disadvantaged before they can attempt to teach the children necessary skills. They state that unless feelings of alienation are overcome, unless the psychological strain of broken or overcrowded homes is attended to, and unless a sense of individualism and self-expression is fostered, learning will not take place. While some efforts in these directions are indeed desirable, there are, nevertheless, severe limits to the school's ability to solve economic and cultural problems not of its making. Schools cannot, for example, give work to unemployed fathers, relieve family strains, or cure other ills which impair children's performances. Other social institutions must help here. But schools *should* be able to teach. As S. Alan Cohen in his insightful book *Teach Them All to Read* very strongly asserts, the *raison d'etre* of the schools is not to solve the problems of the family, home, and community, but rather to promote literacy (Cohen, 1969, p. 6). Schools cannot and should not be expected to solve the social ills of society; various social institutions are expected to deal with social and moral problems. The school's unique job is to teach the basic skills of reading, writing, and arithmetic. Despite long-winded discussions about why culturally different children cannot read, we say with Cohen that in order for breakthroughs to occur in the teaching of reading, teachers must concentrate on methodology. Then and only then will the children of the poor be reading as well as the children of middle America.

SEXISM AND RACISM IN CHILDREN'S BOOKS

Content analysis deals with the analysis of both the evident or obvious elements and hidden or subtle elements of content in a piece of literature. It may involve the evaluation, classification, or tabulation of the key themes and symbols. Content analysis is usually performed to determine the meaning and probable effect of a body of literature. The purpose of many recent studies has been to determine if children's trade books and basal readers are discriminating against races and the sexes. Content analysis has also been used to determine the probable effect of this discriminatory process.

Discrimination can take the form of sexist writing, blatant sexism, and/or sex stereotyping. Sexism refers to the expression of beliefs and behaviors which assign an inferior or secondary status to one of the sexes. Sex stereotyping involves designation of a set of interests, career choices, and behaviors to one sex. Schulwitz (1976) states that sexism occurs when attitudes and actions of individuals promote the use of sex as the basis for judging and categorizing people in matters unrelated to actual sex differences. Basal textbooks or children's trade books are sexist if they demean either sex by using degrading language, omit the actions and achievements of women, or if they show only stereotyped roles. Although sexism can function as a discrimination against either sex, the current problem is most evident in the unfair portrayal of females.

Over the past few years, a pattern of categories in which the types of sexist writing fall has emerged. These categories, along with the findings of studies relevant to these categories, are discussed below.

The first category of sexist writing deals with the frequency of occurrence of males and females in children's literature. Theoretically, there should be an equal number of women and men represented in the illustrations, titles, and central roles of children's readers. The majority of the research conducted so far indicates this to be far from true. Wylie (1976) analyzed a total of twenty-two stories which were selected by twenty-one teachers as favorite picture books to use with young children. Each picture book was found to contain about twice as many illustrations of male children than female children. In another study (Weitzman 1972) of Caldecott Medal winners, the ratio of titles featuring males to those featuring females was found to be 8 to 3. In the analysis of 325 stories from a prominent basal, Schnell and Sweeney (1975), two thirds of the illustrations were found to feature boys, and somewhat over one third featured girls. In an earlier study (Frashner and Walker, 1972) males were found to be the main characters in more than three times as many stories as females. The number of male main characters was found to far outnumber the female main characters across several studies (Schnell & Sweeney 1975; Wylie 1976). These studies show that males and females are not equally represented. More recently McDaniel and Wilcox (1979), in analyzing three current basal primers, found some bias favoring girls. Based on the results of these studies, one might detect a moderation or even a reversal of the earlier trends.

A second category of sexist writing deals with the personality and character traits which are attributed to males and females in the stories. In reviewing some studies a clear pattern of the stereotypic personality traits assigned to each sex emerges. One of the major characteristics attributed to males was that of independence. In a number of different studies (Graebner 1972; Hillman 1976; Schulwitz 1976; Wylie 1976) males were found to be more independent, clever, imaginative and competent than girls. Females seem to be portrayed as the weaker sex, incapable of problem solving and achievements, dependent, and lacking in initiative and competence. Males, on the other hand, seem to show a higher degree of positive and desirable qualities; leadership, independence, initiative, curiosity, bravery, perseverence, and problem-solving ability.

The third category deals with the interests and activities of males and females depicted in the stories. It was the general finding (Graebner, 1976, Frashner and Walker, 1972, and Shirreffs, 1975) that boys are depicted as active and adventuresome, while girls are shown as passive and immobile.

Category four relates to career choices; not only are female career-role assignments fewer in number, they are also much more limited in variety and quality. Stewig (1975), found that 68 percent of the books included women in the homemaking role and only 32 percent in any type of professional roles. Shirreffs (1975) reported that a young child might conclude after reading all but one of the series investigated that a female has three choices: to become a nurse, to become an unmarried teacher, or to become a mother.

A fifth category of sexist writing deals with how the role of the male and female in the family is portrayed in the literature. The roles of the mother and father are clearly described in the literature. The mother figure is typically presented as a pleasant, hardworking, but basically uninteresting person. She is almost always confined to the house and her duties there are not portrayed as difficult or challenging. She is shown as a house-bound servant who cares for her husband and children and is essentially or basically insipid and boring (Weitzman 1972; Frashner and Walker 1972).

Through books children learn about the world outside their immediate environment. Stefflre (1970) states that from the readers used in schools, children derive their first view of the world beyond the schoolroom, the home, and their immediate community. They learn about what other boys and girls do, say, and feel. They learn about what is right and wrong and what is expected of children their age. In stereotyping, the writers' of children's literature cast models for the children to identify with which are limited and unrealistic and do not allow for individual differences. In addition to learning sex-role identification and sex-role expectations, boys and girls are socialized through readers to accept society's definition of the relative worth of each of the sexes and to assume the personality characteristics that are typical of members of each sex (Weitzman 1972). Children learn how to fill stereotypic sex roles, but not how to become worthwhile individuals in their own right.

The rigidity of sex role stereotypes is harmful not only to little girls. Little boys may feel equally constrained by the necessity to be fearless, brave, and clever at all times. While girls are allowed a great deal of emotional expression, a boy who cries or expresses fear is unacceptable. Equally important perhaps, males do not want or should not have the steady diet of attributes they display in the books (Graebner 1972). Some believe that boys' stories should outnumber girls' because boys won't read stories about females. A good reason for this could be that stories about girls consistently show them in dull and inconsequential activities. Two authors (Frashner and Walker 1972) felt that the strongly stereotyped activity picture of boys presented in the reading series was one which might well contribute to, rather than relieve, the greater number of reading problems boys have. By giving the impression that boys should nearly always be playing ball, riding bikes, or climbing trees, little reinforcement is given to the idea that reading and other language related activities are also appropriate and fun for boys. It is evident that the stereotypic roles forced on boys and girls in children's literature could do damage to the development of these children's goals and attitudes.

The following checklist, developed by a committee of the International Reading Association, should be helpful to teachers in evaluating the sex bias in textbooks and trade books.

The Committee on Sexism and Reading of the International Reading Association has developed the following checklist to assist teachers in analyzing educational materials for sex stereotypes and related language usage. All persons responsible for selecting books for classroom, school, or districtwide use or functioning in any capacity as educators should be aware of the implications of sex-role stereotyping and exclusionary language.

Directions: Place a check in the appropriate space. Most items should be evaluated separately for each sex.

	Almost always	Occasionally	Rarely
1. Are girls and boys, men and women consistently represented in equal balance?			
2. Do boys and girls participate equally in both physical and intellectual activities?			
3. Do girls and boys each receive positive recognition for their endeavors? Females / Males			
4. Do boys and girls, fathers and mothers participate in a wide variety of domestic chores, not only the ones traditional for their sex? Females / Males			
5. Do both girls and boys have a variety of choices and are they encouraged to aspire to various goals, including nontraditional ones if they show such inclination? Females / Males			
6. Are both boys and girls shown developing independent lives, independently meeting challenges and finding their own solutions? Females / Males			
7. Are women and men shown in a variety of occupations, including nontraditional ones? When women are portrayed as fulltime homemakers, are they depicted as competent and decisive? Females / Males			

8. Do characters deprecate themselves because of their sex? (Example: "I'm only a girl.") Do others use denigrating language in this regard? (Example: "That's just like a woman.")

Females _____ _____ _____
Males _____ _____ _____

9. Do the illustrations stereotype the characters, either in accordance to the dictates of the text or in contradiction to it?

Females _____ _____ _____
Males _____ _____ _____

10. Is inclusionary language used? (For example, "police officer" instead of "policeman," "staffed by" instead of "manned by," "all students will submit the assignment" instead of "each student will submit his assignment," and so on.)

Females _____ _____ _____
Males _____ _____ _____

Sex Differences in Reading Achievement

Another more subtle aspect of sexism relating to reading and reading instruction which is not discussed extensively in the reported literature is the different opinions about the *reasons* for the differences in boys' and girls' reading achievement scores.

A survey of some studies shows that the emphasis has changed in research from attempts to establish that sex differences in reading achievement exist to attempts to establish why sex differences exist. A common assumption still appears to be that girls are superior readers and boys are superior in quantitative achievement.

In a 1977 review of sex differences in reading, Klein begins with the statement that over the years girls do better than boys in reading, often at significant levels of differences. In an extensive federally funded study, Herman (1975) found support for the findings of many smaller studies in asserting a consensus that the superiority of girls over boys was substantiated. While some writers attempt to show that the difference lies in an inherent physiological base, others remain content to imply that genetic differences are the cause.

The weight of the evidence of the difference in reading between boys and girls falls in two areas: (1) boys are over-represented in remedial reading and learning disabilities classes and (2) girls score higher on tests of reading achievement.

The second major factor on which sex differences in reading are based, test scores, is equally questionable. Maccoby and Jacklin (1974) systematically analyzed and interpreted a massive body of reported research findings in such areas as perception, cognition, achievement, self-concept, activity level, sociability, aggression, competition, dominance, modeling and socialization, hormonal level and genetic factors. These authors found that sex differences in reading and arithmetic achievement are minimal during the early school years. Further, it has apparently been established that differences disappear in adulthood (Johnson, 1976; Herman, 1975). Dwyer (1976), however, questioned the bias of the instruments used to measure the differences.

Assuming that true differences exist, however, has led to the question "Why do such differences exist?" Traditionally, the difference has been said to derive from the apparent tendency for girls to develop superior verbal skills, while boys excel in spatial perception. However, Maccoby and Jacklin (1974) contend that the two sexes are very similar in their interests and in utilization of information that comes to them via hearing and vision.

The nature-nurture controversy continues to be explored to explain the presumed differences. Johnson (1976) compared English speaking children from grades two, four, and six who were from Canada, England, Nigeria and the United States and concluded that culture is a dominant factor affecting sex differences in reading. He reasons that universality, essential to proving biological causation, has been disproved by his study.

Gruend-Slepack and Berlowitz (1977) assert that the United States is making headway against more traditional patterns. American textbooks show more women in a positive light, more often in careers, and an overall tendency toward less male dominance than those in Germany.

Gentile and McMillan (1976), say that such stereotypes as "reading is sissy" have caused Spanish-American boys to have reading problems and they urge the use of male tutors. However, in the same journal issue Lahaderne (1976) argues that the fears of feminized schools leading to boys' reading problems have been refuted by recent studies.

The research literature concerning sex differences in reading achievement raises some questions that stem from the very nature of using sex as a research variable. First, the bias in the instruments used to measure differences combined with the bias of the referral procedure seems to be serious enough for a challenge to the consensus that a significant difference does exist. Second, assuming a difference does exist, surely a more reasonable and fair method of eliminating the differences can be found than that of creating reading material and designing tests to eliminate any factor that is neutral or does not favor boys and creating or leaving intact factors which do not enhance girls' chances of success. No one is helped by artificially inflated scores and, if the research itself contains sexual bias, nothing definitive will come from the findings.

RACIAL BIAS

Subtle types of racial bias and discrimination also occur in children's books. A review of some recent reports dealing with racial discrimination in children's writing reveals some fascinating yet distressing results. Racism, in this case, refers to the actions and attitudes expressed in writing which assign racial and ethnic minority groups to an inferior or secondary status. In literature the idea is often conveyed that the white race is superior. Several categories of studies deal with different types of racist writing. One category deals with the frequency of occurrence of ethnic minorities compared to whites and a second deals with the professional and occupational roles assigned to each in children's literature.

Allen (1971) examined 42 textbooks to determine the frequency of occurrence of pictures of black people. In over one third of the texts, the blacks were completely ignored. In the texts which did not ignore them only an average of 14 percent of the pictures featured blacks. Britton (1975) found that out of 5,242 stories analyzed minority groups were represented in only 14 percent of the stories as main characters or involved in a significant way. Out of a sample of 25 books from 175 purchased for the children's literature section of a midwestern university library, only 25 percent included black Americans as main characters (Wunderlich 1974). Wunderlich also observed, however, that even when blacks are featured as main characters of stories, it is typically the white who resolves the problem of the black, instead of the solution coming from some mutual endeavor.

While the findings of these studies are distressing, there is some evidence that black representation in children's books is increasing and the quality of their representation is being improved. Chall (1978) reports that overall, compared to 1965, definite improvements can be seen in children's books containing black characters. The percentage of books with one or more black characters in text or illustrations doubled. This author goes on to say that the characters were placed in contemporary settings and also had more prominent roles in stories.

What are the children of all races learning relative to racial and ethnic minorities during the teaching of reading? Ignoring blacks and other minority groups may suggest to white children that only their kind is important. Black or minority children may be impressed with their own lack of importance. Minority children see their own ethnic group depicted in only a few skilled positions. The ones that are shown are extremely limited in variety. This does not provide them with the realistic scope of opportunities that are open in life, and may not stimulate them to reach self-actualization. As a result, black children may find it difficult to identify with goals so far removed from what they might become.

What can be done about the sexism and racism in children's readers and picture books? The available literature reflects a concern dating back to 1971. Yet, to date, some educators appear to not be evaluating books selected for use with their young children or trying in any way to help solve this problem. The educator, as a professional, is equipped with an excellent sense of judgment and fair play. Teachers should first become aware of the most common or prevalent types of sexism and racism, and then use their professional judgment in coping with them.

Schulwitz (1976) offers some excellent suggestions about ways in which to cope with the problem. Teachers should first thoroughly examine the reading materials they are using. Knowing the sexist and racist aspects of books will make it easier to deal with them. They can explore and modify racist or sexist attitudes as they come across them in their teaching. The stories they read can be modified and changed. Teachers can help develop critical thinking abilities about the author's sexist or racist language and concepts. Finally, teachers can omit some stories or books which are extremely sexist or racist and substitute some of the newer or existing non-sexist ones.

The accountability movement of the past decade was one of the first indications of public disenchantment with the public schools and public school personnel. Although, as one author points out, accountability is not new it has had a substantial impact on school personnel (Laffey, 1973).

In more recent years there has been further decline in support for public education and an all too apparent drop in the public's confidence in decisions made by educators. There is evidence to support these contentions in the taxpayer's unwillingness to support bond issues and other financial measures to aid public schools and public school personnel.

School superintendents are sometimes viewed with suspicion by the public, school teachers, and school boards. School principals and supervisors are often viewed as adversaries by teachers. School boards and state legislators are often seen as necessary evils. They are there primarily to challenge the professional judgment of educators and to intrude on educational policy decisions. The effect of the decline in support and esteem for public education and educators has resulted in a new demand for quality with some attention being given to output as measured by standardized and criterion referenced tests (Baratz, 1978).[1]

Emphasis on the use of standardized measures, in turn, has resulted in the question raised by Page (1978): "What kind of reading will the law prescribe?" This author goes on to describe three types of reading definitions: (1) the spoken analogue definitions, (2) reconstructing the author's message definitions, and (3) the definitions reflecting a reader's constructive views of the printed message. Each of these definitional viewpoints is questioned in light of its potential as an appropriate legal definition which, in turn, would structure the focus of the school's reading curriculum. Regardless of the final answer to the definitional question, it is all too apparent that critical decisions about the school's reading curriculum can and have been imposed by some state school boards and state legislatures. This could have unfortunate consequences, especially in the instances where legislation is enacted and a state school board enacts the legislation prematurely by imposing standards on students without carefully field testing the evaluation instruments. In fact, in one state, the Board of Directors of the State Reading Association submitted a request in the form of a carefully written memo to the State's Board of Education to delay establishing a test criterion. The memo also recommended that the state board field test the instrument and the test items across the state and among different student populations. The State's Board of Education turned down the Reading Association's Board's request and arbitrarily established a minimal level of performance. As a result of this decision, hundreds of students failed the minimal competency test. It is evident from this experience that although legislatures and state school boards have the right to act and usually are attempting to act in the best interests of students, often premature decisions and consequent actions can and do have an extremely negative effect on students' self-concept as learners.

---

[1] See also the discussion of accountability by Ransom and Mitchell in Chapter Five.

Another author carries the idea of legal influence on the schools one step further by suggesting that legislation should be enacted which would require the schools to acquire, evaluate and, where relevant, implement research findings concerning promising instructional practices in reading (Schember 1978).

In some states teachers and other educators have relatively little influence among politicians and on the legislative process. Some attempts have been made by school personnel to have some input into the type of legislation which should be enacted. The South Carolina State International Reading Association, (I.R.A.) Council in 1977 achieved some very positive results by communicating directly with the governor and other state legislators. The council and some of its officers were invited to make a presentation to a legislative study committee. The study committee was in the process of writing new legislation relating to minimal competency testing in South Carolina. As a result of their meeting and other contacts with the committee, the state IRA president reported that there was quite a change in the committee's attitude and thinking. Of course, the action taken by the South Carolina I.R.A. Council is atypical both to the extent that they were informed ahead of time of the type of legislation that was being considered and also because the council, in fact, did influence the pending legislation. In many other states minimal competency legislation was enacted before educators were fully aware that it was being considered. Regardless of the many unfortunate experiences educators have had with politics and the law, it is apparent that more widespread changes are taking place.

An incident which gives some indication of the change is one which took place recently in Virginia. A new law which would have put a freeze on minimum class size in the primary grades was proposed by one legislator. The Virginia Education Association which had been monitoring the legislation session immediately called forth an array of experts and teachers to contact the legislators and the governor to put a stop to the proposed legislation. Even though by that time the bill had passed the Virginia State Senate by a 40-0 vote, it was nevertheless later defeated in the Virginia House of Representatives. According to the Director of Research for the Virginia Education Association, it was the opposition of the Virginia Educators Association which prevented it from passing. It is apparent that the type of action taken both by the South Carolina State I.R.A. Council and the Virginia Education Association is the type of action that needs to be taken on critical educational issues. Furthermore, it is obvious that educators as voters need to show their displeasure with inappropriate and harmful legislative actions to local, state and national educational policies at the polls.

TELEVISION AND READING

Television has been called the "plug-in drug" (Winn, 1979). The viewer does not need to act or react other than turning on a television set and monitoring the sound level. This passive participation in many ways can affect both parents and children. Television viewing should continue to be a concern of educators and educational researchers. Over the years television viewing time has been under constant study. In a comprehensive report Waters (1977) claims that children under 5 watch over twenty-three hours of television a week. Even though it is less than the forty-four hours of television viewing of adults weekly, it still is an enormous amount of time which could be an influence especially in light of some other statistics relating to the number of commercials (350,000) and murders (18,000) that would be viewed during this time.

Regardless of the time children spend watching television, a more important concern has to be the relationship of reading to television viewing. Winn (1977) analyzed the relationship of reading to television and noted: (1) that reading entails a transformation of symbolic images which television does not often include, (2) that the quality of reading materials was far superior to the quality of television programs, (3) that reading involves and demands a much higher level of concentration than television viewing and, finally, (4) that the reader controls the pace of the experience whereas in television viewing the pace is controlled by the program. The pace in television in turn limits the opportunity for viewers to use their imagination. Even though the limiting qualities of television are well known, it appears almost unreasonable to suggest that teachers need to recommend that children should watch less television or attempt to combat the television viewing habits of their students. It appears that the viewing habits are beyond the control of teachers and the schools. A far more constructive effort seems to be within the reach of teachers. For example, Becker (1973) suggests a rich variety of strategies that teachers can use to help understand their students' interest as a basis for promoting reading through the use of television. By following these suggestions and many others, Becker claims that "Bringing television into the classroom encourages you to become aware of a changing world as depicted through this medium and to use this knowledge as a means of making your teaching more exciting and relevant." Adams and Harrison (1975) suggest a variety of strategies as one way to individualize assignments and as a way to provide supplementary exercises to reading skills lessons. These authors list twenty specific reading skill areas from which the teacher could choose to use as a supplementary skill lesson for reading. Gough (1979) describes a series of television programs which can be used to motivate readers. These instructional television programs have the ability to bring to class outstanding storytellers that are not available through other means. Also, instructional television has the capability to dramatize exciting excerpts from stories to make them come alive. It can also bring authors to life for the students. Finally, instructional television can bring other related arts to the classroom to enhance a production.

Television is here to stay, and for classroom teachers television can be either an enemy or an ally. If viewed as an enemy, it seems that it is one that is untouchable. If viewed as an ally and used as suggested, then television can do nothing but promote more and better reading.[2]

---

[2] See also the discussion of the influence of television by Strickler and Eller in Chapter Thirteen.

SUMMARY

All too often competence in teaching reading to the culturally different is equated with different programs and approaches. There are justifiable reasons for this. A number of different approaches that utilize different published reading programs have proven their potential for success with culturally different students. The success of specific programs depends less on the quality of the instructional programs and the different approaches than it does on the quality and competency of the teacher. The key to high quality reading instruction for culturally different students is teachers who are well-prepared professionally, who are sensitive, and who sincerely care for their students.

The evidence regarding sex bias in basal readers and trade books is conflicting so teachers must review materials carefully. If books which present biased or stereotyped treatment of either sex must be used, teachers and children should be aware of this discrimination in the literature. Data reviewed in this chapter suggest that sex differences in reading achievement appear to be diminishing.

Teachers are encouarged to be more active politically and to work for legislation they consider essential for education of high quality.

In data reported regarding the influence of television on children's reading it was suggested that teachers and parents work with children to establish criteria for program selection, and that television be used to encourage and stimulate reading. The two media can be and should be mutually reinforcing.

REFERENCES

Adams, A. H. and Harrison, C. B. "Using Television To Teach Specific Reading Skills." *The Reading Teacher,* Vol. 29, No. 1, October, 1975, pp. 45–51.

Alatis, James E. "Teaching Standard English as a Second Language or Dialect." In *Teaching English as a Second Language and as a Second Dialect,* edited by Robert P. Fox. Washington, D.C.: National Council of Teachers of English, 1973.

Allen, V. S. "An Analysis of Textbooks Relative to the Treatment of Black Americans." *The Journal of Negro Education,* 1971, *40,* 140–145.

Bailey, Beryl L. "Some Principles of Bilingual and Bidialectal Education." In *Teaching English as a Second Language and as a Second Dialect,* edited by Robert P. Fox. Washington, D.C.: National Council of Teachers of English, 1973.

Baratz, J. C. "Policy Issues in Education: Reading and the Law" in *Reading and the Law,* edited by Harper and Kilaar, IRA/ERIC, 1978, pp. 11–15.

Becker, G. J. "Television and the Classroom Reading Program." Reading Aid Series, International Reading Association. Newark, Delaware: 1973, pp. 1–32.

Billingsley, Andrew. *Black Families in White America.* Englewood Cliffs, New Jersey: Prentice-Hall, 1968.

Britton, G. E. "Danger: State Adopted Texts May Be Hazardous To Our Future." *The Reading Teacher,* 1975, *29,* 52–58.

Caudill, Harry M. *Night Comes To the Cumberlands.* Boston: Little, Brown, 1962.

Chall, Jean S. "Blacks In the World Of Children's Books". *The Reading Teacher,* Vol. 32, No. 5, February, 1979, pp. 527–533.

Cohen, S. Alan. *Teach Them All to Read,* New York: Random House, 1969.

Crow, Lester D.; Murray, Walter I.; and Smythe, Hugh H. *Educating the Culturally Disadvantaged Child.* New York: David McKay Company, 1966.

DiPietro, Robert J. "Bilingualism and Bidialectalism." In *Teaching English As a*

Second Language and As a Second Dialect, edited by Robert P. Fox. Washington, D.C.: National Council of Teachers of English, 1973.

Dwyer, Carol. "Test Content and Sex Differences in Reading." The *Reading Teacher,* 1976, *29,* 753–757.

Elam, Sophie L. "Acculturation and Learning Problems of Puerto Rican Children." In *The Disadvantaged Learner,* edited by Staten W. Webster. San Francisco: Chandler Publishing Company, 1966.

Ford, Thomas R. *The Southern Appalachian Region: A Survey.* Lexington, Kentucky: University of Kentucky Press, 1962.

Frashner, R. & Walker, A. "Sex Roles in Early Reading Textbooks." *The Reading Teacher,* 1972, *25,* 741–749.

Gentile, Lance M. and McMillan, Merma M. "When Johnny Can't Read But Mary Can, Men Can Help." *The Reading Teacher,* 1976, *29,* 771–775.

Giffin, Roscoe. "Newcomers from the Southern Mountains." *In Culture and School,* edited by Ronald Shinn. Scranton, Pennsylvania: Interest Educational Publishers, 1972.

Glazer, Nathan. "Ethnicity and the School." *Commentary,* No. 58 (1974), pp. 55–59.

Gough, P. B. "Introducing Children to Books Via Television." *The Reading Teacher,* Vol. 32, No. 4, January, 1979, pp. 458–462.

Graebner, D. B. "A Decade of Sexism in Readers." *The Reading Teacher,* 1972, *26,* 52–57.

Grund-Slepack, Donna and Berlowitz, Marvin. "Sex Role Stereotyping In East Germany versus United States Textbooks." *The Reading Teacher,* 1977, *31,* 275–279.

Hall, Mary Anne. *The Language Experience Approach for the Culturally Disadvantaged.* Newark, Del.: International Reading Association, 1972.

Harper, R. J. and Kilaar, G. "The Changing Theory Of the Reading Process: Does Society Really Know How It Reads?" in *Reading and the Law,* edited by Harper and Kilaar, IRA/ERIC, 1978, pp. 53–65.

Harrington, Michael. *The Other America.* New York: Macmillan, 1962.

Harris, Albert, and Serwer, B. L. "The Craft Project: Instructional Time in Reading Research." *Reading Research Quarterly 2* (1966): 27–56.

Herman, Magdalin, ed. *Male-Female Achievement in Eight Learning Areas.* Denver, Colorado: Education Commission of the U.S., 1975.

Hillman, J. S. "An Analysis of Male and Female Roles in Two Periods of Children's Literature." *The Journal of Educational Research,* 1974, *68,* 84–87.

Hillman, J. S. "Occupational Roles in Children's Literature." *The Elementary School Journal,* 1976, 77, 1–4.

Hyman, Herbert. "The Value Systems of Different Classes: A Social Psychological Contribution to the Analysis of Stratification." In *Class Status and Power,* edited by Reinhard Bendix and Seymour Martin Lipset. Glencoe, Illinois: The Free Press of Glencoe, 1962.

Johnson, Dale, "Cross-Cultural Perspectives on Sex Differences in Reading." *The Reading Teacher,* 1976, *29,* 747–752.

Johnson, Kenneth R. *Teaching the Culturally Disadvantaged.* Palo Alto, Calif.: Science Research Associates, 1970.

Klein, Howard A. "Cross-Cultural Studies—What Do They Tell About Sex Differences in Reading." *The Reading Teacher,* 1977, *30,* 880–86.

Kim, Y.; Berger, B.; and Kratochvil, D. W. "Product Development Report No. 14—Distar Instructional System." Palo Alto, Calif.: American Institutes for Research, 1972.

Kluckholn, Clyde. *Culture and Behavior.* New York: The Free Press of Glencoe, 1962.

Laffey, James L. "Accountability: A Brief History and Analysis." in *Accountability and Reading Instruction.* Edited by R. Ruddell, N.C.T.E. 1973, pp. 1–12.

Lahaderne, Henriette M. "Feminized Schools—Unpromising Myth to Explain Boys' Reading Problems." *The Reading Teacher,* 1976, *29,* 776–786.

Maccoby, Eleanor and Jacklin, Carol. *The Psychology of Sex Differences.* Stanford, Calif.: Stanford University Press, 1974.

Malinowski, Bronislaw. *A Scientific Theory of Culture and Other Essays.* Chapel Hill, North Carolina: The University of North Carolina Press, 1944.

Marden, Charles F., and Meyer, Gladys. *Minorities in American Society.* New York: American Book Company, 1968.

Martinez, Armando. "Literacy Through Democratization of Education." *Harvard Educational Review* 40 (1970): 280–282.

Maryland Department of Economic Development. *The Appalachian Region: A Preliminary Analysis of Economic and*

Population Trends in an Eleven State Problem Area. Annapolis, Maryland: Maryland Department of Economic Development, 1960.

Modiano, Nancy. "Where Are the Children?" *Florida F. L. Reporter,* No. 7, 1969, p. 93.

Monteith, Mary K. "Alternatives to Burning Sexist Textbooks." *The Reading Teacher,* 1977, *31,* 346–347.

Naiden, Norma. "Ratio of Boys to Girls Among Disabled Readers." *The Reading Teacher,* 1976, *29,* 439–442.

Narang, H. L. "Improving Reading Ability of Indian Children." *Elementary English,* 51 (1974): 190–192.

Oliver, L. "Women in Aprons: The Female Stereotype in Children's Readers." *The Elementary School Journal,* 1974, *74,* 253–259.

Page, W. D. "What Kind of Reading Will the Law Prescribe?" in *Reading and the Law,* edited by R. J. Harper and G. Kilaar, IRA/ERIC, 1978, pp. 27–35.

Riessman, Frank. *The Culturally Deprived Child,* New York: Harper and Row, 1962.

Rodriguez, Armando. "The Mexican-American—Disadvantaged? Ya Basta!" *Florida G. L. Reporter,* 7, (1969): 35.

Rosenthal, Robert. "The Pygmalion Effect Lives." *Psychology Today,* September, 1973.

Schnell, T. R. & Sweeney, J. "Sex Role Bias in Basal Readers." *Elementary English,* 1975, *52,* 737–742.

Schulwitz, B. S. "Coping With Sexism in Reading Materials." *The Reading Teacher,* 1976, *29,* 768–770.

Science Research Associates. "Summaries of Case Studies for the Effectiveness of the Distar Instructional System." Palo Alto, Calif.: Science Research Associates, 1971.

Shirreffs, J. H. "Sex-Role Stereotyping on Elementary School Health Education Textbooks." *Journal of School Health,* 1975, *45,* 519–522.

Stefflre, B. "Run, Mama, Run: Women Workers in Elementary Readers." The *Vocational Guidance Quarterly,* 1970, *18,* 99–103.

Stewart, William A. "Urban Negro Speech: Sociolinguistic Factors Affecting English Teaching." *Florida F. L. Reporter,* 7 (1969): 58.

Stewig, J. W. "Sexism in Picture Books: What Progress?" *The Elementary School Journal,* 1975, *76,* 551–555.

Stuart, Jesse. *To Teach, To Love.* New York: World Publishing-Times Mirror, 1970.

Waters, H. F. "What T.V. Does To Kids." *Newsweek,* February 21, 1977, pp. 62–70.

Whitman, L. J. "Sex-Role Socialization in Picture Books for Preschool Children." *American Journal of Sociology,* 1972, *77,* 1125–1149.

Winn, Marie. *The Plug In Drug.* New York: Viking Press, 1977, pp. 1–231.

Wunderlich, E. "Black Americans in Children's Books." *The Reading Teacher,* 1974, *28,* 282–285.

Wylie, R. E. "Sex Bias in Children's Books." *Childhood Education,* 1976, *52,* 220–222.

Yawkey, T. D. & Yawkey, M. F. "An Analysis of Picture Books." *Language Arts,* 1976, *53,* 545–548.

PREVIEW

Professional educators have given a considerable amount of attention to the implications of language learning for teachers of reading. The experts very seldom deny the importance of the relationship between language development and the reading process even though their viewpoints and interpretation of research findings may be different. They recognize that the facility with which individuals use language will have an impact upon their reading achievement. They discuss the parallels in the development of reading and writing skills.

Goodman and Burke have made extensive contributions to the fields of psycholinguistics and sociolinguistics. These contributions are evident in topics such as language as a graphophonic system, a semantic system, and a syntactic system. They state their position on the influence of dialects on reading achievement—a matter of considerable professional concern. Although the chapter is basically theoretical, it does include suggestions you will find practical as a teacher of reading.

4

Language and Psycholinguistic Bases

Yetta Goodman, University of Arizona
Carolyn Burke, Indiana University

OBJECTIVES

After you have read this chapter, you should be able to:

1. **From personal recent language experiences describe the differences between receptive and productive language.**

2. **Make a chart to show the similarities and differences among listening, speaking, reading, and writing.**

3. **Provide evidence from children's language samples to show that the purpose of language is communication.**

4. **Provide evidence from your own experience to show that reading is an active language process.**

5. **Explain the essential interrelationships of the semantic, syntactic, and graphophonic systems of American English.**

6. **Match concepts and language structures of children to the concepts and language structures of selected reading material for children.**

Since the beginning of the twentieth century, psychologists and linguists have studied and analyzed language and how people use it. Psychologists have emphasized the use that people make of language, the ways that language relates to learning and thinking, and how language controls people's behavior. Linguists have analyzed the structural components of language, explored the meanings of words and sentences in different settings, and described how language changes are based on historic, economic, age, geographic, or racial differences.

Around 1960, it became obvious that neither linguistics nor psychology, as separate fields, had an understanding of the scope of the issues and problems involved in how people use language. Linguists began to look to psychology and psychologists began to look to linguistics to learn more about language from each other. The disciplines of communication theory, sociology, and anthropology were also investigated for their contributions to the study of language. As the concepts from all these fields became interrelated, the new field of psycholinguistics emerged.

Much of language difference is related to the social status and role orientation of language users. The study of human reasons for language differences and their functions in society added another field of study known as sociolinguistics. Its development closely parallels that of psycholinguistics, and the fields have many concerns in common.

About 1960, the word *psycholinguistics* began to be used frequently. Now it appears in books and in prominent dictionaries. There are courses at universities in the field of psycholinguistics, and there are professionals who refer to themselves as psycholinguists.

Psycholinguistics is the study of the interrelationship between thought and language processes. It is the study of how people use language, how language affects human behavior, and how language is learned.

Reading is language—and it is the responsibility of those who will teach reading to understand the significance of that statement. Therefore, this chapter will discuss the interrelationship among reading, writing, speaking, listening, language development, and the factors affecting language and cognitive development in the school setting. It will also suggest ways to apply the growing knowledge of psycholinguistics in the classroom.

LANGUAGE: SYSTEMS AND PROCESSES

Teachers and students are speaking, listening, writing, and reading continually during the school day. Whenever the term *language* is used in relation to school instruction, all four aspects of language are implied. It is through these four aspects of language that much of human communication takes place. The listener or reader must actively process that which the writer or speaker has actively produced or there will be no communication.

Language Systems

In order to communicate, speakers, listeners, readers, and writers must follow a similar set of rules. These are not rules of which the language user is consciously aware. In fact, in most cases, people cannot state or explain the language rules they use.

For centuries linguists, or more specifically grammarians, have constructed models of these rule systems to show how languages operate. These models are called grammars. All models, including models of language, change as new knowledge is discovered. When, for example, views of the earth became available from space travel, the globe—a scale model of the earth—was changed by geophysicists to accommodate those recent discoveries. Grammatical models, too, have changed over the years as linguists found out more about language. First attempts at explaining the structure of English were made by borrowing archaic Latin grammars (the Romans having already borrowed from earlier Greek grammars). Where differences existed between the two languages, the English was forced into the pre-existing Latin structures (Gleason, 1965, pp. 28–31).

At about this time anthropological linguists began to turn their attention to mapping the structure of a number of languages which did not possess writing systems. This study, focusing its attention upon the unique structural qualities of individual languages, legitimatized describing language as it is spoken in a particular place at a particular time. As a result, the next attempts at explaining English used the techniques of descriptive linguistics (Gleason, 1965, pp. 37–57).

More recently, the "transformational-generative (TG)" model has become regarded by some linguists as the most promising for describing the features of language. First introduced in 1957 by Noam Chomsky, the TG model has undergone a number of significant revisions. All versions, however, are looked at as models of *linguistic competence,* that is, our tacit knowledge of the rule system of a language. *Linguistic performance,* that is, speaking, listening, writing, and reading, makes use of this linguistic competence, as well as other cognitive abilities. All versions are *generative,* that is, the rule system is capable of generating all the sentences of the language, and only the sentences of the language. For example in an informal conversation, an English speaker would not produce a sentence such as *wear I shoes yellow.* Evidence that we have this linguistic knowledge is the fact that speakers of English understand that *we called up mary* and *we called mary up* have the same meaning, even though they are different on the *surface.* We know this because these two sentences have the same *deep structure,* which is an underlying, abstract level where meaning is determined. The rules that transform the single deep structure of these sentences into two surface structures are called *transformational rules.* This is the view according to Chomsky's 1965 model of transformational grammar called the *standard theory.*

There are other types of generative grammars such as case grammar (Fillmore, 1968); but the importance all generative grammars have for language learning is the notion that children do not imitate and memorize every sentence of their language but rather they learn the *rules* of that language. These rules involve all components or systems of the grammar. Linguistics is in a very dynamic time period so these models are undergoing continuous rethinking and updating.

Three interrelated language systems are necessary for written and oral communication to take place. Oral language utilizes the phonological, syntactic, and semantic systems and written language utilizes the graphophonic, syntactic, and semantic systems. The word *system* emphasizes the fact that rules are involved.

Phonological System   The phonological system consists of the rules that govern the sound patterns of language. For example, speakers of English recognize that "tr" is a permissible word initial sound sequence (trip, try) but not permissible as the final sounds of words. *Trup* or *trop* might be English words but *nutr* or *retr* could not be. Speakers of English can also recognize the systematic difference in stress for nouns and verbs in pairs such as "pérmit", "permít", "cónvict" and "convíct", "ínsult" and "insúlt".

Graphophonic System   In languages such as English, the visual representation of language or the graphic system uses alphabetic symbols. Although there is a relationship between the graphic system and oral language, it is not the case that each alphabetic symbol or groups of symbols systematically represents particular sounds of the language.

Other languages, such as Chinese, may not utilize an alphabetic system but rather an idiographic one in which each symbol represents a meaningful unit.

The Semantic System   The relationship that words, phrases, clauses, and sentences have to objects and functions as well as to abstract ideas (such as meanings and thoughts) comprises the semantic system of language. This system is the core of the language process.[1] Communication is a language's reason for being. The other two systems of language exist to facilitate this purpose.

The Syntactic System   The graphophonic system and the semantic system can be fully related through the order and rules of the syntactic system. The rules which are used to indicate the interrelationship of syntactic structures (words, phrases, clauses, and sentences), the order of these language units, and how these language units are changed to indicate tense, number, and gender are the syntactic, or grammatical, system of language. Meaning (the semantic system) can only be communicated through the graphophonic system by employing the rules of syntax.

These three systems are truly interrelated. For example, the words *boy, runs, mother, to, his,* and *the* can be assigned meaning. But presented as individual words separated by commas, they do not actually communicate what the writer was thinking when they were written. However, when the words are placed in a syntactic pattern "The boy runs to his mother", the reader has some understanding of what the writer had in mind. A change in word order or in the inflectional system can convey different meanings. For example: "His mother runs to the boy," or "The boys ran to his mother."

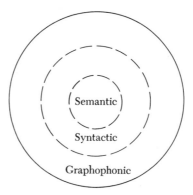

Figure 4.1
The Language Systems.

---

[1] Sometimes the study of how language is used by humans constrained by the social settings in which it occurs and the social interactions between groups and individuals is called pragmatics. In our discussion, we include these interrelationships in the semantic system.

Language Processes

Reading, writing, speaking and listening make use of semantics, syntax and either phonemic or graphophonic representation. When speakers or writers are producing language, they are actively doing many things to make sure that their listener or reader will understand what they have produced. For communication to take place, readers and/or listeners must be actively trying to get the message. They use their own language, background, and experience to try to understand the message of the speaker or writer. Language —both oral and written—is an active process.

Oral Language   During speaking and listening, it is the phonological system that communicates meaning. Without some kind of mechanical recording device, oral language is fleeting and cannot be recalled exactly as it occurred. Any ideas conveyed through oral language must be recreated if they are to be discussed again later.

Oral language occurs in all human societies. Each language is spoken within a contextual setting common to its speakers, who are together in the same place and know something about the people with whom they are communicating. They share similar experiences; and they can watch each other in order to know whether or not their message is being understood. They use various kinds of body language to enhance their verbal communication. The speaker and listener can interact, ask questions, and explain things to each other when there is a lack of understanding or a breakdown in language communication.

Written Language   In writing and reading, the graphic system represents language. Written language is a more permanent system than oral language. It can be perused again and again. An author can continue to rewrite something until it is exactly what he or she would like to express. A reader can reread a passage in order to rethink or redefine it. In written language, the other participant (the reader) is usually not immediately available to the writer. Written language, therefore, must include information regarding people, places, and times, so that whoever comes in contact with the written language will have enough context available to understand the message.

Although reading and writing have the written system in common and listening and speaking have the oral system in common, reading and listening operate in ways that speaking and writing do not.

When people communicate language to others they are producing language. Speaking and writing are the *productive* forms of language. Language producers are concerned with making themselves understood.

Reading and listening are the *receptive* forms of language. When people are on the receiving end of language, they concentrate not on production but on understanding. They use strategies to gain the meaning of what the speaker or writer is saying.

By the time children come to school, they have spent at least five years of their life using strategies to make themselves understood and to understand others. They have usually been successful in communicating with those around them.

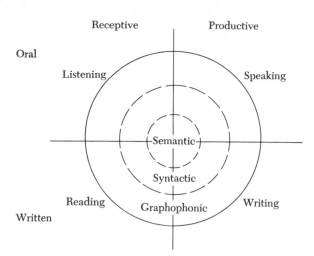

Figure 4.2
The Language Processes

LANGUAGE AND CULTURE

Another aspect of language which teachers of reading must understand clearly is the concept of *dialect*. One way to explain this concept is to draw an
analogy. Just as everyone belongs to a particular group of human beings, so
everyone speaks a particular dialect of a language. No one is *the* human
being or the *normal* human being, with others belonging to a subhuman
species. We are simply of various types, which can be classified by differences
like sex, race, national origin, or occupation. In the same way, no one speaks
the language or *a* standard language with all other variations of the language
considered substandard or disadvantaged. Each dialect is equally capable of
carrying the message of the speaker to others who use the same dialect.

Dialects can be classified by their differences. There are differences between the phonological systems of various dialects, as well as differences
between the syntactic and semantic systems. There are different dialects in
different geographic regions and for different racial and socioeconomic
groups. However, just as there are no clear and distinct lines by which to
categorize human groups, there are no clear and distinct lines among dialect
groups (Wolfram and Fasold, 1974).

Some dialects are considered to have greater prestige than others and
are referred to as standard dialects. Dialects which are not considered prestige
dialects are sometimes called non-standard dialects. Socioeconomic criteria
—not the "goodness" or "correctness" of the language—usually determine
which dialects are prestige or standard. The language of the people who are
considered the socioeconomic leaders of a particular community is most often
the standard language of that community, even if those people comprise only
a small minority. There are probably as many different standard dialects
spoken by middle- and upper-class speakers in this country as there are
non-standard dialects spoken by poor people.

Speakers of American English dialects can understand each other with a
minimum of effort. In general, people can receive a wider range of dialects

than they can produce. Speakers of non-standard dialects, particularly in urban areas, usually have broader experiences in receiving standard dialects than speakers of standard dialects have in receiving non-standard dialects. In other words, non-standard speakers probably understand standard speakers better than standard speakers understand non-standard speakers.

The important bond between language and culture is often reflected in the differences between dialects, as well as in the development of thought. Language and thought are shaped by cultural experiences. When cultural groups lack certain experiences, there is no reason for the people to have concepts or language expressions related to those experiences. American middle-class, nuclear families, for example, have little understanding of terms related to extended family relationships—terms like "Big Daddy," "second cousin twice removed," or "kinfolk."

Experiences stimulate people to think about what is happening to them, and this thinking creates a need for language. At an earlier time in American history, when children were usually looked after within the home, a person needing outside help might have strolled over to a neighbor and said, "Will you sit with my baby while I am gone?" As it became more common for parents to be away from their babies, new language was developed to meet these new experiences, and the term *babysitter* became common: "Will you be my babysitter while I'm gone?" As the concept of babysitting expanded to include various types of roles and duties, it became possible for someone to say: "Will you babysit my dog when I go on my vacation?"

Snow skiing provides another example of the interrelationship of experiences and language. Skiers realize that the way they ski depends on the quality of the snow. When they talk about *corn snow, powder snow,* and *hard packed snow,* they understand—as most non-skiers do not—the significance of such terms.

As children grow up in a particular culture and dialect group, they learn not only to speak the language of that particular group, but also to think and organize their ideas according to the view of the world shared by those with whom they are most intimate (Britton, 1970). *By the time children enter school they have been communicating successfully in the dialect of their home community for at least three years.* Since language, thought, and cultural view are inextricably intermeshed, attempts to change children's dialect or to reject the way they think about the world will disrupt their learning. The teacher must reach out to understand both the children and the world from which they emerge. This acceptance and respect for what the children are will in turn *encourage children* to extend their learning and to expand their language (E. B. Smith and others, 1976).

ORAL LANGUAGE DEVELOPMENT

There is a growing body of research which describes what children do as they learn language. These descriptions are significant for teachers, since they show how the learning of oral language is related to the learning of written language.

Preschool Years

In early infancy, babies babble in a wide range of sounds, many of which do not appear in their mother tongue (Brown, 1973; Dale, 1972). Some are sounds that belong to other languages. At about the age of two, children are just starting to speak; but they have been listening for a long time. They have *receptive* control over their language long before they have *productive* control. They have been listening to a multitude of sounds around them. In order to learn to speak, they have distinguished the particular sounds which belong to the language of their own families and have eliminated others from their oral production. They have learned to understand a great deal of what their parents are saying. Even before the age of two, young children will get things that someone asks for, or will point to objects when requested to do so. They indicate specific people when asked to identify "mommy" or "daddy."

As children begin to organize their world, their need for language grows. In turn, their expanded use of language gives them greater opportunities for discussing, interacting, and thinking. And their use of language develops very quickly. They start out with one or two word sentences and before they are five are speaking in sentences almost as complex as those spoken by their parents. Though it is very complicated for linguists to describe the syntactic and semantic system of any child's or adult's language, it is not difficult for human beings to learn a language during infancy and early childhood. Children's language learning is so precocious that some researchers have been led to hypothesize that language is not learned but is innate (Smith, 1966). It is not necessary to accept the "innate" theory, however, to be impressed with how sophisticated children's language competence becomes.

Children do much more than simply imitate the language they hear. As soon as they begin to produce understandable language, they are generating new language structures which follow systems of rules. When a four-year-old says "He gots my ball," the child is showing control over the rule concerning the *s* endings on verbs following third person singular nouns. But unlike adults' grammar, the child's grammar may not contain the irregular verb form. When children produce language which does not conform to adult language, that language often shows that the child is applying a regular rule to an irregular case. Because children have a social need to communicate and interact, their language moves closer to that of the majority of speakers around them. They accommodate their language to the language of the people with whom they wish to interact.

In addition to learning the rule system of their language, children begin to expand the use of language to serve a variety of purposes. Halliday (1975) found that young children will use language for personal recognition, social interaction, to regulate the behavior of others, to fill their personal needs, to learn about their environment, and to create a world of make-believe and imagination. These functions of language develop and expand as children become effective communicators.

During the preschool years, children are actively developing concepts about the world around them. Sometimes, the child's concepts do not match those of adults. For instance, five-year-olds will often laugh and think you are telling them a joke if you say that people are animals. They see it as totally incongruous to categorize people within the concept of "animal" that they have developed. Children may call all women "mommy" at two, but within a year they call only their own mother "mommy" or "mom" and begin to put other women in other categories. When they play house, they portray the roles and activities of members of their family, showing that they understand what each one does. They recognize voices and distinguish those they know well from strangers' voices. All these things show that preschoolers have already begun to categorize, to differentiate, and to organize their environment (Vygotsky, 1962; Flavell, 1964).

Early School Years

Regardless of community, race, or nationality, all children come to school with language, with a way to think about the world, and with a variety of experiences. Although they acquire some complex aspects of English grammar during the elementary school years, a more significant development is their growing understanding of the relationships among words and what these relationships have to do with their own experience. At age five, children's meanings and concepts do not yet match those of the adult world around them. Any discussion among a group of five-year-olds can reveal the way children view the world.

Mrs. B., a beloved first-grade teacher, started one morning's discussion with "I am a grandmother now." Then she showed the children some pictures of a newborn infant. Pat said, "Now you're old." Barbara said, "Where is your pantsuit and long earrings?" Jimmy, looking unhappy, said, "Now you won't be our teacher any more, and you will have to stay home and babysit the baby."

Each child revealed a different concept of *grandmother*, based on individual experience. Now they began to accommodate into their own thinking the views that the other children and their teacher had about grandmothers. Mrs. B. helped to stimulate this thinking process by asking, "What is a grandmother?" Other children's concepts were added to the discussion. Tom's "grandmother" was an aging widow who lived next door to him and was always giving him fresh baked cookies. But Tom's "grandmother" was not a relative. Jerry's grandmother worked at a factory and was a boss.

The teacher encouraged the children to ask their parents about the term *grandmother,* and they returned the next day with pictures and more ideas. Betty called her mother's grandmother "Grandma" and her own grandmother "Ma." Andy's grandmother didn't like being called "Grandmother" and preferred to be called "Stella." The children talked about all their experiences with grandmothers. No single definition of *grandmother* could fit all they knew, and all they knew did not yet match the concept they would eventually have of grandmothers. But thinking and talking about their experiences expanded their concept of *grandmother,* and the language they used to talk about their new learning was expanded and extended as well.

The greatest aid to children during the elementary school years is a wide range of experiences and a great deal of opportunity to discuss them through a variety of language activities. By the time children complete the elementary school years, they have developed more differentiated thought categories and an ability to handle more abstract ideas.

Middle School Years

The move into adolescence adds new dimensions to the student's thought and language. Not only do teenagers want to talk about the things they know, but they begin to examine and evaluate the ideas they have heard around them and the notions about life they have begun to develop. Their thinking becomes more abstract as they examine philosophies of life, religious questions, and political, scientific, and moral issues. This concern about the world and their place in it often brings adolescents into conflict with adults' more stable view of the world. Often adolescents find themselves in conflict with parents and teachers. As teenagers come together to talk about similar problems and concerns, they often develop unique language that fits some new view of the world which they believe they have discovered. This examination of the world can put the adolescent in the position of a catalyst for cultural change; and this change is often reflected in the dynamic quality of the language of the youth culture. The dialects of the surfer, the motorcycle buff, and the disco dancer exhibit this dynamic quality. The groups farthest removed from the established center of society are less likely to be inhibited in their use of innovative language. It is therefore not surprising that linguistic change seems to be most dynamic among young people.

But adolescents still want and need to communicate with the adult society around them. Although they can use the dynamic language of their peer group, they can also switch easily to the language which is demanded in the classroom or by the adult culture. Teachers who genuinely want to understand and communicate with teenagers will need to show as much respect for and give as much attention to the youth culture as they do to the various ethnic cultures they find represented in their classroom.

WRITTEN LANGUAGE

Language in its written form plays a central role in technologically advanced cultures. It is chiefly through writing that we communicate with, regulate, and appeal to one another.

Central governments, regulating millions of people over billions of acres of land, are made efficient by rapid communication and rapid transit, and this is made possible by *written* language. The president can appear on television and announce a new tax program. However, because of complexities like long and short form schedules, taxation rates based on varying income, deductions, and capital gains, he can enact the program only through written instructions. In fact, without his own ability to use written language, he could not have "held in mind" the complex relationships necessary to have created the program. While the act of taxation is not dependent upon written language, sophistication of taxation is.

We can't take a bus, go shopping, drive, or vote without dealing with written symbols. Often the limits of our ability to participate in the culture are determined by the limits of our ability to deal with written language. Some drivers, for example, seldom or never use the freeways; they are disturbed not only by the speed of traffic, but also by the speed with which they must make decisions to change lanes, exit, or merge, based on some rapidly perceived and minimally cued written information. It can be argued that the most efficient means of discriminating against individuals within our society is to make sure that their facility to receive written language (to read) is not sufficient to meet general public need.

The acquisition of oral language allows people to organize their amorphous perceptions and feelings, to relate their experiences, and to share these experiences with others. The acquisition of written language allows people to reliably expand their relationship to those beyond their physical reach in time and space. Just as a certain complexity of thought is beyond our grasp without the mediating factor of oral language, a level of cultural complexity is dependent upon the use of written language (Winkeljohann, 1973).

It is our culture's ever increasing dependence on written communication which motivates our concern about the teaching of reading. Recent psycholinguistic research has much to contribute to an examination of written language. We will focus on three of these contributions: the role of perception in reading, a view of written language development, and the relationship of writing to reading.

Perception and Reading

Because reading involves the processing of visual information (letters, spaces, words, punctuation marks), a reader's visual acuity and visual perception are often diagnosed as factors of reading difficulty.

Visual acuity is simply a measure of how clearly and distinctly visual images are picked up by the optic nerve. Some limitations on visual acuity are corrected by glasses or by surgery. While such common problems as nearsightedness might cause the reader to tire easily, recent studies have indicated that many minor visual acuity problems do not directly affect success in learning to read (Lindsay and Norman, 1972).

Some cognitive psychologists describe perception as selective attention to and use of stimuli in the environment. Based on our previous experiences and knowledge we predict or anticipate what we will perceive, thereby increasing our perceptual efficiency. We are immersed in a world of color, shape, and texture. If we tried to pay equal attention to all of these stimuli, we would overreach the brain's capacity to accept, organize, store, and retrieve information. You might say we would "blow a fuse." If we were not selective about the visual stimuli which we take in, we would live in a kaleidoscopic world, with lots of color, texture, and movement but no recognizable or stable relationships (Neisser, 1976).

School age children have already developed highly effective visual perception. They have learned to categorize by characteristics instead of paying attention to surface variations. Five-year-olds will recognize as dogs such physically different breeds as chihauhuas, collies, dobermans, and poodles. They will classify a semi, a pick-up, and a van all as examples of truck.

They have intuitively learned to operate by seeking significant characteristics; but if they are to successfully identify the relevant information for any specific category, they must have some previous experience and knowledge of the items which are to be classified. A childhood experience of Carolyn Burke's illustrates this point.

At the age of eight I was a very practiced grocery shopper. It was my job to go to the corner store with a list and pick up all of the miscellaneous items my mother needed between her regular weekly shopping trips. I would always read the list and select the items from the shelves myself. One day I arrived home with the listed items only to have my mother discover that I had bought a cabbage instead of lettuce. I didn't know how to tell the difference between them.

I didn't lack direct contact with these two vegetables. My mother bought one or the other each week and I usually accompanied her to the store. I didn't need perceptual training—I'd been reading since the age of five. I simply had never paid attention to cabbages and lettuces. They had been in my line of vision, but not in my line of perception.

Many adults in our Western culture cannot perceive the differences between makes of cars. They can't tell a Chevrolet from a Ford or a Dodge, much less distinguish between the many different available models. Yet there are ten-year-olds who can use fender shape, grill design, and general lines to make just such distinctions. The adult has simply chosen not to attend to these distinctions.

Some children labeled "culturally different" or "disadvantaged" or "learning disabled" do very poorly on perceptual tasks assigned by the school. They seem unable to consistently identify the one duck who is going in the wrong direction out of a line of four ducks,

or to note correctly which letter is different:

h   n   h   h

Yet these same children can tell the difference between a bowl full of collard greens and one of turnip greens. They can learn the steps to a new dance by simply watching someone else perform them once or twice or learn to whack a baseball out of the park. What they lack is not perceptual training but experience in perceiving the specific distinctions which the school intends to use in the teaching of reading. Exposure to these phenomena for a period of time enables them to apply their perceptual strategies to this new experience.

Learning to read need not be dependent, however, upon becoming proficient at these new perceptual tasks. Later in this chapter we will suggest an approach to initial reading in which the perceptual distinctions are developed as an aspect of the reading process.

Visual Images and Meaning   One other aspect of perception and its relationship to reading should be considered. Because readers are concerned with the message, they perceive not just the visual images but also meanings.

Paul Kolers, a psychologist, found that when bilinguals read a passage which contained sentences of both French and English such as:

Une violente brise was blowing

they were able to comprehend the passage easily. However, they were unable to recall which information had been contained in which language. They had been concerned with the meanings rather than with whether the lexical item was in French–"brise"–or English–"wind" (Kolers, in F. Smith, 1972).

What Paul Kolers discovered when he had people read bilingual text can also be observed through miscue analysis. Sometimes the words that a person reads orally differ from the words in the text. When these unexpected responses are collected from oral reading and examined, they are often found to retain the meaning of the text. The following examples of such reading variations were collected by Kenneth Goodman and his associates as they studied the reading process (Goodman, 1973):

1   She had a hypodermic syringe in one hand. *(needle)[1]*

2   Wait a moment. *(minute)[1]*

3   They put the hoses on the fire truck. *(engine)[1]*

4   His class was having an outside project. *(they)[2]*

5   This(is) all I'(ve) got for you tonight. [3] [3]

In each of these cases the reader varied the text without changing the meaning. Like the bilingual readers in Kolers's experiment, these readers have perceived the meaning without concern for its exact surface level representation.

The fourth and fifth examples used above were produced by black dialect speakers. They demonstrate that Kolers's concept of reading meaning and not words works just as well within dialects of a single language as it does between two languages. Recent studies seem to indicate that oral language dialects create no linguistic barriers to reading. *Readers need only be receptive to an author's dialect in order to deal with meaning in print* (Goodman and Buck, 1973).

The Reading Miscue   K. Goodman is interested in the unexpected responses produced by readers. He has developed a procedure for studying reading which makes use of two facts:

1   The reader is a language user and must employ the three language systems in order to gain meaning from printed material.
2   All readers create unexpected responses.

---

[1] Substitution of one word for another
[2] Insertion of a word
[3] Omission of a language unit

He believes that a reader employs the same language cues in producing an unexpected response as in producing an expected response. Therefore he calls these unexpected responses *miscues.*

Through miscue analysis Goodman has developed a psycholinguistic view of the reading process (Goodman and Goodman, 1978) which suggests that readers predict on the basis of selected cues. (In example 1 listed earlier, the reader predicted *needle* on the basis of the semantic cue *hypodermic.*) If their predictions are confirmed by subsequent cues, they continue reading. However, if those cues indicate that the previous predictions did not produce acceptable language, readers will use various correction strategies. As they predict and confirm, readers simultaneously and continuously integrate the meaning they construct into their own system of knowledge. There is one point upon which most people who study reading and reading instruction are agreed—reading is a very complex process. The first section of this chapter pointed out that reading involves using all three of the language systems (phonological, syntactic, and semantic) used in speech, plus learning to relate the set of speech sounds to a set of written letters. Awareness of this complexity has made people very cautious about the initial reading programs which they plan.

A quick look at initial reading programs commonly in use within the schools reveals two major focuses: one on lexical items or words; the other on sound/letter relationships.

Emphasis on Word Attack The first approach directs beginning readers' attention to words. The relationship between oral language units (morphemes) and their written representations (words) becomes the focus for instruction. Readers are encouarged to memorize the written symbols so that they will immediately recall them on sight. The reading text facilitates this recall task by repeated use of selected vocabulary items. Vocabulary is selected on the basis of usage frequency, so that with a small sight vocabulary students are able to read a great deal. They are frequently encouraged to distinguish root words within larger inflected (-ed, -s, -ing), derived (-tion, -ment, -al), and compounded (bird-house, table-cloth, hair-brush) words.

The second approach focuses the students' attention on the relationships between the letters of the alphabet and the sounds of the language. Readers are encouraged to handle or "attack" new words by applying these sound/letter relationships. Individual programs offer varying means for accomplishing this task. Some stress a direct correspondence between individual letters and individual sounds (a one-to-one correspondence); some stress relationships between combinations of letters and possible sequences of sounds (a spelling pattern); some limit themselves to short monosyllabic (one-syllable) words, while others make use of syllable-length units in varying combinations; some use the traditional alphabet, while others introduce an artificial "teaching" alphabet. All of them make exclusive use of the graphophonic system to instruct beginning readers.

These two different approaches to initial reading instruction have the same objective: to enable the student to "read" words. They differ only in their means of accomplishing this goal. Both minimize the reader's use of the syntactic and semantic systems of language. They do this not because they think these systems are unimportant to reading, but because they think that young readers would become confused if they were called upon to pay attention to all three language systems at once. They both conclude that the word is the most simple and direct key to reading—if you can recognize enough words you can string them together like beads and make sentences.

Psycholinguistic Contributions   Evidence from psycholinguistic research indicates that these two approaches to initial reading instruction are limited; they fail to take into account information about how people think and about how they learn language.

In planning methods of reading instruction, we need to consider the way that language develops. The following are key aspects of oral language development which seem particularly relevant to reading:

1   From birth, infants are surrounded by the ongoing speech of adults.
2   Infants become proficient receivers of oral language long before they effectively produce it.
3   The first speech efforts of toddlers are related to specific ongoing situations which hold great significance for them.
4   Toddlers' first speech reflects their own rule-governed syntactic structures, which they have developed by thoughtfully distilling order from the speech of surrounding adults.

But we must also be aware of aspects of written language in this society which have impact on beginning reading.

In our highly literate society, children are surrounded by a great deal of written language as well as oral language. They experience print on television commercials and programs, road signs, billboards, store and restaurant signs. When accompanying adults to the supermarket, preschoolers are surrounded by print on food and household product labels and may even be allowed to pick their own favorite brands from the shelves. They observe their parents write or read in order to get money, attend a meeting, or get news from friends.

Researchers have begun to examine the extent to which preschoolers are aware of and reacting to print found in the environment. Traditionally, children who have been observed as readers have been considered as exceptional; but studies by the authors of this chapter and others (Torrey, 1969; Ylisto, 1978; Forrester, 1978) suggest that many children of various ethnic, linguistic and socioeconomic backgrounds begin to read before receiving formal instruction. In these studies, preschoolers are asked to respond to print in natural settings as it is found on food and household product labels, street signs and store signs. They find that the preschoolers are able to react meaningfully to the print in such contexts. Most of the children can correctly identify the items when the print is embedded in familiar contexts and point to the print rather than the pictures or symbols when showing where it "said that". They also find that children have developed awareness that print has directionality.

These studies demonstrate that children react to printed symbols in the environment—the cereal name, "STOP," the signplate; that the symbols act as recognized placeholders for meaningful experiences—a food they like, an expected behavior, a need; and that their inexpert use of the symbols is supported by the use of other situational clues—the tiger on the box, the red eight-sided sign at street corners, the door with a signplate in a public building.

The school does not have to initiate reading, but only to support a process which the children have already initiated. Children have used situational context to begin to organize print and to assign meaning to it. They have done this intuitively and naturally as part of a constant effort to understand and participate in the surrounding world.

The language and thought processes which children are using are abstract and complex. But as a language user they are not called upon to understand them, only to make use of them. This they do in much the same way that people become expert drivers without knowing anything about the operation of the gasoline engine, or create and use electrical power without being able to explain its existence. Models of the language process, theories of propulsion, the relationship of electrons and protons are all very abstract. But cereal names, cars, and lamps are concrete. They are known and understood by the way in which they are used and in relation to the need and purposes of the learner. In the same way, context makes written language concrete and allows readers to gain reliable meanings for words they do not recognize.

Imagine that you are twelve years old and the teacher has placed the following word on the blackboard and asked you to read it:

krait

You have very few methods available for dealing with this item. You either recognize it or you do not. If you do not recognize it, you cannot even be sure that it is a real word. Because the letters seem to be organized in familiar combinations, you can use the graphophonic system of language. That is, you can try to pronounce the item.

Even your attempts at pronouncing an unknown item will be kept in the context of other items which you already know how to pronounce. So you will try *crate* because you know the word *bait,* or *krite* because of *aisle,* or *kret* because of *said.* But you will not know which one of these pronunciations, if any, is the conventional one, and the pronunciation will not tell you the meaning of the word or its grammatical function. Is it a verb?

I could krait all day if I had to.

Or an adjective?

I'll take the krait balloon.

Now imagine that the teacher erases the word from the board, and in its place she writes the following:

The krait is only about 10 inches long.
But even though it is small, it is deadly.
It is a cold-blooded animal and seeks warm
places to stay. The krait is a relative
of the cobra.

This does not help you decide which of your attempted pronunciations was correct—only the dictionary or other people's usage can do that—but it does answer more important questions. Krait must be a noun because it is used in slots where nouns are used:

The krait is . . .
(car)
(hose)
(trunk)

If you know the cobra, you will assume that a krait is a snake. Not knowing the cobra, you can still guess that it is a poisonous reptile (*deadly* and *cold-blooded*).

Now imagine that you are six years old and the teacher places this word on the board:

dog

You groan to yourself. There's that darn letter again. It looks so much like that other letter, *b,* and you can never remember which sound is associated with which letter. Is the word on the board *bog* or *dog?*

But then the teacher surrounds the item with the following context:

The dog was Sam's pet.

And now you know. You can read the word and be assured of your choice, without having to be dependent on an isolated component of the process.

In both of these instances the context made all three of the language systems available for the reader's use. Inexpert functioning in one system could be compensated for and supported by cues from the other two systems. The basic criterion for an initial reading program might be stated this way: *Keep written language in context, and keep the structure and meaning predictable.*

DEVELOPMENT OF WRITING AND ITS RELATIONSHIP TO READING

At one time it was believed that children were not biologically ready to read or write prior to school. Delacato (1959) stressed the importance of neurological development and Heffernan (1960) and Betts (1936), among others, supported the idea that instruction in both reading and writing were futile before a given age, usually about six-years-old. However, researchers have long noted that the development of writing does begin prior to formal instruction and shares many of the same characteristics as oral language learning.

As early as 1932 researchers such as Legrün and Hildreth note that "writing" may develop from the ages of three to six without direct instruction. Legrün even outlined stages in early writing which included development from unorganized scribbles to better articulated forms showing some variations of structure but not broken up into parts and finally further differentiation with occasional interpositions of true letters and figures (Gibson and Levin, 1976, pp. 230–239).

More recently, Lavine, Wheeler and Gibson and Levin (1976, p. 233) among others, support the notion that children's writing gradually develops characteristics of alphabetic writing such as linearity and horizontal orientation, without any direct formal instruction.

In *What Did I Write,* Marie Clay (1975) encourages adults to view children's writing as a developmental language system. Clay suggests that many "errors" are actually signs of progress reflecting the use of rules or ambitious attempts to communicate meanings.

Clay also stresses the notion that children learn to write on all language levels (letters, words, sentences) simultaneously. Children's writing does not develop such that letters are learned before words, words before sentences, etc. The child's writing reflects development at all these levels prior to instruction.

Within recent years, researchers in written language development such as Read (1975), Lamb (1979) and C. Chomsky (1971, 1975) have focused attention on the "invented spellings" which children initiate in their early writing. Analysis of "invented spellings" reveal that when children's writing is allowed to develop naturally without formal instruction, their spelling attempts are not haphazard or random, but rather rule governed, systematic and logical. C. Chomsky observes that: children often spelled words consisting of a /ê/ sound (as in the initial sound of chair) with an "h" because its letter *name* includes the /ê/ sound as part of its pronunciation. She also notes that "*gr*" (pronounced like "*jr*") substitute for "*dr*" and "*tr*" in words like "dragon" and "train". The letter name for "*g*" seems to bear a close resemblance to "*tr*" and "*dr*" sounds in those words. Thus children's spellings demonstrate a sophisticated knowledge of the speech sounds of English.

There has been some discussion in research studies concerning the order in which reading and writing develop in relation to each other. It seems logical that, as in the development of oral language where listening precedes speaking, in the development of written language the receptive ability (reading) should precede the productive ability (writing). Some researchers such as C. Chomsky (1971, 1975) argue that the opposite is true. She contends that writing develops before reading and suggests that instruction should also proceed in that order. Chomsky states that "writing is an exciting and, for some children, a much easier first reading activity" (Chomsky, 1975). The authors of this chapter believe, however, that reading and writing do not develop in a sequential order, but rather in a parallel fashion. In this view, reading and writing are mutually supportive. Strengths in one build strengths in the other. Further research is needed to fully clarify this interesting issue. However, what is important is that the teacher be aware that the child has been organizing and developing concepts about written language prior to coming to school.

A four-year-old will very deliberately sit and fill a page with a series of squiggles, loops, and wavy lines. At times she will choose to do this in place of drawing the houses and trees and people which she has become fairly proficient at representing. Her page filled, she is apt to approach an adult and inform him that she has written a story. Upon request she can then "read" the story she has just written.

This little scribbler has just told us several very important things about her language development.

1   She has grasped the language relationship of reading and writing. She

understands that the marks on the page carry meaning.

2   She is developing a feeling for the purpose of writing. She went to seek a second person because she has some notion that what the author puts down on the page should be accessible and meaningful to some other person who approaches the page as a reader.

3   She is aware of the limitations of her "writing." The person she has sought out is expected to act as a listener/reader. At this point the "author" is the only one who can gain meaning from the page.

4   She has perceived a difference between the written symbols of language and pictures. For this experience she has abandoned her newly developed talents as an artist. She is aware that the symbols of writing do not "picture" the meaning.

5   She has preferred to re-enact a whole message in context rather than to create a piece of "writing" by sitting and meticulously trying to reproduce individual letters from some master copy. She is not interested in the detail.

Informal Learning Experiences   By the time children reach school they have already invested five years of intensive study into language learning. As listeners/speakers they are most accomplished. They can listen to and, in varying degrees, understand different dialects, and they can respond to these communication situations effectively with their own dialect. Their oral communication is limited more by lack of experience and conceptual development than by language development.

As readers/writers they already respond to written symbols in context. They expect written symbols to carry meaning and are willing to guess at that meaning on the basis of the life situation in which they find it.

For these five years children have supervised their own learning with only occasional intervention from "outside experts." They were born into a world where everyone was a member of a private club which they could not immediately join. The entrance requirement was language. The club members were receptive to them. They talked, read, and wrote in front of and to the children, but generally left it up to them as to how they could best sort, organize, and develop understanding for the language process.

Children deal with whole messages and always keep them in the context of the situations which generate them. The planned learning experiences of the school will be most supportive to language users if the learning format closely resembles the one the children have already devised and very successfully used in their initial language learning.

IMPLICATIONS FOR THE TEACHER

Any kind of instructional program for children must take place in an environment in which the student feels respected and accepted. This must include the acceptance and respect for the child's language, culture, and learning style. School should be a place where the teacher as well as the student is willing to learn. A teacher who shows an interest in learning from the students will give the students reasons for sharing their experiences with the teacher and the rest of the children. Through this open give and take, the teacher can learn a great deal about how children learn, about their language and their culture.

The following seven psycholinguistic principles are the ones we believe deserve the greatest attention from teachers, since they may have the most significance for the development of reading programs in the classroom. With each principle, we suggest specific classroom applications.

Principle: *Written language development begins prior to school.* Children come to school with a great deal of experience and knowledge about written language. Instruction should be aimed at extending and expanding this knowledge in a way that is consistent with the natural developmental process. Children must continue to view written language in meaningful and functional settings. This can be achieved by providing a literate classroom environment that contains a variety of written materials. Setting up play stores and model neighborhoods in the classroom will encourage children to use the information they have already found about print in the environment. Children should be read to individually or in small groups in order to increase their understanding of the function of print in books.

Language should *never* appear in total isolation as this confuses a child who has already developed the concept that print is meaningful, purposeful language. Teaching abstract units of language, such as sounds, word parts, letter names, words or sentences with no relationship to a written language context relevent to the child, confuses the beginner about the purpose and function of written language.

Principle: *Language communication involves the transmission of meaning from a language producer to a language receiver.* Reading is language. Therefore, any reading program which is used in the classroom must show readers that searching for meaning is their main concern. The major criterion that a teacher uses to screen reading materials or programs must be: *Does this program help my students focus on understanding the meaning of what they read?* Many of the programs now used in schools would pass such a criterion. Language experience programs, for example, concentrate on the students' gaining meaning. Suggestions in the teacher's manuals of basal reading programs emphasize comprehension. Individualized or personalized reading programs (Veatch, 1966) which permit the students to select their own reading materials are also based on the notion that what students read must concern them personally and make sense to them. A teacher who understands the significance of readers' search for meaning can incorporate all aspects of the above programs to develop a comprehension-centered or meaning-centered reading program.

Principle: *Reading is a receptive but very active language process.* Too many instructional programs are designed to provide readers with the notion that reading is telling exactly and carefully what is on the printed page, or that reading is dramatic oral presentation of what an author has written. The first view will only impede the development of readers' efficiency. The second view makes one seldom-used purpose of reading into a primary goal. But reading is a receptive process, and readers must be concerned primarily with constructing a message from their reading. This can happen only in independent reading.

Only silent, independent reading should be called reading. A third-grade teacher recently instituted an individualized reading program. By the fourth week of the program, most of the children were reading independently and silently from thirty to forty-five minutes a day. Many of these children would come up to Ms. Curtis, the teacher, and ask, "Why aren't we having reading today?" Joan's mother came to school one day and asked Ms. Curtis why she was not having reading in school any more. Joan had come home and said that there was no reading going on. Ms. Curtis began to realize that most of the children thought reading was the time spent in a twenty-minute reading group, where everyone reads orally two or three minutes with the teacher and then does exercises of some sort.

Reading instruction activities should be called seat work, follow-up activities, or reading instruction. Oral reading should be called interpretive or dramatic reading. Group discussions to interpret a story should be called group activity or discussion time. All activities which surround the reading experience should be called other things—*only the time for independent silent reading should be called reading.*

Principle: *What is read is language. Reading materials must always involve the interaction of the three language systems: graphophonic, syntactic, and semantic.* Since what is read is language, reading should be taught using "real" or "natural" language as its medium of instruction. Reading must be a means to an end for the learner, not an end in itself. It might be best not to relegate reading to a separate reading class but instead to incorporate it within the wide range of activities and subject matter which students explore during the school day. As readers use materials written for social studies, science, math, music, and so on, they will have to develop a range of reading strategies which are appropriate to the particular syntactic, semantic, and graphophonic systems used to express the differences within these various fields.

Teachers in content areas must realize that many of the concepts from their particular fields take on appropriate meaning only in the context of the language of that field. A vocabulary item like the word *axis* is not the same in math as it is in social studies. Even within the field of social studies the term can refer either to the pole around which the earth turns or the powers that fought the allies during the Second World War. Only within the "natural" context can the reader reconstruct meaning.

Attempts to separate the graphophonic system from the syntactic system or meaning system provide readers with artificial language. Artificial language is too abstract for children who use language for knowledge and social interaction. Reading material must be presented in a form that readers recognize as language, so that they will treat it as something they know and can read.

Principle: *People can understand what they read when the material is expressed in language with which they are familiar.* The closer the written language is to the oral language of the reader, the more easily the material will be understood. The written language does not have to represent exactly the oral language of the student, however. It can also represent the oral language of the people around him. Children can understand a wider range of dialects than they can speak. But the teacher must become aware of the language the students speak and hear in order to provide appropriate beginning language materials, as well as to expand the students' receptive control of a variety of written styles.

Using a language experience approach (Van Allen, 1976, Lee and Rubin, 1979) is one way that teachers can achieve this purpose. One type of language experience activity is the language experience story which is a planned activity making use of children's own language.

1   The lesson is built directly upon a meaningful experience which the learner has had. This can be done either by encouraging the learner to call to mind something from the past or by planning an activity in which learner and teacher will both participate.
2   The learner is given time to organize and evaluate the experience. Through discussion—thinking out loud—the learner's attitudes can be fully developed and alternate ways of sharing them can be considered.
3   The learner's thought and language are preserved. The teacher and/or student writes what the learner wants shared in the language of the learner.

The writer and the reader of the first language experience stories are often the same person. The focus is on the interrelationship of speaking, listening, reading, and writing. The learners come to understand how these support each other and realize that strength in one kind of expression can be used to develop another. At first the teacher offers strong support. By encouraging the students to look for topics that really interest them, by listening and questioning, the teacher helps to focus and deepen the students' understanding of the topic.

Gradually, the focus and teacher support are altered. Goodman and Watson (1977) suggest that students be encouraged to become authors who may write about their out-of-school as well as in-school experiences, keep journals, and write letters. They suggest developing book making and editing activities in the classroom, so that students begin assuming responsibility for the quality of their writing. The students should be encouraged to begin producing stories with other readers in mind, at the same time becoming readers of the writing of others. As the children write with others in mind, they develop a concern for the experiences and language which a reader might bring to the material. When they read the writing of others, they begin to predict the material on the basis of the way they know the author thinks and writes.

At the same time, the teacher should expand the receptive language of the students by reading to them daily from the rich variety of literature for children and youth. Writers of such literature use a variety of literary styles (Huck, 1976; Reid, 1972), and their syntax and vocabulary often represent a variety of oral dialects. Some authors are now using dialects which were not previously expressed in written language (Steptoe, 1969; Graham, 1970). There are also books, magazines, and comics which use print variations to indicate dialect differences. These give students many opportunities to deal with variations in written language.

Principle: *People can best understand what they read when the material is related to their own background and experience.* It is very difficult, if not impossible, to read something which is totally foreign to one's own background. Reading a legal contract is a common example. The solution to the problem is to consult a lawyer; but this does not provide readers with appropriate strategies for reading future legal contracts on their own. Only an appropriate background can help the student deal with many new concepts in reading.

All written materials contain words or phrases which authors do not explain because they assume that the reading audience is familiar with the ideas expressed or the words used. It is, therefore, the teacher's responsibility to make sure the students have a variety of prereading experiences to prepare them for any unfamiliar concepts which they may read about. Such experiences will take on more meaning if the activities involve the learners in a concrete and active manner and permit the learners to think and talk about what is happening. These kinds of prereading experiences may be more necessary for the reading of informational material than for fiction. However, sometimes a piece of fiction that was written at a different time in history or in a unique culture can be quite foreign to the students. In these situations, the teacher may need to help the students bridge the cultural or time gap.

In some cases authors build the concepts related to the words, phrases, or ideas through their story or article. For the teacher to explain such terms or concepts prior to reading would interfere with the interaction between the reader and writer. *One of the purposes of reading is, in fact, the extension of knowledge through new learning.* It will take teachers who are sensitive to the language as well as the background and experience of their students to know which concepts need to be presented prior to reading and which concepts should be left to the readers' own strategies.

Principle: *People can best understand what they read when the material is interesting, functional, and purposeful.* When students are interested in what they read, all aspects of their reading become a great deal easier. Motivation is built in. Since students' interests vary, a wide variety of reading material must be available in the classroom. Readers must be involved in planning their own reading experiences and in selecting appropriate materials. In addition to paperback and hardback books, newspapers, magazines, comics, and so on should be available. There should be opportunities for students to read and follow directions—for construction of various kinds, for cooking, sewing, knitting, or crocheting. Song sheets of popular music which students can follow as they listen to records or sing, science corners with written directions for experimentation, or mathematics tables with suggestions for problems are all a legitimate part of such a program. These activities should always serve some function for the student and should reflect the wide range of purposes for which written language is used in society.

SUMMARY

Linguists, psycholinguists, and sociolinguists have studied language and think-ing and their effect on learning and on society. Only teachers, however, can apply this knowledge to the classroom. Not only must they be aware of the most up-to-date information from the scientists who study children, their language, and how they learn, but teachers must build a framework or a philosophy to understand the implications for classrooms of the emerging knowledge and ideas. It becomes their responsibility to decide the best ways in which to develop this knowledge into instructional programs for children. This is, indeed, the most significant part of the teacher's professional role.

REFERENCES

Allen, R. V. *Language Experience in Communication.* Boston: Houghton Mifflin Co., 1976.

Britton, J. *Language and Learning.* Florida: University of Miami Press, 1970.

Brown, R. *A First Language: The Early Stages.* Cambridge, Mass.: Harvard University Press, 1973.

Chomsky, N. *Aspects of a Theory of Syntax.* Cambridge, Mass.: Massachusetts Institute of Technology Press, 1965.

Chomsky, C. "Write First, Read Later." *Childhood Education,* March 1971, pp. 290–295.

Chomsky, C. "How Sister Got Into the Grog." *Early Years,* November 1975.

Clay, M. *What Did I Write?* New Zealand: Heinemann Educational Books, 1975.

Dale, P. S. *Language Development: Structure and Function.* Illinois: The Dryden Press, Inc., 1972.

Delacato, C. *Treatment and Prevention of Reading Problems.* Illinois: Charles C. Thomas, 1959.

Fillmore, C. J. "The Case for Case" in *Universals in Linguistic Theory,* Bach, E. and R. T. Harms, eds. New York: Holt, Rinehart and Winston, 1968.

Flavell, J. H. *The Developmental Psychology of Jean Piaget.* New York: Van Nostrand, 1964.

Forrester, A. "What Teachers Can Learn From 'Natural Readers'," in *Reading Teacher,* Vol. 31, Nov. 1977, pp. 160–166.

Gibson, E. and H. Levin. *The Psychology of Reading.* Cambridge, Mass.: The M.I.T. Press, 1965.

Gleason, H. A. *Linguistics and English Grammar.* New York: Holt, Rinehart and Winston, 1965.

Goodman, K. and Buck, C. "Dialect Barriers to Reading Comprehension: Revisited." *The Reading Teacher,* October 1973.

Goodman, K., and Burke, C. *Theoretically Based Studies of Patterns of Miscues in Oral Reading Performance.* Final Report, Project No. 9-0775, Grant No. OEG-0-9-320375-4269. U.S. Department of Health, Education, and Welfare, Office of Education, Bureau of Research, May 1973.

Goodman, K. and Y. Goodman. *Reading of American Children Whose Language is a Stable Rural Dialect of English or A Language Other Than English.* U.S.O.E. No. NIE–C–00–3–0087, 1978.

Goodman, Y. and D. Watson. "A Reading Program to Live With: Focus on Comprehension." *Language Arts,* Nov./Dec. 1977, pp. 868–879.

Graham, L. *David He No Fear.* New York: Thomas Y. Crowell, 1970.

Graham, L. *Every Man Heart Lay Down.* New York: Thomas Y. Crowell, 1970.

Halliday, M.A.K. *Learning How to Mean.* London: Edward Arnold Publishers, 1975.

Huck, C. S., *Children's Literature in Elementary School,* 3/e. New York: Holt, Rinehart and Winston, 1976.

Lamb, P. "Pre-School Children's Knowledge of Phoneme-Grapheme Correspondencies," Paper presented at AERA meeting, San Francisco, 1979.

Lee, D. and J. Rubin. *Children and Language: Reading and Writing, Talking and Listening.* Belmont, Calif.: Wadsworth Publishing Co., 1979.

Lindsay, P. H., and Norman, D. *Human Information Processing: An Introduction to Psychology.* New York: Academic Press, 1972.

Neisser, U. *Cognition and Reality.* San Francisco: W. H. Freeman and Co., 1976.

Read, C. *Children's Categorization of Speech Sounds in English.* Urbana, Illinois: NCTE, 1975.

Reid, V. M. *Reading Ladders for Human Relations.* Washington, D.C.: American Council on Education, 1972.

Smith, E. B.; Goodman, K. S.; and Meredith, R. *Language and Thinking in School.* New York: Holt, Rinehart and Winston, 1976.

Smith, F. *Psycholinguistics and Reading.* New York: Holt, Rinehart and Winston, 1972.

Smith, F., and Miller, G., eds. *The Genesis of Language.* Cambridge, Mass.: Massachusetts Institute of Technology Press, 1966.

Steptoe, J. *Stevie.* New York: Harper and Row, 1969.

Torrey, J. W. "Learning to Read Without a Teacher: A Case Study." *Elementary English,* May 1969, pp. 550–556, 658.

Veatch, J. *Reading in the Elementary School.* New York: Ronald Press, 1966.

Vygotsky, L. *Thought and Language.* Cambridge, Mass.: Massachusetts Institute of Technology Press, 1962.

Winkeljohann, Sister Rosemary, ed. *The Politics of Reading: Point Counterpoint.* Newark, Del., and Urbana, Ill.: International Reading Association and National Council of Teachers of English, 1973.

Wolfram, W. and Fasold, R. W. *The Study of Social Dialects in American English.* New Jersey: Prentice-Hall, Inc., 1974.

Ylisto, I. "Early Reading Responses of Young Finnish Children" in *Reading Teacher,* Vol. 31, Nov. 1977, pp. 167–172.

STRATEGIES

PREVIEW

The preceding chapters have dealt with the theoretical, psychological, and sociocultural aspects of the reading process. In Chapter Five the focus changes and the authors approach the teaching of reading in the context of the school. Ransom and Mitchell describe the characteristics of the mature reader and outline a comprehensive curriculum with guidelines for establishing long-term and short-term objectives. Components of Developmental, Applied, and Corrective/Remedial programs are presented. They discuss the use of oral reading in the curriculum, the role of teachers, paraprofessionals, and others who are often involved in the reading program. Considerable attention is given to organizing and planning both the reading program and specific reading lessons. Ransom and Mitchell, in allowing for individual teaching styles and programs, emphasize that the essence of the reading program is direction and focus.

5 Curriculum and Objectives

Peggy Ransom, Ball State University
Ronald W. Mitchell, International Reading Association

OBJECTIVES

After you have read this chapter, you should be able to:

1. **List three specific aspects of self-actualization in reading. For each of these, suggest at least one teaching strategy which should encourage self-actualization in general and reading achievement specifically.**

2. **What are the concerns in the "Back to Basics" movement?**

3. **List three of the most significant characteristics of a mature reader.**

4. **Suggest a teaching procedure which should help develop each of the characteristics you listed in number three.**

5. **List similarities and differences among the four types of reading programs presented in the chapter: developmental, functional, recreational, and corrective-remedial.**

Reading instruction is one of the most important parts of the school curriculum. Through it teachers influence not only their students' ability to read but also their ability to achieve their full potential as individuals and as members of society (Wilkins, 1976; Dworkin and Dworkin, 1979; Merton, 1948). One way teachers exert this influence is through expectations they have for their students.

"I really like to read," says Betty, a fourth-grade pupil. "My teachers tell me I'm an excellent reader, and they help me find interesting books in the library. I hope some day I can be a teacher and help children to read, too!" This enthusiastic reader has obviously encountered success in reading throughout her school years, and her reading skills have been supported by teachers. She is an example of a successful reader.

Jim, however, says, "I can't read." When asked, "Why can't you read, Jim?" he is apt to answer, "Because the teacher told me I can't read." The teacher's expectations—whether for the success or failure of the students—are likely to be fulfilled.

Because teachers have different expectations for children from the middle and lower socioeconomic levels, it is not surprising that these children are often low in academic performance and are frequently classified as discipline problems (Rosenthal and Jacobson, 1968). The teachers' expectations for mastery in reading can and should be high, regardless of the social class of the students. Children who go to school where teachers expect them to master the material do indeed succeed. "It is difficult to estimate precisely the value of a positive teacher attitude or the damage of a negative one; however, the value and damage are real" (Wilson, 1972).

Teachers' responses to the question, "How well do you think your pupils should be reading?" reveal a great variety of expectations. A first-level teacher in a school enrolling pupils classified in the middle socioeconomic range answered this way: "I expect most of the students to be reading at the end of the school year. However, some of them who have scored low on tests might not be able to read until the end of first reading level or beginning second reading level. You understand, I don't expect them all to be at the same place, for children progress at different rates."

Another first-level reading teacher responded to the same question as follows: "Most of these children will not be able to do much reading at the end of the first year in my room, but when they reach a stage of wanting to read, I will teach them." This teacher must search for specific indications that a child wants to read and is "ready" to do so.

Still another first-level reading teacher gave this response to the question: "I expect every child to read to the best of his abilities. When they start school with me, I try to continually assess their reading abilities and needs in order to provide a teaching program adjusted to each individual. Some children need more help than others, but with my additional aid and guidance, they will become both effective and efficient readers. I try to keep in mind that reading can be fun, and help children to enjoy it."

Stop and think about yourself: Where did you go to school? What were your teachers like? Were you given rewards by teachers for succeeding academically? Did you like school better some years than others because of the teachers you encountered? Why are you preparing to be a teacher, or to improve your teaching skills? Did you have teachers who led you to self-actualization in reading?

Then ask yourself: What will I expect from children? Do I have plans for helping them reach their potential? Am I (or will I be) giving them all the help I can, enabling them to learn to the best of their abilities? It is to be hoped that you will become a teacher of reading who helps students meet their own goals and those which society has set for them.

Meeting Society's Needs

In 1968, Dr. James E. Allen, Jr., then U.S. Commissioner of Education, made the following discomfiting disclosures:

1   One out of every four students nationwide had significant reading deficiencies.

2   In large city school systems, up to half of the students read below expectation.

Dr. Allen stated: "The tragedy of these statistics is that they represent a barrier to success that for many young adults produces the misery of a life marked by poverty, unemployment, alienation, and, in many cases, crime" (Allen, 1969, p. 2). Allen was so concerned over these results that he set a goal: by the beginning of the 1980s no one would leave school without the skill and the desire necessary to read to the full limits of their capabilities. Dr. Allen left office soon after this proclamation, but the total national commitment to the Right to Read Effort is being implemented to some degree throughout the United States.

Right to Read is designed to coordinate all reading-related efforts now being made at the federal, state, and local levels into a united attack on the nation's reading problems. The Right to Read Effort has (1) identified some of the most effective reading programs in the nation and packaged information about them, (2) shared these packages with Right to Read sites, so they can use components from the models to build their own effective programs, and (3) retrained teachers and community leaders so they can cope with a variety of reading problems, rather than just a few. The basic principles of Right to Read are:

1   With the exception of the small portion of the population which is considered uneducable, all people can learn to read if they are provided with programs designed to meet their needs.
2   Teachers will adopt new methods of teaching reading if they are convinced that these will help them teach more effectively.
3   The United States has the resources necessary to at least ease, if not solve the reading crisis.

These principles remain to be translated into better teaching training, as well as innovative and effective educational programs.

All classroom teachers are part of the Right to Read Effort, for every time teachers help children in reading, they have helped them realize their right to read. Teachers can further assist the effort by making a personal commitment to find and implement better ways of teaching reading.

To be an effective citizen today, one must be able to read at least minimally. Applying for a job, obtaining a driver's license, and even buying groceries all require functional literacy. The Adult Basic Education Act of 1965 established programs to aid adults in reading and other areas. As the teaching of reading in elementary school classrooms improves, however, the need for programs to counteract adult illiteracy should diminish.

The School's Accountability

Increasingly, educators are being held accountable for the literacy of their students. They are accepting responsibility for the results of their teaching. Some school districts have accepted this accountability by establishing systems analysis. They review student data from standardized tests and informal reading inventories, gather data regarding students' attitudes and interests, and survey standardized test scores. With this information school personnel can more adequately assess the reading achievement of the pupils. They can compare test scores from pupil to pupil within individual schools (districtwide comparison is probably unfair because of the differences among schools), and the resulting analysis helps teachers improve their reading programs. Faculties and administrators can then compare changes which result from systems analysis.

Each day, the effective teacher of reading diagnoses children's weaknesses, strengths, and needs, and adjusts teaching plans, materials, and procedures in terms of these diagnoses. This process represents acceptance of the principle of accountability. It is important that teachers decide at the beginning of the year how they will demonstrate their accountability for the teaching of reading. The school and community will not question teaching techniques when they can see the results of an evaluation of diagnostic-prescriptive procedures of teaching reading for each individual pupil.

Open communication between the school, teachers, and community will also help establish accountability lines. When the teacher has the records of students in reading, knows their weaknesses and strengths, attitudes and interests in reading, it becomes much easier to produce evidence to parents and the community when they become concerned about the school's reading program and more especially their children.

Teachers and schools should also have open communication lines (like newsletters, parent meetings, advisory boards, volunteers, parent teacher organizations, etc.) with parents so the community is aware of the school's concerns, especially teachers' concerns over students' reading abilities. The open communication allows teachers and the school another avenue to provide evidence of their accountability in the teaching of reading to students.

As has been stated, educators and the public are stressing teachers be accountable for the literacy of their pupils. This accountability usually means that teachers know where their students are in reading ability, and thereby develop teaching strategies that are suitable for each individual student. This also indicates that there be some measurable methods, usually testing, that prove the students have progressed in their reading skills. The testing aspect has made the terminology change in the last few years from accountability to "Back to the Basics."

BACK TO THE BASICS

Concerned with a steady decline of college entrance test scores through 1975, disturbed by articles in the public press indicating today's schools are turning out an alarming percentage of functional illiterates—and perhaps with their judgments somewhat clouded by the nostalgic misconception that things were better in the good old days—many parents, employers and legislators are suggesting that the solution to today's educational decline is a swift and judicious return to the "basics."

While the "Back to the Basics" movement has received some support from the public and from several state legislatures, many educators have expressed serious concerns for a variety of reasons. First of all, the implication that schools today ignore the basics seems difficult to defend, at least as far as reading instruction is concerned. A recent study in Indiana, for example, indicates that sixth and tenth-grade students studied in 1976 received 50 percent more instructional time in reading than did the 1944–1945 students with whom they were compared (Farr, Fay, and Negley, 1978).

A second concern relates to the premise that children today are not being taught to read as well as they were in the past. This premise is based at least partially on reports that scores on a college entrance examination, the Scholastic Aptitude Test (SAT) have been declining markedly over the past 20 years. While this decline in scores has been documented, educational writers (Farr, 1978; Jencks, 1978) are quick to point out that the SAT is an aptitude test designed to predict a student's success in college. It was not intended to, and probably does not, provide a valid evaluation of achievement in the basic skills. Perhaps the major reason for the decline in SAT scores relates to the fact that a higher percentage of high school students are entering college, many of whom are less academically inclined. Including less able students in the test population would, of course, have the effect of lowering the average test scores for the group.

To answer the "then versus now" question in reading, it would seem wiser to compare results on achievement tests rather than aptitude tests. Several such comparisons have been made and, while the results are by no means conclusive, many of the studies reject the assumption that today's children are poorer readers than their counterparts in the past. In the Indiana study mentioned earlier for example, the investigators conclude:

> Because there was little difference in the grade equivalent performance of the 1944–1945 and 1976 students on the *Iowa Silent Reading Tests* and because the age-adjusted performance of the 1976 students was markedly higher than their 1944–1945 counterparts, the assumption that the reading abilities of students is declining is unsupported by this study.

Farr and Tone (1978) and Jencks (1978) refer to additional studies that indicate students, particularly in the elementary grades, are showing continued progress in reading achievement. In perhaps one of the most extensive studies, the National Assessment of Educational Progress (1976), a government supported assessment project, compared 9-, 13- and 17-year-old students in 1971 and 1975 on literal comprehension, inferential comprehension and reference skills. The achievement of the 1975 9-year-olds was higher on all measures. The total reading scores of the 13- and 17-year-olds showed little difference between 1971 and 1975, although the 1975 students scored slightly higher in literal comprehension and slightly lower in inferential comprehension. The results of these investigations seem to indicate today's students are no less able and, in fact, students at the lower levels may be outperforming their counterparts in the past.

Perhaps the greatest concern with the "Back to the Basics" movement, however, lies in the interpretation of the word "basics." If, in reading, the basics are conceived narrowly as a program concerned primarily with the teaching of phonetic elements and rules, of drill on isolated words and word families, on exercises that ignore the child's linguistic background and cognitive processes, on dull materials that fail to take into account the child's tastes, interests and relevant needs and the affective aspects of the reading programs, surely reading instruction in this country will suffer greatly.

ORAL READING

Oral reading is widely used in elementary school reading programs. Therefore, a classroom teacher needs to know what the process requires of readers, and its value and limitations.

Oral Versus Silent Reading

Oral reading, the process of reading printed material aloud, is complex. To achieve a better understanding of the process, one can compare it to silent reading, which in itself, involves more than simply reading material silently. The basic goals of oral reading are quite different from those of silent reading. Whereas silent reading requires a reader's reaction to printed ideas, and at a rate commensurate with the reader's ability to think (Spache and Spache, 1977), oral reading requires correct pronunciation of printed words and, hopefully, comprehension. In other words, oral and silent reading are somewhat contradictory. Silent reading can include vocalizations of some sort for many readers. Nevertheless the major goals for silent reading are comprehension, integration and assimilation. Oral reading, on the other hand, involves correct enunciation, inflection and pronunciation of words, which usually indicate that the reader understands what is being read.

Oral reading can be a distracting process. Because readers are intent upon reading aloud with proper pitch, volume and rhythm, etc., they may easily lose sight of what the material is conveying. They may find it difficult to read eloquently and at the same time react cognitively to the printed message. Because the silent reader is intent upon comprehending, unimportant words or word parts are often skipped or quickly glanced at. Consequently, the silent reading rate is often faster than for oral reading. Durrell (1956) found that sixth graders could read silently at a rate of 210 words per minute, but these same pupils when reading orally, the rate decreased to 170 words per minute. This difference is normal because good oral readers must slow their rate of presentation so the audience can process the message. It's also true that the eyes and mind can process print faster than the voice, ears and mind.

A reader's eyes move differently across a line of print during silent reading than during oral reading. Durkin (1978) reports this to indeed be the case. Consequently, eye movements for oral reading predictably show more and longer fixations, and an increased number of regressions.

Obviously, oral reading requires spoken utterances and silent reading does not. Mature silent readers avoid most subvocalizations, which are pronunciations of words which can range from whispers to inaudible lip movements. Subvocalizations can reduce speed and distract the reader.

Mature readers spend considerably more time reading silently than orally. To verify this recall when you last read something aloud. Possibly a phone number, a recipe, or a want ad provided the opportunity for you to read aloud to someone. Yet you read large volumes of materials silently each day, whether it be business reports, textbooks, the newspaper, or television ads.

Oral Reading: Its Uses and Abuses

Oral reading has several valuable uses in a school reading program. However, its abuse can create several unfortunate consequences. These will be detailed in the following sections.

Diagnostic   Oral reading provides a good opportunity for teachers to informally assess the reading performances of their students. Strengths and weaknesses in word recognition, including the development of sight vocabulary and other phonics and structural analysis skills can be readily detected. Comprehension can also be checked informally following oral reading by the teacher asking specific questions over the passages read. However, for oral reading to be a useful diagnostic tool, a teacher needs to do more than make a few mental notes about the difficulties a student is having. Classroom teachers often have their students read aloud, make a few checks, and plan corrective strategies accordingly. A more productive approach, for diagnostic purposes, involves the assessment of oral reading on an individual basis rather than through group reading. Teachers need to make written observations of abilities detected, and they must also realize that comprehension following oral reading may not be as high as following silent reading. A teacher should be systematic about assessing oral reading, and use an approach similar to informal reading inventories.

Instructional   Oral reading can convey information effectively to an audience. However, for full communication to be achieved, both the reader and the audience must work to attain it. The reader must be prepared to present the material smoothly and meaningfully, and the audience must actively listen and respond to the information presented. All too often classroom teachers require students to read aloud without initial prereading or practice. In such cases, the reader is unprepared to present the information in the most communicative fashion, and the audience has little incentive to attend to the reader. For oral reading to be of instructional benefit, both the reader and the audience must be willing to communicate. Round robin reading, the practice of having pupils take turns reading aloud, is prevalent in many elementary classrooms. This process does not achieve these communicative purposes and is discouraged as a teaching strategy.

Oral reading plays a special role for the beginning reader. For such a student, or one having reading difficulties, oral reading brings immediate assistance. A teacher can detect difficulties and offer immediate help, whereas such problems are not readily identifiable in a silent reader.

Facile decoding ability enhances comprehension. As decoding skills become automatic, silent reading should be emphasized. Thus, oral reading has a special place in a beginning reading program, but loses instructional significance as readers mature in their decoding skills.

Motivational   Oral reading is an excellent way to motivate students to read more. Teachers who read aloud to their students or have their youngsters read aloud to one another often find an increase in recreational reading. Librarians can frequently detect from increased circulation when a book or book parts have been read to a class. However, if used inappropriately, oral reading can be devastating to students, especially those with reading difficulties. In the all too prevalent round robin approach students quickly become disinterested, especially if the oral reader falters. Ridicule or laughter may erupt, resulting in increased anxiety and feelings of inadequacy for the reader.

Students brought up on group reading practices, especially round robin reading, often tend to think of reading as simply reciting words on a page without much thought to what the words convey. Teachers themselves often lose sight of the reading process, or they would not reward parrot-like reproductions of texts and ignore comprehension, evaluation and assimilation. For oral reading to be motivational, both the reader and the audience must be prepared to accept its benefits.

Aesthetic   Although much material is written for the purpose of conveying information, some, such as poetry, drama and some aspects of humor, are written for the enjoyment gained through speaking and listening. Such materials lend themselves well to oral reading; they are created for the human voice and ear and cannot fully be appreciated unless read orally. Teachers can do their part in developing appreciation for such art forms in their students. Choral reading of poetry and student participation in plays are two such means of developing an awareness and enjoyment for such material in children. As in other activities of oral reading, teachers must plan them properly. Students must prepare their reading parts in plays beforehand and must present them to an attentive audience. Choral readers must also prepare for their readings so that appreciation for the author's use of rhythm, timbre and verse can be achieved. The aesthetic values of oral reading are particularly significant for older pupils.

Teaching Strategies

Oral reading is an effective teaching tool if properly handled in the classroom. For it to be of benefit, both the reader and the audience must be prepared and willing to relate to one another. The following activities suggest ways in which such communication can be accomplished.

1   Children are asked to share parts of their favorite books with one another or with younger children. Following preparation, they read aloud the chosen parts to a small group of students.

2   One child is asked to act out a part of a story which has just been read. Other students guess at the part portrayed and locate it in the story. One child then reads the part out loud for the benefit of the others.

3   The students write a radio newscast or program pertaining to class events. Several students practice reading their parts and then present the program to the other students.

4   Students study their parts and then act out the scenes of a play. The dialogue is read from small cards or easily handled books.

5   Based on material previously read, students compose and read riddles to the rest of the class. Other students guess the answers to the riddles and read aloud the parts of the material that helped them to decide upon the answers.

6   Students compose poems, short stories, or articles for a class newspaper. The material then is read aloud or put on tape. Students listen to the tape individually or on a small group basis.

7   Poetry is read aloud by a group of students who have practiced reading it beforehand.

8   An author is introduced by several students who have collected and researched this author's books. Passages or reviews are prepared and read aloud. Students discuss what they have learned about the author from listening to the material read to them.

9   Students compose short passages which are used to introduce various members of the class. The passages contain information about the students' hobbies and interests. Once the introductions have been read, the students themselves read aloud material which particularly interests them.

SUMMARY

A good oral reader is intent upon conveying information to some listener and so will pronounce words carefully, using proper pitch and intonation. Too much concern for good elocution can be distracting. Although comprehension aids in the presentation of the material, readers, especially beginners, may be unable to focus on proper diction and comprehension at the same time.

Oral reading is a valuable teaching tool in a school reading program. It has diagnostic, instructional, motivational and aesthetic values, if properly utilized. Oral reading is most effective when both readers and listeners are prepared and willing to communicate.

READING AND LANGUAGE ARTS

As could be noted in the preceding section, activities designed to enhance oral reading reflect the interrelationship of reading and other language arts.

The child's language facility, much of it developed in preschool years, contributes to the development of skills in reading, listening, speaking, writing, spelling, and literature. What facilitates and fosters growth in one area also facilitates and fosters growth in the others. The teacher's responsibilities, therefore, include the following:

1   Being flexible enough to allow for the range of language abilities children have when they come to school.

2   Understanding the language of the community from which the children come.

3   Valuing and appreciating the language of every child.

4   Developing widening experiences with children, thereby fostering language development (Smith, Goodman, and Meredith, 1970, p. 165).

Language-related instruction has progressed far beyond that offered under the headings of reading, spelling, written composition, and speech only a few years ago. Reading is seen as a facet of communication, not as an isolated fragment of the language arts. Teachers who attempt to teach listening, speaking, writing, spelling, reading, grammar, and literature as isolated elements appear to be ignoring natural relationships that exist among these areas of the language arts.

The medium through which teaching and learning take place is language. When children comes to school, they have already learned much about the grammar and vocabulary of the language spoken in their home. Teachers, therefore, can "use the oral efficiency that children bring to school as the means of developing a complementary efficiency in reading and writing" (Burrows, 1972, p. 96).

Courses relating the language arts to one another will help pupils improve their ability and flexibility in communication. Listening and reading, for example, involve related skills, as do writing and speaking. When students work in small groups on activities related to the reading program, there is more opportunity for speaking and listening than there is if pupils are called upon individually. These communication skills are an important initial step toward skill in reading.

For the same reason, a listening center is an important part of the classroom. Materials in the listening center can include taped stories with questions to be answered at the end. The answers to the questions could become the basis for dramatizing a story using puppets, or for preparing a tape recording to be heard by other pupils. The result will be an integration of the various aspects of the language arts, including reading. This kind of integration should be the classroom teacher's goal.

CHARACTERISTICS OF THE MATURE READER

One of the major goals of a reading program is to help students develop into mature readers. Mature readers (1) reflect on what they are reading; (2) effectively organize and utilize materials; (3) think critically about the *content* of what they read; (4) try to determine the qualifications of authorities consulted; and (5) select authors who fulfill their own immediate needs (Bond and Wagner, 1966).

Gray and Rogers add the following characteristics to the list:

1   A genuine enthusiasm for reading.
2   A tendency to read
    a   a wide variety of materials that contribute pleasure, widen horizons, and stimulate creative thinking.
    b   serious materials which promote a growing understanding of one's self, of others, and problems of social, moral, and ethical nature.
    c   intensively in a particular field or materials relating to a central core.
3   Ability to translate words into meanings, to secure a clear grasp and understanding of the ideas presented, and to sense clearly the mood and feelings intended.
4   Capacity for and habit of making use of all that one knows or can find out in interpreting or construing the meaning of the ideas read.
5   Ability to perceive strengths and weaknesses in what is read, to detect bias and propaganda, and to think critically concerning the validity

and values of the ideas presented and the adequacy and soundness of the author's presentation, views, and conclusions. This involves an emotional apprehension, either favorable or unfavorable, as well as a penetrating intellectual grasp of what is read.

6 Tendency to fuse the new ideas acquired through reading with previous experience, thus acquiring new or clearer understandings, broadened interests, rational attitudes, improved patterns of thinking and behaving and richer and more stable personalities.

7 Capacity to adjust one's reading pace to the needs of the occasion and to the demands of adequate interpretation (Gray and Rogers, pp. 54–55).

Few readers ever achieve full maturity in reading, but many make continuous progress toward the achievement of each of the stated characteristics. The teacher's role is to assist and encourage this progress.

Students' progress toward maturity in reading should be evaluated in terms of their potential. A teacher must try to develop the potential of individuals so that their lifetime reading habits may be made more worthwhile and personally satisfying.

THE READING CURRICULUM

The reading curriculum must encompass specific reading programs which will help pupils develop into mature readers. We use a somewhat technical language when discussing reading curriculum or programs. Some of the terms used are *developmental reading, functional reading, recreational reading,* and *corrective-remedial reading.* In comprehensive reading programs, instruction, guidance, and media are provided in all these areas. What do these terms mean, and how do they relate to an effective instructional reading program?

The most important goal of the *developmental reading* program is learning to read. Developmental reading programs teach (1) skill in the mechanics of reading, and (2) skill in reading comprehension. The mechanics of reading include developing sight vocabulary; developing skills in identifying unfamiliar words through structural analysis, context clues, dictionary work, and phonics; developing efficient eye movements; developing speed in silent reading; adjusting to the types of material one reads; developing oral reading skills such as phrasing, expression, pitch, and enunciation.

Reading comprehension skills include development of a more extensive reading vocabulary; development of the ability to remember, evaluate, and generalize from what one has read; the ability to note and recall details; and the ability to understand the author's ideas and point of view.

The primary objective of *functional reading* programs is to enable a reader to obtain information from various types of reading, or just to read to learn. It sometimes is called study-type reading as well as functional reading. The skills important in functional reading include the following:

1 the ability to locate needed reading material by means of an index, table of contents, encyclopedia, library card file, or other bibliographic aid.

2 the ability to skim or scan material in search of information.
3 the ability to comprehend informational materials which require the application of the comprehension skills for developmental reading, and development of specific skills required by special subject areas, such as reading for social studies content, reading arithmetic problems, reading maps, charts, and graphs.
4 the ability to select the materials needed to gain specific information.
5 the ability to organize what is read—to summarize, for example, or to outline chapters within books.

The major purpose of *recreational reading* or free reading is enjoyment or appreciation. The skills involved in this kind of reading are (1) developing and raising the level of interest in reading, and (2) developing literary judgment and taste (Harris, 1970). Teachers can develop students' interest in reading by demonstrating their own enjoyment of reading as a leisure time activity. They can also help pupils select reading materials for themselves. To help them develop deeper literary judgment and taste, the teacher must establish different learning strategies for fiction and nonfiction, prose, poetry, and drama, and also develop an appreciation for the style and beauty of language.

Developmental, functional, and recreational reading cannot be completely separated. Developmental reading will often be taught with a recreational reading activity or a functional reading assignment. Programs which are truly comprehensive include all these types of reading, and also provide for pupils who need corrective-remedial help.

Corrective-remedial reading programs are usually planned as supplements to the regular developmental program. Whereas the other three types of programs described are group oriented, the corrective-remedial program operates on an individual or small group basis. It usually involves skills in the mechanics of reading and in reading comprehension, for the students are usually weak in one or both of these. The teacher frequently must develop new ways of teaching the basic skills in order to help the students learn to read. As much as possible, the teacher should also provide remedial students with functional and recreational reading; but since these students lack the basic reading skills, the emphasis is placed on the developmental program, adjusted to individual differences.

Even though corrective-remedial reading is related to developmental, functional, and recreational reading, there are some differences. The goals of a corrective-remedial program and of a regular program are the same: (1) teach every child to read to the best of his abilities; (2) permit a more open atmosphere for learning; (3) diagnose students for specific learning difficulties; (4) give daily individualized instruction; (5) motivate children to want to read. But in a regular classroom, with thirty or more students, these are often only verbalized, while in a corrective-remedial program, where teaching is on a one-to-one basis, they become an actuality (Heilman, 1972).

Curricular Determinants

Teachers and administrators often differ from each other in attitudes and philosophy. Controversies exist over such issues as teaching children at their own reading level, permissiveness in individual instruction, and emphasizing interest in reading. Other areas of controversy concern the appropriate number of conferences with parents, the need for diagnosing children more thoroughly, and techniques for allowing them to set noncompetitive reading goals.

The school's position on such issues will influence the curriculum. For this reason, teachers should be familiar with the philosophy of schools where they apply for teaching positions. What the teacher believes should, ideally, be in general agreement with established school policies. When teachers see the need for a change of philosophy or practice, however, they have a professional obligation to try to effect such a change.

The way the teacher organizes the reading program will depend on the materials and techniques he or she uses and on the structure of the classroom—whether it is a self-contained, nongraded, or team-teaching situation. The first step in setting up the program is to set long range goals, such as, "Children will be able to read to the best of their ability during this year." The next step is to diagnose the children's reading skills, and, according to the results, select the techniques and materials to be used and set specific objectives for each child, either daily, weekly, or monthly. The most effective diagnosis makes use of as many sources of information as possible. Standardized tests, teacher observations, informal reading tests, and cumulative cards can all be valuable.

It is often helpful to organize an individual reading folder for each student. Table 1 shows one system for recording skill development data. Teachers may modify this to suit their own teaching situations.

A completed table will indicate what reading skills the child possesses, and which ones yet need to be taught or practiced. Teachers can develop specific teaching objectives from this information. They can decide how to group pupils, determine which pupils need individual instruction, and select appropriate materials and teaching techniques.

Table 2 shows one teacher's plans for a day's reading program. This teacher has grouped the students into four reading groups. The teacher tries to work with three groups each day. The teacher has a tutor and a paraprofessional to help in the classroom. The same type of daily program could be used in a team teaching situation. Table 2 also shows another daily plan for teaching reading. There is more time allotted and the teacher has no aides. The teacher utilizes the allotted time for the language arts/reading program.

Table 2 represents only two types of lesson plans. Each teacher needs to adjust his or her lesson plans to meet the individual needs of the students. Effective reading instruction is based on careful planning. The plans suggested in the guides which accompany basal readers, while helpful, can never accommodate all the needs represented in a typical reading group.

OBJECTIVES OF THE READING CURRICULUM

Since reading is highly complex and involves the learning of many specific skills, very specific objectives should be planned for the reading program. Vague objectives will yield poor results. A good set of objectives indicates the reading skills that children should demonstrate as a result of the reading

Table 1

INDIVIDUAL READING FOLDER FOR STUDENTS

Name _____   Grade Level _____

Teacher _____

Reading levels	Standardized test scores	Reading capacity

Informal reading inventory
Independent   _____ _____ _____

Instructional   _____ _____ _____

Frustration   _____ _____ _____

	Introduced	Practiced	Applied

1. Prereading skills
   a. Letter names
   b. Listening
   c. Speaking vocabulary
   d. Visual discrimination
   e. Auditory discrimination
   f. Left-to-right orientation

2. Word analysis skills
   a. Sight vocabulary (level)
   b. Phonic analysis
      1. Initial consonants
      2. Final consonants
      3. Blends
      4. Digraphs
      5. "Long" vowels
      6. "Short" vowels
      7. Vowel generalizations
      8. Contractions
   c. Structural analysis
      1. Prefixes
      2. Suffixes and endings
      3. Compound words
      4. Syllabication

3. Comprehension and study skills
   a. Vocabulary
   b. Details
   c. Main ideas
   d. Sequence
   e. Inference
   f. Dictionary
   g. Book parts
   h. Other

4. Recreational Reading

Table 2

PLAN FOR A DAILY READING PROGRAM

	Group 1	Group 2	Group 3	Group 4
9:00–9:30	(With Teacher) Introduce new story and read silently.	(With Tutor) Practice on vocabulary phrases and sentences. Oral reading from science textbook.	(Alone) Pupil goes to kdg. to read a story to them, or reads independently.	(Alone) At listening center. Tape with a practice story prepared by the teacher, who has already taught the story.
9:30–10:00	(Alone) Listening center. Tape with a reading (mystery) story that has the ending omitted.	(With Teacher) Individualized reading. Teacher works with 5 students individually.	(With Tutor) Play games on initial consonants since the students need to practice this skill.	(With Paraprofessional) Work on writing sentences with new vocabulary presented by teacher on previous days.
10:00–10:30	(With Teacher) Each write his own ending to the taped mystery story.	(With Teacher) Listening center. Tape on spelling worksheet to follow. Writing spelling words in sentences.	(With Teacher) Read a story from a linguistic series.	(Alone) Record the written sentences on tape recorder or read independently.
9:00–9:30–	(With Teacher) Introduce vocabulary. Read a story.	(Alone) Learning Activity. Crossword puzzle. Skill activity. Practice spelling words.	(Alone) Listening Center. Tape on Listening skills.	
9:30–10:00	(Alone) Practice book. related to vocabulary. Practice spelling.	(With Teacher) Review practice book. Teach vocabulary of new lesson.	(Alone) Practice spelling words. Write words in sentences.	
10:00–10:30	(Alone) Write a story or poem with vocabulary bank (Students' words on index cards).	(Alone) Listening Center. Tape on "How to Listen."	(With Teacher) Review story. Find answers to questions, for oral reading. Review sentences they wrote.	
10:30–11:00	Teacher works with individuals, checks seatwork, or adjusts time to fit the needs of the individual students.			

program, and thus guides the teacher in the types of learning activities and evaluation procedures used (Barrett, 1969).

The *major objective* of a reading program might be, "At the end of the school year, pupils will be reading to the best of their reading ability." A *specific objective,* however, is related to the teacher's diagnosis of the pupil's strengths and weaknesses and the day-by-day activities which follow the diagnostic and prescriptive analysis. One specific objective, for example, might be, "Today a pupil will read a paragraph at that pupil's instructional level, missing only one word and answering questions about content with 75 percent accuracy." The specific objective helps the teacher know when a student has mastered a particular skill.

The major goal of the developmental program is learning to read; for the functional program the goal is reading to learn; for the recreational program the goal is reading for enjoyment or appreciation. Under each of those goals some specific objectives can be listed, and these objectives (or behaviors) will be the specific plans for reading lessons. Table 3 shows an example of a comprehensive goal, a major objective resulting from that goal, and the specific objectives established for lessons.

When the objectives of the reading program are stated concretely and specifically, progress can be made and assessed. Pupils as well as teachers can see where they are going and what they have accomplished.

Pupils will frequently set up their own objectives. Pupils' objectives, however, are more likely to be specific skills and knowledge and less likely to involve the development of positive attitudes, interests, and appreciations. Since students often do not see the applications of reading to real situations in school and life, it is important that they, as well as the teacher, be aware of and work toward specific objectives.

To encourage pupils to develop initiative in making choices, teachers may want to suggest rather than prescribe goals. Pupils can be led to develop their own objectives, perhaps in this way: Have the pupils make a study of their own reading needs and achievement; then ask them to select the goals most appropriate for them from a comprehensive list. Each goal should be accompanied by specific objectives, so that the students can see exactly what they will be working on. The pupils should mark the objectives they want to work toward and identify those specific objectives on which they think the most progress can be made. This not only helps the pupil, but adds focus to the pupil-teacher conference on reading.

In order to develop effective objectives, the teacher should answer the following important questions: (1) What is it that must be taught? (2) How can the teacher know when it has been taught? (3) What materials and procedures will work best in teaching what is to be taught? If further guidelines are needed, those listed by Mager (1962), including steps to follow in the development and use of behavioral objectives, might be helpful:

1   A statement of instructional objectives is a collection of words or symbols describing one of your educational intents.
2   An objective will communicate your intent to the degree you have described what the learner will be doing when demonstrating his achievement, and how you will know when he is doing it.
3   To describe terminal behavior (what the learner will be doing):
    a   identify and name the overall behavior act.
    b   define the important conditions under which the behavior is to occur.
    c   write a separate statement for each objective; the more you have, the better the chance you have of making clear your intent.
    d   if you give each learner a copy of your objectives, you may not have to do much else (Mager, 1962, p. 52).

If an objective is not stated in behavioral terms, the teacher and pupil will have no way of telling whether or not the objective has been attained. "A student can follow written directions" is a nonbehavioral objective. It does not identify the specific behavior that is expected of the student: With what degree of accuracy can the student follow directions? What materials will the student use? How will the teacher and the pupil know when this objective has been accomplished? A good behavioral objective will answer questions like these.

The Authors' Viewpoint

It is important for teachers to establish both major objectives and specific behavioral objectives in order to understand what is to be taught and the direction the learning process should take. When a teacher has established behavioral objectives, it will be easier to develop learning activities to meet students' needs and to evaluate their performance. Teachers should not rely on only one learning activity for all students before an evaluation is made. When students do not understand a behavioral objective after one learning activity, there should be two, three, even four other activities they can do to achieve a successful performance. Students build on successes, and repeated failure to meet a behavioral objective can be devastating. Therefore teachers need to have, for each objective, many learning activities and different types of performances.

Teachers have often failed to understand the sequence in which reading skills should be taught throughout the elementary grades. Having to set goals and define expected behaviors forces them to recognize and follow this sequence.

Clear objectives can also assist pupils' self-actualization. If teachers understand what they want pupils to achieve in a reading lesson, then they are better able to predict what each individual child will successfully achieve. Success will raise pupils' self-esteem and allow them to proceed to the next reading skill in the program.

If teachers are to be accountable for the results of their teaching, then they must develop goals and objectives which delineate specific behaviors, so they can demonstrate that their objectives have been met. Goals and objectives should also be established for each school, and these should closely relate to the philosophy of that school. This will give the teacher insight into the school's entire reading program.

ORGANIZING A READING PROGRAM

Most reading curricula consist of developmental, functional, recreational, and corrective-remedial teaching programs. Within each of these areas teachers establish objectives and specify behavior for obtaining those objectives. Then they select the materials best suited to their program.

Basal readers with workbooks are frequently used in developmental reading programs, because they are built upon the sequential learning-to-read process. Publishers of these readers usually list the objectives and outline the scope and sequence of their programs. They also provide tests and suggestions for supplemental reading. Other materials, however—such as programmed learning materials—are also designed sequentially and can be used for developmental reading. Teachers can make their own materials, too, as long as they are prepared according to a correct developmental sequence. Work on basic sight words, for example, should come at the beginning levels of reading and throughout the first year of reading instruction. Developmental

Table 3

GOALS, OBJECTIVES, AND BEHAVIORS OF A READING PROGRAM

This is an example of a page that could be given to students. Other goals and objectives could be added according to the teaching situation and the needs of the individual students. Teachers could benefit by keeping records of the reading achievements of individual students.

Student _____   Teacher _____

Level _____   School _____

Goal	Major Objectives	Specific Objectives and Behaviors
1. Development of vocabulary skills	a. To use many different kinds of firsthand experiences to gain understanding of words.	1. Read a newspaper, locate new words and write them with meanings. 2. Be able to write ten new words and their meanings every two weeks for six weeks.
	b. To learn key words in studying other school subjects.	1. Listen to three TV programs and write unknown words. Locate meanings in the dictionary. Try for 5 new words in two weeks. 2. Write a story after six weeks using all new words for this time. 3. Read three library books in six weeks and locate new words and their meanings.
	c. To consult dictionary for exact meanings of words.	1. Start a pupil dictionary to enter new words of the six weeks. 2. In six weeks the dictionary should contain 50 new words and their meanings.
	d. To learn word origins and the different meanings of the same word in different contexts.	1. After six weeks take a test of 50 new words and be able to give the meanings of 45 words. Also write the 45 words in sentences.

2. Development of word recognition skills

   a. To identify words through context clues.

      1. Be able to identify new words through context clues four out of five times.

   b. To identify words through phonics.

      1. Be able to identify orally the initial consonant letters and sounds of selected words.

      2. Be able to identify all the final consonant letters and sounds of these same words.

      3. Be able to identify blends and digraphs in words selected.

   c. To use the dictionary efficiently.

      1. Be able to locate ten new words and write their meanings in fifteen minutes.

      2. Be able to use three different types of dictionaries.

      3. Be able to write ten new words correctly in sentences after locating them within twenty minutes.

   d. To identify words through structural analysis.

      1. Be able to locate prefixes and suffixes in five stories.

      2. When given four stories, be able to identify the compound words in all five of them.

      3. Be able to tell why words are divided into syllables (or divide them correctly ten out of ten times).

3. Development of comprehension skills

   a. To use a variety of comprehension strategies.

      1. Be able to identify new word meanings in ten stories, using the dictionary.

      2. State main ideas and supporting details.

      3. Be able to follow written directions ten out of ten times.

      4. Be able to give a sequence of events for all stories read in a six-week period.

   b. To comprehend sentences accurately.

      1. Be able to recall the ideas of sentences ten out of ten times.

      2. Be able to identify word meanings in sentences ten out of ten times.

      3. Be able to sequence a set of sentences into a story at least five times.

4. Development through reading

   a. To read for personal growth and enjoyment.

      1. Be able to select many different types of materials related to ideas to be read about (maintain a written list of these).

      2. Read for appreciation and enjoyment when given extra time (observation by teacher). Make a list of books read with a short summary of each.

programs organized on an individualized basis depend for success on the teacher's awareness of appropriate sequences for the pupils. The students read daily in material which they have chosen. The teacher utilizes the time to have teacher/pupil meetings whereby the teacher checks the students' reading abilities, word recognition, comprehension and study skills. This time also can be used for teaching small groups reading skills for which they show a need. This approach allows students to read what they desire and to pace themselves in reading, but it does mean that a classroom must have many (at least twenty books per student) books for students. Other reading approaches for developmental reading are discussed more thoroughly in Chapters Seven and Eight.

One way of using a developmental reading program is to follow carefully four basic steps in teaching a lesson: readiness, silent reading, oral rereading, and reaction to and application of what has been read. This sequence can be adapted to any type of material used in the classroom and can be used with small groups or with the whole class.

Each major publisher's basal reading program presents a sequence of steps to be followed in teaching a reading lesson. An outline of steps in a reading lesson, including readiness, reading, and response, is presented in Table 4. All steps need not be accomplished in one reading lesson, but setting the purpose for reading is very important and should be done before pupils read. The remaining steps can occur within a day, two days, or even a week.

The functional reading program is the application of the developmental program. The materials used in functional reading are usually content area books, maps, charts, and teacher-prepared materials, especially those designed to promote study skills. The same approaches are recommended for content area reading as are appropriate for the developmental reading program. The lesson consists of a readiness stage, a reading stage, and rereading and application stages. It is a teach, practice, and apply process. The program can be organized for whole classes, interest groups, tutorial groups, or research groups.

A list and description of reading materials to be used with a developmental, functional, or corrective-remedial reading program can be found in *Learning to Read: The Great Debate* (Chall, 1967). Chall also presents a classification chart of twenty-two reading programs, which can be helpful to teachers looking for programs to meet particular needs. A selected bibliography of materials for teaching comprehension, useful for developmental and functional reading programs, is given in *Reading Instruction for Classroom and Clinic* (Fry, 1972).

Most of the materials in the recreational program will be trade books—paperbacks especially, which tend to excite pupils about reading. Books the pupils prepare themselves can also be included. Teachers and pupils talk together about the books the pupils have read. Recreational reading programs usually do not include direct reading instruction unless the developmental reading program is individualized, in which case the two programs become one. Time should be allotted for recreational reading in every teaching day. Too often, recreational reading is neglected, and this is unfortunate; few things are more exciting than to read books that provide important experiences and information.

Table 4

STEPS IN TEACHING A READING LESSON

1. Readiness	2. Reading	3. Response	4. Reteaching
a. Motivation (Build interest)	a. Silent/Oral Reading (Always silent first unless in a diagnostic situation)	a. Continued Discussions	a. Only when students cannot understand (in test out)
b. Background (Build associations	b. (Guide students through reading) Discussion	b. Study Skill Skill development (Follow-up activities)	
c. Vocabulary (Teach new words)		c. Learning Activity	
d. Purpose for reading (Set stage for reading; always done just before silent reading)		d. Transfer-Application (use in other areas)	
		e. Mastery Are the students ready to proceed to the next lesson?	

Source: William Powell, University of Florida.

In many schools, the corrective-remedial program is organized and managed by the classroom teacher. In some schools, however, special reading teachers are available. When this is the case, coordination between the class room and the remedial programs is important. Too frequently, the remedial teacher loses contact with classroom teachers. Some authorities believe that a remedial reading specialist can best work with individuals or small groups *within* a classroom, where the classroom teacher can observe the teaching situation and use it to the advantage of the pupils during the day. Occasionally, the reading specialist might meet with pupils separately, individually or in groups. The classroom teacher, too, should work with small groups of pupils who need additional corrective-remedial reading instruction.

The four steps as shown in Table 4 of a reading lesson are: 1. readiness; 2. reading; 3. response; and if necessary 4. reteaching. To illustrate these steps in teaching a reading lesson, one can think of the story of Cinderella and how it would be taught in first or second grade.

1   Readiness
  a   Motivation
    Today we are going to read a story about a girl who was not liked by her sisters or mother. (Discuss with students their feelings about sisters, brothers, mothers, and fathers.)
  b   Background
    This family lived in a little house in a country where there were kings and queens. Is this what we have in America? (Build association)
  c   New Vocabulary
    There are some new words in our story today. In this slipper (have an actual shoe with slipper written on it and the new vocabulary written on strips of paper in the shoe) are the new words in our story used in sentences. Let's see if you can read them. (Each

student takes one slip. Use the blackboard for more in the teaching lesson if necessary.)

2 Reading

   a Silent/Oral Reading

   Always silent reading before oral reading except in a diagnostic setting. Read according to the students' reading abilities. Some can do the entire story alone, while others need guidance with each page, maybe each paragraph.

   b Guide students in their reading. As we read today we may find the answers to these questions. Write them on board. Set purposes for reading.

   Where was the story?

   Who were the important characters?

   What was exciting about the story?

   How did you feel about the story?

   Could the story have really happened? Why?

3 Response

   a Continued Discussions

   Find the answers to the questions used in setting purposes. Students must scan for the answers and read them orally when it fits the questions. The teacher should also ask factual, inferential, and critical questions.

   b Study Skill—Skill Development

   Teach skill lessons that relate to the story. Skill lessons may be before or after the reading of the story. Workbook pages may be either skill related or story related.

   c Learning Activity and (d) Transfer-Application

   Throughout the day, week and year, the teacher watches to see that students use the skills taught in the reading lesson. The teacher utilizes workbooks and other learning activities to reinforce the teaching lessons of Cinderella.

   e Mastery: Teachers determine if students have learned all the elements of the teaching lessons of Cinderella through evaluation techniques.

4 Reteaching

   If the students do not develop the vocabulary, the reading skills, nor understand the questions of the story, a teacher must reteach the same lesson again.

Table 5 provides a comprehensive organizational pattern including all the types of programs discussed so far.

Paraprofessionals and Volunteers in the Reading Program

Paraprofessional and volunteer help can be valuable in all of these types of reading programs. When students need additional practice, the supervision of such practice can be assigned to paraprofessionals, aides, parents, or older students in the school. The professional teacher becomes the one who plans

Table 5

Organization for a Reading Program

	Developmental	Functional	Recreational	Corrective-Remedial
Curriculum	To learn to read	To read to learn	To learn to enjoy reading	To try to balance skills needed in reading.
Materials	Basal readers Programmed reading Linguistic reading Language-experience Teacher-made materials Individualized reading	Content text Maps, charts Teacher-made materials Supplementary books	Library books Microfiche Paperback novels Newspapers Magazines Student-made books	All the materials mentioned, but many high interest, low vocabulary books. Materials adjusted to individual needs.
Method	Steps in teaching a lesson	Steps in teaching a lesson: 1. Survey 2. Question 3. Read 4. Recite 5. Respond	Independent teacher-pupil cooperation	Steps in teaching a lesson, but geared to meet the needs of individual pupils.
Personnel	Teacher: Professional leader, planner, decision-maker			Special cases: Reading specialists
	Aided by: Paraprofessionals, cross-age tutoring, volunteer tutors, parents			

and selects appropriate methods and materials, initiates the lessons or exercises, and evaluates the degree to which the learners have advanced in their reading skills. The teacher formulates all assignments given to aides, basing them on specific objectives set for individual pupils, so that each aide understands what is to be done and what the end result should be. At the end of each session, the teacher confers with the aides in order to understand problems they encountered or to adjust assignments for future days.

The teacher should keep in mind that aides and volunteers do not have the professional expertise of a teacher. Therefore, they should not be expected to make decisions for which they are not equipped. The materials they will use must be carefully evaluated. Are the directions too complicated for them to deal with? Do the materials require direct instruction which should be done by the teacher? Has the aide or volunteer been given sufficient on-the-job training to carry out certain specific instructional tasks?

With proper guidance, aides and volunteers can be a vital part of the school reading program (Cooper & Ransom, 1973). Such differentiated staffing is becoming more and more common in our school districts. Helpful materials on the subject can be found in the *Handbooks for the Volunteer Tutor* (International Reading Association, 1969).

The following are some of the advantages of additional personnel within a school:

1   Additional help is provided for pupils.
2   The pupil-teacher ratio is reduced.

3 Better public relations are established when parents and neighborhood people assist in the classroom.
4 Such personnel are less expensive than additional hired teachers.

There are some disadvantages, too, however:

1 Teachers are given additional responsibilities.
2 In-service training may not be provided for aides and teachers.
3 The administration may enlarge classes, assuming the aides perform the same job as teachers.
4 A professional teaching position may be filled by an aide, who can be paid a lower salary.
5 Because of large class assignments, teachers are sometimes forced to behave as though their additional personnel had professional preparation.

Only when in-service training for teachers and paraprofessionals is provided and the roles and responsibilities of teachers and aides are carefully defined can pupils gain the full benefit of differentiated staffing.

SUMMARY

Schools today offer a variety of organizational patterns, additional personnel to assist the teacher, and a flexible reading curriculum, adjusted to the individual needs and interests of the pupils. This variety and flexibility is necessary for meeting pupils' differing needs; but variety alone does not ensure a successful reading program. Research has generally shown that the single most important factor contributing to the success of a reading program is the teacher—the trained and experienced teacher who is open to new designs in reading instruction and who is willing to implement these approaches in the classroom. Such a teacher—whether in a self-contained classroom, a nongraded classroom, or an open classroom, with or without additional personnel—will be most likely to achieve the major goal: to teach all children to read to the best of their abilities.

REFERENCES

Allen, James E., Jr. "The Right to Read—Target for the 70's." Washington, D.C.: U.S. Department of Health, Education, and Welfare, Office of Education, 1969.

Barrett, T. C. "Goals of the Reading Program: The Basis for Evaluation." In *Elementary Reading Instruction,* edited by A. Berry, T. C. Barrett, and W. R. Powell. Boston: Allyn and Bacon, 1969.

Betts, E. A. *Foundations of Reading Instruction.* New York: American Book Company, 1957.

Bond, G., and Wagner, E. B. *Teaching the Child to Read.* 4th ed. New York: Macmillan, 1966.

Burrows, A. T. "Children's Language: New Insights for the Language Arts." In *Language Arts Concepts for Elementary School Teachers,* edited by P. C. Burns, J. E. Alexander, and A. R. Davis. Itasca, Ill.: F. E. Peacock Publishers, 1972.

Chall, J. *Learning to Read: The Great Debate.* New York: McGraw-Hill, 1967.

Cooper, J. D., and Ransom, P. *Local Concerns.* Unpublished manuscript. Ball State University, 1973.

Dworkin, Nancy and Dworkin, Yehoash. "The Legacy of *Pygmalion in the Classroom." Phi Delta Kappan.* 60: June, 1979.

Farr, R. "The Potential Misuse of Tests" in *Minimum Competency Standards,* Newark, Del.: International Reading Association. 1978.

Farr, R.; Fay, L.; and Negley, H. *Then and Now: Reading Achievement in Indiana (1944–45 and 1978).* Bloomington, Ind.: School of Education, Indiana University, 1978

Farr, R., and Tone, B. "What Does Research Show?" *Today's Education* 69: Nov./Dec. 1978.

Fry, E. *Reading Instruction for Classroom and Clinic.* New York: McGraw-Hill, 1972.

Gray, W. S., and Rogers, B. *Maturity, Its Nature and Appraisal.* Chicago: The University of Chicago Press, 1956.

Hafner, L. E., and Joy, H. B. *Patterns of Teaching Reading in the Elementary School.* New York: Macmillan, 1971.

Harris, A. J. *How to Increase Reading Ability.* 5th ed. New York: David McKay, 1970.

Heilman, A. W. *Principles and Practices of Teaching Reading.* 3rd ed. Columbus, Ohio: Charles E. Merrill, 1972.

Jencks, C. "The *Wrong* Answer for the Schools Is: Back to Basics". *Washington Post,* Sunday, February 19, 1978.

Lapp, D. *The Use of Behavioral Objectives in Education.* Newark, Del.: ERIC/CRIER and the International Reading Association, 1972.

Lavatelli, C. S. "An Approach to Language Learning." In *Language Arts Concepts for Elementary School Teachers,* edited by P. C. Burns, J. E. Alexander, and A. R. Davis. Itasca, Ill.: F. E. Peacock Publishers, 1972.

Mager, R. F. *Preparing Instructional Objectives.* Palo Alto, Calif.: Fearon Publishers, 1962.

Merton, R. K. "The Self-fulfilling Prophecy." *The Antioch Review,* Summer 1948.

National Assessment of Educational Progress. *Reading in America: A Perspective of Two Assessments.* Denver: The Assessment, 1976.

Popham, W. J.; McNeil, J. D.; Baker, E. L.; and Millman, J. "Measurable Objectives Collections." Los Angeles, Calif.: Instructional Objectives Exchange, 1970.

Rauch, S., ed. *Handbook for the Volunteer Tutor.* Newark, Del.: International Reading Association, 1969.

Rosenthal, R., and Jacobson, L. *Pygmalion in the Classroom.* New York: Holt, Rinehart and Winston, 1968.

Sebesta, S. L., and Wallen, C. J. *Readings on Teaching Reading.* Chicago, Ill.: Science Research Associates, 1972.

Shane, H. G.; Redder, M. E.; and Gillespie, M. C. *Beginning Language Arts Instruction with Children.* Columbus, Ohio: Charles E. Merrill, 1961.

Smith, E. B.; Goodman, K. S.; and Meredith, R. *Language and Thinking in the Elementary School.* New York: Holt, Rinehart and Winston, 1970.

Smith, J. A. *Creative Teaching of Language Arts in the Elementary School.* Boston: Allyn and Bacon, 1967.

Smith, J. A. *Creative Teaching of Reading and Literature in the Elementary School.* Boston: Allyn and Bacon, 1967.

Spache, G. D., and Spache, E., *Reading in the Elementary School,* Fourth edition, Boston: Allyn and Bacon, 1977.

Strang, R. "The Reading Process and Its Ramifications." Invitational Addresses, Tenth Annual Convention. Newark, Del.: International Reading Association, 1965, pp. 49–52.

Strang, R., et al. *The Improvement of Reading.* Newark, Del.: International Reading Association, 1961.

Whipple, G. "Characteristics of a Sound Reading Program." In *Reading in the Elementary School,* 48th Yearbook of the National Society for the Study of Education, Part II. Chicago, Ill.: University of Chicago Press, 1949.

Wilkins, William E. "The Concept of a Self-Fulfilling Prophecy," *Sociology of Education* 49: April, 1976.

Wilson, R. M., and Hall, Maryanne. *Reading and the Elementary Child.* New York: D. Van Nostrand, 1972.

PREVIEW

The problems of reading assessment have become more critical for you as a teacher, in this era of accountability in education.

In this chapter Karlsen presents a framework of assessment procedures and their application to the reading program at several levels. Included in the chapter are practical suggestions for the use of tests, manuals, and the interpretation of data. We hope that this chapter will not only increase your knowledge about reading assessment, but also help you synthesize the content of the chapters that follow.

Though in the past testing was used primarily to assess pupil progress, Karlsen believes that the new thrust in this phase of education is assessment to improve instruction. Emphasis is placed on the uses of tests in a diagnostic-prescriptive approach to reading instruction. Formal testing has also become more common since government-sponsored programs at all levels now require some type of formal assessment. Local districts generally have annual testing programs, which makes it imperative that you be knowledgeable about testing. This chapter deals with these testing problems which will be of particular interest to you as a reading teacher.

Assessment and Diagnosis of Reading Abilities

Bjorn Karlsen, Sonoma State College

OBJECTIVES

After you have read this chapter, you should be able to:

1. Describe the diagnostic teaching of reading and demonstrate this approach with pupils.

2. Name five common types of reading tests and describe all in some detail.

3. Describe the difference in diagnostic usefulness between a standardized survey test and a standardized diagnostic test.

4. Make correct judgments about the appropriateness of answer sheets for a group of pupils.

5. Explain the three most common types of norms and explain, in general, how they are derived.

6. After administering and scoring a standardized test, demonstrate the use and interpretation of the appropriate norm tables.

7. With respect to reading readiness assessment, delineate the main differences between the prognostic and the diagnostic approach.

8. List at least ten different situations in which one of the assessment techniques described in this chapter will help a teacher of reading.

The concept of evaluating children with tests has been a subject of considerable debate in recent years. It has been a confusing debate, since it has rarely been exactly clear which tests were discussed and why they were supposed to be detrimental to children. Many of the stated opinions have been contrary to rather well-established facts. Some writers have been unhappy with certain uses of IQ tests and, as a result, suggest the abolishment of all tests. There have been school districts which have placed a moratorium on all testing only to reinstitute testing after the issues were studied, finding the main difficulty generally to be that the educators applying the tests were poorly prepared to use and interpret test results properly. Formal tests are very helpful periodically in obtaining some objective information about children's achievement; they can be used with advantage by teachers, administrators, and boards.

Until recently tests were administered at the end of an instructional period, usually at the end of the school year. It was a kind of educational *post mortem.* Now, the emphasis in testing is toward the future; it has become an inextricable part of instruction, no longer something being done *to* children at the end, but something to do *for* children to improve their education. In reading, there has been a significant shift from single-score survey testing to an increased emphasis on diagnostic assessment.

Reading instruction is most efficient when it is aimed toward the needs of each individual student in a classroom. But before reading instruction can be individualized, it is necessary to determine how each student reads, what skills need help, and what new skills the student is ready to learn. This process is generally referred to as *diagnosis,* and the systematized diagnose-teach-diagnose-teach approach to reading instruction has been called the *diagnostic-prescriptive* approach. Diagnosis, then, is not simply analysis of the basic causes of reading problems. It is oriented toward the future and is most effective when it helps the teacher arrange meaningful and efficient learning experiences that will help each student become a skillful reader.

When it is part of an intensive case study of each child, diagnosis precedes instruction. But the classroom teacher has one big advantage over the clinical diagnostician: the teacher can observe the child every day, so that diagnosis becomes an ongoing process, interacting at all times with instruction. When a child makes a mistake, the teacher notices the nature of this mistake and decides what remediation is necessary. When it is time to teach the next skill in the reading program, the teacher has already had many opportunities to observe how a child functions with respect to that skill. As a result, a teacher can decide how intensively the new skill should be taught. This is *diagnostic teaching*—an approach in which instruction and diagnosis interact continually.

There are times when the teacher will need to stop and analyze the reading abilities of an individual, or a group, or the entire class. At that point, the teacher will need to know some specific techniques with which to test for such abilities. We will refer to this process as *assessment.* The techniques of assessment chosen will depend on the purposes for which the results will be used. Some techniques are appropriate for the evaluation of individual students' needs; the assessment of the overall growth of a class calls for an entirely different approach. Reading materials which are specifically designed to make assessments are generally referred to as reading *tests.*

A DIAGNOSTIC VIEWPOINT FOR TEACHERS

The need for diagnosis in a broad sense is stressed throughout this chapter, since teaching is most efficient when the pupils are being taught what they need to know in order to develop. Assessment techniques are necessary for effective diagnosis.

The single most complex task in reading assessment is that of determining what instruction should be initiated. Just because a child has a specific difficulty does not necessarily mean that attempts should be made to remedy that problem. Diagnostic systems which list all the items or objectives that a child had difficulty with are generally confusing. Such listings are confusing because instructional priorities are generally not stated. The basic tenet of educational diagnosis is that the child should master prerequisite skills before going on to more advanced skills. Such an approach demands teachers who have a good grasp of the reading process and the hierarchy of reading skills.

The fundamental viewpoint, then, is that we must determine where children are and then teach them from that point at a rate which is sufficiently comfortable to give feelings of success and self-confidence. Poor readers are not challenged by reading material that is very difficult for them; they are frustrated by it. This is often a problem in testing, in which we are trying to determine what a student knows and doesn't know; a difficult test can be very frustrating. Instructional material, however, need not elicit this reaction.

STUDENT ATTITUDES TOWARD TESTING

Many teachers have created unhealthy attitudes toward tests among their pupils. Sometimes, when these pupils grow up and become teachers, they are reluctant to subject their own pupils to the "ordeal of being tested." They blame the tests for these attitudes rather than their teachers, who have perceived testing as something done *to* children rather than *for* them. Teachers should explain assessment techniques to children before administering tests, and they should explain the results afterwards. Eventually, the pupils themselves might administer and score some of the tests, so that they can become involved in self-diagnosis. It is natural for children to want to improve; this is as true of reading and school achievement in general as it is of physical and social activities. If they don't, we must deal with their attitudes and their self-concepts.

SOME COMMON TYPES OF READING TESTS

A great many approaches to the testing of reading are currently being used. These assessment techniques range all the way from simply having teachers sit and listen to the child read out loud to very elaborate diagnostic tests. No attempt will be made here to cover every possible technique; instead, we will concentrate on what are probably the seven most common approaches to reading testing in a typical school setting. This section will deal with the types of tests, and the following section will deal with their most common applications.

Several tests now come with practice tests, which the children take a few days prior to testing. This makes them familiar with the test format and gives teachers time to explain the testing procedure. Some teachers let the children take these practice tests home so that their parents can see what the test looks like. This procedure is particularly recommended for the primary grades.

Teacher-made Tests

The main advantage of a teacher-made test is that it is specific; it covers exactly what has been taught in the classroom, using the vocabulary and the specific content of the reading lessons, including even the teacher's particular style and emphasis. The main drawback of such tests is that they are often poorly constructed. They may contain items that are ambiguous and simply do not work for a given group; multiple choice questions may include distractors that are also correct; or, for some questions, there may be no clearly correct answer at all. Also, there are times when pupils have difficulty understanding the directions. It is useful, therefore, after administering such a test, for the teacher to find out exactly which children had difficulty with what items. The best teacher-made tests are generally those designed for specific groups within the classroom, rather than tests which are given to everybody. Students should be tested on what specifically has been taught through group-individualized instruction (Wood, 1960; Nelson, 1970; Educational Testing Service, 1961b). The instructional technique generally referred to as "individualized reading" particularly requires a great deal of teacher testing (Harris and Smith, 1972). Since the children work so much on their own, the teacher will need to plan an instructional program for each child, which necessitates periodic reevaluation of the students' abilities and instructional needs.

Basal Reader Tests

The vast majority of American children are taught from a basal reader or by some sort of reading instructional system (Aukerman, 1971). These systems generally include printed tests which are used mainly to determine how well the students have learned the content of a specific unit of instruction. Such tests are generally more carefully constructed than teacher-made tests, but they are specific to each reader, and norms are ordinarily not supplied. Occasionally, a basal reader test will be accompanied by a set of "tentative norms," which have often been obtained from a few relatively small school districts within a narrow geographical area rather than from a national sample, as is the case with a standardized test. Basal reader tests have a definite place in the assessment program, since they can help teachers determine if students have actually learned the content of a specific unit. The teacher can then determine who needs specific remediation, who can be advanced at the usual pace, and who might be accelerated somewhat.

Since the basal reader test is generally given immediately following a unit of instruction and covers the basic objectives of that unit, such tests tend to be fairly easy for the students, a fact which makes for ease of test administration but inadequate assessment of the very high achievers. However, the tests do show up the problems of those children who have not achieved well in a particular unit.

Some basal readers have tests built into their workbooks. These tests are sometimes limited to a specific skill, and they can serve some very useful diagnostic purposes. The teacher will also find that analyzing a student's workbook is another way of getting good insights into the kinds of problems the student has. However, a word of caution is necessary about using workbook performance to diagnose reading problems. Because the difficulty of workbooks is often not carefully controlled, the teacher should determine if a particular exercise was especially difficult for all students before jumping to conclusions about one student's specific problem. There are two main determiners of student performance on a reading test—reading ability and item difficulty. Only standardized tests control and publish the difficulty of each individual item, the index of difficulty being the percentage of students who pass each item.

Criterion-referenced Tests

In recent years we have seen the advent of the so-called "criterion-referenced tests," also referred to as "objectives based" tests because they attempt to determine the extent to which the pupils have reached specific objectives or certain performance criteria in reading (Wrightstone, 1971). Behavioral objectives state the behaviors pupils should exhibit after they have reached a particular objective. See, for example, the behavioral objectives at the beginning of this chapter. The criterion-referenced test simply attempts to determine if each child or class has reached a given objective (Kibler, 1970). Part of this approach consists in stating exactly at what point a child has reached a certain level of behavior or a class has reached a certain level of proficiency in a given skill. One can say, for example, that a class has reached a certain objective if 80 percent of the class can perform a given task, this percentage being the criterion of achievement mastery. (These tests are also called "mastery tests.")

These tests are used to determine if a given child has reached a certain level of performance in a given skill. For this purpose, attempts are being made to specify each individual skill and subskill in every single subject. Needless to say, in order to determine whether students have learned these hundreds if not thousands of skills, we need tests which can determine the extent to which each objective has been achieved. The criterion-referenced test often determines whether a child has reached a certain criterion by means of a single item, sometimes a couple of items. From a measurement point of view, this is not a good practice, because children's performances on a task which they have just learned are not stable enough to warrant making decisions about their accomplishments on the basis of one or two test items. Also, it has been found in measurement studies that the percentage of children who can perform correctly on a given task will vary, depending on the particular words that are being used to measure the particular skill in question (Madden, 1972). The 80 percent criterion, then, can be reached either because children perform well on that task or because easy words have been chosen with which to test that task.

Maybe an example will help illustrate this point. For the author's own research, a national tryout was made of several thousand test items. One of the subtests was a decoding test containing an item designed to determine the knowledge of the /oi/ diphthong. One would expect sixth-graders to know this, but that depends on one's criterion. These three test words were used, yielding the following percents passing: *joy*—90 percent, *toy*—86 percent, and *point*—78 percent. With an 80 percent criterion level, the students have passed if either of the first two items is used, but only the use of *joy* as a test word enables them to read the 90 percent criterion level. On specific skills like this, there were variations within one grade of as much as 30 percent and even occasionally 40 percent, demonstrating time and again the need for many items to assess a specific educational attribute.

There is a further problem associated with the criterion-referenced test. It has often been assumed that children at a given grade level ought to perform at the 80 percent level of proficiency in those tasks which are being taught at that grade level. The author has presented evidence that this is not so in a paper entitled *"There is No Such Thing as a Third Grade Word."* (Karlsen, 1979). This study dealt with both spelling and reading, and the notion that 80 percent of the children in a class should know the "third grade words" by the end of third grade. Figure 6–1 presents some spelling words, showing the model or theoretical growth curve going from virtually zero to 80 percent in the third grade. Plotted onto this figure are the growth curves for three "third grade words," *doing, need,* and *through.* The first word seems to be learned mostly in grade 2, the second word shows a gradual increase from grade 2 to grade 6, while *through* was mastered by only a few children in the third grade. It was pointed out that there are *no words* which have a growth curve which coincides with the theoretical growth curve. Similar results are presented in reading. The lesson to be learned here is that teaching and assessment must be carried out at a somewhat higher cognitive level. This study also points to one of the weak spots of the "management systems." They teach and assess at a level of unnecessary specificity. The 80 percent criterion is actually an arbitrarily chosen figure for which there appears to be no particular scientific basis. Some people use other percentages, but 80 percent appears to be the most common figure quoted in the professional literature.

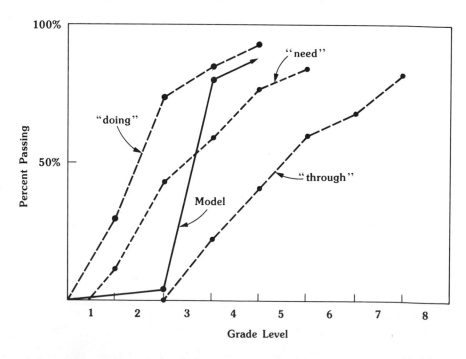

Figure 6.1
Third grade words

The criterion-referenced test has been embraced as a replacement for the "norm-referenced" test. This is a meaningless dichotomy, since a normed test is simply a test for which norms have been obtained. There is no reason at all why we could not have a criterion-referenced, normed test; all we would have to do would be to standardize a criterion-referenced test. One often hears a teacher say, "Now that I have found out what my students can do, what does it mean? How do they compare with those in other schools and in other classes like mine?" Such questions indicate a continuing need for some kind of comparison information, some sort of norm.

A compromise position is being sought by both the *Iowa Test of Basic Skills* (1973 edition) and the 1973 *Stanford Achievement Test.* These tests are designed along the lines of criterion-referenced tests, but they have been normed. They both speak of criterion-referenced interpretation of norm-referenced tests.

The entire issue of criterion-referenced tests is very current and controversial; we will hear a great deal of discussion about it in the next few years. And, in all likelihood, these tests will find their place among the many different kinds of evaluation instruments at the teacher's disposal.

Informal Reading Inventory

The informal reading inventory is a versatile and useful instrument. It is a way of determining the child's ability to handle the instructional material being used with a class and is often used for a quick evaluation of children new to a school or class, or as a periodic reevaluation of children's reading abilities. Ordinarily, the teacher will have the child read silently and orally from the instructional material, having picked selections of varying degrees of difficulty to determine the level at which the child functions for instructional purposes. The process has been worked out in great detail, and there are extensive references on how to make up informal inventories (Johnson and Kress, 1965), the different uses of the informal reading inventory, and so on, which are covered in detail in Chapter Twelve.

The informal reading inventory usually covers a wide range of skills, from rather easy material to rather difficult. But the main advantage is that children are reading the actual material from which they are going to be instructed. This avoids the problem of determining the relationship between a separate test and the specific set of instructional material to be used with the student. Since this is an individual test, it also offers the teacher many opportunities to observe the student's lip movements, eye movements, problems with comprehension, handling of words they are unable to decode, and so on. The procedure is somewhat difficult to handle at first but most teachers have found it very useful to learn. The observational techniques involved with the informal reading inventory are described in considerable detail in the section of this chapter called *The Individual Diagnostic Conference.*

Standardized Survey Tests

Of all the formal printed reading tests taken in the United States, the standardized survey test is by far the most common. There are over thirty such tests on the market, although those most frequently used tend to be part of an achievement test battery. These batteries include such well-known tests as the *California Achievement Test, Comprehensive Test of Basic Skills, Iowa Tests of Basic Skills, Metropolitan Achievement Tests, SRA Achievement Series,* and *Stanford Achievement Test.*

Survey tests usually assess two or three relatively broad reading objectives, such as comprehension, word study skills, and vocabulary. The tests are typically developed from lists of instructional objectives, which the test items sample. After the tests have been written, they are tried out to determine the adequacy of each individual item. The final test is then assembled and *standardized* (Burrill, 1972). This means that it is given to a sample of American children which is representative of the country as a whole. Information from this process is used in establishing national *norms,* making it possible to compare the scores of an individual child with children in general. For this reason, these tests are sometimes said to be "norm-referenced."

Standardized tests are generally used once a year as a periodic check on the educational growth of each child and of a class as a whole. The norms of different levels of the same test battery are comparable. One will, however, find some variation in norms from one test battery to another. This variation is the result of different samples being used for standardization, different content, and variations in the year of standardization. Within the last several decades we have seen considerable fluctuation in the scholastic achievement of American children, so that the date when a test was standardized is a crucial piece of information for those evaluating test results (Kelley, 1966; Stanford Research Report, 1974).

Since a major purpose of giving a survey test is to determine the reading level of each individual student, such a test must of necessity cover a rather wide span of reading ability, individual differences in reading within a single grade being rather extensive. It is important for teachers to realize that the survey test is probably the most difficult test children will take. Most of the students' test-taking experiences have been with easy tests, and to those who are used to obtaining perfect or near perfect scores, the survey test can be a frustrating experience. Hence the need for the teacher to explain the purposes of such a test. Several of the achievement test batteries alleviate this problem by providing practice tests.

Individual variability among students increases with age so that, by the sixth grade, we find a few students reading at the third-grade level, a few as high as the eleventh-grade level, and the rest scattered in between. It is impossible to get accurate assessment of all these students with a single test of reasonable length. To deal with this problem one can go to *out-of-level testing,* where the next more difficult level is used if one is testing a group of high achievers, or the next easier level of the test for a group of low achievers. This needs to be studied carefully, however, before it is done.

One of the controversies surrounding survey tests has to do with their diagnostic usefulness. Since the items generally sample the main objectives of reading instruction, would it not be possible to look at each item to find out which skills a student has or has not learned? Most measurement specialists are of the opinion that more than one or two items are needed to make a diagnosis which can be used as a basis for remediation of an individual student (Mehrens and Lehmann, 1978). But the procedure can be used for an entire class; that is, one can find out which specific skills a class as a whole seems to have a great deal of difficulty with. Obviously, every bit of information we can gather about a student is useful in gaining a better understanding of the student's reading characteristics and instructional needs. But if we are going to place a lot of weight on reading test results for educational planning, we will have to use a test which evaluates all major aspects of reading thoroughly. Since such a test is used to "diagnose" reading instructional needs, it is referred to as a diagnostic reading test.

Standardized Diagnostic Reading Tests

The main purpose of the diagnostic test is to assess students' strengths and weaknesses in the major aspects of reading, so the teacher may plan an instructional program for them. However, such tests do not diagnose the basic causes of reading handicaps in students. Instead they are a tool for the "diagnostic-prescriptive" approach to reading, described earlier in this chapter. They are used to diagnose each individual student's reading characteristics, and the results lead to a prescription for the student's main instructional needs.

There are two main types of diagnostic reading test: those which require individual administration and those which can be given to an entire class simultaneously. The individual test has the obvious disadvantage of being time consuming, requiring up to one and a half hours of testing time, but also has the advantage of not subjecting the very poor reader to extensive testing with items which are much too difficult. This problem is minimized if the group test emphasizes mainly those areas in which a student shows weaknesses, which also means that the test is relatively easy.

The two main individual diagnostic tests are the *Durrell Analysis of Reading Difficulty* and the *Gates-McKillop Reading Diagnostic Tests*. These tests are so technically difficult to administer and interpret that they are used primarily by reading specialists who have been trained in their application.

There are several group diagnostic reading tests in use at present. The one most commonly used is the *Stanford Diagnostic Reading Test;* some other well-known diagnostic tests are the *Diagnostic Reading Scales, Metropolitan Reading Instructional Test, Prescriptive Reading Inventory,* and the *Silent Reading Diagnostic Tests*. These tests are relatively easy to administer, and most of them can be machine scored. But, in order to assign instructional priorities to the various needs identified by the test, the teacher must have a good grasp of the hierarchy of reading skills and must know enough about these skills to be able to select the appropriate instructional materials for each student. This process can be done by machine or by hand for the *Stanford Diagnostic Reading Test,* which also has available a handbook that lists published materials appropriate for each child and, in addition, describes instructional techniques which teachers can use.

The norms of a standardized diagnostic reading test are used somewhat differently from those of a survey test. With the diagnostic test, the teacher makes intertest comparisons to determine the student's relative strengths in the various subskills. Both kinds of tests can be used to measure growth, but for instructional grouping they are used quite differently. Survey tests are often used to group students by reading *level* (high, middle, low), while diagnostic tests are used for grouping according to *needs* (phonics, comprehension, speed, vocabulary). Because diagnostic tests are used for intertest comparisons, the subtests must be long enough to provide a stable assessment of each skill (test reliability). This makes the tests rather lengthy—a problem that is perhaps the most commonly criticized aspect of diagnostic tests. Such tests require two to three hours for administration and, in cases where teachers hand score the tests for an entire class, several hours for scoring and interpretation.

Accountability Tests and Competency Tests

The early 1970s saw the advent of the accountability trend in education (Lessinger, 1970). Because of the extreme importance of reading, much of the discussion of accountability centered around reading instruction. How well are the children reading? How much better do they read as the result of additional federal funding? How well do the children in this state read as compared to children in other parts of the country? These questions inevitably led to the initiation of large-scale testing programs, which are costly and time consuming since they require the administration of fairly lengthy tests to enormous numbers of children.

As we mentioned earlier, the accuracy of measurement for a single child (test reliability) is directly related to the number of items in a test. An accurate group *average,* however, can be obtained with fewer items. Since the politicians and school board members who wanted testing for accountability purposes were only interested in averages, they could get this information by sampling the test; that is, they could give only part of a test (item sampling). An equally stable average could be obtained by giving the entire test to only some of the students (student sampling). These two approaches could be combined by giving, say, every fifth student one fifth of the test (matrix sampling), thus giving good group data on an entire school population, but requiring relatively little testing time. The main drawback, of course, is the lack of individual pupil data.

By the late 1970s, about 70 percent of all the states had some sort of state assessment program. But a new concept had emerged: *Minimum Competency Testing.* The large scale testing programs had revealed that quite a few students were graduating from high school without even a bare minimum of academic competency. As a result, many states now require that students must pass a test in order to graduate. This brought to the fore a question which test people and others have been struggling with for years: What is the reading level required to get along as an American adult? This may seem a simple question, but no agreement has been reached as to the answer. How, then, can we determine who is to fail a competency test? Schools, generally, have decided this by arbitrarily choosing a point so that between, say, five and ten percent of the students fail. (Notice here that a *normative* approach is used to answer what is basically a criterion-referenced question.) Merely failing a student is not enough; we must provide remediation. So, this testing has been moved down into lower grades in order to give the students an opportunity to catch up and graduate. In California, such competency testing became mandated for as early as the elementary grades.

The minimum competency movement may not be as viable as initially conceptualized. Many worry that minimum will become maximum competency, and the political ramifications are horrendous. Characteristically, when a certain cut-off score is set for minimum competency, several times as many minority students will fail as whites. Further, many students and parents feel that the twelfth-grade test is much too easy, since it can generally be passed by a majority of eighth graders.

Perhaps the most unfortunate thing about these developments is that testing has become a political tool, thereby possibly diminishing its educational usefulness. In California where the average reading scores for every district are published in the newspapers every year, the test scores are used by realtors to sell homes in high scoring districts. This approach totally ignores the fact that such test scores are probably a better index of the socioeconomic status of a school than the quality of its instruction. Even school people feel that their school ought to be at least "average." But it is in the nature of averaging that half be below and half above a national or state average. This fifty-fifty situation exists regardless of what that average is (Mehrens and Lehmann, 1978).

SOME COMMON USES OF READING TESTS

Any one of the tests described in the preceding section could be used for a great many purposes. But many of them would be inefficient for certain uses, and so the teacher is faced with the job of selecting the most suitable test for each of a variety of purposes. This section will describe six common situations for which teachers will need some type of test and make suggestions as to which type of test will do the job. The main idea is, of course, to get the most useful information with the least expenditure of time and money.

In many phases of education, one can see examples of false economy, and testing is no exception. One will find teachers making up their own tests because the school can't afford to spend five dollars to buy them. So the teachers spend one weekend, ten ditto masters, and two hundred sheets of ditto paper to develop their own. The writer once reviewed a "diagnostic notebook" which a teacher had made up; she wanted to show him the test and how she analyzed and applied the test results. When asked how much of her spare time she had used to develop this material, she said, "About one month." That service could have been purchased for twenty-five cents per student. There are some advantages in having teachers score tests if they do item analyses (Ahmann and Glock, 1971), but this also can now be done very quickly by computer. An item analysis is a study of how each student in a class performed on every single item of a test. When done by hand, this typically means that the teacher would go through a test booklet and review the kinds of errors each student made. The computerized item analysis can do an even better job, because it will print out the number of the item options that the members of the class chose, enabling the teacher to analyze the various errors or misconceptions of a group, an entire class, or a school. It should be mentioned here that an item analysis done by hand is time consuming and prone to error. Item analysis by computer is cheaper and much more accurate and the teacher's time can be spent on the most important aspect of test analysis, planning for improvement of instruction.

Organizing the Class into
Reading Groups

The most usual scheme for grouping within the classroom is based on the reading levels of the students. Typically, there is a high, a middle, and a low group. Such grouping is global, and is ordinarily not based on any kind of diagnostic study. In its simplest form, this grouping requires that the students be ranked from highest to lowest, then split into groups. The teacher can make some readjustments later, based on observations.

The standardized survey test is often used for grouping purposes. If the students have taken such a test at the end of the preceding year, and if there is not a great deal of mobility in the school, the teacher can have a tentative grouping on the first day of school. The *Metropolitan Achievement Test* will actually yield an instructional reading level similar to that found by means of an individual reading inventory.

Another rather common approach is to give a pretest or placement test which is part of the basal reader, and place the students in the readers indicated by the test results. This approach can result in more than three reading groups.

Organizing the Class by
Instructional Needs

This approach to grouping is used either for the basic reading instruction or as part of a supplementary reading program. Some schools will have one reading period in which the class is divided into the typical groups and another session in which the class is divided according to needs.

This approach requires that the teacher make a rather careful study of the reading needs of each student. The standardized, diagnostic group test is perhaps the most efficient way of doing this. It will cover the main skills which the students need to know to develop adequately in reading and will help teachers pick suitable instructional materials. One problem to be alert to is the possibility of such a test being too difficult. When teachers feel that something must be done to deal with the students individually, it is typically because many of them are having problems with reading. It is probably safer to select a test according to students' approximate reading levels than their grade levels (Educational Testing Service, 1961a).

If the class is to be grouped according to need, a criterion-referenced test could also be used. This requires that the teacher have a good grasp of the skills needed at different grade levels because, after the testing, the teacher will need to make decisions as to which specific needs of each student have instructional priority.

The informal reading inventory can also be used in this situation, although it is more appropriate when instruction according to needs is to be entirely individualized. This technique requires a good deal of background and is rather time consuming.

Evaluating Individuals and
Small Groups

Periodically, the need arises to evaluate one student, or maybe a small group. A transfer student might suddenly arrive, or the teacher may feel that one specific student belongs in a different group or needs to have some problems reevaluated. Here the informal reading inventory, or what is described later in this chapter as the individual diagnostic conference, is an appropriate assessment technique. It will tell the teacher whether what has recently been taught has actually been learned, and also how to plan subsequent educational experiences for the student.

When the time comes to reevaluate a small group, a criterion-referenced test, covering the specific skills that the teacher has been trying to teach, is appropriate. Some people also give such a test for the next skill to be learned, to determine the need for such instruction. The criterion-referenced test should be reviewed carefully to ascertain that it indeed does cover the skills it claims to cover, and to make certain that the number of items is sufficient for diagnosis.

Teacher-made tests of a great variety can be used for this type of evaluation. In many instances the teacher will have accumulated enough observations to make a formal test unnecessary.

Correcting Specific Difficulties

There are times when the teacher needs to study an individual child in more depth than usual—a child who is not responding to classroom instruction, for example. If the school has a school psychologist who is knowledgeable about reading diagnosis (many of them are not) or a reading consultant, a referral to one of these specialists would be appropriate. An individual diagnostic reading test would be helpful in planning remedial instruction, although many reading specialists are now administering group diagnostic reading tests to individuals. Such individual administration works well and it can be accomplished in much less time than group administration. This is a procedure which the classroom teacher can also carry out.

Criterion-referenced tests can also be used in this situation, if the teacher knows which ones to use to determine the most pressing instructional needs of a student. But workbooks could probably be used with as much success. The teacher has the child do those pages designed to teach the specific skills the child seems deficient in. It will be necessary to go into the workbooks for the grades below the student's own grade level, but pages can be used by means of a sheet of acetate and a transparency marker, which avoids marking up a workbook just for a few pages.

The biggest problem in this area is knowing which skills to analyze and test for. The most common mistake is not going low enough in the skills hierarchy. Just because a child does not know a specific skill does not necessarily mean that it should be taught at that time. A child who has difficulty with vowel digraphs, for example, should be tested on long and short vowels, then consonants, then auditory discrimination. Children must be able to discriminate among similar sounds before they are taught to associate sounds with the letters representing them.

Every teacher will encounter children with very severe reading problems, intermediate grade pupils whose general reading level is two or more years below their grade placement. One can even find students in the secondary school whose reading level is below fourth-grade level. These students need an intensive clinical diagnosis, followed by lengthy individualized remedial reading instruction. Their problems are typically of such a complex nature as to take more skills and time than the classroom teacher has. A referral through the school principal is recommended.

Assessing the Instructional Program

When it comes to trying to assess the effects of a reading program, the standardized survey test remains the main instrument. In fact, over half the schools with a testing program use the tests primarily to measure the results of schooling. They do this by administering a survey test in the month of May. Many have argued that this is not a particularly good time to test because such testing is almost completely retrospective; by May nothing can be done to rectify problems, and there is often so much shifting and moving among the pupil population during the summer that the May data might not be very useful the next year. Some test people have argued that testing should be done about two thirds of the way through the year in order to leave some time available to remedy problems of the instructional program.

It has often been said that the survey test should not be used to evaluate teachers because of the great many variables which affect school learning. But teachers certainly ought to use test data, along with everything else they know about their students, to evaluate their own reading programs. Such evaluation is particularly critical when there has been a change in methods or materials and is most useful if the testing is done annually, giving the teacher some basis for comparing the results from one year with those from preceding years.

Recently, a great many schools have begun giving standardized diagnostic tests in the fall and often again in the spring. This gives much more information about the effects of a particular program on a great many skills, rather than just one or two. Other schools follow up fall diagnostic testing with a spring survey test. In either case, they are interested in educational growth. From a measurement point of view, this is a particularly difficult problem to deal with; a separate section of this chapter has been devoted to it.

Some schools use basal reader tests to evaluate the effects of their reading program. Such an assessment is all right for determining if the material in a specific reader has been learned. But most educators prefer to evaluate with a test that is completely separate from the instructional material. They want to know how their students, going through the particular reading program they have chosen, compare with other students throughout the country. In some experimental programs, the sponsoring agencies insist not only on the use of an independent test but also on a program evaluation made by an independent, outside organization. Such an assessment program is called an "external audit" (Lessinger, 1970).

School-wide Reading Assessment

In recent years we have seen a great increase in school-wide, system-wide, and even state-wide reading assessment programs. In fact, there is also a nationwide systematic testing program called National Assessment of Educational Progress (Womer, 1972). This latter program has developed its own tests. In practically all other large-scale programs, however, the standardized survey test is the common approach. Much of this testing has not proved to be of direct benefit to the students (NAEP, 1972); results have been used mostly for accountability purposes. Therefore a great deal of controversy has arisen over this type of testing program. It is fairly easy to determine how well a system is performing in comparison to the state or national norms, but how does one evaluate the results? There is no test made to tell administrators and politicians how children *ought* to perform. And what does it mean for a system to be below the national average in reading? It could be a result of poor teaching, but it is also possible that this district spends less time or money on reading and more on other activities. Improving reading usually means spending more time doing it. Since the length of the school day is fixed, that time must come from somewhere. Should it be taken from art, music, social studies, physical education?

In the wake of accountability testing we are seeing a new process coming to the fore, that of *priority setting*, which is an attempt to decide where a school should place its emphasis in effort and finances. For example, if tests reveal low average scores, school boards may decide that since reading achievement is their first priority, resources must be taken from other school efforts such as art, music, athletics, and other activities to pay for special reading programs. A danger with such an approach is that the school may overemphasize those educational objectives for which pupil achievement can be readily measured. Such assessment over time is an important aspect of a school testing program in order for all concerned to make intelligent decisions. The section in this chapter dealing with the assessment of growth should help develop an appreciation of some of the difficulties entailed by that process.

Large-scale testing programs tend to be time consuming, expensive, and cumbersome when done with an achievement test battery. The short accountability type test that will yield only averages is more efficient. But if a district or a state has already adopted a standardized reading test, this could also serve well as an accountability test. At least one achievement test battery now has a group norm, which would enhance the test's usefulness in the study of groups. This special norm will be discussed later in this chapter.

ADMINISTRATION AND SCORING OF TESTS

The term *assessment* has been used here in a broad sense. When teachers ask students to read a paragraph out loud to determine if a book they have selected is of suitable difficulty, the teachers are engaged in assessment. It is informal, and is approached casually both by teacher and student. But these day-by-day observations are very useful in studying student behavior over a long period of time. They are also a way of communicating to the child that assessment is an integral part of education and that it is done to help the student advance; it is oriented toward the future. So it is important that the teacher spend some time explaining to each child how the results of all assessments, formal and informal, are being used to help. The teacher should make some effort to communicate to the students that "this test will help us plan what you should learn next," rather than give the students the impression that "this is a test to find out how smart (or dumb) you are."

A few specific problems of testing will be discussed in this section. These pertain, in part, to all sorts of tests, but the main emphasis is on the standardized test. The reader who has never reviewed a standardized reading test would find it beneficial to do so before proceeding with this chapter.

Test Administration

Most of the questions teachers have about test administration are answered in a good test manual. It is imperative that the teacher study this manual carefully before giving a test. This is particularly crucial for a standardized test, since part of the standardization process is the standardization of the directions. It is only when the standardized directions are being followed that the norms are applicable. Deviating from the directions to the point of allowing additional time for completion of a timed test or giving help with the answers invalidates a standardized test.

The teacher should try to maintain as normal a class situation as possible in order to ensure valid results. And it should be kept in mind that the purpose of a reading test is to determine the students' reading ability, not their skill at following directions. It is appropriate, therefore, to explain the directions again to those who do not understand how to take the test. If they fail to turn the page, they can be told to do so, and if they mark the answer in a wrong way, this can be rectified while they take the test. It should not be counted as a mistake if it is not discovered until the test is scored. The teacher should keep extra pencils handy in case a student needs one.

When a particularly difficult test format is encountered, the directions should be followed rigidly. In all likelihood, the author has experimented with different sets of directions, and the test has been standardized with those directions which appear in the manual.

The biggest test administration problem arises when answer sheets are being used, but this problem will be discussed in the next section.

Test Scoring

It is exceedingly difficult to score a batch of tests with one hundred percent accuracy, especially if done by hand. The sources of error are numerous. For example, the erasures of one student might be heavier than the regular marks of another student, a fact which some test scoring machines adapt to by having a mechanism which first determines the density of each pupil's handwriting and then adjusts the machine to that particular marking. Some children will mark two options; some will actually write answers onto the answer sheet. The teacher can do several things to improve the validity of test scoring.

1　Inspect the answer document for obvious and gross problems such as writing out the answers, crossing out wrong answers rather than erasing them, and so on. Verify the marking of name grids, etc.
2　When hand scoring, score twice.
3　Score only one subtest at a time for the whole class.
4　When several forms of a test are available, make sure the form of the scoring key matches the form of the test.
5　Rescore all near perfect and near zero scores; rescore the tests of

those students whose scores are grossly at variance with their classroom performances.

One comment should be made about the "chance score" concept (Fry, 1971). This score is obtained by dividing the number of items in a test by the number of options per item. A 36-item test of four-choice multiple choice items would give a "chance score" of 9; that is, if a student took the test by simply guessing rather than reading the items, he should obtain a score of 9 on the average. Most students do not behave this way. The typical pattern is a series of correct answers at the beginning of the test, then some items which are mixed correct and incorrect, then a few incorrect answers in a row, and then stop. But a few students guess throughout; they tend to have low achievement. One can easily discern their test-taking pattern after scoring their test booklets, because the items they answer correctly are scattered rather evenly throughout the test, their total scores being fairly close to the "chance score." Such tests should be considered invalid.

Record Keeping

The evaluation of a pupil's growth in reading is particularly meaningful when it is done on the basis of a large variety of data over time. The elementary school teacher has the necessary material for such an evaluation. But it is important that data collected over a period of time be gathered in such a way as to be maximally useful.

The simplest form of assessment is the informal observation. Its main strength is that it can be used to gather information regularly. After listening to a child read one day, the teacher might make a note that "John is still having trouble with final e making the preceding vowel long, as in mad and made." Such an observation should be verified from time to time to determine if the same problem occurs in spelling and other written work. The persistence of the problem over several months is cause for remedial action.

Student performance in workbooks and on worksheets is also a potent source of evaluative information, and it is useful to save worksheets periodically. Worksheets often provide the best evidence a teacher has that students are making progress—proof that they can do something now which they couldn't do before. They can also show a teacher when a student has a unique problem which has persisted over a period of months despite rather specific teaching; such evidence suggests that the student might possibly have a specific learning disability.

Perhaps the single most useful piece of information in a cumulative folder is the results of a standardized reading test. In fact, many schools purchase pregummed labels with each child's test results in conjunction with the machine scoring of the tests. These are then pasted directly into the child's folder. It is important that the recording of test results be made in such a way as to facilitate interpretation. One such record is the "class analysis chart." This chart tabulates the scores of the students in one class in all subtests onto a single one-page chart.

Another approach to record keeping is the "bivariate distribution." This can now be purchased along with machine scoring in the cases where both an achievement test and scholastic aptitude test have been administered. Such charts, worked out and printed by a computer, permit the comparison between aptitude and achievement in all achievement areas tested. The most recent development is the use of a measure of children's language competency as a basis on which to compare achievement (Madden, 1972). This approach is promising since it should assist educators in making the kind of diagnosis which will most readily lead to remedial instruction.

Test Norms

The "raw score" on a test, usually the number of items marked correctly, carries little meaning in and of itself. Converting it to a percentage is not very meaingful either, since the percentage score obtained on a test is as closely related to the difficulty of the questions as to how well the students perform. The fact that a student received a 90 percent on a test could mean either that the student did quite well or that the test was very easy. The 90 percent could have been the highest or the lowest score in the class. The solution to making a score more meaningful has been to provide norms whereby the performance of each student is compared to the performance of a national sample of students.

There are two basic approaches to the development of test norms. First, we can have a kind of growth scale where the raw scores are compared to the norms for successive grade levels. A *grade norm* of 5.4 on such a scale means that a given child's raw score is the same as the average score for students who are in the fourth month of the fifth grade, regardless of the student's present grade level. There are some problems, however, with the grade norm, particularly with students at the extreme ends of the distribution of scores. If, for example, a test is designed primarily for second grade, it lacks meaning to say that a pupil has done as well as an average fifth grader because we don't know that the fifth-grade curriculum was sampled. A second type of norm avoids this difficulty by comparing the child's performance only to that of a national sample of students who are at the same grade level. For many years, this *percentile norm* was used extensively.

Percentiles are points in a distribution of raw scores. At or below each point, one will find the percent of students indicated by the given percentile. For example, if Sally had sixteen items correct on a test and the percentile table showed this to have a percentile rank of 45, we would know that 45 percent of American children score 16 or less, while the remaining 55 percent would score 16 or higher. (Those scoring 16 are usually divided in half.) In addition to national norms, some tests have norms for a given state or for a local school district, all generally referred to as *local norms*.

As was the case with grade norms, percentile norms were used because they seemed easy to interpret. But these norms were deceptive and cumbersome in some ways. Because children tend to be about average, the scores would pile up in the middle and so would the percentiles. Percentiles of 45 and 55 were quite close together on the distribution, while 5 and 15 were separated by quite a margin. The farther from the mean (average) we went, the farther apart were the percentile points. The scale is divided into one hundred unequal percentile units, meaning that intertest comparisons are very difficult to make and scores cannot be averaged (Anastasi, 1968). To solve this problem, several scales have been devised that are relative to the mean but in equal units of deviation from the mean. They are based on the *standard deviation,* a commonly used unit of variability, and are generally referred to as *standard scores.* The most common standard score in use with reading tests is a relatively brief, nine-point scale called stanines, an abbreviation of "standard nine."

A new norm has been developed for use in federally sponsored programs. It is a standard score based on a normal curve and is called *normal curve equivalent* (NCE). It is a scale which goes from 1 to 99, these two end scores coinciding with percentile ranks of 1 and 99, as does also the mean of 50 coincide with 50. But the in-between points are different. While the percentiles tend to pile up around the middle and spread farther apart as we get to the more extreme scores, the NCE scores are in equal units.

The relationships among stanines, percentiles, and NCE scores are shown in Table 6. Remember that we are comparing the test performance of one child with that of all children enrolled at the same grade level, without regard for any other variable such as location of school, type of school, or method of reading instruction used. Ordinarily, special norms for such groups as "inner-city" school children or bilingual students are not available. But special editions of tests are sometimes available for handicapped children.

Norms have sometimes been criticized for not telling exactly how well children read; they merely tell how their reading scores compare with those of other children. The criterion-referenced tests were designed to meet this criticism. But they, in turn, are being criticized for not relating reading performance to some sort of standard or norm (Mehrens and Lehmann, 1978).

The question of standards of performance is a difficult one. While norms tell us how well children *are doing,* standards specify how well they *ought to be doing.* The idea of setting standards of achievement has only recently entered the testing scene in the form of minimum competency tests, as mentioned previously. It is closely related to the issue of *expectancy,* which has often been determined by means of IQ tests and, more recently, by a measure

— THE RELATIONSHIP BETWEEN STANINES AND PERCENTILES —————— **Table 6**

Stanines	NCE	Percentiles	Percent per stanine	
9	86–99	97–99	Highest 4%	
8	77–85	90–96	Next highest 7%	Above average 23%
7	66–76	78–89	Next 12%	
6	56–65	61–77	Above middle 17%	
5	45–55	41–60	Middle 20%	Average 54%
4	35–44	24–40	Below middle 17%	
3	24–34	12–23	Next 12%	
2	15–23	5–11	Next lowest 7%	Below average 23%
1	1–14	1–4	Lowest 4%	

of language competency. This problem is discussed in a later section of this chapter.

HOW TO READ A TEST MANUAL

The typical standardized reading test consists of the test itself, the manual, and auxiliaries such as scoring keys , charts, and lists for recording scores. The test manual will cover the details of test administration, interpretation, and a variety of technical information. When the reading test is part of an achievement test battery, there might be separate manuals for administration and interpretation, as well as a "technical supplement." These manuals are virtual gold mines of factual information often overlooked by educators. They answer most questions commonly asked about tests. The main problem appears to be that most educators have a great deal of difficulty reading and interpreting the manuals, particularly the more technical ones. In this section, therefore, we will provide some background for understanding these manuals, including some practical suggestions as to how to interpret the information they ordinarily contain.

Test and Item Format

The degree of difficulty a student has with a test is influenced by the particular item format the test uses. This is especially true in the primary grades. Some test publishers provide a practice booklet in order to familiarize the students with the particular item formats used. In achievement test batteries, one will sometimes find a change in item format from one subtest to the next, which slows down the testing and is potentially confusing to the student.

Generally speaking, the more students have to switch around in order to respond to a test, the more difficulty they will have. The biggest contributor to low test scores resulting from the test format is the separate answer sheet. Below grade four, most students have some difficulty with answer sheets; but even in grades four, five, and six the poor readers have difficulty with some answer sheets (Clark, 1968). Then why are answer sheets used if they tend to lower some students' scores? There are two main reasons: economy and scorability. The use of answer sheets makes it possible to reuse the test booklet and, since answer sheets are generally single sheets of paper while the test booklets may have eight to thirty-two pages, the use of answer sheets can reduce the cost of a testing program by as much as 50 percent. Also, even if a test is hand scored, it is much easier to score a single-page answer sheet than a test booklet. And answer sheets can be filed much more readily. Further, all answer sheets available for standardized reading tests can be scored by a test scoring machine; many school districts even have their own machines.

Around 1970 we had a new development in test scoring which greatly benefits those students who have difficulty with an answer sheet. It is called the machine-scorable test booklet. There is a machine that can score the test booklet itself by cutting off the spine of the booklet and then running each page through an optical scanner. If this scoring system is tied in to a computer, the computer can tabulate data, calculate group statistics, plot charts, interpret the data to the teacher, and even send back sets of instructional suggestions for each student in the class. The computer performs this analysis with such incredible speed as to make the entire process economically feasible.

Test Validity

The most important question to ask oneself when evaluating a reading test is, "Does this test measure what is being taught as reading?" Or, in test terminology, "Is this a valid test?" One must determine what instructional objectives the test covers and if these objectives coincide with the major objectives of the reading program used with the students. This can be done by reviewing the test's objectives or by a direct analysis of the test items.

There are also some statistical ways of determining the validity of a reading test; one of these is to correlate it with other reading tests. Before going into that problem, we will briefly discuss the concept of correlation.

The *correlation coefficient* is a number which indicates the degree of relationship between two variables. It can range from -1.00 to $+1.00$. Zero correlation indicates that two variables have no relationship whatever. The farther from zero, the higher the correlation. The sign shows the direction of the correlation. A negative number reveals a negative correlation; that is, a high score on one variable tends to be associated with a low score on the other. For example, the score on a reading test and the number of errors on a spelling test might correlate $-.70$. But if the spelling test were scored by counting the number of words spelled correctly, the correlation would be $+.70$. The two coefficients are of the same magnitude, but in different directions. Most correlation coefficients found in test manuals are positive. One way of deciding on the significance of a correlation coefficient is to make a rough estimate of what percentage the two variables have in common. This is done by simply squaring the coefficient. For example, a correlation of .70 would give $.70 \times .70 = .49$, or about 50 percent commonality between two variables. It would be considered a fairly substantial relationship (Ahmann and Glock, 1971).

Two tests of reading comprehension should correlate on the order of about .80. If the correlation is substantially less than that, one might suspect that the two tests measure somewhat different aspects of reading. When looking at the intercorrelations among several subtests, a good rule of thumb is to assume that intercorrelations among tests of different aspects of reading should be within the .40 to .70 range, showing that they do measure different aspects of reading but are still positively correlated.

The intercorrelations among the subtests of the *Stanford Diagnostic Reading Test,* Level Green, grade 4 are given in table 7. The table shows, for example, that Auditory Vocabulary and Auditory Discrimination correlate .67 (second number in the top line in the matrix.) This indicates that the two skills are only moderately related to each other. Phonetic Analysis has its highest correlation with Structural Analysis, which one might have expected. The opposite situation would have cast some doubt on the validity of either of these two tests. Of considerable interest is the high correlation between Literal and Inferential Comprehension (.91), leading us to believe that those two skills are probably not much different. The children who can do one would

Table 7

INTERCORRELATIONS AMONG SDRT–GREEN SUBTESTS FOR GRADE 4

Subskill	1	2	3	4	5	6	7
1. Auditory Vocabulary	(.90)	.67	.66	.66	.65	.69	.68
2. Auditory Discrimination		(.93)	.69	.70	.68	.69	.70
3. Phonetic Analysis			(.92)	.75	.66	.71	.70
4. Structural Analysis				(.95)	.79	.80	.81
5. Reading Comprehension					(.96)	.98	.98
6. Literal Comprehension						(.93)	.91
7. Inferential Comprehension							(.91)

Source: Manual for Administering and Interpreting Stanford Diagnostic Reading Test, Green. Reprinted with permission of Harcourt Brace Jovanovich, Inc.

tend also to be able to do the other. Tables such as this are found in all good test manuals; they should be studied carefully.

Test Reliability

If a teacher were to give the same test twice, he or she would want some assurance of getting rather consistent results. This consistency is referred to as *reliability* and can be determined by actually administering the same test twice. The correlation coefficient between these two sets of scores is referred to as the *reliability coefficient.* Examples of these are found in Table 7, the coefficients appearing in parentheses. As a general rule, reliability coefficients of .90 or better are considered highly adequate. If they are less than .85, one should assume that the scores obtained on that subtest are subject to more chance fluctuation than the rest (Madden, 1972).

These generalizations about reliability pertain only to the scores of individual students. Group averages will show much higher reliability than individual scores, since individual chance fluctuations tend to wash out in the means. Also, it should be understood that the single most important factor in reliability is the number of items in a test. The longer the test, the more reliable (Anastasi, 1968). The problem of reliability is one of the main reasons why many test experts reject the idea of measuring the achievement of specific objectives with one or two criterion-referenced test items.

When studying a test manual, one should also make sure that the reliability coefficients reported were obtained for a single grade level. Pooling the data for several grade levels will yield inflated values. In most manuals, one will also find, next to the reliability coefficients, a statistic called the *standard error of measurement.* This is a measure of the degree of precision of each test; it provides an exact basis for evaluating changes in test scores. It tells us something about the magnitude of such chance fluctuations (Mehrens and Lehmann, 1978). As an example from everyday life we can use the reading of a thermometer. Many outdoor thermometers lack precision, so if one were to say that it is 30.5° outside, one's certainty would be quite low, since there are no marks between 30 and 32, and those two numbers are quite close together on the scale. However, the certainty with which one could say that it is between 30 and 32° outside would be much greater than for 30.5°. And one could state with even greater confidence that the temperature is between 28 and 34 degrees. In educational testing we have actually gone one step further and specified in probabilistic terms the degree of precision of a test score or the extent to which a score is subject to chance fluctuations from one day to the next. Two examples from educational testing are shown in Table 8. First, in grade five, the standard error of measurement in grade scores is 0.5. The table shows the magnitude of the chance fluctuations as we encompass, successively, one, two, and three standard errors of measurement on each side of the mean. As we increase the certainty (probability) of our statements, the range increases considerably. The test upon which this is based had a reliability of .93. The second example, shown in the last three lines in Table 8, pertains to an IQ test with a reliability of .90, a fairly typical situation.

Table 8

INTERPRETATION OF STANDARD ERROR OF MEASUREMENT

If standard error of measurement is	the probability is about	that a score of	could fluctuate by chance from
.4 years	68%	grade 5.5	5.1 to 5.9
.4 years	95%	grade 5.5	4.7 to 6.3
.4 years	99%	grade 5.5	4.3 to 6.7
5 points	68%	IQ 90	85 to 95
5 points	95%	IQ 90	80 to 100
5 points	99%	IQ 90	75 to 105

Reliability is certainly an important concept in interpreting individual scores and changes in such scores, but, again, these are individual data. If we look at the mean for a typical class, the error of measurement is reduced to about half of that shown in Table 8. If a student was tested in the middle of grade five (5.5) and again in the middle of grade six (6.5), and in that year had "grown" only 0.2 year, one could easily ascribe this change to chance. The same holds if a student had "regressed" 0.2 year in that time, since such minor fluctuation could easily occur from one day to the next. But suppose this student had gained 1.0 year in this time. The probabilities that this has occurred by chance are so small that it could safely be ascribed to "growth." The probability of a mean changing 1.0 year because of pure chance fluctuations is extremely remote.

It is the responsibility of those who use tests to understand that test scores are subject to chance fluctuation, and that of the test author to report in the manual the exact magnitude of this fluctuation.

Norm Tables

Test manuals contain norm tables which are used to convert one kind of score to another; for example, they permit conversion from raw scores to scaled scores to percentiles to stanines. But they also contain a wealth of very interesting and useful information. For example, a large school system decided that a certain standard of reading proficiency should be required for their entering (grade ten) high school students. One member of the board of education, having heard something about eighth-grade proficiency being a kind of minimum level of "functional literacy," proposed that students scoring below 8.0 grade score on a standardized reading test should enroll in a course called "Remedial English." This became a regulation; in each high school they set up such a class and the students were tested at the end of grade nine. The selection was to take place during the summer so that the students could be enrolled in Remedial English upon entering the tenth grade.

A look at the table of norms for the test they were using reveals that a grade score of 8.0 in reading has a percentile equivalent of 32 at 9.9; that is, in a national sample, about 32 percent of the population will, at the end of grade nine, score 8.0 or lower. Since nobody had taken a look at these tables beforehand, one can well imagine the amazement of the school administrators when they discovered that, as one of them put it, "about one third of the students entering high school lack functional literacy." The fact of the matter was that the students were doing about average.

The norm tables found in test manuals show that, as we go up the grades, variability among the students increases, indicating that the need for individualization in reading increases with the age of the students. Actually, the typical elementary teacher handles this variability well in reading, but less well in other subjects. There is no argument in favor of individualization of instruction as powerful as that put forth by test results, since they tend to reveal that the achievement levels of the highest and the lowest achievers in most classrooms differ by a number of years.

THE INDIVIDUAL DIAGNOSTIC CONFERENCE

The more teachers know about the procedures for teaching reading at many levels and how to pick appropriate instructional techniques and materials, the less they need to rely on periodic evaluation with highly detailed, standardized reading tests. A perceptive teacher can get a great deal of insight into a child's reading characteristics through an individual diagnostic conference. A great many techniques can be applied in this situation; some of them, however, require extensive practice.

There are several observational systems and checklists available commercially which are generally designed to help teachers cover all major skills. The *Barbe Reading Skills Check List* (Barbe, 1961) contains the main objectives for grades one through six, which teachers can check off as they listen to children read and recall what was read. A much more formal and systematic analysis of children's oral reading characteristics is the *Reading Miscue Inventory* (Goodman and Burke, 1972); it is a very complex observational system, although it is not norm referenced.

The individual diagnostic conference to be described here is loosely structured and is considered an adjunct to other assessment techniques. Its purpose is the analysis of an individual child's reading characteristics. The following paragraphs describe some techniques for observing the major aspects of reading. The material used is ordinarily the book which is being used for reading instruction, or it could be a book the student has selected to read. The teacher may have worked out a form, dittoed, which is filled out and filed in each child's folder, or may simply take notes, as with the individual reading inventory. The former procedure will ensure more systematic coverage, of course. The teacher can have the child read silently, then orally. Under both circumstances, the teacher can time the child to determine silent and oral reading speeds.

The Student's Behavior
While Reading

During the silent reading part of the diagnostic conference, the teacher should sit across from the child. It is helpful to have the student hold up the book so that student's eyes can be observed across the top.

Start timing when the child starts to read silently. At the outset, it is important to observe the student's eyes (Wilson, 1971). When the student first looks at the page, are both eyes together? If not, or if one leads, the other following perceptibly behind, the student might have eye coordination problems. Make note of characteristics such as lip movements, finger-pointing, whispering, and so on. If the reading material is fairly simple for the student, there should be little such extraneous behavior; but nearly all children exhibit some of these behaviors when the material is difficult or if they are under stress.

It takes a lot of practice to be able to count eye movements, but some problems can be observed readily. Of particular interest is the student's eye behavior when unable to decode a specific word. Some will keep looking at the same word, trying to "sound it out," often with accompanying sound effects. Others will look around for picture clues. Those who start the sentence over again, or who try to read farther, are generally searching for context clues.

Two kinds of fingerpointing can be observed: the students may follow along as they read, or they may use their finger as a line holder to make sure that their eyes will hit the next line after the return sweep from the previous one. These are often found in pupils in the primary grades; if this occurs in the intermediate grades, it might indicate problems of eye coordination. Ordinarily, children who have persisted with fingerpointing will discontinue it by the end of third grade; the same holds true for whispering. Lip movements might persist a bit longer.

Comprehension

After students have read silently for three to five minutes, they should be stopped when there is a natural break. At this point, the teacher should ask a few questions to determine their comprehension of what was read. It is important that this questioning go beyond the very obvious and superficially literal content of the material. (See Chapter Eleven by Guszak and Hoftman for a detailed discussion of teacher questioning techniques.) When students cannot answer a question, the teacher might ask them to find the answer in the book. It is useful to find out what it was they did not understand. Questions of inference should be asked of all pupils, although for younger pupils they should be fairly simple.

The teacher must be sure to ask comprehension questions that the pupils cannot answer unless they have read the story. It is necessary, therefore, that the teacher be well acquainted with what the child has been reading and see to it that questioning goes beyond a superficial "What was this story about?"

Vocabulary

Lack of comprehension is sometimes caused by vocabulary problems, of which there are several kinds. First, the child might not have previously encountered a specific word like *beneficial, inflammable,* or *perquisite.* Many teachers limit their vocabulary instruction to this level. But children also have problems understanding the multiple meanings of words. To test for this, the teacher might point to a word in the story just read and ask what meaning of the word was used in that particular sentence.

A third type of vocabulary problem to consider is the ability to deduce the meaning from context. When a student does not know the meaning of a word, the teacher should ask, "What do you think it means?" Such questioning will encourage the use of context. A related set of skills pertains to the meanings of affixes and root words. The meaning of a word can often be deduced from a combination of context and knowledge of word parts. For example, if you did not know the word *affixes,* but you did know the meaning of the prefix *a-,* the root *fix,* and the suffix *-es,* you would probably be able to figure the word out.

This illustrates another aspect of vocabulary teaching—the morphemic unit. The student should know from the final *-s* or *-es* that the word *affixes* might be either a plural or the present tense of a verb. When testing for vocabulary, it is useful to determine if the student understands common morphemes such as *-er* (a person who), *-ed* (past tense), *-less* (without), and so on.

Bright students are often interested in words, their derivations, and their origins. With the less able student, one should probably be quite specific when diagnosing and remedying deficiencies in vocabulary.

Decoding

We now come to the oral reading phase of the individual diagnostic conference, where problems of decoding can most easily be diagnosed. When students encounter an unknown word, exactly what do they do? What they should be doing depends on their level of reading ability; primary pupils may try letter-by-letter sounding, while intermediate students will often try syllabication first. The decoding process has been analyzed in many ways, none of which is completely satisfactory because of the interaction of several simultaneous processes. One analysis says that a student must go through three processes. First, the word must be divided visually into units such as letters, digraphs, and syllables. Second, each unit must be pronounced. Third, these pronunciations must be blended together.

When children are reading orally, the teacher has many opportunities to observe the kinds of errors they make, but it takes quite a bit of experience to translate this information into remedial action. A review of the scope and sequence chart found in most teacher's editions of basal readers will help in determining the hierarchy of the phonics skills taught.

The oral reading situation is also a good place to determine the students' ability to transfer recently taught skills to their independent reading. This will also give the teacher feedback as to the effectiveness with which the skills were taught.

Asking students comprehension questions after their oral reading will sometimes reveal rather limited understanding of what was read. This is particularly true when the student has a tendency to become self-conscious or nervous in an oral reading situation. If this is the case, it is usually the attitude rather than reading skills which requires remediation.

Reading Rate and Efficiency

Students should be timed during both the silent and oral reading. The easiest way to do this is to note how far they have read at the exact minute you stop them; that is, if they are close to finishing after four minutes, note the exact word they are reading at that time and divide the number of words read by four. The longer the student reads, the more reliable this rate measure will be. The same procedure should be followed with both the silent and oral reading. This will give a comparison between the two.

Typically, the two rates coincide until about the end of third grade, at which time the rate is close to 140 words per minute. The oral reading rate might level off at 130 words per minute and increase little from then on. But the silent reading rate will increase about fifteen words per minute each year up to junior high school. From then on, the increase is about ten words per year; the average high school senior is reading about 250 words per minute (Taylor, 1963).

Many people feel that a measure of reading rate is not much help in diagnosing the reading of primary graders. But reading rate becomes a significant bit of information if viewed not just as a measure of speed but as a measure of *decoding efficiency*. Some children can decode practically every word put in front of them, but at a rate so slow as to make the reading deficient. By the end of second grade, the typical pupil will read about two words per second. Less than one word per second is considered inefficient. Clinical experience with children with extreme reading disabilities has also revealed that the most stubborn cases are the word-by-word readers. These children, when confronted with repetitions of the same word on the same line of print, would read it the second or even the third time just as slowly as the first. Extremely laborious reading, even if mostly correct, is generally symptomatic of a reading deficiency.

THE ASSESSMENT OF READING READINESS

The assessment of a child at the prereading level presents certain unique problems, many of which will be discussed in the later chapter on reading readiness. This chapter will concern itself only with the specific problem of readiness testing and not with the assessment of the many physical, social, and other maturational characteristics relating to readiness.

At one time, reading readiness was thought of as a rather specific stage of development, a point in a child's life when he or she was ready to be taught to read. Some researchers in the 1930s tried to determine that crucial moment, and some school administrators worked out schedules showing when each child would reach a certain mental age as determined by an intelligence test. Later on, readiness testing was used to predict success in beginning reading instruction; one could call it prognostic testing. And it was found that both intelligence tests and reading readiness tests were good tests for predicting school success of a group of children, although individual prediction was subject to some fluctuation (Mehrens and Lehmann, 1978).

By the early 1970s, however, teachers become increasingly impatient with the prognostic approach. As teachers, they wanted to know what to do. If a child made a low score on a readiness test, how could they negate the prediction of low achievement? In other words, the teachers wanted a diagnostic approach to readiness testing. But what should be diagnosed? Scholastic aptitude? Or some of the skills and abilities which are necessary for learning to read? Both approaches are currently in use and will be discussed in some detail.

Scholastic Aptitude

The main purpose of most intelligence tests is to determine the student's probability of success in school. This is particularly important at the time of school entry, since we do not have any past scholastic records with which we can predict later success. Some schools, therefore, use group intelligence tests in the first grade for purposes of prognostication. There are many such tests on the market; two of the more commonly used are the *Cognitive Abilities Test* and the *Otis-Lennon Mental Ability Test,* group intelligence tests which contain several batteries extending from kindergarten through high school. Such tests are generally administered to small groups and depend rather heavily upon the comprehension of language, a factor which is a particularly good predictor of success in school.

Attempts have also been made to assess the particular cognitive abilities which are required for success in school. A good example of a test for this purpose is the *Analysis of Learning Potential,* which yields prognostic scores for both reading and arithmetic.

Most aptitude testing in kindergarten and first grade is done with the readiness tests, since they tend to show a higher correlation with later reading ability than do the more general intelligence tests. The readiness tests include the measurement of such abilities as matching symbols and other visual discrimination skills, auditory discrimination, aural comprehension, letter recognition, and other reading-related abilities. A very commonly used readiness test is the *Metropolitan Readiness Test.*

The prognostic approach to readiness testing has been criticized by teachers who feel that the results do not tell them what to do for the students. Some first grade teachers, however, use the results of prognostic tests to group the children by level, providing prolonged readiness instruction for the low scorers, a normal period of readiness instruction for those with about average scores, and little if any such instruction for the high scorers. Such differentiated instruction from the beginning has been shown to be beneficial to the children at all levels of reading readiness (Spache, 1966).

Readiness Diagnosis

The diagnostic approach to readiness instruction is similar to the behavioral objectives approach in that the teacher first lists all those abilities which are necessary for learning to read, then determines (with a diagnostic readiness test) if each student has those skills and abilities to a sufficient degree, and finally teaches those skills which each student is lacking by means of an individualized readiness program. It is an orderly scheme which obviously makes a lot of sense. It has only one drawback: we don't know exactly all of the skills and abilities which are prerequisites for learning to read, even though the major factors have been studied extensively (Harris and Sipay, 1975).

Some research and a great deal of rhetoric can be found on this topic, the two often being contradictory. For example, learning to read obviously requires visual acuity; certainly the child must be able to see the print. However, research with visually handicapped children has shown that children with equal degrees of measured visual handicap differ greatly in their ability to utilize their vision (Jones, 1961); they range from functionally sighted to functionally blind. There are even some "legally blind" children, whose visual acuity is so limited as to be unmeasurable with a Snellen Chart, who can actually read large print. Since many "legally blind" children can learn to read from basal readers, visual acuity is probably grossly overrated as a problem in learning to read (Benton, 1970).

Visual acuity is a relatively simple concept, and certainly an attribute we can all agree on as being a prerequisite to learning to read. A great many others—such as attention, auditory discrimination, and language development—also enter into the act of learning to read. It seems safe to conclude, therefore, that a comprehensive diagnostic readiness test is a long time in the future. Some tests are approaching this type of diagnosis, but on a very limited scale. Examples of such tests are the *Murphy-Durrell Reading Readiness Analysis* and the *Stanford Early School Achievement Test*.

Even if we could test for all of the prerequisite abilities, we would still not have a complete picture. We must also take into account students' ability to compensate for their deficiencies and the degree to which their motivation will override some of their poorly developed skills. Many experts feel that, while the teacher should employ many techniques, it is just as important that he approach the job of diagnosis with a flexible and imaginative attitude.

Teacher Evaluation of Readiness

Several studies of readiness tests have shown that teacher prognostication correlates as highly with later reading ability as do scores on readiness tests (Karlin, 1971). The data have often been cited as evidence that teachers' judgment is really quite good. They can also be used as evidence in favor of the tests, however, since the teacher needs a couple of months of experience with the children to make such a prediction, and the test can do it in about one hour of testing time. But, as has been pointed out earlier in this chapter, the teacher is in the unique position of being able to use those testing techniques we have described, observe how the students respond to the instruction designed for them, alter this instruction as the need arises, diagnose again, and so forth. In fact, this possibility is perhaps the strongest argument we have in favor of the self-contained classroom.

THE ASSESSMENT OF GROWTH

Teachers have always been interested in growth and improvement; in a way, that is what education is all about. But in the past most educators have been satisfied when they thought a student was improving. Assessment of the student's improvement was based on teacher judgment not only of how much each student had improved, but also of how much improvement each student was capable of making. Along with the accountability trend have come demands for more quantitative measures of growth. Statisticians are pointing out some of the difficulties of measuring growth, giving the general impression that the measurement of growth might not be particularly reliable or valid as a single measure of status (Wrightstone, 1971). For example, it was pointed out earlier that tests are not perfectly reliable. When we then calculate the difference between two not perfectly reliable measures, the difference (growth) has lower reliability than either of the two individual test scores. But these are problems beyond the scope of this chapter. What will be discussed here are some of the very specific curriculum problems relating to the assessment of growth in reading. More detailed discussions of these measurement issues can be found in Farr (1970).

The Reading Growth Curve

Children grow at different rates with regard to a great many variables. If we plot a specific measurement against the children's age, we get their growth curve. Such growth curves have been plotted for height, weight, strength of grip, head circumference, and so on. When we plot averages, say every six months, for a large, randomly chosen group of children, we get a norm, or normal growth curve. These normal growth curves often show that growth is not even; for example, in most areas we often find the familiar "adolescent growth spurt." Plotting such curves is a fairly easy task when dealing with inches and pounds, but how can it be accomplished in reading?

The unit of measurement most commonly used to determine growth in reading is the reading grade equivalent norm. This norm has been worked out as part of the standardization process. The average score for, say, the end of grade four is set equal to 4.9, the same for grade five. The in-between points are interpolated, assuming this growth to be linear. It is also assumed that the growth from 3.9 to 4.9 is the same as from 4.9 to 5.9. The whole scale is based on the assumption that growth in reading is linear. Further, the scale implies that children grow on the average 1.0 units per year—that is, for example, that growth from 2.9 to 3.9 is the same as from 10.9 to 11.9. The scale also has the advantage of being decimalized and easy to handle statistically.

Many reading experts believe, however, that this assumption of a linear growth curve is wrong, that there is a levelling off in the secondary school. In fact, there are many variables which make the plotting of a reading growth curve difficult. Different aspects of reading develop differently; there is disagreement as to which characteristics to include on a growth curve; and we have not had the proper scale with which to measure reading in terms of units which represent equal steps in "functional reading ability." Various statisticians have attempted, however, to develop a continuous scale which measures achievement in approximately equal units. Such a procedure was applied to the 1973 *Stanford Achievement Test* (Madden, 1972). This scaled score, as it is called, can be used to measure growth and also to plot a reading growth curve. The author has done so for reading comprehension by consulting the various *Norms Booklets* for this test, plotting the mean grade level against the mean scaled score obtained by pupils of various grades. The result is shown in Figure 6.2.

According to this growth curve, the greatest amount of gain in functional reading occurs in grades two, three, and four. The growth tapers off in junior high school and even more in senior high school, but it does continue. In other words, more growth takes place in second grade than in tenth, on the average. Therefore, when attempts are made to evaluate the amount of growth achieved by a group of pupils, one needs to know not only the amount of growth, but the group's mean score. The class whose average has gone from 2.0 to 3.0 has gained more than one which has gone from 8.0 to 9.0. In scaled score units, the former has gained fourteen points, the latter has

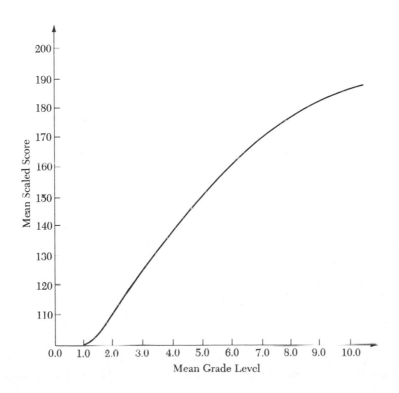

Figure 6.2
*The Scaled Score Growth
Curve for Reading
Comprehension.*

gained six. (It should be pointed out that the material presented here is in many respects original, representing the author's thinking about this issue. It is presented here in the belief that we now have a technique which can resolve one major problem in the measurement of growth and that this will become a common approach in the future.)

In the past, we have used the linear measuring scale—the grade equivalent—to measure growth in reading, which is curvilinear. The grade equivalent score was introduced because of its apparent simplicity; we are now saying that it is deceptively simple, leading to many erroneous conclusions. We hope that the scaled score will replace grade equivalents as a measure of growth, though this is not likely to happen in the near future.

Growth According to Capacity

Growth in reading is usually evaluated by comparing the amount of growth that *has* taken place against the amount of growth that *ought to have* taken place, or against what educators have usually referred to as *expectancy*. This gets us into the very difficult problem of prediction. We can actually make fairly good *group predictions*—that is, we can predict how well a class average will come out at the end of the year. There are several factors which influence the outcome of education, such as the socioeconomic background of the students, the educational level of their parents, the extent of bilingualism in a school, and the average IQ level. Actually, the single best predictor is the mean reading score which the group obtained the year before, assuming that they will continue at the same rate. But it is very difficult to make *individual* predictions—that is, to be able to predict how well each child will do. And to use this prediction as a determiner of what a particular child ought to be doing is going a bit beyond our data.

The single most common predictor of reading success is a measure of capacity, ordinarily determined with an IQ test. To say that students must read at a level commensurate with their IQ is to say that there ought to be a correlation of + 1.00 between IQ and reading ability. In reality, that correlation turns out to be around .70. Obviously, the two factors go together, but there is also a great deal of individual variation. There is too much variation to warrant making this type of one-to-one prediction; there are too many variables entering into the picture. The teacher needs to look at each child in totality and then try to estimate what would be a "reasonable" expectancy. This issue is an exceedingly complex one (Madden, 1972), much beyond the scope of this book, but the beginning teacher should know enough about the concept of "learning capacity" to realize that there are many factors in addition to the IQ which relate to school achievement.

Even though we cannot specify exactly how well students at different IQ levels should do, there is a great deal of empirical data available which specify how students at different IQ levels actually do perform in reading. Such a table has been compiled to show how well the bottom fourth, the top fourth, and the total of a national sample on an IQ test perform in reading.

Table 9 shows that, as a group, the bottom fourth of the population will gain, on the average, about 0.7 year per year in grades four through eight, while the top fourth averages 1.3 years per year. (These figures were com-

Grade	Low 25%	Total	Top 25%
4	3.2	4.6	6.2
5	4.1	5.6	7.2
6	4.7	6.6	8.7
7	5.4	7.6	10.3
8	6.2	8.6	11.4
Mean Gain	0.7	1.0	1.3

Source: Adapted from Stanford Achievement Test, Technical Supplement. New York: Harcourt Brace Jovanovich, Inc., 1966.

piled from Kelley, 1966.) Since we are talking about a growth rate, the differences between the average group and these extreme groups will increase with age. It might appear that the lower IQ students are getting farther behind the longer they stay in school. But the fact is that they are improving every year.

The main reason for testing and evaluating students is not to classify them but to help plan the best possible educational experiences for all students. To do so, we must know them well, and IQ tests add one more dimension to our understanding. But we must realize that there are students whose reading is quite different from the predictions made from IQ tests. If children perform better, they are not "overachievers"; we made the error of "underprediction." If they do poorly, we should not label them "underachievers," but see it as an error of "overprediction" (Thorndike, 1963). But, in either case, tests will help because we know that all students can improve with time. That is the nature of a child's development. Therefore, testing must be done with an eye toward the future.

A Year's Growth in a Year?

The average American child gains a year in reading ability each year, by definition. That is the way grade equivalent norms are made. This fact has led some school administrators to the erroneous conclusion that not only should the average go up a year each year, but each child should gain at least a year per year.

Again, we are back to talking about what children *ought* to do, which is essentially a philosophical issue, and, again, we are back to the problem of prediction. It is a well-known principle of educational psychology that past performance is the best single predictor. If one wishes to predict a student's success in a particular subject, the simplest approach is to look at how the student is doing in that subject at the present time. There is an abundance of such data in the various test manuals.

Table 10 was constructed from the various manuals of the 1973 *Stanford Achievement Test,* but it would be essentially the same if it had been taken from another achievement test battery. It shows normal growth in the total population for grades one through seven, as well as for the lowest fourth

Table 10

NORMATIVE GROWTH IN READING GRADE SCORE BY READING
LEVEL

Grade	Low 25%	Total	Top 25%
1	1.1	1.9	3.0
2	1.7	2.9	4.4
3	2.3	3.9	6.2
4	2.9	4.9	7.4
5	3.5	5.9	9.3
6	4.2	6.9	10.5
7	4.5	7.9	11.8
Mean Gain	0.6	1.0	1.5

Source: Adapted from *Stanford Achievement Test Manuals.* New York: Harcourt Brace Jovanovich, Inc., 1973.

of the class, in terms of reading ability, and for the highest fourth. One can see that, on the average, the lowest quarter gains only 0.6 year per year as a group; the highest quarter gains 1.5. Again, it must be kept in mind that these are averages and that there is much individual variation within each of these groups. But the data give us some idea of how children do develop with respect to reading.

The top and bottom 25 percent were chosen arbitrarily. Had more extreme groups been picked, deviations from the average gain of 1.0 would have been greater. For example, had we chosen to use the top and bottom 8 percent, the data at the end of grade five in Table 11 would read: 3.0, 5.9, 10.5.

To expect every class to gain at least one year on the average on a reading test is often unreasonable. Many will gain more, many gain less. There are simply too many variables which affect reading. And to hold teachers *accountable* for an average gain of this magnitude is often unfair, besides creating unnecessary anxiety in teachers and a poor relationship between teachers and administrators. But, even though standardized test results should not be used to evaluate teachers, the teacher should use these data, along with other forms of evaluation, to make some judgments about the adequacy and appropriateness of his or her methods and materials. Again, the emphasis should be upon the future. It is for the purposes of educational planning and individualization that the many forms of evaluation described in this chapter should be most helpful.

The Student and Behavioral Objectives

A list of behavioral objectives was provided at the beginning of this chapter. Readers should now reread these objectives to determine, as a form of self-diagnosis, if they can exhibit the behaviors called for. Should there be some objectives about which readers are uncertain, they should study further the appropriate sections of this chapter. Some of the items in the list of references might be helpful in case the reader wishes to study a given topic in more depth.

MAJOR PUBLISHERS OF READING TESTS

167
Assessment
and Diagnosis
of Reading
Abilities

Information about current reading tests can be gotten free by writing to the test publishers for catalogs. A list of the major publishers of reading tests is given below:

1. American Guidance Service, Inc.
   Publishers' Building
   Circle Pines, MN 55014

2. Bobbs-Merrill Co., Inc.
   4300 West 62nd Street
   Indianapolis, Ind. 46268

3. California Test Bureau
   Del Monte Research Park
   Monterey, Calif. 93940

4. Educational Testing Service
   Cooperative Tests and Services
   Princeton, N.J. 08540

5. Follett Educational Corporation
   1010 West Washington
   Boulevard
   Chicago, Ill. 60607

6. Houghton Mifflin Company
   110 Tremont St.
   Boston, Mass. 02107

7. Lyons & Carnahan
   407 East 25th Street
   Chicago, Ill. 60616

8. Personnel Press, Inc.
   20 Nassau Street
   Princeton, N.J. 08540

9. The Psychological Corporation
   Harcourt Brace Jovanovich, Inc.
   757 Third Avenue
   New York, NY 10017

10. Science Research Associates, Inc.
    259 East Erie Street
    Chicago, Ill. 60611

SUMMARY

All tests published are reviewed in Buros (1978), *Mental Measurements Yearbooks;* every standardized reading test is described and reviewed by at least one authority in one of the yearbooks. They are extremely valuable resource books which are published every three or four years, the latest, the eighth, having been published in 1978. When a test is published, it is usually reviewed in the next *Yearbook* in some detail, but may not be reviewed in subsequent books unless the test is revised. In these *Yearbooks* one will find a description and a critical review by at least one authority of every standardized test published.

Below is a bibliography of the tests mentioned in this chapter and of some additional reading tests which are commonly used in American schools.

TEST REFERENCES

Adult Basic Learning Examination. Adults achieving at grades 1–12. B. Karlsen, R. Madden and E. Gardner. New York: Harcourt Brace Jovanovich, 1967, 1970.

Analysis of Learning Potential. Grades 1–12. W. N. Durost, E. F. Gardner, R. Madden. New York: Harcourt Brace Jovanovich, 1970.

California Achievement Test. Grades 1–12. E. W. Tiegs and W. W. Clark. Monterey, CA.: California Test Bureau, 1977–78

Cognitive Abilities Test. Grades K–13. R. L. Thorndike, E. Hagen, I. Lorge. Boston: Houghton Mifflin, 1978.

Comprehensive Test of Basic Skills. Grades

2–12. CTB. Monterey, Cal.: California Test Bureau, 1973–75.

Cooperative Primary Tests. Grades 1–3. Cooperative Tests and Services. Princeton, N.J.: Educational Testing Service, 1965–67.

Diagnostic Reading Scales. Grades 1–8. George D. Spache. Monterey, Cal.: California Test Bureau, 1963.

Durrell Analysis of Reading Difficulty. Grades 1–6. D. D. Durrell. New York: Harcourt Brace Jovanovich, 1955.

Gates-MacGinitie Reading Tests. Grades K–12. A. I. Gates and W. H. MacGinitie. New York: Teachers College Press, Columbia University, 1978.

Gates-McKillop Reading Diagnostic Tests. Grades 2–6. A. I. Gates and A. S. McKillop. New York: Teachers College Press, Columbia University, 1962.

Gilmore Oral Reading Test. Grades 1–8. J. V. Gilmore and E. C. Gilmore. New York: Harcourt Brace Jovanovich, 1968.

Iowa Silent Reading Tests. Grades 6–12. R. Farr, ed. New York: Harcourt Brace Jovanovich, 1973.

Iowa Test of Basic Skills. Grades 3–9. A. N. Hieronymus, et al. Boston: Houghton Mifflin, 1978.

Metropolitan Achievement Test. Grades 1–9. G. A. Prescott, et. al. New York: The Psychological Corporation, 1978.

Metropolitan Achievement Test. Reading Instructional Tests. Grades 1–9. R. Farr, et al. New York: The Psychological Corporation, 1978.

Metropolitan Readiness Test. Grades K–1. G. H. Hildreth, N. L. Griffiths, and M. E. McGauvan. New York: Harcourt Brace Jovanovich, 1964–65.

Murphy-Durrell Reading Readiness Analysis. Grades K–1. H. D. Murphy and D. D. Durrell. New York: Harcourt Brace Jovanovich, 1964–65.

Otis-Lennon Mental Ability Test. Grades K–College. A. S. Otis and R. T. Lennon. New York: Harcourt Brace Jovanovich, 1967.

Prescriptive Reading Inventory. Grades K–6. Monterey, CA: California Test Bureau, 1972–77.

SRA Achievement Series. Grades 1–9. L. P. Thorpe, D. W. Lefever, and R. A. Naslund. Chicago: Science Research Associates, 1954–69.

Silent Reading Diagnostic Tests. Grades 2–6. G. L. Bond, B. Balow, and C. J. Hoyt. Chicago: Lyons and Carnahan, 1970.

Stanford Achievement Test. Grades 1–9. R. Madden, E. F. Gardner, H. C. Rudman, B. Karlsen, and J. C. Merwin. New York: Harcourt Brace Jovanovich, 1973.

Stanford Diagnostic Reading Test. Grades 2–13. B. Karlsen, R. Madden, and E. F. Gardner. New York: Harcourt Brace Jovanovich, 1966–74.

Stanford Early School Achievement Test. Grades K–1. R. Madden and E. F. Gardner. New York: Harcourt Brace Jovanovich, 1969–70.

Tests of Achievement and Proficiency. Grades 9–12. D. P. Scannell et. al. Boston: Houghton Mifflin, 1978.

REFERENCES

Ahmann, J. Stanley, and Glock, Marvin D. *Evaluating Pupil Growth.* Boston: Allyn and Bacon, 1971.

Anastasi, Anne. *Psychological Testing.* 3rd ed. New York: Macmillan, 1968.

Aukerman, Robert C. *Approaches to Beginning Reading.* New York: John Wiley and Sons, 1971.

Barbe, Walter B. *Educator's Guide to Personalized Reading Instruction.* Englewood Cliffs, N.J.: Prentice-Hall, 1961.

Benton, Curtis D., Jr. "Ophthalmologists Recommend Less Emphasis on the Eyes in Learning Disorders." *Journal of Learning Disabilities* 3 (1970): 54–56.

Bloom, Benjamin S., Hastings, J. Thomas, and Madaus, George F. *Handbook on Formative and Summative Evaluation of Student Learning.* New York: McGraw-Hill, 1971.

Buros, Oscar K., ed. *The Eighth Mental Measurements Yearbook.* Highland Park, N.J.: Gryphon Press, 1978.

Burrill, Lois E. "How a Standardized Achievement Test Is Built." *Test Service Notebook #125.* New York: Harcourt Brace Jovanovich, 1972.

Clark, Carl A. "The Use of Separate Answer Sheets in Testing Slow-learning Pupils." *Journal of Educational Measurement* 5 (1968): 61–64.

Educational Testing Service. *Making the Classroom Test: A Guide for Teachers.* Evaluation and Advisory Service Series No. 4. Princeton: E.T.S., 1961(b).

Educational Testing Service, *Selecting an Achievement Test.* Evaluation and Advisory Service Series No. 3. Princeton: E.T.S., 1961(a).

Farr, Roger, ed. *Measurement and Evaluation of Reading.* New York: Harcourt Brace Jovanovich, 1970.

Fry, Edward. "The Orangoutan Score." *The Reading Teacher* 24 (1971): 360–362.

Goodman, Yetta M., and Burke, Carolyn L. *Reading Miscue Inventory.* New York: Macmillan, 1972.

Harris, A. J. & Sipay, E. R. *How to Increase Reading Ability.* 6th Edition. New York: David McKay, 1975.

Johnson, Marjorie S., and Kress, Roy A. *Informal Reading Inventories.* Reading Aids Series. Newark, Del.: International Reading Association, 1965.

Jones, John W. *Blind Children, Degree of Vision, Mode of Reading.* Bulletin 24. Washington, D.C.: U.S. Office of Education, 1961.

Karlin, Robert. *Teaching Elementary Reading.* New York: Harcourt Brace Jovanovich, 1971.

Karlsen, Bjorn, *There's No Such Thing as a Third Grade Word.* In Proceedings of the California Reading Association Convention, 1979.

Kelley, Truman L., et al. *Stanford Achievement Test: Technical Supplement.* New York: Harcourt Brace Jovanovich, 1966.

Kibler, Robert J., et al. *Behavioral Objectives and Instruction.* Boston: Allyn and Bacon, 1970.

Lessinger, Leon M. *Every Kid a Winner: Accountability in Education.* Palo Alto, Calif.: Science Research Associates College Division, 1970.

Madden, Richard. "Assessing the Total Reading Program." In *Administrators and Reading,* edited by Thorsten R. Carlson. New York: Harcourt Brace Jovanovich, 1972, pp. 110–134.

Mehrens, William A., and Lehmann, Irvin J. *Measurement and Evaluation in Education and Psychology.* 2nd Ed. New York: Holt, Rinehart and Winston, 1978.

National Assessment of Educational Progress. *Reading: Summary.* Report 02-R-00. Denver: NAEP, 1972.

Nelson, Clarence H. *Measurement and Evaluation in the Classroom.* Toronto, Canada: Macmillan, 1970.

Silvaroli, Nicholas J. *Classroom Reading Inventory.* Dubuque, Iowa: Wm. C. Brown, 1973.

Spache, George D. *A Study of a Longitudinal First Grade Reading Readiness Program.* Research Project 2742. Washington, D.C.: U.S. Office of Education, 1966.

Stanford Research Report. *Equivalent Scores for the 1973 Edition of Stanford Achievement Test and the 1964 Edition of Stanford Achievement Test in Terms of Grade Equivalents.* #5. New York: Harcourt Brace Jovanovich, 1974.

Taylor, Sanford. *Eye Movements and Reading.* Reading Newsletter 30. Huntington, New York: Educational Developmental Laboratories, 1963.

Thorndike, Robert L. *The Concepts of Over and Underachievement.* New York: Bureau of Publications, Teachers College, Columbia University, 1963.

Wilson, John A. R., ed. *Diagnosis of Learning Difficulties.* New York: McGraw-Hill, 1971.

Womer, Frank B. *What Is National Assessment?* Denver: NAEP, 1972.

Wood, Dorothy Atkins. *Test Construction.* Columbus, Ohio: Charles E. Merrill, 1960.

Wrightstone, J. Wayne, et al. "Accountability in Education and Associated Measurement Problems." *Test Service Notebook* #33. New York: Harcourt Brace Jovanovich, 1971.

PREVIEW

*Alden Moe and Dale Johnson worked with each other in very close coopera-
tion as these chapters were being revised, and so they will be viewed as a unit
rather than as separate chapters.*

*In Chapter Seven the authors begin with a brief treatment of the history
of reading instruction in the United States, tracing it to its antecedents in
Greece and Rome. You will certainly understand more clearly where we are
in reading after noting where we've been. Because basal reading programs
are so extensively used in elementary schools in the United States, they
receive extensive and objective treatment. Linguists and psycholinguists have
had a great deal of influence on reading programs in recent years, and their
contributions and different beliefs are discussed in some detail. Programs
involving orthographic variations (i.t.a., Unifon, etc.) are given some attention, and Chapter Seven concludes with a discussion of multi-media
approaches to reading instruction.*

7

Current Approaches, Part One

Alden J. Moe, Purdue University
Dale D. Johnson, University of Wisconsin

OBJECTIVES

After you have read this chapter, you should be able to:

1. Describe some of the historical antecedents of current approaches in reading instruction.

2. Recognize the strengths and weaknesses of the most common approach to the teaching of reading—the basal reader approach.

3. Describe the rationale behind each of the approaches.

4. List the characteristics which typify each of the approaches discussed.

5. Identify characteristics of one or more approaches which may be used in conjunction with or in place of other approaches, such as the basal approach, even though each approach is considered independent of others.

Although the reading process is not fully understood, a variety of approaches to the teaching of reading have been developed and are currently in use in North American elementary schools.

In this chapter the history of reading instruction will be briefly summarized, so that current practices may be viewed in a historical perspective. The most widely used approach to the teaching of reading, the basal reader approach, will be described and discussed. In addition, four other approaches and related materials will be examined. The approaches reviewed in addition to the basal reader are (1) linguistic approaches, (2) intensive phonics approaches, (3) orthographic variations, and (4) multi-media approaches.

Several thousand years ago the Greeks, coming in contact with Phoenician traders in their economic dealings, learned that the Phoenicians had developed a writing sytem for their Semitic language. Greek scholars began to devise a graphic system for their own language and borrowed freely from Semitic. Since the two languages, Greek and Semitic, belonged to different linguistic families, some Greek sounds were not represented in the Semitic system, so it was necessary to devise unique graphic symbols. Eventually the Greeks produced a system of written symbols with which they could represent each phoneme in their language. Each letter had a name (*nomen*), an appearance (*figura*), and a "power" (*potestas*) or sound. By the fifth century B.C. the Greeks had achieved a uniform phonemic alphabet and had established the left-to-right, top-to-bottom direction in writing.[1] Other peoples had used various pictographic writing systems long before the Greeks established their alphabet. The Greeks, however, were quick to comprehend that words are combinations of sounds and all speech sounds, therefore, must be accounted for in writing.

> Other peoples, such as the Babylonians and the Egyptians, had caught glimpses of the desirability of having signs represent *sounds,* not *things,* but were never able to break with convention to the extent of setting aside picture writing in favor of letter writing. The fundamental defect of picture writing was that it was not based upon sounds at all. The Greeks saw this basic weakness and by avoiding it achieved everlasting distinction (Mathews, 1966, pp. 7–8).

So, several centuries before Christ, the necessity arose for reading instruction. First instruction in reading was in names and forms of letters. Though the printing press would not be invented for centuries—so written symbols were in no way standardized—the task was not as difficult as it may seem, since all letters were capitals. Students learned them in alphabetical order and practiced by searching through written materials for occurrences of letters they had mastered. They recited the alphabet backward and forward, sang alphabet songs, and drilled at length on meaningless but pronounceable syllables (*ab, ob, ub, eb*). Mathews cites a statement made by a Greek school boy as reported by W. Rhys Roberts:

> When we are taught to read, first we learn all the names of the letters, then their forms and their values, then in due course syllables and their modifications, and finally words and their properties, viz., lengthenings and shortenings, accents, and the like. After acquiring these things we begin to write and read, syllable by syllable and slowly at first . . . (Mathews, p. 6).

---

[1] See I. J. Gelb, *A Study of Writing* (Chicago, 1952), and Martin Sprengling, *The Alphabet* (Chicago, 1931) for a complete discussion of the development of the Greek alphabet.

These early methods were to reappear many times in later days and in other societies.

The Romans borrowed the Greek letters from the Etruscans. Instead of using the Greek letter names, however, they named the vowels after their sounds and the consonants from close approximations of their sounds. Their method of instruction was basically oral and leaned heavily upon syllabication.

As a result of more than three centuries of Roman rule, many people in England learned the Latin language. When the English language was first put into writing in the seventh century A.D., Latin letters were naturally selected to represent English sounds. Since new letters had to be added, the English alphabet used today is quite different from its ancestor. Little is known about reading instruction in the first several hundred years after a writing system was developed for English. One of the earliest discussions of the English writing system was Alexander Hume's *Of the Orthographic and Congruities of the Britain Tongue* (1617). Hume concerned himself with spelling patterns and sounds of Latin and English.

Earliest records of reading methodology in fourteenth- through seventeenth-century England indicate that the methods used originally by the Greeks and Romans—learning letter names, then sounds, then combinations and syllables—were still in use. After extended drill children would begin to read by first spelling and then pronouncing *each* word—before moving on to the next.

This "alphabetic" method of reading instruction, which dates back thousands of years, was no doubt the *initial* means of reading instruction once alphabets were developed. It was brought to the new world in the 1600s, along with the famous "hornbook," which was mentioned in a poem written in the 1400s (Wright and Halliwell, 1841, p. 63):

> *When a child to school shall sent be*
> *A book him is brought*
> *Nailed on a board of tree*
> *That men call abc.*

The hornbook was a small wooden paddle with a protective sheath of cow horn covering a piece of paper on which the ABCs were written (often in the form of a cross), as well as some syllables and the Lord's Prayer or some other religious selection. Hornbooks were widely used for reading instruction in England and colonial America.

The *New England Primer* was the first published book designed for American schools. It went through more than twenty editions in the mid-1700s. According to Smith (1965) the book was called a *primer* because of the primary essentials of religious knowledge it contained (Psalms, Commandments, the Creed) rather than from the fact that it was the child's first book. The approach to reading instruction found in the Primer was essentially alphabetic, as described earlier.

The "whole-word" method, developed in Germany during the eighteenth and nineteenth centuries, began to receive attention in America and elsewhere. The whole-word approach—also referred to as "Normal-Word" method—involved the following basic steps:

1 Presentation of an object or picture of an object denoted by the word to be taught.
2 Presentation of the written word.
3 Analysis of the sounds and syllables within the word (letter *names* were not mentioned).
4 Reformation of the complete word.
5 Finger-tracing the word shape.
6 Writing the word on a slate.
7 Reading the word orally.

The first American book utilizing the whole-word method was *My Little Primer,* written by Josiah Bumstead in 1840. With the advent of the graded school, the development of graded series of reading books was encouraged. One of the most popular series was *The McGuffey Readers,* published and reissued between 1836 and the early 1900s, which sold over 122 million copies.

Many heated debates developed between proponents of the alphabetic method and the whole-word method—forerunners of the methodology arguments heard throughout the past 100 years. Horace Mann was probably the most eloquent American proponent of the whole-word or "look-say" approach to teaching reading. In a series of noted lectures he scathingly deplored the alphabetic approach. In supporting the whole-word method he said,

> The acquisition of the language, even from its elements, becomes an intelligible process. The knowledge of new things is introduced through the knowledge of familiar things. At the age of three or four years, every child has command of a considerable vocabulary consisting of the names of persons, of animals, articles of dress, food, furniture, etc. The sounds of these names are familiar to the ear and the organs of speech, and the ideas they represent are familiar to the mind. All that is to be done, therefore, is to lead the eye to the like familiarity with their printed signs. But the alphabet, on the other hand, is wholly foreign to a child's existing knowledge . . . (Mathews, p. 80).

A third method of reading instruction began to gain popularity in the late nineteenth and early twentieth centuries—the phonic method. In this method attention was called to letter *sounds,* not *names,* and the children's task was to "sound out" or pronounce words by applying the rules they had learned. This ability was encouraged by presenting "regularly spelled" words first (*rat, cat, hat, pat*). The phonic method was sometimes used concurrently with the whole-word method.

In summary, reading instruction in America has gone through five rather distinct but overlapping periods.:

1 About 1600 to 1840—the alphabetic or "spelling" approach.
2 About 1840 to 1880—the whole-word approach.
3 About 1880 to 1920—the phonics approach, which, unlike the alphabetic approach, stressed letter *sounds* rather than names.
4 About 1920 to 1960—the "Basal" Era. This was principally a whole-word approach with an emphasis on meaningful reading. Research

studies during the phonics period showed children could pronounce words, but could not read well silently. Language experience charts, discussed later, came to be widely used. The alphabetic method virtually disappeared and supplementary phonics instruction was minimal.

5   About 1960 to the present—basal reading with an increased emphasis on "decoding." The basal reader and decoding programs are discussed in detail in this chapter.

More than ever before, reading methodology is based upon research findings in child development (language acquisition), human learning, psycholinguistics, and reading pedagogy. Dozens of reading "approaches" and countless published programs are in use today. The most widely used approach, the basal approach, will be examined in the following section.

THE BASAL APPROACH

The most common approach to reading instruction, the basal reader program, is used in an estimated 80 to 95 percent of American schools (Chall, 1967; Staiger, 1969). In a sense, basal reading materials and programs have been with us since the days of the hornbook, which contained what was considered to be basic (essential) content. Since those early days basal programs have greatly expanded and contain many components. A number of publishing houses produce basal programs, which have both common features and differences.

The basal reader approach was until recently referred to as the "look-say," "controlled vocabulary," or "whole-word" method. None of these terms is totally accurate or comprehensive enough to include the many features of basal reading programs. With the evolution of the graded school in the middle of the last century, a need arose for grade-levelled reading materials. Through the years basal programs expanded from one book to several and further expanded by adding workbooks, teacher's manuals, supplementary materials, and more recently audio-visual aids such as tapes, cassettes, and transparencies. Generally, though, the overall purpose has not changed: to provide a *comprehensive, sequential* program aimed at teaching reading to all children.

Basal reading programs introduce vocabulary gradually and usually include words that various researchers have identified as occurring frequently in children's vocabularies. Words are repeated often to assure mastery. Word analysis skills are introduced gradually and sequentially. Each aspect of the total scope and sequence of the program is tightly controlled and interwoven so that children progress through a learning-refining-broadening continuum.

What Is the Basal Program?

As comprehensive reading programs designed to introduce nonreaders to beginning reading skills and then facilitate their development into mature readers, the programs typically consist of the several components described below.

Reading Readiness Books and Materials Readiness materials usually consist of workbooks, kits, games, charts, and activities designed to improve visual and auditory discrimination, language and experiential background, directionality, and story development. Visual discrimination activities give practice in visually perceiving similarities and differences in graphic shapes: pictures, geometric designs, letters, real and nonsense words, and longer units. A typical exercise might be: "Circle the letter that is not the same as the others."

1. o   o   e   o
2. t   f   t   t

Auditory discrimination exercises are included to develop ability to perceive auditory similarities and differences. Typical exercises require identifying pairs of words which begin or end with the same sound (such as *books* and *bat*). Other readiness components include picture books without words, from which the child is to tell the story, activities (such as "show and tell") for developing oral language, and objects for categorizing and classifying.

Pre-primers Pre-primers are the pupils' first books. They are very thin and usually have paperback covers. Very few words are introduced—perhaps twenty or twenty-five in each pre-primer—and the words are frequently repeated. Many illustrations are included, and the characters are usually the same ones the children "met" in the readiness program. Because of the tightly controlled vocabulary, the stories sometimes lack any kind of literary merit. However, few authors or teachers could compose anything resembling a literary masterpiece with a vocabulary of two or three dozen words. Furthermore, the purpose of these books is to expose children to a limited number of words and to repeat these words frequently so the children will master them. Development of literary appreciation is not the goal.

Primers Following a series of two to four pre-primers, children begin to read the primer—usually the first hardback book in the series. The primer is built on the vocabularies, and sometimes the story line, of the pre-primers. Typically one hundred or more new words are introduced.

The Readers After completing the primer, children advance to the readers. In some series they are tightly grade-levelled. For example, the two second grade books are "two[1]" and "two[2]," and so on. Most publishers, however, prefer to identify their books by "level" rather than by grade; thus, the "level seven" book is the seventh book in the series and is to be followed by the "level eight" book, etc. After third grade there is usually one reading book per year in these series. The newest basal series have abandoned these tight grade-level notations, primarily because of the stigma attached to them. It is often embarrassing for the slow reading fourth-grade child to be seen with a book marked "two[1]." However, even in the newer series the materials are gradated. In one series there are at least thirteen books intended for the first four grades—each expanding and building on the vocabulary and skills presented in the previous one. In another series, a number of thin paperbacks are coded at varying levels of difficulty. These series of small books are based on the belief that some children are frustrated by the thickness of a hardback book and are motivated to read a small paperback because they feel they can finish it.

Until recently most basal readers did not introduce more than 400 words by the end of first grade, but vocabulary size has greatly increased in some of the newer series.

Workbooks Workbooks usually accompany each reading book in the series, including the readiness materials. Contained in the workbook are decoding activities in phonics, syllabication, structural analysis, and contextual analysis, as well as comprehension activities related to the stories in the readers. Vocabulary building exercises and work with dictionaries and other reference materials are sometimes provided. The workbooks in some series are not related to the reading books and can be used as separate supplementary programs.

Proponents of basal reading programs believe that children need sequential introduction to the basic word recognition and comprehension skills and that workbooks are a sensible vehicle for assuring that none of the essential skills is missed. Teachers are sometimes cautioned that not all pupils need to do every workbook page. Pretests or checkpoints are sometimes provided to help determine which children would profit from the workbook exercises. Workbooks have received considerable criticism both from pupils and reading authorities. Children have been heard to say, "I like to read, but I hate reading," meaning they particularly dislike completing workbook pages. Many reading authorities feel that the term *work* should be removed from the activity books to make them less foreboding.

Teacher Manuals These guide books contain numerous suggestions to teachers for using the materials. Some are so detailed that they list specific questions for each of the stories. They also explain how teachers may use the materials diagnostically and indicate particular workbook pages to be prescribed when a student makes certain errors in oral reading. Typically there is a separate manual for each of the reader-workbook pairs. An acquaintance of one of the authors who is a teacher in New Zealand complains that American teachers are "spoiled" by the teacher's manuals. She believes there are so many suggested activities, questions, games, and the like that the teachers really do not have to think for themselves. Whether or not this is the case, beginning teachers are usually most grateful for the manuals as a thorough resource for instructional planning. More experienced teachers learn how to choose activities selectively.

Supplementary Materials Type, amount, and quality of supplementary materials vary greatly among the published basal reading programs. Supplementary story books built on the vocabulary and skills presented, filmstrips, charts, posters, kits, audio tapes, and games are included to some degree with most current programs. They are intended to add interest and variety.

Tests   Most basal reading programs include an assortment of pre- and post-tests for assessing students' accomplishments of the materials and skills covered and for diagnosing students' reading weaknesses in order to place them within components of the program.

CURRENT PUBLISHERS OF BASAL READERS

In a recent volume of the *Educational Products Information Exchange Materials Report* (1978), 24 published reading programs were identified. These programs were published by sixteen different textbook publishers and most are comprehensive basal series and are available today.

Although the name of a basal series may change, the publishers generally do not. Most of the major basal publishers of today were producing materials thirty or forty years ago. The current publishers of complete elementary (kindergarten through grade six or eight) basal readers, together with the names of the most recent editions of their textbooks, are listed below:

Allyn & Bacon, Inc.
Pathfinder: Allyn and Bacon Reading Program (1978)

American Book Company
American Book Reading Program (1977)

The Economy Company
Keys to Reading (1975)

Ginn and Company
Reading 360 (1969–73)
Reading 720 (1976–1979)

Harcourt Brace Jovanovich, Inc.
The Bookmark Reading Program: Second Edition (1974)

Harper & Row, Publishers
Reading Basics Plus (1976–77)

Holt, Rinehart and Winston
The Holt Basic Reading System (1977)

Houghton Mifflin Company
Houghton Mifflin Reading Series (1976)

Laidlaw Brothers
The Laidlaw Reading Program (1977)

J. B. Lippincott Company
Basic Reading Series (1975)

Macmillan Publishing Company, Inc.
The Macmillan Reading Program (1967–74)
Series R: The New Macmillan Reading Program (1975)

Charles E. Merrill Publishing Company
Merrill Linguistic Reading Program (1975)

Open Court Publishing Company
The Headway Program (1979)

Rand McNally & Company
Young America Basic Series (1978)

Science Research Associates, Inc.
The Basic Reading Series (1976), for K–2
The Comprehensive Reading Series (1971), for 3–6

Scott, Foresman and Company
Basics in Reading (1978)
The New Open Highways Program (1973–74)
Reading Unlimited (1976)

In addition to the elementary reading programs listed above, where there are materials for all grade levels, several publishers have prepared materials just for the primary grades. Although some of these programs vary a great deal from the typical basal reader series they are listed here because they *are* published programs, they are often referred to as basal programs, and they are currently in use. Among these primary programs are the following:

Crane Publishing Company
Crane Reading System (1977)

Harcourt Brace Jovanovich, Inc.
The Palo Alto Reading Program: Sequential Steps in Reading, Second Edition (1973)

Macmillan Publishing Company
The Bank Street Readers (1967–74)

McGraw-Hill Book Company/ Webster Division
Programmed Reading: Third Edition (1973)

Science Research Associates, Inc.
Distar Reading I, II, III, Second Edition (1972–76)

The major components of a basal reader series have already been identified and discussed. It should be emphasized, however, that most publishers provide numerous components and an evaluation of any published program can only be accomplished by a careful examination of each of the many parts.

TRADITIONAL CRITICISMS OF BASAL MATERIALS

Basal reading programs have undergone substantial changes during the last fifteen years and many of the criticisms previously levelled at them are no longer valid. Throughout the 1940s, 1950s, and even most of the 1960s, basal reading programs tended to be very much alike. Today the programs vary considerably. Before discussing the classroom uses of basal programs and related instructional strategies, we will cite several early and recurring criticisms and show how basal reader authors and publishers have responded.

1. *Story content and illustrations portray an all-white, middle-class world in which minority groups do not exist except in service roles.*

This scathing criticism was valid until the past decade. Virtually all characters were white and lived in rural or suburban areas. They were clean, well-fed, and well-clothed, and children possessed only unbroken toys. Father usually worked in an office or in some occupation requiring a white shirt and necktie. Mother never worked outside of the home but was always well-dressed and usually found in the kitchen. Black, American Indian, and Mexican-American families were not included.

Early in the 1960s this began to change. At first light tan faces began to appear, but the environments remained the same. The Bank Street Readers (1965) and the Chandler Language-Experience Readers (1966) were more realistic. Urban environments replaced suburban, and blacks as well as other ethnic groups came to be represented. However, in a study of environmental settings, multi-ethnicity, and success failure outcomes reported by Waite (1968), it was found that of seven basal reading series published in 1965 and 1966 only *two* had more than 19 percent of the stories located in urban settings, four contained 40 percent or more "white-only" stories, and in three series, 30 percent or more of the stories ended in failure rather than success for the characters. However, a more recent evaluation by Lapp and Flood (1978) led them to conclude that most publishers now present a culturally diverse content in their materials.

Today nearly all of the recently published basal reading series have multi-ethnic characters and a variety of environmental settings. With respect to race and ethnicity, *basal reader content is much more realistic* and representative of life in America than in previous years. This is less true with regard to women. Sex-role stereotyping continues to be prevalent. A study of sex stereotyping in children's readers (*Dick and Jane as Victims,* 1972), revealed the following facts. Of the 2,760 stories from 134 books, boy-centered stories outnumbered girl-centered stories 5 to 2, male biographies outnumbered female 6 to 1, and men were shown in 146 occupations compared to 25 for women. In a more recent study of sex-role stereotyping, Britton and Lumpkin (1977) found that in textbooks which were published during 1974–76 that 61 percent of the stories had males as the major characters and that females held the major role only 16 percent of the time. Females continue to be shown as docile, passive, and dependent. It appears that even now the content of basal reading materials needs considerable overhauling to eliminate sexism.[2]

2. *Syntactic structures in basal reader stories do not closely match language usage of children.*

Some publishers, in emphasizing vocabulary control and by (or through) extensive repetition of words, have often ignored syntactic structures. What we know about language development in children is not always applied by authors and publishers. For example, Shuy (1971) points out that one basal author used the construction, "Over the fence went the ball," though few if any children use sentences which begin with a prepositional phrase followed by a predicate. It is encouraging to note that many of the recently published programs show improvement in the inclusion and manipulation of varying syntactic structures, perhaps to the point of increasing the readability level of the material.

3. *Insufficient attention is paid to the development of letter-sound relationships in beginning materials.*

Since most authors and publishers of basal readers take a "whole-word" approach, phonics materials have tended to be supplementary and have been introduced late and treated lightly. However, the most recent basal program authors and publishers have sought the advice of teachers and linguists and have considered research findings, resulting in increased treatment of the decoding skills. Though most programs still begin by teaching sight words, attention is given very early to the development of letter-sound correspondence strategies.

---

[2] See Chapter Three for a more detailed discussion of this issue.

4. Story content is repetitive and dull.

Efforts have recently been made to include a wider variety of stories both in terms of realism and fantasy. Illustrations, photographs, and drawings are more varied today and even the use of print has become more innovative. Various sizes and types of print as well as modification of left-to-right sequence (for example, in one program print goes up the stairs and down in a story and around in a circle in another) are found in the newest books. Furthermore, in most of the basal materials published recently the stories are interesting to read for both students and teachers. Authors and publishers appear to be providing content that is timely, exciting, and relevant.

In general, then, authors and publishers of basal reading programs are sensitive to professional and lay criticisms. Recently they have made many changes in the content and format of their materials. Though further improvements are needed, current materials appear to be far better and more diverse than those of a decade or two ago.

Using the Basal Approach

After a certain period of readiness work—its length depends on the needs of the children—instruction with the reading materials begins. With most basal reading programs a four-step instructional format is followed each day, or with each lesson or story: (1) background development, (2) prescribed reading, (3) skill development, and (4) extended reading.

The teacher begins the lesson by developing background. This usually includes a discussion of the story's topic in relation to the lives of the children in the group. If the story is about subways, the teacher might ask, "How many of you have been on a subway?" "Who will tell us about it?" and other related questions. New vocabulary is introduced during this discussion. If three new words *(subway, tunnel, turnstile)* are presented in the story, they might be written on the chalkboard within context:

> The *subway* train is fast
> a *tunnel* under the city
> a *turnstile* gate . . .

In addition to sharing experiences and introducing new vocabulary, the discussion establishes purposes for reading. The teacher asks questions or gives directions related to the story: "When you read the story, see if you can learn why Tom's friend wasn't with him."

Prescribed reading takes a variety of forms. Most often the teacher asks the group to read the story silently. Then a discussion is held and the teacher asks comprehension questions. These discussions can be very interesting if questions are asked beyond the literal level. It is certainly more fun to respond to an inferential question like, "Do you think Tom will ever ride a subway alone again?" than to, "How big was Tom's ticket?" Following the discussion the teacher may have the children read the story orally. There are usually two purposes for this oral rereading. One is simply that most children enjoy reading aloud. The other is that the oral reading allows the teacher to diagnose problems children might be having.

Basal reading instruction is often criticized for "round-robin" reading, in which children in a small group of six to twelve take turns reading orally, with everyone focused on the same line. Some children read slower and some faster than others, which can cause boredom or confusion. Likewise it can be embarrassing for the child who reads poorly. One remedy to this legitimate criticism is to divide the group into "reading pairs" for oral reading. The paired children can alternate reading each paragraph or page. In this way every child will have more opportunities to read. The teacher can move from pair to pair to listen and give assistance if needed. The two children can help one another with words and check with the teacher if both are stumped. There may be a louder noise level in the room, with four or five children reading aloud instead of one, but it need not be a problem.

For skill development, teachers may use both the reading book story and the accompanying workbook exercise. Letter-sound correspondences are taught or reinforced by calling attention to words within the story that have identical letter-sound relationships. Structural analysis (play, play*ed,* play*ing*), contextual analysis, and comprehension strategies are presented.

The teacher can encourage further reading by calling attention to books or records within the classroom or library which relate to the content, theme, location, or some other aspect of the story just read. Many children are interested in doing related reading but need suggestions as to what is available and where to find it.

Classroom Organization in a
Basal Program

According to information gained from pretesting and observation, the teacher forms a number of groups consisting of children reading at approximately the same level. The range of children's abilities will be wide. In one class of fourth graders, for example, there may be both nonreaders and children who read at a high school level. Forming groups based on reading ability reduces the range within any one group—though it is important to remember that there will still be a range. The number of groups may range from one to six or more, though for some reason, most basal reader teachers form three reading groups. Each group, the high, the middle, and the low, works with a different set of materials. Some school systems use three separate basal series—a different series for each group. In other schools, different levels of the same series are used with each group.

The three-group plan has been often criticized for its rigidity. It has been found that there is little mobility between groups within a school year or even within a child's several years in an elementary school. Once assigned to the low group in grade one, a child may continue in the low group for many years. Bosman (1972) found that 80 percent of the children in fifth grade in her school were in the same reading group level (high, middle, or low) they had been in since first grade. The three-group plan is also criticized for the potential psychological damage it can do to children who are labelled "dummies" and are daily identified with the low group. Many teachers attempt to camouflage the groups by using neutral names like "red, blue, and green" groups or "Bill's, Mary's, and Sandy's" groups or euphemistic terms like "bluebirds, sunbursts, and twinkle-stars." But children are not fooled by labels; everyone knows who is in the low group.

Smith and Barrett (1974) have proposed forming flexible groups. Interest groups would form and dissolve frequently during the year, skill groups would be formed as needed and then disbanded, and basic groups could continue. Different types of groups would meet on different days. In this way no one would be continuously affiliated with only one group. During a typical reading period of about one hour, the teacher spends fifteen or twenty minutes with each group. In the meantime other children, individually or as groups, do workbook exercises, read independently, prepare for the session with the teacher, or work on projects. Clearly, individualization is possible within the framework of a basal program.

SUMMARY

The basal reading approach encompasses a number of series or programs, commercially produced, which provide continuous reading instruction throughout the elementary grades. Vocabulary is controlled and introduced gradually, and skills are presented sequentially. Children progress from the familiar to the unfamiliar, ever broadening their reading ability. Reading materials are levelled; each new book builds on vocabulary, concepts, and skills presented earlier. Children are usually grouped according to reading ability, and small group instruction prevails.

After an examination of other approaches to the teaching of reading, the authors will present more personal viewpoints concerning the use of basal readers on page 233.

LINGUISTIC APPROACHES

As background for considering the linguistic approaches to the teaching of reading, it is helpful to know the characteristics of language as viewed by the linguist.[3] Bishop (1971) offers the following principles as representing the current attitude among linguists:

1 Language changes constantly.
2 Change is normal.
3 Spoken language is *the* language.
4 Correctness rests upon usage.
5 All usage is relative.

As we shall soon see, it is the third principle, that spoken language is primary, which has been most emphatically stressed in the development of published linguistic reading materials.

Readers who desire an overview of linguistic applications in reading and other language arts are referred to *Linguistics in Proper Perspective* (Lamb, 1977) for a thorough but nontechnical treatment of the subject.

---

[3] See Chapter Four for a more complete discussion of the issues briefly noted here.

A Brief History of Linguistics and Reading

Although Mathews (1966) reports that a book which presented what might now be called a linguistic approach to the teaching of reading was published in 1913, he states that this book "appears to have failed utterly in arousing either interest or understanding" (p. 153). Credit for presenting the first linguistic approach to the teaching of reading has generally been given to Leonard Bloomfield, a well-known linguist (Heilman, 1977; Ives and Ives, 1970; Lamb, 1977).

Bloomfield became interested in reading instruction in the 1930s, when his son was about to begin school. Bloomfield reasoned that since his son could understand and speak several thousand words he knew the language; therefore, he saw reading as decoding—transferring the printed symbols into speech sounds which were already familiar to the reader.

In two articles Bloomfield (1942) outlined procedures which he believed should be followed in teaching children how to read. Although Bloomfield and his colleague, Clarence Barnhart, experimented throughout the 1940s and 1950s with materials they had devised, it was not until 1961 that their reading program was published as *Let's Read: A Linguistic Approach.* Two other notable publications appeared at about the same time representing similar philosophies: *Sound and Spelling in English* by Robert A. Hall, Jr. (1961), and *Linguistics and Reading* by Charles C. Fries (1962). Bloomfield, Hall, and Fries all viewed reading as essentially a decoding process, and it is this view that has become known as the linguistic method of teaching reading.

Another book, *Linguistics and the Teaching of Reading* by C. A. Lefevre (1964), took a much broader approach to reading instruction. Whereas Bloomfield and Fries were concerned primarily with the decoding of words, Lefevre points out that "it is not enough to consider only phonemic-graphemic correspondences and the ordering of difficulties of spelling patterns" (Wardhaugh, 1969, p. 27). Lefevre's concern was with structures and patterns, particularly sentence patterns. His views consider more complex aspects of language than either Bloomfield's or Fries's, and have only recently appeared in published reading materials.

Other writers have written extensively on various aspects of linguistics and reading; among the more notable are Goodman (1967, 1968), Goodman and Burke (1970), Shuy (1969a, 1969b), and Wardhaugh (1969), all of whom discussed the complexities of language and reading.

Since 1961, when the first linguistic materials appeared on the market, the emphasis has been largely on decoding; only recently has a different linguistic approach become apparent. Therefore, our discussion of published linguistic materials will examine two general types: (1) the more traditional linguistic approaches, which emphasize decoding—particularly the decoding of words, and (2) linguistic approaches which consider syntactic structure—phrases and sentences.

Decoding Emphasis
Linguistic Programs

Bloomfield and Fries advocate a linguistic approach which defines reading as essentially a decoding process. Their approach relies primarily on only one aspect of linguistic science, phonology, the study of the sounds of a language. Hence, they view reading as the ability to make the proper phonemic-graphemic matches—that is, saying [cat] for the word which appears in print as *cat*. They claim further that, since the child has already mastered oral language by the time he comes to school, his main task is learning to break the coded relationships between sound and symbol.

An examination of four published decoding emphasis linguistic programs will show, however, that while they are grouped here under a common heading, there are a number of differences among them.

Let's Read was published in 1961 as one large 465-page volume by the Wayne State University Press and had a very limited distribution (Aukerman, 1971). In an effort to market the program, Clarence L. Barnhart formed his own company and divided the large volume into nine smaller, more easily handled books which were first published in this form in 1963. Examples of the *Let's Read* materials are found in Figures 7.1 and 7.2. The following are the major characteristics and special features of the program:

1   There are nine books in the program.
2   It is intended for grades one to three.
3   Reading instruction begins with the teaching of letter names.
4   Reading is viewed as a process of decoding from print to sound.
5   Emphasis is placed on mastery of the alphabetical code—whereby each letter of the alphabet possesses but one phonemic value.
6   There is stress on learning phonemic-graphemic relationships with individual words.
7   Words are always pronounced as wholes, never letter by letter.
8   Sound-letter correspondences are established by phonemic contrasts, as with *hat–cat, rip–zip, kid–kit.*
9   Mastery of spelling patterns is stressed.
10   Motivation for student learning is provided by the act of decoding.
11   No pictures are used in any of the texts.
12   Nonsense words such as *din, dib, jin, lin, nin,* and *zin* are used.
13   Word length is controlled.
14   No sight words are presented in the initial reading.
15   There is little story content with which the reader can identify.

The 1966 edition of the *Merrill Linguistic Readers* (Fries, Wilson, and Rudolph) was probably the most widely used of the published "linguistic" approaches. Because of the 1975 edition of the *Merrill Linguistic Readers* with a new authorship team, the 1966 edition is no longer available. However, because of their historical value and their widespread use for a decade, the Fries materials will be described here briefly. Also, beginning levels of the 1975 edition are only a little different from the 1966 edition. It is apparent, however, that throughout the series there is a much greater emphasis on comprehension.

Like Bloomfield, Fries viewed reading as a decoding activity and put little emphasis on comprehension. During the course of the development of the Merrill Linguistic Readers, however, Fries became somewhat more concerned with reading for meaning than he had formerly indicated (perhaps because of the influence of his coauthor, Rosemary Wilson). The words and sentences in the Merrill Linguistic Readers do form stories, whereas the Bloomfield content often does not; this is especially apparent in the books prepared for the very early stages of reading. Furthermore, Fries did not employ nonsense words and did introduce several function words (*is, a, the*) at the very beginning of the program. The major characteristics of the program are as follows:

1 There are six books in the program.
2 It is intended for grades one and two, and possibly grade three.
3 Reading is viewed primarily as decoding, although some emphasis is placed on reading for meaning.
4 Letters and letter names are learned prior to the introduction of first words.
5 Stress is placed on the learning of phonemic-graphemic relationships with individual words and words in sentences.
6 Sound-letter correspondence is established by minimal phonemic contrasts, as with *cat–fat, man–fan,* and *sad–bad.*
7 Mastery of a very limited number of spelling patterns is expected.
8 A few irregularly spelled structure words are introduced early (*the, to,* and so on) as sight words.
9 No illustrations are used in any of the texts.
10 Word length is controlled.
11 Stories are generally set in a familiar background.

A pig had a wig.

Dan had a big map.

Sal had a big pig.

A cat ran. A rat ran.

Pal can dig. Dig, Pal, dig!

Pam had a big fig.

Nat had fig jam.

Can Nan jig? Can a cat jig?

Can a big, fat pig jig?

Figure 7.1
Let's Read, Part 2,
Experimental Edition.

The Linguistic Readers (formerly Harper and Row Linguistic Readers, 1965) are now published by Benziger, Inc., a subsidiary of Crowell Collier and Macmillan. This program looks like the traditional basal reader, since pictures are used and the sentence construction is like that found in the usual reader. However, Aukerman (1971) states that "there *is* a significant difference. It is to be found in the consistency with which new words are introduced" (p. 174).

Although the early materials stress the use of words which fit a very limited number of spelling patterns, the story content is more interesting than that found in the Bloomfield or Fries materials. Major characteristics of the program are as follows:

1 Materials include three pre-primers, one primer, one first reader, one second reader, and one third reader.
2 Reading is decoding, but there is emphasis on meaning also.
3 Stress is on phonemic-graphemic relationships with individual words and words in sentences.
4 Whole-word recognition of initial sight vocabulary is stressed.
5 Illustrations in earlier editions were one color, but in later editions are multicolor.
6 Content of pre-primers is concerned completely with familiar animals.
7 Vocabulary is introduced more rapidly than in the usual basal reader.

Playing Gold Rush Days

Lizzie and Willie, who live in an
apartment, have a game they play on
rainy days. It is called Gold Rush Days.
They are settlers going West to seek gold.
Willie makes a wagon from old bo......d
blankets, and Lizzie gets several of Mom's
dented tin pots and plates to eat from. If
they are lucky Mom lends them a milk
bottle to keep water in and gives them a
tin box to keep cookies in.

They have six oxen to haul their wagon
along over the dusty trail and across
rivers. They are bold and brave, going
West in terrible rain and cold.

When Mom calls both of them in to
lunch, they crawl away from their wagon
and hunt bear on their way to the kitchen.

Source: Reprinted by special permission from *Let's Read 8* by Leonard Bloomfield and Clarence L. Barnhart, © 1965 by Clarence L. Barnhart, Inc. All rights reserved.

The Miami Linguistic Readers (Robinett, Rojas, and Bell, D. C. Heath, 1964–1966) were developed during the early 1960s in an effort to meet the need of the many refugees who left Castro's Cuba. In his description of the

Figure 7.2
Let's Read, Part 8,
Experimental Edition.

program, Robinett (1965) states that it is a language program and not just a reading program. Aukerman (1971) summarizes well:

> The rationale for the Miami Linguistic Readers was, consequently, two-fold: (1) to develop books which were "culture-free," and which would have themes with which children of any background could relate; (2) to develop books which would provide an approach to American English with the least amount of phonemic irregularity—this being necessary, especially for children who already had some knowledge of a relatively regular phonemic language: Cuban-Spanish (p. 209).

Characteristics of this program are as follows:

1 It consists of twenty-one small paperback booklets and sixteen work-books.
2 It is intended to be used for the first two years of school.
3 Decoding is preceded by language experience activities.
4 Reading is reinforced by writing.
5 There is some emphasis on spelling patterns.
6 The program emphasizes the learning of letter names in the initial stages.
7 Content of stories is familiar to children.
8 Initial regular words are introduced as sight words until the child gains insight into spelling patterns.
9 Word length is generally not controlled.
10 Illustrations are black and white cartoon-type drawings.

Summary of Decoding Emphasis Linguistic Programs It should be apparent that while the four programs are all described as decoding emphasis programs, they are not the same. Some authors are concerned exclusively with decoding, while others emphasize comprehension as well. Nevertheless, we can list the distinguishing characteristics of the decoding emphasis linguistic approach in general:

1 Pupils are taught a systematic decoding system at the beginning of their reading experience rather than after they have acquired a sight vocabulary.
2 Letters and letter names are introduced early.
3 Sound-letter relationships are established by repetition of known words and through the use of minimal contrasts (*fat–cat*), but sounds which make up a word are never presented in isolation.
4 The introduction and patterning of consonant and vowel combinations are systematically controlled through the use of common spelling patterns.
5 Pictures and context clues are not considered part of the decoding system, although some programs introduce them as separate skills.

For those who have reservations about the linguistic programs just described, Lamb (1972) provides this caution:

> To criticize the authors and publishers of these materials because they obviously do not emphasize meaning is to accuse them of not achieving

an objective they never had. If one considers meaning an important factor in reading at the beginning levels, then one selects different materials or supplements these more narrowly conceived reading materials, choosing ones designed to achieve broader goals (p. 15).

Linguistic Approaches That Emphasize Sentence Structures

Whereas most linguistic approaches have been concerned with words and their systematic presentation in orderly spelling patterns, other linguists have argued for an emphasis on meaning and an examination of units of language larger than the word. Perhaps the earliest case for such an examination was presented by Lefevre (1964). In the preface to his book, *Linguistics and the Teaching of Reading,* he states that the method he proposes "is a whole-sentence method that applies a scientific description of American English utterances to the problems of teaching reading. No one can get meaning from the printed page without taking in whole language patterns at the sentence level, because these are the minimal meaning-bearing structures of most written communications" (p. vii). In agreement with other linguists, he rejects the teaching of the sounds of letters in isolation and advocates that only complete words be pronounced.

Lefevre's approach develops reading comprehension by building students' ability to understand sentence sense. He stresses that readers must be able to translate written language back into its primary form, the spoken language. For Lefevre, therefore, intonation is more important than other aspects of the reading process. While Bloomfield and Fries emphasized the importance of word identification, Lefevre emphasizes the importance of word comprehension.

In contrast to Bloomfield and Fries, Lefevre argues strongly that the single word is not a principal language unit, and that most English words "are 'chameleon' in both structure and meaning" (p. 5). He explains that a concrete noun may be used in a sentence as a noun, a verb, an adjective, or an adverb. So he concludes that "each 'word' discovers its meaning and use in every sentence where it occurs" (p. 5). Following this premise, he provides the following observations:

1　The basic fault in poor reading is poor sentence sense, which is often demonstrated orally in word-calling.
2　True reading requires that isolated words be brought back into the larger patterns that function linguistically and carry meaning.
3　Reading should be taught by language patterns that carry meaning. Intonation and word order provide reliable clues to the total meaning-bearing pattern.
4　The most significant structures in English are syntactical word groups, intonation patterns, grammatical word groups, clauses and sentences (Lefevre, 1964, pp. 5–6).

In agreement with Lefevre, Goodman (1963) states "that at all levels reading materials should have meaning, that words should have meaning, that words should never be introduced in isolation unless they are individually communicative, that the child must be provided opportunities to learn the signals of structural meaning, and the child must be taught to utilize these signals in obtaining meaning from his reading" (pp. 295–296).

Although we now see the influence of Lefevre and Goodman and others (Shuy, Bormuth, Ruddell, and Wardhaugh, most notably) in many of the newer basal materials, the first effort in this direction was made in the *Harper and Row Basic Reading Program* (O'Donnell and Van Roekel, 1966). While the program was similar in format to a typical basal program, the authors emphasized the following linguistic exercises:

1 Exercises dealing with pitch, stress, and juncture to help the child bridge the gap between spoken and written language.
2 Activities focusing attention on noun phrases, verb phrases, and prepositional phrases in order to promote the reading of groups of words.
3 Exercises dealing with word substitution in sentence patterns.
4 Sentence building exercises stressing the function of word types such as descriptive words, noun markers, and so on.

It is apparent to most observers that the linguists who *currently* write about the reading process and reading instruction are primarily interested in meaning. That is, they are concerned with how a reader processes larger units of language like sentences, paragraphs, and stories. The materials for the late 1970s were concerned with larger units of language than the word and the sentences found in basal readers and are now much more representative of the sentences children speak. For their interest in reading instruction and their tenacity in encouraging educators to learn about language and language learning, the linguists deserve much credit.

THE INTENSIVE PHONICS APPROACH

Since all—or almost all—approaches to the teaching of reading employ the use of phonics to some degree, this discussion will be restricted to those methods and materials which advocate intensive training in phonics; this approach is often referred to as the *total* or *intensive phonics approach* to the teaching of reading. Advocates of this approach believe that phonics should be introduced either before a sight vocabulary is established or concurrent with the introduction of sight words in the beginning reader. The approach requires much work with isolated words and phonic elements, and such work is usually begun at the initial stages of reading instruction. Word recognition skills are taught in a variety of sequences. The order in which the various phonic elements are introduced varies from one publisher's program to another's; some begin with short vowels, others with long vowels, others with consonants.

Programs which take the linguistic (decoding emphasis) approach and those which take the intensive phonics approach are not always easily distinguished from each other. We will briefly discuss, therefore, some of their similarities and differences.

Phonics and Linguistics:
Some Comparisons

There are more similarities between the phonics and linguistics approaches than differences. (The reader must continue to bear in mind that *linguistic approaches* here refers to those that emphasize decoding.) Indeed, several years ago, Chall (1967) stated that materials appearing with the "linguistics" label were advocating methods identical to materials with the "phonics" label and that a number of current materials could be classified as either phonic or linguistic. The characteristic the approaches hold in common is that they both emphasize decoding from the initial stages of instruction. The means by which they teach the decoding system, however, differs markedly.

Linguistic approaches emphasize the primary of oral language. Proponents of phonics approaches, however, have never completely agreed; while viewing competency in oral language as necessary for success in beginning reading, the proponents of phonics view the *printed word* as their primary concern. It is how this printed word is decoded into familiar speech that brings out the differences in the two approaches.

1   Many phonics proponents would teach the student to break up a word into parts. The word *cat* may be broken up in the decoding process as *c-at, ca-t,* or *c-a-t.* The linguist, however, would view this breaking up of words into isolated parts as a corruption of our language.

2   While both approaches emphasize the learning of letter-sound relationships, the linguist would have the child compare known whole words with unknown whole words. For example, the unknown word *mat* might be compared with the known words, *fat* and *man,* and through the use of such minimal contrasts, the student would learn new letter-sound relationships and subsequently be able to decode new words. The phonics approach, however, may emphasize individual letter-sound relationships. The teacher might state, for example, that the letter *b* stands for the sound you hear at the beginning of *boy, bounce,* and *bird* (which a linguist would support) or the letter *b* stands for the [buh] sound, the letter *d* stands for the [duh] sound (which a linguist would not support).

Analytic vs. Synthetic
Phonics

The analytic method of teaching phonics begins with the introduction of sight words before the student begins to learn letter-sound relationships. For example, after the words *run, rabbit, real, red,* and *ride* have been learned as sight words, the student is guided to realize that (1) the words all begin with the same sound when spoken, (2) they all begin with the same letter, and (3) the same written letter represents the same sound at the beginning of each word. It is probably safe to say that in many respects the linguistic approach leads children to learn letter-sound relationships in the same manner as the analytic approach.

The synthetic approach establishes letter-sound correspondence by drill on individual letters and letter combinations. For example, after the student has learned the letter-sound relationship for *m, a,* and *t,* the sounds may then be blended together to form the word *mat.*

For a more detailed description of analytic and synthetic phonics, see Chapter Ten.

Intensive Phonics Materials

Teachers may purchase a number of different workbooks which teach children to use phonics in decoding new words. Such workbooks are rarely used as total programs, however; they are generally used to present information the teacher may find lacking in the basic program. Examples of such phonics workbooks are the following:

1 *The Phonics We Use Series,*
   Rand McNally, 1978

2 *Phonics Is Fun,*
   Modern Curriculum Press, 1970, 1971.

3 *Merrill Phonics Skilltexts,*
   Charles E. Merrill, 1979.

There are also several basal reading programs which employ an intensive phonics approach. Some representative samples of those basal series follow:

1 *Keys to Reading,*
   The Economy Company, 1975.

2 *Lippincott's Basic Reading
   Program,*
   J. B. Lippincott Company, 1975.

3 *Open Court Basic Readers,*
   Open Court Publishing
   Company, 1976.

Phonics materials are neither inherently good nor inherently bad. But if the materials are used to teach phonics to the exclusion of other word recognition techniques, children may not learn those other important word recognition techniques. For this reason, approaches which emphasize only phonics must be carefully examined and used with discrimination.

ORTHOGRAPHIC VARIATIONS

The traditional orthography of the English language has been much criticized because of the inconsistencies with which it represents spoken English. A number of attempts have been made to change the traditional orthography in order to help beginning readers acquire a rapid mastery of sound-symbol correspondence. In some cases the changes have been relatively minor; in others the changes have resulted in sets of symbols which bear little resemblance to the twenty-six letters of our regular alphabet. Such changes are referred to here as orthographic variations.

Initial Teaching Alphabet

The Initial Teaching Alphabet, or i.t.a., is an attempt to establish a one-to-one relationship between grapheme and phoneme. Instead of the twenty-six letters of traditional orthography (T.O), i.t.a. uses forty-four characters to represent the sounds of our language. While i.t.a. is presented here as an approach to the teaching of reading, strictly speaking, it is not; the proponents of its use are quick to state that it is simply a new alphabet which regularizes the sound-letter correspondence and as such may be used with a variety of approaches.

The Development of i.t.a.   Credit for the development of i.t.a. is generally given to Sir James Pitman, an Englishman, although his grandfather, Sir Isaac Pitman (inventor of the Pitman Shorthand System) actually began work on an alphabet in 1842. And though James Pitman had been interested in a new alphabet for many years, it appears that the support he received from George Bernard Shaw in 1947 provided the impetus he needed to complete the project (Pitman and St. John, 1969, pp. 111–114). It was not until 1960, however, that Pitman convinced school officials in England that an experiment should be conducted whereby i.t.a. could be compared with T.O. (traditional orthography) in the initial stage of reading. With some difficulty he found twenty schools willing to try i.t.a. There was no problem in finding

Figure 7.3
Initial Teaching Alphabet.

Source: i.t.a. bulletin 4, 1 (Fall 1966), p. 12.

schools to provide control groups. Thus, the first experiment began in September 1961.

The early experiments provided highly satisfactory results for the students who learned to read with i.t.a. (Harrison, 1964, Chapters IV, XV, and XVI, pp. 127–161), and the alphabet became quite widely adopted in other English schools during the 1960s. During this early period John Downing became the chief spokesman for i.t.a.; he is now its major international proponent.

How It Is Used   The i.t.a. is a writing system—not a system for teaching writing, but a "system of ink marks on paper to represent the primary system of sounds in air which is the spoken language" (Downing, 1968). It is a forty-four-character alphabet with an almost one-to-one correspondence between sound and symbol. Of the forty-four characters, twenty-four are borrowed directly from the traditional alphabet. The letters *q* and *x* are omitted; the sounds usually associated with them in T.O. are represented by *kw* and *ks*, respectively, in i.t.a. spellings. Fourteen of the i.t.a. characters are combinations of familiar letters:

$$æ \ ɛ \ ie \ ue \ ch \ th \ th \ ʃh \ ŋ \ au \ ou \ wh \ œ \ oi$$

and six are peculiar to i.t.a.:

$$r \ ꜱ \ ʒ \ ɑ \ ω \ ꭐ$$

Woodcock (1966) offers the following additional principles as a guide to understanding the i.t.a. approach:

1   A capital letter is indicated in i.t.a. by writing the sound-symbol approximately one and one-half times the size of the lower-case symbol.
2   The abbreviations *Mr.* and *Mrs.* are spelled out in i.t.a.:

$$mister \ missꭐ$$

3   Foreign words and names retain traditional spellings in i.t.a. material.
4   Consonants are doubled in i.t.a. spellings if the corresponding letters in T.O. are also doubled *(ball, better, stuff)*.
5   Short vowel sounds are represented by traditional letter forms in i.t.a. *(a, e, i, o, u)*.
6   Long vowel sounds are represented by special double characters:

$$æ \ ɛ \ ie \ œ \ ue$$

Proponents maintain that the consistency of i.t.a. makes it possible to introduce letter sounds and letter combinations earlier than with T.O. An example of i.t.a. consistency between sound and symbol is provided here:

T.O.	i.t.a.
I	ie
eye	ie
by	bie
buy	bie
bye	bie
hide	hied
high	hie
tie	tie

Basically, once children learn the i.t.a. symbols, they are ready to read any word written with these symbols. If they see an unfamiliar word, they "spell" the word, an operation of pronouncing every sound in the new word. Therefore, the reader reads exactly what is written.

Several different programs using the i.t.a. approach have been developed in America and England since 1961, which allows a teacher of i.t.a. some freedom of choice. There are four basic types of i.t.a. programs as described by Downing (1968):

1 The most familiar is a transliterated i.t.a. version of T.O. basal readers. In this program the methods and content remain the same as in the T.O. edition. Only the alphabet used to print the words is changed from T.O. to i.t.a. One benefit of this program is that it is ideal for basic research comparing i.t.a. with T.O.

2 Another program easily converted to i.t.a. is the language-experience approach. Again, the only modification needed is the use of i.t.a. instead of T.O. in the teacher's and pupil's writing and reading of experience charts and booklets.

3 The Creativity-Discovery Approach is designed especially for use with i.t.a. The materials are written only in i.t.a. and emphasize a child's need for self-expression in creative writing. The Downing Readers provide an example of an i.t.a. basal series that uses the creativity-discovery approach.

4 There is a more formal expository approach, written specifically for i.t.a. as a teaching method. An example of this formal teaching approach is the *Early-to-Read* i.t.a. series by Albert Mazurkiewicz and Harold Tanyzer. The *Early-to-Read* series emphasizes the learning of individual sounds and corresponding i.t.a. symbols. It is based on the premise that children should first learn the individual sound symbols before being taught to synthesize them into words, sentences, paragraphs, and eventually stories.

While many school systems tried the i.t.a. approach in the mid 1960s and a number continued through the early 1970s, there are relatively few schools in North America where the initial teaching alphabet is currently used. Its use

lemonæd, lemonæd,
fiev sents a glass!

wun dæ polly, molly and jack wer
plæiŋ in ŧhe frunt yard.

up ŧhe street cæm a big truck. ŧhær
wos a sien on ŧhe truck ŧhat sed "**sircus.**"

mueꝣic cæm from ŧhe truck.

ŧhær wer ŧhree clouns on ŧhe back
ov ŧhe truck.

"ŧhe sircus iꝣ in toun!" caulld ŧhe
first cloun.

"wun week œnly!" caulld out
ŧhe second cloun.

"cum wun, cum aull!" caulld out
ŧhe ŧhird cloun.

Figure 7.4
Early-to-Read, Book 4,
Rev. Ed.

Source: Find A Way, (Book 4, Early-to-Read i.t.a. Program) by Albert J. Mazurkiewicz and Harold J. Tanyzer. Copyright © 1966 by Initial Teaching Alphabet Publications. Reprinted by permission of Fearon Pitman Publishers, Inc., Belmont, California.

in Great Britain is similarly diminishing. The i.t.a. approach is introduced in kindergarten or first grade and is intended to encourage early reading without frustration. It is not meant to be a panacea for all reading problems.

UNIFON

Like the initial teaching alphabet, UNIFON is an attempt to establish a one-to-one correspondence between sound and letter. The UNIFON system, also called the single-sound alphabet, consists of forty characters with which the child learns to read and spell in his initial school experiences.

Origins   The developer of UNIFON, John R. Malone, was an advocate of radical spelling reform both for faster mastery of the writing system and also for simplification of electronic data processing of language (Malone, 1962). By

1960 Malone had the system developed, and it was used experimentally with preschool children. Most of the experimental studies involving the use of UNIFON appear to have taken place in the period 1963–1966; there is little recent mention of the method in the literature.

The Method The forty characters of the UNIFON include twenty-two upper-case letters from the traditional English orthography plus eighteen additional characters which in most cases appear to be modifications of traditional letters. The letters are large block type (no upper- and lower-case), and all words are spelled exactly as they sound with no silent or double letters used. All words which sound the same are spelled the same; therefore context must determine the meaning of many words.

DMS

The diacritical marking system, usually referred to as DMS, is another attempt to eliminate the problem of inconsistency in the letter-sound relationships of English. With DMS, traditional orthography is maintained although modified somewhat by slashes, lines, dots, and asterisks. Edward Fry, who devised DMS, stated that its purpose is to "regularize orthography for beginning reading instruction by adding marks to regular letters. The marks are used because basic word form is preserved. They can later be vanished as the reading habit is established" (Fry, 1964, p. 528).

The basic rules for modifying the traditional orthography with DMS are as follows:

1 Regular consonants and short vowels are unchanged.
2 "Silent" letters have a slash mark (*ẃrīte, rīght*).
3 Long vowels have a bar-over mark (*mādé, māíd*).
4 Schwa vowels have a dot-over mark (*ȧgo, lemȯn*).
5 Other consistent sounds than those above are indicated by the bar under (*is, aṵtō*).
6 Digraphs have a bar under both letters (*shut, chat*).
7 Exceptions to the above basic rules have an asterisk above the letter (*̇of, ̇oncé*) (Fry, 1964, p. 528).

The major advantage of the DMS over other modified alphabet systems like i.t.a. and UNIFON is that the regular letters of our alphabet are maintained. DMS has not become widely used, however, and Fry (1967) himself has reported that his method was no better than the traditional orthography.

Words in Color
Another method devised to overcome the inconsistencies of letter-sound relationship is one devised by Caleb Gattegno. Called *Words in Color*, it is an attempt to simplify the English language for the beginning reader (Gattegno, 1968).

Origins In 1957, while working for UNESCO in Ethiopia, Gattegno devised this method for teaching illiterate adults to read and write. In 1958 Dr. Gattegno's experimentation with English came to the United States, first in

Texas with kindergarten children and later in California (Gattegno and Hinman, 1966).

In studying the English language, Gattegno identified forty-seven distinctive phonemes. He divided these forty-seven phonemes into twenty vowel sounds and twenty-seven consonant sounds. As a way to make the language more phonetic, he introduced the aspect of color into the program. Each of the forty-seven vowel and consonant sounds was coded to a different color shade so that each phoneme could be distinguished from the others on the basis of color alone. *Words in Color* does not change the traditional spelling of words or introduce any new graphic symbols into the language.

The Method   Classroom materials consist of twenty-one charts which progress from the regular to the irregular spelling of words, eight phonic code color charts which present a systematic organization of vowels and consonants and their varied spellings, and a set of word cards which introduce words of different parts of speech.

The eight colored phonic wall charts are hung around the classroom to be used as a constant reference for the children. The charts are divided into forty-seven columns, each representing one of the unique phoneme sounds. Under each vowel or consonant heading is a vertical listing of all the different ways that particular phoneme sound can be spelled. For example under the [ʃ] phoneme sound (coded in mauve) are listed f, ff, fe, ph, lf, gh, ffe, pph, and ft also color coded in mauve (Gattegno, 1968). The child learns that the sound [ʃ] can be spelled in at least nine different ways. A distinctive sound is always represented by the same color regardless of its spelling. The short sound of [a], for example, is white whether it is in *pat* or *laugh*. It is Gattegno's belief that children use these color clues to help fix the image of the sound in their mind.

Advantages   Bentley (1966) states that there is no problem with reversals (such as *on* for *no*) "since the criteria of spoken speech (in which we do not reverse words) are connected to written speech from the beginning" (p. 517). *Words in Color* may also have some value as a motivational device for teaching children who have experienced difficulty by another method. The introduction of color and the novelty of the presentation may provide motivation for slow learners and less interested students. *Words in Color* may also be more suited for slower children because initially all the words presented are regular and the students are not confused by spelling irregularities. However, this spelling regularity can be maintained *without* the use of color.

Disadvantages   Because of the similarity in hues, some children may have trouble discriminating one color from another. Another disadvantage is that initial reading instruction must be restricted to the classroom, where the child has access to the phonic color-code charts. The child never reads words printed in color outside of the classroom charts and the few words a teacher may write with colored chalk on the blackboard. Clearly, the color blind child is at a real disadvantage if this approach is used. Furthermore, there is no evidence to indicate that learning to read with color is superior to any other method of learning to read.

Peabody Rebus Program

The *Peabody Rebus Reading Program* is a beginning reading program which uses pictures—the rebuses—in place of words in teaching children how to read. The development of the program began in 1964 as a method of teaching reading to mentally retarded children. Authors of the program, which is published by American Guidance Service, Inc., are Richard W. Woodcock, Charlotte R. Clarke, and Cornelia Oakes Davies.

The first characters the child "reads" are almost exclusively pictures with the exception of a few symbols which stand for common function words; for example, the symbol + represents the word *and*. As the child reads, pictures rather than words are read; as the child learns to comprehend the rebuses, words are introduced which gradually replace the rebuses.

The basic materials consist of three paperback workbooks and two paperback readers. By the time the child completes the program he or she should have a sight vocabulary of approximately 120 words and should be able to read primer materials from most published basal reading series.

MULTI-MEDIA APPROACHES

Through the 1950s the materials used for reading instruction were almost exclusively books and workbooks. In the 1960s a number of programs which employed machines for the teaching of reading became popular. In the 1970s the use of computer chips—tiny circuits on which information is stored—made devices which could rapidly display letters and words available at a relatively low cost. In this section the use of such machines to teach reading will be described as multi media approaches, and the discussion will be limited to those multi-media approaches that use machines to a major or minor degree for teaching reading.

The EDL Program

The Educational Development Laboratories, better known as EDL, market several machines to be used for reading instruction. Among the most widely used of the EDL machines is the *Tach-X* tachistoscope, a sophisticated film-strip projector which can be used to project images on a screen for as long as 1½ seconds or as briefly as $\frac{1}{100}$ of a second. The *Tach-X* is intended for group use; a smaller hand-held tachistoscope, the *Flash-X,* is designed for individual use.

Perhaps the most popular EDL machine is the *Controlled Reader,* which is also an elaborate filmstrip projector. For use with the *Controlled Reader* there is a variety of filmstrips which range in difficulty from prereading activities to college level instruction.

EDL also markets what it intends to be a total reading program, which includes filmstrip projectors, filmstrips, audio tapes, workbooks, and books. While some teachers have expressed reluctance to use mechanical devices in the classroom because they are difficult to operate, it has generally been the contention of EDL that most first-grade children can be taught to use their machines, thus freeing the teacher for other teaching responsibilities. At the prereading and beginning reading stages, however, many teachers prefer not to use such devices until students have a mastery of essential word recognition and comprehension skills.

Responsive Environment

The responsive environment began as an approach to teach reading to pre-kindergarten children through the use of a special typewriter. This typewriter became popularly known as the "talking typewriter" and received much attention among educators and child psychologists. Its inventor, O. K. Moore, developed the machine in order to provide the learner with an environment in which to explore and interact freely in problem-solving situations.

According to Moore, a responsive environment meets the following conditions:

1 It permits the learner to explore freely.
2 It informs the learner immediately about the consequences of his actions.
3 It is self-pacing—that is, events happen within the environment at a rate determined by the learner.
4 It permits the learner to make full use of his capacity for discovering relations of various kinds.
5 Its structure is such that the learner is likely to make a series of interconnected discoveries about the physical, cultural, and social world (Aukerman, 1971, pp. 424–425).

As children operate in Moore's "responsive environment" they are seated in front of a typewriter and—in the initial stages—are encouraged to freely explore the keyboard. Free exploration is followed by matching exercises and later by word construction, reading, and writing.

Other Machines for Reading Instruction

Several machines have been marketed as supplementary aids for the teacher. Perhaps the most widely used is the *Language Master* by Bell and Howell, which allows students to see a word on a card and then hear that word pronounced. The students may then record their pronunciation of the same word and compare it to the prerecorded voice. The *Language Master* is easy to use and has applications at all achievement levels.

The *Craig Reader,* which presents a filmstrip on a small screen, has been a popular addition in situations where students experienced difficulty with other methods. Its use, however, is by no means limited to remedial students.

In the late 1970s the *Speak and Spell Reader* by Texas Instruments became popular for both home and school use. The device has several hundred words stored in memory chips; these words are used in a variety of word games which the user plays by pressing the appropriate buttons. It is likely that many similar devices—with a greater capacity for word and sentence storage—will become available in the 1980s.

Machines have been designed to increase speed of reading, to combine audio instruction with the printed word, and to improve word recognition skills in a variety of ways. Although they are more costly than software and may occasionally break down, they have the decided advantage of having unlimited patience. Furthermore, they give the teacher more time for doing the things that only a human being can do.

Because both this chapter and the following chapter are coauthored by the same writers, the authors' viewpoint is found at the end of Chapter Eight.

REFERENCES

Aukerman, R. C. *Approaches to Beginning Reading.* New York: John Wiley and Sons, 1971.

Bentley, H. "Words in Color." *Elementary English* 43 (1966): 515–517.

Bishop, M. "Good Usage, Bad Usage, and Usage." In *The American Heritage Dictionary of the English Language,* edited by W. Morris. Boston: American Heritage Publishing Co., and Houghton Mifflin, 1971, p. xxiii.

Bloomfield, L. "Linguistics and Reading." *Elementary English Review* 19 (April 1942): 125–130; (May 1942): 183–186.

Bloomfield, L., and Barnhart, C. L. *Let's Read: A Linguistic Approach.* Detroit: Wayne State University Press, 1961.

Bloomfield, L., and Barnhart, C. L. *Let's Read,* Levels 1–9. Bronxville, N.Y.: Clarence L. Barnhart, 1966.

Bosman, D. R. *Mobility in Basal Reading Groups.* Unpublished paper, University of Wisconsin, 1972.

Britton, Gwyneth E. and Lumpkin, Margaret C., "For Sale: Subliminal Bias in Textbooks". *The Reading Teacher,* Vol. 31, No. 1, (October, 1977), pp. 40–45.

Buchanan, C. D., and Sullivan Associates. *Programmed Reading.* New York: McGraw-Hill Book Company, 1963.

Chall, J. S. *Learning to Read: The Great Debate.* New York: McGraw-Hill Book Company, 1967.

Dick and Jane as Victims (Sex Stereotyping in Children's Readers). Princeton, N.J.: Women on Words and Images, 1972.

Downing, J. "Alternative Teaching Methods in i.t.a." *Elementary English* 45 (1968): 942–951.

Educational Products Information Exchange Materials Report, Selector's Guide for Elementary School Reading Programs.

Volume 2, No. 83m. New York: EPIE Institute, 1978.

Fries, C. C. *Linguistics and Reading.* New York: Holt, Rinehart and Winston, 1962.

Fries, C. C.; Wilson, R. G.; and Rudolph, M. K. *Merrill Linguistic Readers.* Columbus, Ohio: Charles E. Merrill Books, 1966.

Fry, E. "A Diacritical Marking System to Aid Beginning Reading Instruction." *Elementary English* 41 (1964): 526–529.

Fry, E. "First Grade Reading Instruction Using Diacritical Marking System, Initial Teaching Alphabet and Basal Reading System—Extended to Second Grade." *The Reading Teacher* 20 (1967): 687–693.

Gattegno, C. *Teaching Reading with Words in Color.* New York: Educational Solutions, 1968.

Gattegno, C., and Hinman, D. "Words in Color—The Morphologico-algebraic Approach to Teaching Reading." In *The Disabled Reader: Education of the Dyslexic Child,* edited by J. Money. Baltimore: Johns Hopkins Press, 1966.

Gelb, I. J. *A Study of Writing.* Chicago: University of Chicago Press, 1952.

Goodman, K. "A Communicative Theory of the Reading Curriculum." *Elementary English* 40 (1963): 290–298.

Goodman, K. *The Psycholinguistic Nature of the Reading Act.* Detroit: Wayne State University Press, 1968.

Goodman, K. "Reading: A Psycholinguistic Guessing Game." *Journal of the Reading Specialist* 4 (1967): 126–135.

Goodman, K., and Burke, C. "When a Child Learns to Read: A Psychological Analysis." *Elementary English* 48 (1970): 121–129.

Hall, R. A. *Sound and Spelling in English.* Philadelphia: Chilton Books, 1961.

Harrison, M. *Instant Reading: The Story of the Initial Teaching Alphabet.* London: Pitman, 1964.

Heilman, A. W. *Principles and Practices of Teaching Reading.* 4th ed. Columbus, Ohio: Charles E. Merrill Publishing Co., 1977.

Ives, S., and Ives, J. P. "Contributions of Linguistics to Reading and Spelling, Part 1: Linguistics and Reading." In *Linguistics in School Programs,* editied by A. H. Marckwardt. The Sixty-Ninth Yearbook of the National Society for the Study of Education. Chicago: University of Chicago Press, 1970.

Lamb, P. *Linguistics in Proper Perspective.* 2nd ed. Columbus: Charles E. Merrill Publishing Co., 1977.

Lamb, P. "Linguistics and the Teaching of Reading." *Indiana Reading Quarterly* 4 (1972): 14–16.

Lapp, Diane and Flood, James. *Teaching Reading to Every Child.* New York: Macmillan Publishing Co., Inc. 1978.

Lefevre, C. A. *Linguistics and the Teaching of Reading.* New York: McGraw-Hill Book Co., 1964.

Malone, J. R. "The Larger Aspects of Spelling Reform." *Elementary English* 39 (1962): 435–445.

Mathews, M. M. *Teaching to Read, Historically Considered.* Chicago: University of Chicago Press, 1966.

McCutcheon, Gail; Kyle, Dian; and Skovira, Robert. "Characters in Basal Readers: Does 'Equal' Now Mean 'Same'?" *The Reading Teacher,* Vol. 32, No. 4, January 1979, pp. 438–441.

O'Donnell, M., and Van Roekel, B. H. *The Harper and Row Basic Reading Program,* Evanston, Ill.: Harper and Row, 1966.

Pitman, J., and St. John, J. R. *Alphabets and Reading: The Initial Teaching Alphabet.* New York: Pitman, 1969.

Robinett, R. F. "A Linguistic Approach to Beginning Reading for Bilingual Children." In

First Grade Reading Programs, Perspectives in Reading No. 5.* Newark, Del.: International Reading Association, 1965, pp. 132–149.

Robinett, R. F., Rojas, P., and Bell, P. W. *Miami Linguistic Series.* New York: D. C. Heath and Co., 1964–1966.

Shuy, R. W. "A Linguistic Background for Developing Beginning Reading Materials for Black Children." In *Teaching Black Children to Read,* edited by J. C. Baratz and R. W. Shuy. Washington, D.C.: Center for Applied Linguistics, 1969(a).

Shuy, R. W. "Some Language and Cultural Differences in a Theory of Reading." In *Psycholinguistics and the Teaching of Reading,* edited by K. S. Goodman and J. T. Fleming. Newark, Del.: International Reading Association, 1969(b).

Shuy, R. W. "Some Things That Reading Teachers Need to Know About Language." Paper presented at IRA Conference, Atlantic City, April 1971.

Smith, N. B. *American Reading Instruction.* Newark, Del.: International Reading Association, 1965.

Smith, R. J., and Barrett, T. C. *Teaching Reading in the Middle Grades.* Reading, Mass.: Addison-Wesley, 1974.

Staiger, R. C. "Basal Reading Programs: How Do They Stand Today?" In *Current Issues in Reading,* edited by N. B. Smith. Newark, Del.: International Reading Association, 1969, pp. 283–293.

Waite, R. R. "Further Attempts to Integrate and Urbanize First Grade Textbooks: A Research Study." *Journal of Negro Education* 7 (Winter 1968): 62–69.

Wardhaugh, R. *Reading: A Linguistic Perspective.* New York: Harcourt, Brace and World, 1969.

Woodcock, R. *ITA for Teachers.* New York: ITA, 1966.

Wright, T., and Halliwell, J. O., eds. *Reliquiae Antiquae.* London: 1841, p. 63.

PREVIEW

In Chapter Eight, the language experience approach and individualized reading are given detailed attention. After reading this chapter you will better understand both the underlying principles and the teaching strategies involved in these two widely used approaches to reading instruction. Some of the more significant issues related to individualized reading are discussed and Alden Moe's and Dale Johnson's positions on these issues become clear. We live in an age in which computers are assuming increasing importance. Appropriately, then, the use of computers in reading instruction and reading program management is discussed. Team teaching and plans involving departmentalized reading instruction are briefly discussed, and Chapter Eight concludes with a statement of Moe and Johnson's viewpoint. There is a large amount of material in these two chapters and it is presented in a readable, interesting style.

8

Current Approaches, Part Two

Dale D. Johnson, University of Wisconsin

Alden J. Moe, Purdue University

OBJECTIVES

After you have read this chapter, you should be able to:

1. Describe the similarities and differences between two current instructional approaches in reading: The language-experience, and the individualized.

2. Specify the instructional practices appropriate to each of these approaches.

3. Describe three levels of participation for individualized reading instruction.

4. Identify three intra-class and intra-school organizational arrangements.

The preceding chapter presented a brief history of reading instruction and then described in detail several approaches used to teach reading in American schools. Included was a discussion of basal reading, linguistic, phonic and multi-media materials and orthographic variations.

In the present chapter, approaches, techniques, and materials are discussed that are more pupil and teacher created and directed. These approaches make less direct use of the types of commercially published materials discussed in Chapter Seven. A description of the Language Experience Approach and Individualized Reading forms the heart of the contents of this chapter; but attention is also given to other ways in which children are organized for reading instruction.

The label *language-experience* is, in itself, a hint as to what this approach entails. In essence the term implies that reading should be based on the language and experiences of the learner. In her book *Teacher* (1963), Sylvia Ashton-Warner describes her work with the Maori people of New Zealand. She entitles her method "Organic Reading" and considers it a bridge between nonreading and reading. In defining the "Key Vocabulary," the first words a child learns to read, Ashton-Warner articulates a fundamental tenet of the language-experience approach. She states: "First words must have an intense meaning. First words must be already part of the dynamic life. First words must be made of the stuff of the child himself, whatever and wherever the child" (p. 32). The language-experience approach is a method in which the reading materials are developed by recording the spoken language of the child, so that what the child reads reflects experiences as well as language patterns. The four language arts—listening, speaking, reading, and writing—are integrated.

The language-experience method is, at least *at the outset,* a whole-word approach. Further, it is a whole-word approach in which the words are obtained from the child. But it is much more than that. Mary Anne Hall (1972) discusses the relationship between oral language and reading, and cites four implications for reading instruction based on the relationship between oral and written language.

1 The language of initial reading material should represent the child's speech patterns.
2 Reading instruction should build upon the relationship between spoken and written language.
3 Reading experiences should be taught as communication experiences even in the beginning stages.
4 Reading instruction must be related to the total language program (p. 18).

Children come to school with highly developed language facility. They can use and understand thousands of words in conversation. They have command of most syntactical structures and can understand and generate countless utterances new to their experience. With the language-experience approach children are given the opportunity to use their private storehouses of language abilities. The language-experience approach has been viewed as both a *group* and an *individual* method. When used most effectively, it is really both. Individual interests, needs, and experiences are accommodated and group processes are developed.

Procedures
The language-experience method is most often used in *beginning* reading, commencing in either kindergarten or first grade. In some schools the approach is used for a few months only, while in others it is the basic program throughout first and into second grade. It may also be used with older children needing remedial instruction. Some of the comments in this section, though primarily pertaining to initial instruction, may also apply to older children.

Vocabulary   Proponents of the language-experience approach believe that children learn to read more easily if the initial vocabulary is important and interesting to them. They believe that "first words" should come from the child, not from some external source. In this they disagree with the phonics enthusiasts and structural linguists such as Bloomfield who believe first words should be highly patterned and have consistent letter-sound correspondences to make decoding easier. They also differ with the approach taken by the authors of many basal readers, which build vocabulary according to frequency: those words that are thought to occur most often in the pupil's speaking and understanding vocabularies are taught first.

With the language-experience approach, the teacher regularly asks the children to suggest or list words that they would like to learn to read. This may be done daily, twice daily, or more often. When the child tells the teacher a word, it is written on a blank piece of paper or a card and given to the child, who then practices reading the word, tracing it with a finger, and perhaps writing it.

Many teachers have each child develop an alphabetized vocabulary book. As each new word is learned the child copies it into the vocabulary book. This becomes a personal list of words used when writing sentences or stories. Others have the child keep the word cards in a "word bank," usually a sturdy file box. As words accumulate, the child can be tested informally. Sylvia Ashton-Warner believes that if children cannot remember one of their words, the card should be destroyed because the word was apparently not important to them. In pairs or small groups, children can take turns reading their words to the other children and can then try to read the other children's words. Some children may wish to draw pictures or do other artwork to illustrate their words. They can label their pictures and display them about the room.

Individual Dictation   As time permits, children should be given the opportunity to dictate short stories, observations, poems, beliefs, questions, or the like to the teacher or teacher's aide. The teacher or aide serves as "secretary" or "recorder" and writes the child's dictation, legibly, on a sheet of paper or newsprint with a marker, pen, or crayon. The child may then read the story to the teacher, who can help with unlearned words, if necessary. Children can practice reading the story at their desk, or illustrate it, or record words in the vocabulary book while others in the class are dictating their stories. When all the children in the group have finished the dictations, some children may want to read their stories to each other or to the group, and they may also want to read someone else's story.

There is a disagreement about vocabulary and syntactic control in these stories. Psycholinguists generally believe that the stories should be recorded in the language patterns of the child, whether grammatically "correct" or not. Some reading specialists, on the other hand, believe sentences, no matter how dictated, should be simplified and rendered grammatically correct. Heilman contends that the difficulty of controlling vocabulary is a weakness in dictated stories. He believes that too many words may be introduced at one time and basic sight words may not be repeated frequently enough to ensure mastery (Heilman, 1972, p. 210). Few people would advocate altering the spelling of words to match the dialectal pronunciation of the child. For example, if the child says "hep" for *help,* it should still be spelled *help.*

It is our contention that dictated stories should be recorded, as closely as possible, in the syntactic structures of the child. This means a teacher must be acutely aware of the dialects of pupils. Nothing is more frustrating to a child, or potentially injurious to self-concept, than to have one's language "corrected" when, in a social milieu, it is perfectly acceptable. On the other hand, since all of us talk in thought clusters that contain run-on sentences and repetitions, it will be necessary for the teacher to determine sentence boundaries and punctuate accordingly.[1]

One of the greatest advantages of the language-experience approach is its ability to match printed with oral language to facilitate interest and comprehension. It would be an error to destroy this advantage by being overly concerned with vocabulary control and repetition.

Many children will need motivation for dictating stories. The following short list of topics can be used for individual or group dictation. These topics can be mentioned in class, listed on a bulletin board marked "Topics for the Day" (or week), displayed about the room, or posed as questions.

Some Topics for Dictation

animals	toys	mother	father
sister	brother	home	friends
church	synagogue	parades	teacher
ghosts	rainy days	lazy days	games
vacations	school room	summer	our principal
winter fun	night time	airplanes	seasonal holidays
trains	boats	sledding	favorite books
basketball	school work	policemen	the grocery store
Yom Kippur	Christmas	Easter	the family car
Valentine's Day	monsters	TV shows	other countries
magazines	dreams	submarines	school programs

Teachers can easily expand this list by discovering the interests of their pupils and by being attuned to timely topics and events. While many children will be able to select their own topics, others will need suggestions to get started.

Group Experience Stories   Though individually dictated stories are generally preferable to group stories, the teacher cannot be available to twenty or more children individually very often. As an alternative to individual stories, group experience stories are often very successful. Some children respond better in a group situation and may contribute more freely. Developing group stories is often a good way to introduce reading on the first day of school, and is often used as part of a basal reader approach.

Construction of group experience stories develops from group discussion about meaningful *shared* experiences or interests. Some examples follow.

Experiences for Group Stories

a class pet or animal
plans for a class trip

---

[1] Refer, again, to the discussion of the teacher's editorial role in Chapter Four.

a recurring activity:
coming to school
recess time
the hot lunch menu
a TV show the group has seen
a recent field trip
favorite food
grandmothers
If I could go to the moon . . .
If we sailed across the ocean . . .
If it was always night time . . .
If Pooh Bear visited our classroom . . .

Discussion topics can be in the realm of reality or fancy. The main concern for the teacher is to discover topics interesting to the *children*. The constraints of time and interest will determine how long and involved the discussions become.

The group stories can be written as the discussion is under way or as a summary to a completed discussion. The latter is often preferable, since discussions can deteriorate when frequently interrupted for recording sentences. It is useful, though, to keep an abbreviated record, either on the chalkboard or on note paper, of the main points being discussed. The disadvantage to writing stories summarizing discussions is that the spontaneity and originality of the children's thoughts and language may be lost.

After a certain period of discussion, the teacher might say, "Now, let's write about what we've been discussing. Let's write a story about what we've said. Who can think of a good title for our story?" After an agreement is reached, the title can be recorded. While some teachers write group experience stories on the chalkboard, many others prefer to write them on large newsprint, tag board, or poster paper so they can be saved and perhaps illustrated.

The following dialogue from a first-grade class shows the procedure followed in writing a group story about a discussion of "favorite foods."

Teacher: Do we all agree that "Hamburgers and Malts" will be the title of our story?

Class: Yes.

(Teacher writes "Hamburgers and Malts" on a large piece of paper, using a felt-tipped pen.)

Teacher: How shall we begin our story?

Lisa: Let's say, "Some food tastes *icky*." (Class giggles)

Teacher: Shall we begin "Some food tastes *icky*"?

Class: Yes.

Kirk: No, let's start, "Down with gravy!" (Class giggles)

Julie: I like "Some food tastes *icky*."

Others: Me too. Let's begin that way.

(Teacher writes "Some food tastes icky.")

This group experience story session continued for about fifteen minutes—after an earlier fifteen-minute discussion of favorite foods. The final product was:

Hamburgers and Malts

Some food tastes icky.
Prunes, potatoes, beets and corn.
Pizza is good.
Breakfast cereal, too.
Also hot dogs, coke, and steak.
But, we could eat hamburgers and
  malts every single day.

The teacher's role, in addition to writing the story, is to ask questions and interject comments to help the children recall their discussion. The story is written in the children's own language.

Once the story is written, the teacher reads it to the class, pointing to each word. Children are then asked to read the story in unison along with the teacher. Finally, children can volunteer to read different lines or the entire story by themselves.

In one elementary school, four first-grade classes discussed the same topic, a field trip they had all been on. Each class constructed its own experience story and then shared it with the other classes. The stories were so different that a reader might have wondered if the children had been on the same trip!

Many teachers who use the language-experience approach like to prepare mineographed books for each child. After each story has been completed, the teacher writes or types it on a ditto master and duplicates a copy for each child, leaving space for illustrations. Each child can make a cover of heavy construction paper and write a title on it—"Our Stories" or "Words of Wisdom from Wilson School" or something else. In addition to the individual duplicated books, a class "big book" will grow as each story is completed on large paper. Some teachers make an additional copy of the large experience story, which can be marked or cut up for use in developing word identification and comprehension skills.

Thus at the end of the first day of school children may take home a story they have helped write and read it to their family—often with a great deal of excitement and pride.

Developing Reading Comprehension An effective means of developing reading comprehension is by asking questions. In his "Taxonomy of Comprehension," T. C. Barrett (1979) describes four levels of comprehension questions: Literal, Inferential, Evaluative, and Appreciative. Too often teachers (and test makers) ask only literal questions, which simply require the recognition or recall of specific facts and details from a story. Asking questions *beyond* the literal level (such as, "What would have happened if . . .?" "Do you think this could really happen?" "Have you ever had a bad dream? What was it?") can provoke much more thought and generate far greater interest than using such questions as "What color was the hat?" The suggestions about reading comprehension in Chapter Eleven are particularly pertinent to the use of group experience stories. In any approach, considerable attention must be devoted to the development of reading comprehension. In Chapter Eleven, Barrett's taxonomy is discussed in detail and this most important aspect of reading is given thorough treatment.

Word Recognition Skills The language-experience approach is often criticized for being too "whole-word" oriented and for neglecting the development of needed word recognition skills. Most beginning readers need practice in auditory and visual discrimination and with the basic decoding skills of phonic, structural, and contextual analysis. All are examined in detail in Chapters Nine and Ten. In the language-experience approach these skills are taught *as the child needs them* and as the experience stories provide opportunities for teaching them, rather than in the arbitrary sequences found in basal reading programs.

The teacher can develop students' visual discrimination by asking them to find a word in the story that begins, or ends, or has the same medial letters as a word the teacher writes on a flashcard or on the chalkboard. One way to increase auditory discrimination is to say and repeat a word, for example *dog.* Then read a group story in unison and ask children to raise their hands when they hear words that begin (or end) like *dog.* The procedure can be repeated with other words.

In describing the word recognition development in her first-grade language-experience class, Dahl (1971, p. 16) said:

In the Language Experience approach, the number of words and sentences in beginning stories lends itself to presenting many skills in an incidental manner. For instance:

1 Example of a Group Skill
After we recorded stories about our gerbils, students were asked to locate the word *gerbil.* When some of the children pointed to the word gerbils, a lesson in forming simple plurals was a natural thing and was easy for the class to understand. We then made plurals of many known words:

rat	bed	carrot	tail	cage
rats	beds	carrots	tails	cages

2 Example of an Individual Skill
A little girl dictated the sentence—"Harriet can drink from a bottle."

As *drink* was printed, the little girl said, "*Drink, dream, drive*—they all start the same, don't they?" Thus, our first lesson on blends was taught to an individual early in October.

3 Example of an Individual Skill
   Student (dictating): "The rat didn't like her, so he went away."
   Teacher (printing): "The rat did not. . . ."
   Student: "Not *did not,* I said *didn't.*"
   This provided a perfect opportunity to present contractions!

can not   did not   is not   have not

Through similar experiences and activities nearly all phonics generalizations (letter-sound correspondence), structural components, and syntactic and semantic contextual clues can be taught. Since there is no research evidence supporting any *particular* sequence of word recognition features, and since children often learn best those things that have immediate application, there is no reason why the language-experience approach cannot be an effective vehicle for developing decoding ability. It will be imperative, however, for the *teacher* to have a thorough understanding of word identification skills and techniques so they can be introduced when opportunities arise.[2]

Creative Writing   Creative writing is an integral part of this method of reading instruction. Children begin to write by copying words from their vocabulary cards and by copying individual or group experience stories. Some children will write two or more words and combine words into thought units (which may or may not be grammatically "correct") about themselves or their experiences. Handwriting, spelling, punctuation, and grammatical accuracy should not be criticized during the first several months of writing, since this can stifle creativity. But the teacher can give help and suggestions while the children are writing. Often children will ask the teacher to help them spell words or to suggest alternate words. Many teachers provide the children with desk copies of the alphabet for reference.

Since story building and language usage are inherent to this approach, children begin to write very early. Before long children will be writing their own small books, often with the help of the teacher or a classmate. Soon after beginning to write and illustrate short books, children may become interested in sharing their books with other pupils and in reading books written by their classmates. Reading and writing thus reinforce each other again. The teacher's role is to be a resource person—answering questions and providing suggestions—and a listener. As children increase their writing efforts and read more works of their classmates, they will feel the need for accuracy in capitalization, punctuation, and spelling. The list of topics presented earlier (p. 208) provides possibilities for creative writing as well as story dictation. Other topics are presented in the next section, "Individualized Reading" (p. 217).

Printed Materials

Children cannot go through life reading only materials written by themselves, their teacher, or their fellow pupils. The ability to read published printed

---

[2] One might question how a teacher handles this for every child in a class. (The editors.)

matter is as important in school as it is useful in life, and it opens countless doorways to knowledge and pleasure.

Teachers using the language-experience approach see to it that large numbers of magazines, paperback books, school newspapers, trade books, pre-primers, primers, and early readers are available in the classroom. These materials afford the children an opportunity to reinforce skills they have learned, locate words from their experience stories, and develop wider interests. Children should be encouraged to visit the school library if there is one, and urged to get a library card for the nearest public library, to which most language-experience teachers arrange an early field trip. Usually by the end of the first grade most children are reading widely in published materials within the framework of an individualized reading program, which naturally follows a beginning language-experience approach.

One criticism levelled at the language-experience approach is that it makes evaluation difficult. Although there are relevant evaluation and record keeping techniques (discussed in the next section), end of chapter tests are unavailable, and with individualized vocabularies, standardized achievement tests are not really applicable. In these authors' opinions, however, the *development of reading ability* should take precedence over the *measurement of it.*[3]

Summary

The language-experience approach to reading instruction is based on the belief that children will learn best when they are *interested* and when reading material originates with children themselves and reflects their own experience and language. Though this approach is most often used as a beginning reading method in kindergarten or first grade, it can also be used successfully with older children needing remedial help and with children of culturally or linguistically diverse backgrounds.[4]

INDIVIDUALIZED READING

An individualized reading program is a natural extension of the language-experience approach to beginning reading. The essential difference between the two is that most of the reading material in an individualized program is published—books, magazines, newspapers—while most of the materials in the language-experience method are prepared by the children or their teachers. Individualized reading with prepared materials is rarely used as an *initial* reading method. Teachers usually begin individualized reading *after* children have achieved a certain independence in reading—that is, when they possess a reasonable sight vocabulary and basic word recognition skills. So most schools do not begin using this method until late in first grade or in

---

[3]One might ask how one knows a skill is developing unless it's measured. (The editors.)

[4]One might ask whether there are any weaknesses in the language-experience approach, as there are of all other methods/approaches discussed. (The editors.)

second or third grade. It can follow virtually any initial program: basal, modified alphabet, programmed, linguistic, or language-experience.

The term *individualized reading* means many things to many people and is consequently hard to define. Most elementary teachers individualize their reading instruction to some degree. Many proponents of individualized reading view it more as a belief about reading than a method.

In an individualized reading program, the pace is determined by each child's strengths, interests, and needs as assessed by a discerning and knowledgeable teacher. These same factors determine the material selection for reading. During reading time in an individualized classroom, children will be reading alone, not in groups with the teacher, and each child will probably be reading from a different self-selected book. The teacher is free to provide skill instruction as it is needed, to help with words, and, very importantly, to engage in private conferences with each child as often as possible. Sharing periods will be held occasionally, and special skill groups will be formed when more than one child shows the same need. Interest groups are sometimes formed, but all grouping is flexible, and groups are dissolved when no longer needed.

Individualized reading is not new; its origins can probably be traced to the very beginning of reading instruction prior to the advent of mass education. During the past decades, interest in individualized reading instruction has greatly increased. Several books, countless journal articles, a variety of conferences, topics, and seminars at professional meetings, and a number of research studies have resulted from this renewed interest. Terms such as *Individually Prescribed Instruction, Individually Guided Education, Computer-Assisted Instruction, programmed reading* and *skills management systems* have been the most recent manifestations; their application to reading instruction will be discussed later in this section.

Individualized reading is based on the recognition that children differ greatly in many ways: children have their own abilities, motivations, wishes, drives, thoughts, and interests. Reading is recognized as a very personal, individual, often private experience. It is common knowledge that most children (and adults) work long and hard when they have the opportunity to choose their own tasks and set their own goals. Similarly, it seems logical that children enjoy reading more and can sustain their interest longer when they select their own materials.

Individualized reading is a belief about reading rather than a method. Individualization means many things and one can visualize a continuum of individualization both in degree and kind. The following definitions of individualized reading distinguish three categories or levels of participation. The categories are not totally discrete:

1. *Partial or occasional individualization is the first category.* This refers to the class in which the teacher primarily uses a basic, published program. This may be one of the many basal programs, a phonic/linguistic program, or a more unique program such as the use of a modified alphabet. From time to time children read independently and individually. This individual reading may take the form of supplementary reading (before or after a group story or activity), a replacement for seatwork skill pages, a periodic reinforcement for a

part of a unit in language arts, or some other subject, reward, or any number of other forms. The point is that in this category individualized reading occurs occasionally and as a supplement to a basic, published reading program.

2. *A second category of individualized reading pertains to a prescriptive, teacher-directed program.* Children in groups, for example, do not read the same basal story as others, or do the same workbook pages; but they *are* directed in their individualized program. What they do is prescribed for them. In such a program a good deal of diagnostic testing is done, and the teacher identifies and assigns the most beneficial books, stories and skill-development materials. In recent years management systems in reading have become very popular. Program independent management systems such as *Fountain Valley* and *The Wisconsin Design,* and program dependent management systems, which are integral to many of newest basal programs such as Ginn 720, facilitate individualization of reading at the prescriptive level. Children do things independently but with direction. Of course, prescriptive individualized programs also make use of independent, free reading activities on occasion. Management systems are discussed later in this chapter.

3. *The third category of individualized reading stipulates that children should be permitted to read when and why they wish.* Its proponents argue that unless a child is ready to read and is interested in it, instruction of any sort will not be very meaningful. In the *laissez-faire* approach, the teacher functions solely as a resource person or consultant who can provide help and suggestions when requested. Children decide what to read, when to read and what skill work to do, if any.

These are the three broad categories of individualized reading: *Partial, prescriptive,* and *totally student-directed.* If you will visualize a continuum with an infinite scale, partial individualization is at one extreme (in fact most teachers would not refer to it as an individualized program); *the laissez faire-* "do your own thing"-approach would be on the other extreme (in fact with the exception of some free schools and alternative classrooms, a totally pupil-oriented reading program would likely be viewed as a dereliction of a teacher's duty); and the prescriptive category of individualization would be somewhat in the middle.

This section will present suggestions for conducting an individualized program, analyze such a program, and examine research and recent developments.

Procedures

Some individualized programs in reading are highly prescriptive and teacher directed; others are more *laissez-faire.* We will describe here an individualized program that is not totally prescriptive.

Materials Materials are basic to an individualized program. No ideal number of books or other printed materials has been empirically verified, but estimates of the number of different books needed for each child range from ten to thirty to one hundred. Remember, there are many printed materials other than books. If children are going to be free to read, a large quantity of materials must be available. Where will these materials come from?

Begin in the classroom and in the old closets, workrooms, and offices of the school. Multiple copies of outdated reading books, magazines, newsletters, and supplementary materials are probably around. Remember that even if materials are old, were written for older (or younger) children, or are not of interest to you, they may still be of interest to a child in the class. Teachers will probably want to exert some selection control over materials furnished by parents and children; but "self-selected" materials are basic to individualized reading, and the child's judgment must be trusted. This is not the occasion for rigid censorship.

Many school libraries and public libraries will make available rotating collections. A group of twenty-five to fifty books, exchanged for another group every two or three weeks, adds another supply of reading material.

Teachers of individualized reading often become great scavengers. The attics, garages, storerooms, basements, and bookshelves of their friends, coworkers, and themselves can be good sources of suitable printed matter. Some teachers send notes home to the parents of their pupils asking for the donation or loan of books and materials belonging to older brothers and sisters, which may be seldom read anymore. Children feel great pride when they bring a box of books from home to share with their classmates.

There are many paperback book clubs for children. Such books are relatively inexpensive, and some clubs give free books in proportion to the number purchased—which adds to the class collection.

In addition to books, current magazines, and newspapers, teachers may subscribe to children's magazines and newspapers. Travel literature, advertising matter, maps and globes, encyclopedias and dictionaries, phone books, musical scores, airline flight schedules, cookbooks, driver education manuals, filmstrips—all these and many more add to the quantity and variety of printed material for the classroom. While some teachers do not permit them, many members of the "over-thirty" generation developed their reading interest and ability with comic books!

Organization   Reading materials can be organized according to topic, level of difficulty, or type. Grouping materials by reading level may be more time-consuming and potentially harmful than worthwhile. Children tend to seek materials they can handle, and they may feel a stigma associated with materials labelled at given levels.

Organizing by type may be the most useful method. Placing books borrowed from the school library in one area, those borrowed from the public library in another, and those borrowed from pupils or friends in a third will facilitate accounting procedures. Donated books could be in another area, and magazines and newspapers on a table or rack. Materials should be arranged in ways that encourage browsing. Occasionally grouping materials by topic can help children select according to their interests.

Room arrangements will vary according to classroom size and type, available furniture, and other considerations. A relaxed, informal classroom lends itself best to individualized reading. Carpet remnants, cushions, and old living room furniture are more conducive to reading than nailed-down desks. As adults, how often do we read for pleasure while sitting in a straight-backed chair?

Hammerstrom (1972) describes a number of interest centers she used in her individualized program. Depending on room size and furniture availability, some or all of the following may be possible.

Book Nook: This is the area of the room where most of the reading material is located. Colorful carpet samples sewn together, mats, pillows, easy chairs, and other pleasant furnishings will enhance the attractiveness of the area. Some teachers have used pup tents, boxes, and old bathtubs filled with pillows to attract children to reading.

Creative Corner: This area is designed to stimulate creative writing and expression. It should be provided with tables, extra desks and chairs, and a supply of paper, pencils, and dictionaries. A chart or bulletin board entitled "What Should I Write About?" can contain suggestions, which should be changed periodically. The following is a list of suggestions for creative writing topics:

What is red?

If I were a snowball, I'd . . .

What color is happiness? Why?

Which room in your home do you like best? Why?

Write about a dream you have had.

Use all of the following words in a story—*role, press, hard, squeeze, throw, apple, balloon.*

I'm happy today because . . .

Why does a banana have a peel?

If you were a witch, what would you be like?

How does it feel to be blue?

How would it feel to be a pumpkin on Halloween?

If you were a Christmas present, what would you like to be? Who would you like to be given to?

What is spring fever?

What will you do when spring comes that you couldn't do before?

What would it be like to own an elephant?

How would it feel to be an astronaut?

Why do cats have whiskers?

Write a story about "The Robot Who Cried."

What would you do if you were President?

How would it feel to be a bubble?

Poet's Pad: This area is set aside for reading, writing, sharing, and discussing poetry. Books of poetry should be available and children's work displayed. Colorful posters of poems can decorate the walls.

Art Cart: There are days when people do not feel like reading. This area provides an alternative. It contains a table or desks covered with newspaper or oilcloth. Boxes of string, yarn, buttons, scraps of cloth, stones, paper, cardboard, crayons, glue or paste, pipe cleaners, paint, clay, brushes, chalk, and junk will provide ample materials for creative expression. Children can create art work as a way of sharing a favorite book or character with others in the class.

Listening Center: This area could contain a tape recorder, headphones and a jack, a record player, and records. Activities carried on here include (1) making tape recordings to share with others, (2) listening to records and tapes of stories, (3) listening to music, and (4) working on listening skills. Several children at a time—as many as there are headsets—can listen to popular tapes or records.

Patterns and Puzzles Place: The materials in this area encourage reading, thinking, and following directions, as well as adding interest and variety. Items included are crossword puzzles, brainteasers, books of riddles, patterns for making toys, instructions for knitting, blueprints and model kits for construction airplanes, ships, or cars.

Skill Center: Labelled files of practice exercises, games, and lists for improving word recognition, comprehension, and study skills are found in this area. Permanent practice exercises can easily be made by removing workbook pages, mounting them on tag board, and covering them with plastic or transparent paper.

Beginning a Program Some teachers interested in individualized reading begin with the whole class while others start with one group. Some begin gradually—for part of the reading period or only once or twice a week. So that none of the students feel confused or left out, however, it is probably preferable to begin with the whole class and for the entire reading period each day. Before beginning, the teacher should discuss individualized reading with the children, so that they understand how the program will differ from their current or previous program. This discussion should consider roles and responsibilities as well as rewards. Classroom guidelines can be developed and explanations of the various learning centers should be clearly given. Children need to understand the nature of conferences, skill groups, and sharing. Some teachers suggest including only reading and conferences the first week and later starting to develop group activities. In the beginning some children may need a good deal of help in selecting a book. In addition to giving aid and encouragement, the teacher will sometimes need to select a book for a child. If the children are older and have had a year or more in some other program such as a basal reader, it may be difficult to convince them that they really are free to read what they want for interest, information, and personal enjoyment.

Conferences Integral to the success of an individualized reading program is the pupil-teacher conference. The conferences have both diagnostic and instructional value.

Some children will require frequent conferences, perhaps one a week, while others will be happy to read independently, conferring with the teacher as infrequently as once a month. Conference time may range from two to ten minutes, or more. Perhaps the best way for the teacher to determine *who* to confer with is to have children sign on a chalkboard or some other place if they desire a conference that day. The teacher can then meet with each child wherever and whenever seems best. A semiprivate area of the room, off-limits to other children during conferences, can be designated. The teacher should also allow time to stroll about the room looking for children who may need help.

Teachers and children should be prepared for a conference. They should be ready to read portions of their latest book, or one that they especially enjoyed, to answer questions about it, and to describe their feelings and opinions. They should also bring folders of up-to-date records. Specific activities within each conference will vary depending on the needs of the child and the purposes of the teacher. By listening to the child's reading, the teacher may diagnose skill needs and involve the child in a skill group or give directions in self-instructional activities in the skill center. Noting the child's interests will help the teacher to recommend particular materials.

There are many questions a teacher can ask about materials read, even if the teacher has not read the materials. Among them are the following:

1 What was the setting? Where did the story take place?
2 Describe the characters you liked most or least.
3 Briefly summarize the story.
4 What did you learn from it?
5 How did you feel as you read it—frightened, happy, worried?
6 Could it have ended differently?
7 Could this really have happened?

Children should not be questioned about or held accountable for everything they read. As adults, how often would we read a book, article, or news story if we had to answer questions or write a book report about it?

The conference not only allows the teacher to diagnose skill needs, determine comprehension ability, and ascertain interests, it also enables teacher and student to get to know each other better. The rapport established during an effective pupil-teacher conference is an invaluable asset to an individualized reading program.

Sharing Individualized reading is sometimes criticized for being *too* individualistic and for not providing enough opportunity for peer-group interaction. Children—like adults—are social creatures who develop through human contact. Sharing time can be arranged to provide this needed interaction.

Sharing activities can be arranged in a number of ways. A short time each day or perhaps two or three times a week can be set aside for sharing. Attendance can be mandatory or optional. The sharing group might consist of the full class, sharing teams (small groups), or pairs. Temporary sharing groups might be established according to common interests (monsters, model cars, horse stories, and so on), with each child reporting on their favorite reading within the topic.

Sharing time should be worthwhile, interesting, and enjoyable for all involved. Formal oral book reports, which can be very boring, should be avoided. There are many other ways to share a book or story and at the same time exchange ideas and experiences. The following list contains some ways of sharing a book:

1   Try to sell the book or story to the class by arousing their interest in it.
2   Read some parts orally to the group.
3   Show an illustration from the book and explain it.
4   Tell about an interesting, exciting, or amusing part.
5   Explain new and unfamiliar words from the story.
6   Pantomime characters or events.
7   Make puppets and give a puppet show.
8   Demonstrate how to do something you read about.
9   Make a shadow box.
10 Make clay models of some characters.
11 Draw and color a map or a floor-plan.
12 Dress a doll as a character.
13 Write a different ending and read it to the group.
14 Make a book jacket and write the "blurb."
15 Draw a picture of some event.
16 Give a TV show dramatizing parts of the book.
17 Report on interviews with others who have read it.
18 Design a bulletin board portraying several things you have read.
19 Write a simpler version for younger children.
20 Make a diorama of a scene.

Skill Development   Skill needs can be diagnosed during pupil-teacher conferences and through formal or informal testing procedures. Once these needs are determined, instruction can be specifically matched to them. Most students will direct their own instruction, using materials that are self-scored.

Workbooks, textbooks, and other materials can be disassembled by the teacher, aide, or pupils and reassembled as self-directed exercise cards with answer keys. File boxes for vocabulary, phonics, structural analysis, and context and study skills may be constructed to contain these self-directed cards. Each file box may be subdivided (initial consonants, short vowels, and syllabication for a phonics box, for example; prefixes, compound words, and suffixes for a structural analysis box) and each exercise card code-numbered.

In addition to the self-directed exercise cards, an assortment of teaching games, kits, and instructional materials can be included in the skill center. They may be both commercially prepared and teacher or pupil made. Three excellent sources of materials, games, and activities are *Creating a Learning-Centered Classroom* by Howard E. Blake, (1977), *Teaching Reading Vocabulary* by Dale D. Johnson and P. David Pearson, (1978), and *The Learning Center Idea Book,* by Ralph C. Voight, (1976). For a current list of game books in reading and a list of off-beat books and booklets for individualizing reading see Hopkins and Moe in *Reading Horizons,* Fall, 1978, and Moe and Hopkins in *Language Arts,* Vol. 56, 1978.

When more than one child needs work in the same skill area, it is frequently useful to form groups. Depending on the activities and the availability of materials, the teacher's presence with the group may or may not be required.

Record Keeping   With each child reading different materials, participating in varying activities, and practicing individually needed skills, record keeping becomes very important. Children can profit from recording their progress; teachers can use records to make instructional decisions and to clear up parents' misconceptions about the reading program.

Some teachers require pupils to keep a daily log of titles and number of pages read. Others ask that students make and organize a vocabulary book, making new entries as they encounter and learn new words. Records can be kept of each sharing activity, indicating the title of the book and the method of presentation. Reading wheels can be made and marked indicating the type of written material read (book, pamphlet, magazine article, newspaper story) or the topic (careers, animals, mystery, "how to"). Some teachers use dittoed formats, which have places for descriptions, summaries, and impressions. If pupil record keeping becomes too cumbersome, however, it can have a negative effect on reading growth. In one program observed by this writer, children appeared to spend more time on record keeping than reading.

Teacher-kept records note comprehension and skill strengths and weaknesses (formally or informally measured), reading interests, accomplishments, and perhaps summaries of pupil-teacher conferences. Skill group assignments and skill pre- and post-test scores may be needed for children who are not yet

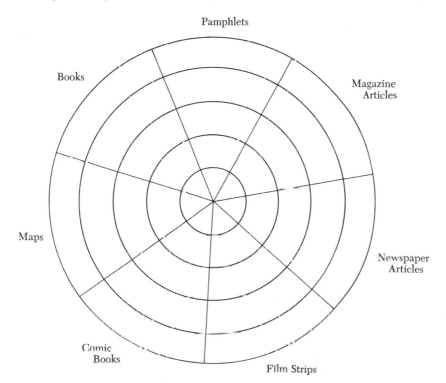

Figure 8.1
*A Reading Wheel.
As the child completes a
reading in a category, he
shades in part of the
appropriate space.*

accomplished readers. Teachers' record keeping, however, should not use time that could be more beneficially spent with children.

Evaluation   Evaluation of reading growth in an individualized program (or a language-experience approach) is of necessity more personal and informal than in other types of programs. There are no end-of-book tests, and standardized measurement instruments may not match the skills being learned. Many of the greatest advantages of this approach are not very easy to measure —there are no grade-level norms for a love of reading.

The most useful evaluation is done through informal observation, diagnostic conferences, examination of exercises and activities completed, and pupil- and teacher-made records. Attitude inventories can reveal interest in reading, and short assessment tests can be given following specific skill instruction. In addition, most schools administer yearly standardized tests of overall reading comprehension and vocabulary.

Teacher Role

Wendell Johnson (1956) has said,

> Reading is something we do, not so much with our eyes, as such, as with our knowledge and interests and enthusiasm, our hatred and fondnesses and fears, our evaluations in all their forms and aspects. Because this is so, a fondness for reading is something that a child acquires in much the same way as he catches a cold—by being effectively exposed to someone who already has it (p. 123).

Teachers serve as models in many ways. If a teacher believes there is value in reading and wishes pupils to value reading, a good beginning is to do a lot of reading, to be seen reading, and to discuss reading interests and experiences with the class. Lyman Hunt (1970) has proposed an idea called "uninterrupted sustained silent reading" (USSR). In essence, the idea calls for a time each day, perhaps the thirty minutes before lunch, when everything else in a school stops and everyone reads: the pupils, the teachers, the principal, the aides and secretaries, the cooks and custodians. Phones go unanswered and teachers *do not* use the time to grade papers or write letters. The writer knows of several schools in which USSR is being used, and it has become the most popular part of the school day. Children read because everyone is reading. This is modeling at its peak.

Another role of the teacher is to read to children. Boys and girls of all abilities, interests, and ages in elementary school enjoy being read to. The unruliest classes become quiet when a story is being read. Any school librarian can tell you what book or story has been read to a class on a given day because of the demands for the book from the children who have just heard it.

Seeing the teacher as a reader and being read to by the teacher are not uniquely advantageous to an individualized reading program, of course; any program can profit from them. Specific to individualized reading is the teacher as a classroom organizer, a gatherer of materials, an arranger of learning centers, an advisor, a diagnostician, a prescriber, a listener, and a friend.

There are a number of issues related to individualized reading, as there also are with any approach. Of the many that could be examined, nine issues which seem to be of special importance will be discussed in this section.

1. *Is individualized reading for everyone?* No; just as children are different, so are teachers and schools. Some teachers are more able than others to achieve a high degree of individualization without becoming disorganized and without running short of materials, time, resources and the patience needed to instruct a group of students on a highly individualized basis. Individualized teaching in reading takes a good deal of knowledge about the reading process and about how children learn. Furthermore, it takes a lot of time, energy, and ingenuity.

In particular, two types of teachers should think carefully before embarking on a highly individualized reading program. The first type is the beginning teacher. In our view most first year and some second and third year teachers need the support and assistance provided by a good basal series. Until a teacher has acquired experience with children and instructional materials, the books, workbooks, accessories and especially the teacher's manual prove to be invaluable assets.

We realize that there are some exceptional beginning teachers who could individualize nicely during their first year of teaching. However, most teachers agree that teacher competence improves with experience.

The second type of teacher who may not want to individualize is the *first grade* teacher. It is extremely hard to have a highly individualized program of *beginning* reading, but it becomes progressively easier with each grade thereafter. First grade is chosen since that is typically where children begin to learn to read. When no one (or few) can read it is efficient to instruct in groups. There are outstanding first-grade teachers who have a totally individualized reading program—and many of them use the language experience approach. The point is that first-grade teachers should not feel guilty if they use a basal series, with its continuity and systematic pacing, and individualize only partially and occasionally. It is probably much easier to achieve high individualization in the intermediate grades and in junior and senior high than it is in any of the primary grades.

2. *Is it necessary that the teacher read every book read by pupils* (in an individualized program)? Some advocates believe that if the child is to be guided in comprehension skills, the teacher must have read the book the child is reading. This is both impossible and unnecessary. Spend time in any second or third grade classroom, or in the upper grades, and observe the quantity and variety of reading: books, stories, magazines, newspapers, film strips and so on. Except, perhaps, in the first few months of first grade, teachers would have to be all knowing to give any degree of comprehensive coverage to the things children read. Furthermore, comprehension can be checked and developed through questions that are general to many kinds of books and stories. For example, ask questions such as those listed on page 219. Nor is it necessary to always check comprehension. How often would you freely choose to read a paperback if you knew you would be quizzed on it

later, or had to do some worksheets on the contents? How would such knowledge affect your reading of it?

3. *How often should conferences be held?* A weekly conference is not always possible. Some children need conferences more often than once a week, some less frequently. When weekly conferences are regularly scheduled and rigorously adhered to, they may become superficial. And a child who needs help on Thursday may not get it until Monday. Conference scheduling, like other aspects of individualized reading, must be individualized.

The approach, in which the teacher meets with a few children at length each day, and then informally strolls about the classroom and engages in short unplanned discussions while providing the other usual kinds of help, seems preferable to the weekly, scheduled formal conference.

4. *Are there any group activities in a highly individualized reading program?* Humans are social creatures. In addition to the social need to function with others, thinking is stimulated, ideas are challenged and interests are expanded through group activities. If children in reading class only sat reading alone, day in and day out, school would be boring indeed. There are many opportunities for full class and smaller group activities—such as movies, field trips, book sharing, discussions of common reading, skill groups, interest groups, project groups, reading pairs, etc., which were discussed earlier in this section.

5. *How does one collect an adequate supply of materials for an individualized reading program?* There is no set number of books or other materials needed for a successful individualized program; but teachers often worry that they just don't have enough in terms of quantity or variety. With a little ingenuity it is amazing how quickly a multitude of materials can be found. Many types and sources of materials were described on page 216 of this section.

6 and 7. *Is there a scope and sequence of skills in reading? If so, how is this dealt with in an individualized reading program?* There are two issues presented here. The first has to do with scope and sequence, the second with skills. Compare any two, ten, or twenty basal series or skills management systems. There is little agreement about the scope and sequence of skills. In no two programs are the sequences identical and in few are they close. Certainly some skills must precede others: the alphabet must be learned before alphabetizing, and alphabetizing before dictionary work. But most sequences are instructional conveniences rather than empirically determined hierarchies. In an individualized program the sequence of skills is based on the needs of the individual learners.

That leads to the second issue. Some teachers believe that skills are not taught at all in an individualized program. Perhaps that is true in the handful of classrooms which have a totally student-run *laissez-faire* program of the type mentioned earlier. It is a fact that most children need instructional help with the basic word identification skills of phonic analysis, structural analysis and contextual analysis. Likewise, most children need help with the development and refinement of the cognitive and literary skills we have clustered under the umbrella called comprehension.

Skill development in an individualized program can and should be organized for instructional convenience. It is individual, it is individually prescribed, and it stems from individual diagnosis. Some programs use skill centers, or individual skill activities and games, while other programs regularly form and disband flexible skill groups. However managed, needed skills should be taught.

8. *Is reading isolated from the other language arts?* Children certainly do read a lot in an individualized reading program. But they do many other things. Learning centers and learning stations are often inherent components of an individualized classroom. Earlier we described the *book nook* with its shelves, books, magazines, carpet remnants, cubby holes and bean chairs; the *creative corner* with children's magazines and suggestions for writing; the *poet's pad,* a place to read, write and share poetry; an *art cart,* a *listening center,* a *patterns and puzzles place,* a *skills center,* a *discovery center* and other special attractions. In an individualized reading program children do read a lot; but they do many other things as well.

9. *Should the teacher read to children in an individualized reading program?* Few children outgrow the love of listening to a good story. At all elementary grade levels (and at junior and senior high also), regardless of the type of reading program in effect, we would encourage you to read to your pupils daily. Librarians can often tell you what books teachers have been reading to their classes by the increased pupil requests for those very books, or others by the same author or on the same topic. Poor readers and disinterested readers cannot help but benefit from the model of good, enthusiastic reading provided by the teacher. We all know that children who enter our schools from reading homes—those with books, magazine subscriptions and library cards, those homes in which parents or older children read to the younger ones —are children at an advantage. Unfortunately, too often as parents who *do* read to our children, we stop this practice once our children learn to read for themselves. We apparently feel we are finally off the hook or perhaps our children can now catch us in the act of skipping pages!

Some teachers are concerned that if they read to a group they are violating the basic philosophy of individualized reading. As stated earlier in this section, we feel that children in any program will benefit from being read to at school. Interests can be increased and an awareness of the value of reading can be generated.

Research Findings

Much of the reported research shows that individualized reading makes no overwhelming difference in increasing reading progress. However, interest in reading and quantity of reading is often greater with children who have been in an individualized program.

A three-year study reported by Rodney Johnson (1965) showed that children in such programs can achieve just as well as children taught with basals, in the aspects of reading measured by standardized tests. An analysis of the results of seven controlled studies comparing individualized reading with basal reading showed that the individualized children did better in four of the studies while the basal pupils performed better in the other three (Vite, 1961). Abbott (1972) found that basal and individualized reading groups did equally well on a test of basic reading skills but that the individualized group had a higher commitment to independent reading. In a study with fourth-, fifth-, and sixth-grade pupils, Karlin (1957) found that the individualized groups showed more interest in reading and read more than the basal group.

Thus there seems to be neither clear-cut evidence favoring individualized reading nor any empirical base for attacking it. A student's ability seems to develop in this kind of program about as well as in other kinds. The 1964—1965 U.S. Office of Education studies showed that there is no *one method* of reading instruction that is superior to all others. There is often more variability in growth *within* a method than *between* methods. This finding further verifies the belief that the key factor in any learning situation is the *teacher,* not the method or material. Proponents of individualized instruction assert that this approach offers a good chance to increase interest in reading and create lifetime readers—*without* loss of achievement.

Summary

There are many degrees of individualization and many kinds of individualized reading programs. Despite vast differences, the thread common to them is the recognition that all children are unique individuals who have different abilities, interests, and potentials. While most teachers individualize in some ways, only a minority of them would classify theirs as a totally "individualized reading" approach. Individualized reading means many things to many people. It is not a discrete program. It varies in hundreds of ways and rarely functions the same way in any two classrooms even in the same building.

The remaining pages of this chapter are devoted to a description of programmed and computer-assisted reading and skills management or monitoring systems, all of which relate to prescriptive individualized reading instruction; and then briefly to other organizational arrangements for reading instruction.

PROGRAMMED AND COMPUTER-ASSISTED READING INSTRUCTION

It is actually redundant to refer to programmed *and* computer-assisted reading instruction, since all computer-assisted reading instruction is in fact highly programmed. Here, however, for descriptive purposes, *programmed reading* will refer to that type of instruction which employs only software (books) as opposed to hardware (computers).

Programmed instruction teaches by means of carefully sequenced steps. Each step leads to increased mastery of the subject with minimum error. Each step is constructed so that the student can confirm the correctness of his response before he progresses to more complex materials.

Programmed instruction differs from the conventional methods in several respects. It is an individual learning process in which the student accepts a far wider responsibility for his own learning and progresses at his own pace; it requires an active response with immediate confirmation of results; and the subject matter is so programmed that the student's learning behavior is shaped in a particular manner (Hughes, 1962).

A Brief History

As early as 1912, Edward L. Thorndike advocated a form of programmed instruction. He said that although students needed to learn by discovery, the content of reading materials should be controlled so that careful reading and understanding preceded the reading of hints or further explanation. In 1925 Sidney L. Pressey demonstrated the first teaching machine to provide an automated feedback to each student in a conventional classroom setting. The same type of questions and examinations used by classroom teachers were written in multiple-choice format for a machine presentation. Since only correct responses permitted the viewing of the following question, students knew immediately whether or not their answers were right. Recently the major proponent of programmed instruction has been B. F. Skinner; a programmed book (Holland and Skinner, 1961) in psychology which he coauthored has now been used for many years.

Programmed reading materials for children came about largely through the efforts of Cynthia Dee Buchanan and her former teacher, M. W. Sullivan. Although they began the development of their program in 1957, it was not until after much experimentation and revision that their materials were finally published by McGraw-Hill in 1963.

Although programmed instruction may be presented by a teaching machine or a computer, it is most often presented in a book. The two major kinds of organization for programmed materials are: *linear,* where the items come one after the other; and *branching,* where items may be skipped or repeated. The linear type of programming is most often employed in programmed textbooks, whereas the branching type is used in computer programming.

Programmed Reading

The Buchanan-Sullivan (1973) materials, *Programmed Reading,* have become synonymous with programmed reading in general, although the materials have also been described as being representative of "linguistic" materials. The program consists of a sequence of twenty-one colorfully illustrated workbooks in which the student writes his response to each item and then checks the correctness of his answer before progressing to the next item.

One of the major advantages of this type of program is that if the material is properly arranged, success is maximized and failure is minimized. Another advantage is that the student is free to work at his own pace. Among the disadvantages, however, is that while repetition and "short steps" from one item to another do, in fact, guarantee success for most students, these things can also be tedious, and the need for a lockstep program through which all students must progress may well be questioned.

An important element of the program is the series of small hard-cover *Storybooks* which the student may read after the completion of the appropriate workbooks. These *Storybooks* are appealing both in content and format; the stories are excellent and the colorful illustrations are delightful. These books provide excellent reading for children regardless of whether the programmed workbooks are used.

It must be emphasized that first grade children do not simply start on page one of the *Programmed Reading* workbooks and begin to learn to read.

They must first master a number of skills in what the publisher calls the programmed prereading stage. Heilman (1977) claims that children must have mastered the following skills:

1   The names of the letters of the alphabet (capital and small).
2   How to print all the capital and small letters.
3   That letters stand for sounds.
4   What sounds to associate with the letters *a, f, m, n, p, t, th,* and *i,* which are used as the points of departure for the programmed readers.
5   That letters are read from left to right.
6   That groups of letters form words.
7   The words *yes* and *no* by sight, how to discriminate the words *ant, man,* and *mat* from each other, and how to read the sentences, *I am an ant, I am a man, I am a mat, I am a pin, I am a pan, I am tan, I am thin, I am fat* (pp. 189–190).

Intended for students in grades one through three, the Buchanan-Sullivan workbooks are now also published by Behavioral Research Laboratories in essentially the same format as the McGraw-Hill program.

While admitting that children do learn to read through the use of programmed materials, several reading authorities (Spache and Spache, 1977; Heilman, 1965) have expressed reservations about widespread adoption of programmed reading as the basic program. The teacher who is considering such a program may wish to ask the following questions:

1   Does this program provide for instruction in the skills I consider essential for my class?
2   Will my students accept the structure of this program?
3   Are the repetitions provided in the program necessary for all of my students?
4   Is pupil-book interaction sufficient, or is pupil-teacher-book interaction necessary?

Computer-Assisted Reading Instruction

Only a few years ago computer-assisted instruction was in its experimental stages. However, with the advent of computer time sharing, which allows for the simultaneous operation of many remote terminals,[5] the use of a computer as the primary instructional aid—rather than a teacher or a book—has become more common, particularly on college campuses where computer terminals are generally more accessible. Since 1978, when portable microcomputers (which are self-contained computers in every respect) became available for under $600, the use of computer-assisted instruction in reading has increased substantially. It is now possible for teachers to purchase their own computers for classroom use.

----

[5] A remote terminal may be miles away from the main computer facility; messages to and from the computer are usually sent over telephone wires.

mat		I am a tan mat. man.
yes		Am I a mat? yes no
yes		Am I tan? yes no
m<u>a</u>t		I am a tan m___t.
no		Am I a mat? yes no
yes		Am I an ant? yes no
no		Am I tan? yes no
yes	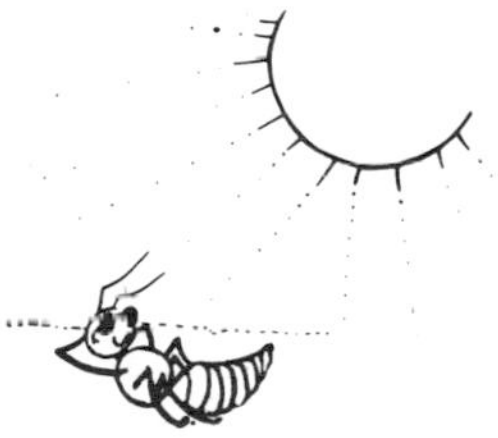	Am I an ant? yes no
yes		Am I tan? yes no
t<u>a</u>n		I am a t___n ant.

Figure 8.2
*Programmed Reading
Book 1, Rev. Ed.*

Source: From *Programmed Reading Book I*, p. 4, 1968. Reprinted by permission of Behavioral Research Laboratories.

A distinction should be made between computer-based, computer-assisted and computer-managed instruction, although the terms are sometimes used synonymously. In computer-based instruction, the computer is the primary source of instruction, whereas in computer-assisted instruction, the teacher provides most of the instruction, and the computer assists with practice exercises. With computer-managed instruction, the computer is used for diagnosis and provides the teacher with recommendations for instruction.

A good computerized instructional program must make available a great many alternate avenues through which the student may be routed to the subsequent phase. It must also have the capacity to assess and use the student's achievement at each stage of the instructional program.

The student receives instruction from a computer terminal called a tele-typewriter, which looks much like a regular typewriter. This teletypewriter provides instructions and sends student responses to the computer.

The use of computers to teach reading came about largely through the efforts of Richard Atkinson and his associates at Stanford University. With the resources of the Carnegie Foundation and the IBM Corporation, they were able to construct and equip a building adjacent to an elementary school near Stanford University. This endeavor soon took on the name of the school (Brentwood Elementary School, East Palo Alto, California) and became known as the Brentwood Project (Atkinson, 1968) and more recently in reading circles as the Stanford Project in Computer-Assisted Instruction in Reading.

In its most recent use, the Stanford Project provided for approximately twelve minutes of supplementary instruction per student each day. The program was marketed commercially for several years; now, however, no computer-assisted reading program is available commercially—although experimentation continues.

The earliest reports of teaching children to read by computer (Atkinson and Hansen, 1966) were greeted with dismay by many educators (Spache, 1967) who felt that computers threatened to replace the normal human interaction of classroom instruction. But computer-assisted instruction in reading is not intended to replace the teacher (although the teacher who *can* be replaced by a computer probably *should* be). Atkinson and Fletcher (1972) state that "on the contrary, it is a tool that can free the teacher for more creative forms of instruction" (pp. 326–327). Within the last ten years, there have been approximately 400 articles published which deal with computer applications in reading. Because the technology of computers is expanding so rapidly, it is difficult to stay current. However, for anyone contemplating the use of computers—including the low-cost microcomputers—a recent book by Mason and Blanchard (1979) is highly recommended.

The Future of Computers and Reading Instruction

For several reasons, it seems likely that the use of computers to teach reading will increase. First, there is now a better understanding of the potential of computer-assisted and computer-managed instruction in reading; though the awe may still be present, the fear is gone. Second, some school systems now use remote terminals (though unfortunately more for record keeping than for instruction). Third, the relatively low cost of microcomputers makes them "affordable" to most teachers. Fourth, present experimentation is providing new and better computer programs. And fifth, observations have shown that computer instruction is efficient, feasible, and humane for at least some of our students during a portion of the daily instruction.

We have examined the language-experience approach and the individualized approach with their individualization and their flexible short-term grouping arrangements. We have also mentioned programmed, computer-assisted, and other skills management approaches to individualization. Three other developments should be mentioned briefly before we conclude this chapter.

The Joplin Plan

So far, we have largely considered reading programs in relation to the self-contained classroom. A modification of within-class (intraclass) ability grouping is the across-class (interclass) ability group plan known as the Joplin Plan.[6] In this scheme children remain in a self-contained classroom with one teacher for most instruction but are grouped across classes for reading instruction. For example, if there are two fourth-, two fifth-, and two sixth-grade classes in a building, six interage reading classes would be formed—based on ability. The very top group might contain mostly sixth graders, some fifth graders, and a few fourth graders, while the reverse might be true for the very bottom group. At a certain time each day children leave their regular classroom and go to their reading class. The method of instruction is usually basal, but other approaches to reading are also found in Joplin Plan schools. Each reading group theoretically has a range of achievement, which is smaller than would be found in any one of the self-contained classrooms. Ranges of ability will still exist, however, as well as varying interests and maturity levels. The stigma of being in a low group may be even greater with this plan since it will become public knowledge to children from other classes. Among others, one recurring criticism of the Joplin Plan is that it deprives classroom teachers of intimate knowledge of their pupils' reading abilities and interests, since many children from one teacher's classroom may be instructed in reading by a different teacher. It might also be noted that Joplin Plan organizational patterns tend to isolate instruction of reading from other areas of the curriculum, the other language arts particularly.

Departmentalized Reading

Like most high schools and middle schools, some elementary schools have done away with the self-contained classroom in favor of subject matter groups. This is often done informally. Mrs. Smith does not like to teach science but enjoys reading. Mr. Jones likes science best, and Mrs. Mott's favorite subject is mathematics. So at the third-grade level Mrs. Smith teaches reading to all three classes, Mr. Jones teaches science, and Mrs. Mott teaches mathematics. They each keep their own class for the remainder of the school day for language arts, social studies, and other areas. While this approach allows teachers "to do their own thing" and therefore, presumably, do it better than the others on the "team," there are some potential problems. Some teachers will not have reading-instructional contact with their home-room pupils, or for that matter, with any other pupils. This lack of reading

---

[6] The arrangement was tried in many schools but became best known after its inception in the Joplin, Missouri, public schools.

contact can have detrimental effects on the teacher's ability to help children in other subjects—nearly all of which require reading ability.

Team Teaching

In schools employing team teaching, two or more teachers generally combine their classes to form one large group of sixty or more pupils. This is sometimes done within a grade, but in the multi-unit, or nongraded, school (increasing in popularity) it is done across grades. The teacher team, usually with the help of paraprofessionals and perhaps student teachers or interns from a nearby university, plans the instructional program. It is possible for them to offer differentiated instruction in the framework of a number of different-sized groups. Any number of reading groups might be formed (as with other curricular areas), and teaching assignments are cooperatively determined.

These three are but a few of the many and varied organizational arrangements currently in use. Although they can all be used successfully, teachers should remember that no organizational plan and no particular reading methodology can ever guarantee success with reading. As we know, the teacher makes the difference.

THE AUTHORS' VIEWPOINT

In this chapter and in the previous chapter we have described a number of approaches that have been used to teach children how to read. While these approaches all have some merit in that they do succeed in teaching children to read, it is our contention that two critical factors determine which approaches are most effective. These two factors relate to teacher competencies in three areas: the first is the extent to which the teacher understands language, particularly as linguistic knowledge relates to the reading process, the second is the degree to which the teacher understands the students and *their* language, and a third area relates to the teacher's understanding of the reading process.

Does this mean that methods and approaches are of little consequence? No, but the employment of method and approach must be based on an understanding of the child's needs, language, interests, environment—and this cannot be done unless the teacher is competent in at least the areas mentioned.

For teachers who know language, their students, and something about the reading process, there are many alternatives available in teaching reading. Teachers who are limited in their knowledge have fewer options. Such teachers may adhere too closely to a manual, a guide, or an approach. The purpose of this book, of course, is to develop competencies that will enable teachers to make intelligent decisions concerning reading instruction.

In presenting our descriptions of some of the many ways of teaching children to read, we have attempted to remain relatively objective and dispassionate. We hope it is clear that none of the approaches examined is a panacea. All approaches to reading are successful with some children and unsuccessful with others depending on the particular mixture of individuals, materials, and classroom environment. Despite the lack of research evidence to convincingly support any one method, and despite the recognition that the classroom teacher is the key ingredient in any reading classroom, we do have a bias.

We can think of no procedure yet devised by educators or lay persons which has had so much success in teaching *so many* children to read as the basal reader approach. We clearly support the use of language experience activities because they make so much psycholinguistic sense; we clearly support intensive instruction in the decoding skills espoused by phonic/linguistic programs; we clearly support individualized reading, both self-directed and prescriptive, especially as children become more competent in reading ability. *But,* we know of no recently published basal reading series which takes all of these factors into account and at the same time presents a *systematic, developmental* set of materials and techniques for reading acquisition and improvement.

And we believe you can't argue with success. The enormous majority of American children are taught to read using a basal approach, and the great majority have learned to read and read well. Basal programs provide the balance of acquisition, development, and appreciation selections, activities, and suggestions which good, thinking teachers can pick and choose from to help most of their children become fluent readers. Until something better comes along, and we can't as yet anticipate what it could be, we support the judicious use of a basal program—with its continuing authorial and editorial revisions and updating which has been a characteristic of the major series over the past decades—supplemented in whatever ways the teacher deems necessary, as an approach to reading instruction that is successful much more often than not.

It is important to emphasize that the approaches to the teaching of reading discussed here need not be mutually exclusive—with one approach used to the exclusion of all others. It is our hope that all teachers will understand the reading process and their students so completely that the approach or approaches selected for instruction will provide the maximum in reading combinations of achievement for each student.

REFERENCES

Abbott, J. "Fifteen Reasons Why Personalized Reading Instruction Does Not Work." *Elementary English* 49 (January 1972): 33–36.

Ashton-Warner, S. *Teacher.* New York: Simon and Schuster, 1963.

Atkinson, R. C. "Computer-based Instruction in Initial Reading." *Proceedings of the 1967 Invitational Conference on Testing Problems.* Princeton, N.J.: Educational Testing Services, 1968, pp. 55–66.

Atkinson, R. C., and Fletcher, J. D. "Teaching Children to Read with a Computer." *The Reading Teacher* 25 (1972): 319–327.

Atkinson, R. C., and Hansen, D. N. "Computer-assisted Instruction in Initial Reading: The Stanford Project." *Reading Research Quarterly* 2 (1966): 5–25.

Bond, G. L., and Dykstra, R. "Interpreting the First Grade Studies." In *The First Grade Reading Studies: Findings of Individual Investigations,* edited by R. G. Stauffer. Newark, Del.: International Reading Association, 1967.

Buchanan, C. D., and Sullivan Associates. *Programmed Reading.* New York: McGraw-Hill Book Company, 1973.

Dahl, S. S. *The Language Experience Approach: A Study and Implementation of the Method.* Unpublished paper, University of Wisconsin, 1971.

Hall, M. A. *The Language Experience Approach for the Culturally Disadvantaged.* Newark, Del.: International Reading

Association, 1972.

Hammerstrom, K. H. *Individualized Reading Instruction: A Third Grade Program.*

Heilman, A. W. "Phonics Emphasis Approaches." In *First Grade Reading Programs,* edited by J. F. Kerfoot. Newark, Del.: International Reading Association, 1965, pp. 65–71.

Heilman, A. W. *Principles and Practices of Teaching Reading.* 4th ed. Columbus, Ohio. Charles E. Merrill Publishing Co., 1977.

Holland, J. G. and Skinner, B. F. *The Analysis of Behavior: A Program for Self-instruction.* New York: McGraw-Hill Book Company, 1961.

Hopkins, C. J., and Moe, A. J. "Game Books for Reading Instruction", *Reading Horizons* (Fall 1977); 75–77.

Hughes, J. L. *Programmed Instruction for Schools and Industry.* Chicago: Science Research Associates, 1962, pp. 8–11.

Hunt, L. "The Effect of Self-Selection, Interest and Motivation upon Independent, Instructional, and Frustrational Levels." *Reading Teacher* 24 (November 1970): 146–151.

Johnson, D. D. and Pearson, P. D. "Skills Management Systems—A Critique." *Reading Teacher* 28 (May 1975): 757–764.

Johnson, R. H. "Individualized and Basal Primary Reading Programs." *Elementary English* 42 (December 1965): 902–904, 915.

Johnson, W. *Your Most Enchanted Listener.*

New York: Harper and Row, 1956.

Karlin, R. "Some Reactions to Individualized Reading." *Reading Teacher* 11 December 1957: 95–98.

Mason, G. E. & Blanchard, J. S. *Computer Applications in Reading.* Newark, Delaware: International Reading Association, 1979.

Moe, A. J., and Hopkins, C. J. "Jingles, Jokes, Limericks, Poems, Proverbs, Puns, Puzzles, and Riddles: Fast Reading for Reluctant Readers," *Language Arts* 56 (November-December, 1978): 957–965, 1003.

Pearson, P. D. and Johnson, D. D. *Teaching Reading Comprehension,* New York: Holt, Rinehart and Winston, 1975.

Smith, R. J. and Barrett, T. C. *Teaching Reading in the Middle Grades.* Reading, Mass.: Addison-Wesley, 1974.

Spache, G. D. "A Reaction to Computer-Assisted Instruction in Initial Reading Instruction: The Stanford Project." *Reading Research Quarterly* 3 (1967): 101–109.

Spache, G. D., and Spache, E. B. *Reading in the Elementary School.* Boston: Allyn and Bacon, 1969.

Terwilliger, J. *Some Problems Associated with the Concept of Mastery.* Unpublished manuscript, University of Minnesota, 1972.

Vite, I. W. "Grouping Practices in Individualized Reading." *Elementary English* 38 (February 1961): 91–98.

PREVIEW

In this chapter, Ollila focuses on young children and their initial reading experiences. He explores a question that has concerned parents, teachers, and educators for many years: When is a child ready to read?

Ollila explains the factors associated with reading readiness and provides a valuable checklist to help you assess the reading readiness of your students. He offers many concrete teaching suggestions in areas such as attention, language training, left-to-right orientation, letters and words, and auditory and visual discrimination. He concludes the chapter with a brief review of preschool and kindergarten training programs and the role of parents and para-professionals at these levels.

Ollila emphasizes that children bring a wide range of abilities and skills to the initial processes of learning to read. This chapter should help you to understand and work with children's varying needs. It covers all aspects of preparing children to read—a complex and controversial topic. You will find Ollila's treatment objective, reasonable and designed to help you reach your own conclusions, rather than to impose the author's viewpoint.

Preparing the Child

Lloyd Ollila, University of Victoria

OBJECTIVES

After you have read this chapter, you should be able to:

1. **Define these words: initial reading readiness and readiness in the broadest sense.**

2. **List and briefly explain at least six factors determining a child's readiness to read and describe how you would evaluate them.**

3. **Discuss some of the diagnostic "tools" available to teachers in preparing children for reading and cite the importance of the teacher's diagnosis.**

4. **Name some of the pros and cons of using commercial readiness materials in the classroom.**

5. **Specify five readiness skills which can be developed and list a few activities to develop each skill.**

6. **Describe some current practices in preparing children for reading including classroom organization, materials, and parent involvement.**

It is Friday, the end of the first week of school at Howard Elementary. The dismissal bell has rung, the children have gone home, and Ms. Lane is sitting in her classroom at the desk thinking about her new class. Slowly she is beginning to know the children as individuals rather than just names on her class list. Some children seemed quite confident, making themselves at home, chatting happily, and enjoying the games and activities. Others seemed shy, hesitant, and a bit frightened. Lee kept moving from activity to activity, never lingering longer than five minutes. Kathy's consuming interest seemed to be painting at the easel. Larry had trouble cutting with his scissors and cried out his frustration. Dick brought his model dinosaur collection to "Show and Tell" and rambled on in detailed discussion about his favorite, Tyrannosaurus Rex. They were all different in background, skills, and abilities. Some of the chil-

237

dren seemed very ready for reading. One girl, Ann, even brought her favorite story, *Green Eggs and Ham,* and read several pages to the teacher. Others seemed totally unable to settle down to any task. *Most,* thank goodness, were somewhere between the two extremes. Almost all of them were neither completely ready nor completely unready to read. Ms. Lane ended her musing on the children. She had work to do. How would she help prepare these children for reading? How would she know who was ready to read?

WHEN IS A CHILD READY TO READ?

Each child's readiness to read gradually develops over a long period of time. As children grow from infant to toddler through ages three, four, and five they accumulate a wealth of background experiences and concepts. Their auditory, tactile, visual, perceptual-motor, and speech skills are being formed and sharpened. They are gradually introduced to the world of objects, symbols, and words. All these various kinds of knowledge and skills help prepare the child for the act of reading. Further preparation may be done at school, but the groundwork begins at home. Since a child's readiness to read is built gradually, we cannot say, "Yesterday this child was not ready to read, but today she is."

A Definition of Beginning Reading Readiness

Reading educators tend to view reading readiness as a match between children and their instructional program. This view is stated by Durkin in *Teaching Them to Read* (1978):

> The question of a child's readiness for reading has a twofold focus: (a) his capacity (a product of an interplay among genetic endowment, maturation, experiences and learnings) in relation to (b) the particular instruction that will be available (p. 162).

This definition takes into account both children and the schools that they attend. In other words, teachers determine whether or not a child is ready to read by asking, "What does this child have to know and do in order to succeed in this particular reading program?" If, for example, the beginning program puts a premium on phonics, they will make sure that the children have sufficient auditory discrimination skills.

Much of the preparation for reading is done at home prior to formal school. But any teacher who just waited around for readiness to occur in the classroom would be negligent. It is the teacher's responsibility to provide activities and experiences that prepare the child for initial reading. Numerous studies have shown that children can be directly trained in different readiness skills and that this training will contribute to their readiness to read (Spache et al., 1965; Blakeley and Shadle, 1961). The teacher should not only prepare the child for a particular beginning reading program but also look for ways to adapt the beginning reading program to the individual differences in the class. If the program is modified, some children may be ready to read sooner. The teacher's goal is to discover the best way of fitting the child to the program and the program to the child.

A General Concept of Reading Readiness

Although we seem to place more emphasis on reading in the first years of school, this concept is important to the entire reading program. The sixth-grade teacher asks, "Are these children ready to learn dictionary skills?" The high school teacher wonders, "Does this class have the background of under-standing necessary to comprehend the chapter in this physics text?" Every teacher has to continually assess the readiness of his class and prepare them for new, more difficult learning. Readiness in the broadest sense is basic to any new learning at any level.

FACTORS ASSOCIATED WITH READING READINESS

Research studies have indicated that a number of prereading skills and abilities contribute to a child's success in beginning reading. However, because of the uniqueness of each child and of the school reading program in which the child is placed, the importance of these abilities and skills will vary from child to child. Reading success is not guaranteed by the presence of all the skills or precluded if some are missing. Our discussion will be limited to a few factors, which are generally regarded as important to the child's learning to read. These factors are grouped arbitrarily into broad categories: physiological, intellectual, environmental, social and emotional, and instructional factors. They are summarized in the chart below. The reader will note that these factors are not only important at the readiness level, but also at other reading levels. To answer the question, "Is this particular child ready to read?" the teacher will observe the child, collect evidence, and assess readiness according to these factors:

Physical Health, Neurological Considerations, and Sex General good health is important for learning to read. A fatigued and listless child is at a disadvantage in any learning situation. Some researchers have pointed out that neurological limitations (various brain defects, mixed domi-nance, etc.) and lack of physical maturity are related to failure in learning to read. Most teachers, however, will not get much practical help from looking for signs of these in their classes.

Generally girls in North America are ready to read earlier than boys. Differences on readiness tests often seem to favor girls slightly (Anderson, Hughes, and Dixon, 1957). Although the teacher can probably expect a few more boys than girls to be immature in reading tasks, most boys and girls will score similarly on readiness tests. Therefore most schools have not felt it necessary to offer separate readiness or reading programs to boys and girls. However, the teacher should be sensitive to the special needs of those boys lacking in readiness. For instance, Downing and Thackray (1975) feel that the female teacher should find ways of letting boys know that reading is important to men.

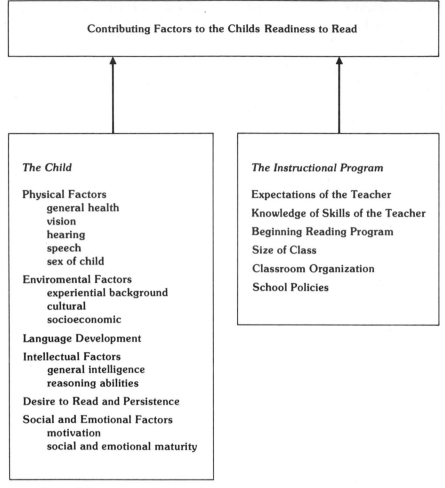

Figure 9.1
Physiological Factors

Speech, Vision, and Hearing Defects Poor speech, hearing, and vision can slow a child's progress in learning to read. For instance, phonic analysis may be hard for a child with a speech or hearing problem. Teachers should be alert for significant signs—constant rubbing of eyes, squinting to see words, needing to have directions repeated again and again—and be ready to refer a child to the proper medical specialist. Most children with one of these handicaps will learn to read quite well if the teacher recognizes the problem and adjusts his instruction accordingly.

Some children's eyes are not fully developed until the age of eight (Getman, 1962). These visually immature children tend to be farsighted. Those who are opposed to early readiness and reading activities often call attention to this fact. They contend that the school is expecting too much from a child physiologically by requiring long periods of close work. Other researchers, however, refute these claims. Eames (1962) found five-year-old children to have more accommodative power than children possess at any subsequent age. He also found that even the most nearsighted child in his investigation had sufficient vision to read commonly used textbooks. The controversy over the effects of reading on young children's eyes is yet to be resolved, but each teacher should be continually sensitive to signs of possible visual problems in the early stages of reading. Each child, especially those at the kindergarten and nursery school levels, should have an eye examination before beginning close prereading tasks. Obviously a thorough test of vision can be done only by professionals.

The teacher should recognize that the commercial vision screening tests available to schools will provide an incomplete picture of the child's vision. Take, for instance, the Snellen test, which has been widely used in schools for years. This test measures visual acuity at a twenty-foot distance. When a child reads books the distance between the eyes and print is much shorter. The child may easily pass the Snellen test, but still have undetected visual problems, which could hinder reading growth. Testing kindergarten children in New Haven, first with the Snellen test and then with more thorough tests, researchers (Peters, 1961) reported that 46 percent had visual problems that had been missed by the Snellen.

Visual Discrimination   Some children who can see adequately in most situations may have trouble learning to read because they have not fully developed their abilities to discriminate between printed symbols such as letters, numerals, and words. For instance, in reading, children are called upon to see the similarities and differences between letters like *b, p,* and *d.* They are asked to notice that the word *dog* is different in length from *something* and different in shape from *pretty.* They are also called on to discriminate between *dog* and words similar to it, like *dig* and *god.* Children who lack these fine visual discrimination skills probably will profit from special training prior to beginning reading.

Auditory Discrimination: Auditory discrimination—the ability to hear likenesses and differences in letter sounds—is often considered a more important factor than adequate hearing in determining a child's reading readiness. Most children hear adequately and distinguish between different sounds by the time they begin school. Many children, however, have not developed this power to the fine degree needed for learning to read. Ollila, Johnson, and Downing (1974), testing kindergarten children's ability to discriminate phonemes in words, found that only five children in a group of 60 were able to recognize all the phonemes in words presented to them. Many children cannot isolate beginning, middle, or ending sounds, distinguish rhyming elements, or blend a number of speech sounds into words. These fine discrimination abilities enable a child to recognize a word in print, such as *cat,* by "sounding out" its elements *(c–a–t).* Children who lack this skill probably will need special training, especially if phonics is stressed in the beginning reading program.

Intellectual Factors

General Intelligence and Mental Age: All things being equal (an unlikely situation), the teacher can expect bright children to learn to read faster than slower children. Numerous researchers contemplating this positive relationship between reading and intelligence have suggested that there is a certain level of intelligence, or minimum mental age, necessary before a child can succeed in learning to read. The influential Morphett and Washburne study (1931) proposed a mental age of six and one-half years. However, most recent studies conclude that it is impossible to say that children must attain a specified mental age before they can learn to read. There are far too many other factors to be considered. Studies such as Davidson's (1931) on teaching dull five-year-olds to read and Durkin's study (1963) of three-, four-, and five-year-olds who learned to read early show that some children with mental ages below six and one-half can learn to read successfully under the right conditions.

The relationship between intelligence and beginning reading success varies from one reading program to another. Gates (1937), in his now famous readiness factor research, concluded that the minimal age concept is meaningless without qualifying information as to the methods, procedures, and materials used in the beginning program plus information on the teacher's ability to individualize the instruction to meet pupils' needs. Two writers, Spache and Spache (1977), expand upon this view, observing, "It is the stereotyped, inflexible, and mass-oriented reading program that demands a higher mental age, and makes intelligence so important a factor in reading success in our primary classrooms" (p. 156).

Conceptual Development and Specific Reasoning Ability: While the general intelligence of a child determines beginning reading success to a certain extent, those facets of general intelligence that are related specifically to reading are an even better predictor. Downing and Thackray (1975) contend that the cognitive factors involving the development of reasoning abilities and concepts of reading "may be the most important of all the foundations of readiness for learning to read." They cite as research evidence several studies, including the extensive review of the research on poor readers by Vernon (1962). Vernon found that the common characteristics of children who failed in reading were "cognitive confusion" and "lack of system about the whole reading process." She felt that the main problem of disabled readers was a failure in developing "a particular type of reasoning process." This reasoning process was necessary in understanding such important concepts as the relationship of written language to speech.

Reid (1966) and Downing (1970), in interviews with five-year-olds in their first year of primary school, found the children confused about the nature of reading and the problem-solving tasks they were required to do. Reid observed that the children showed "a general lack of any specific expectancies of what reading was going to be like, of what the activity consisted, of the purpose and the use of it." Furthermore, the children had trouble understanding abstract technical terms such as "word," "number," "letter," and "sound." Downing reports that at the end of the school year a minority of children remained confused about the reading process while others made "varying degrees of progress towards developing the concept of reading and developing the specific abilities in learning to read." Downing's description of the development of cognitive clarity about the reading process indicates five features: children grow in understanding the communication purpose of written language; their conception of the functions of symbols becomes clearer; their concepts of linguistic segments, such as "word" and "sound," approach those of the teacher; their corresponding spontaneous command of the abstract technical terminology of language increases; their understanding of the process of decoding alphabetic letters to speech sounds and vice versa improves.

Reid's and Downing's studies have an important implication for teachers of young children. Downing points out, "It would be a grave error to assume that the young child's perception of the process of reading and writing is the same as that of the adult who desires to teach him these useful skills."

Environmental Factors

Home Background and Experience   A number of environmental factors both subtle and obvious are at work in shaping the child's personality, experiences, attitudes, values, and language abilities. Conditions in the home influence a child's personal and social adjustment, which in turn may help or hinder that child's learning to read. Children with a stable home life and parents who love and understand them and provide them with a sense of individual worth will have one less stumbling block between themselves and reading.

The home also influences the child's attitudes towards books and reading. Parents who read and own books and who appreciate reading themselves and enjoy reading stories to their children usually produce children who want to read. Parents who take an interest in the school, in what the child is learning and doing there, reinforce this positive attitude.

The quality and extent of a child's experiences at home are also important to progress in reading. Reading should be a meaningful act, and children's past experiences enable them to comprehend what they read. Probably most school beginners have the background of information and experience necessary to handle most beginning reading material. It is, of course, important to remember that the teacher's instruction should be based on the child's previous experiences.

Socioeconomic Class and Culture: There is a tendency for middle- and upper-class children to be ready earlier for beginning reading instruction. However, as Harris (1961) observes, "What counts for child development is not the wealth of the home but the intellectual and social environment with which the child is surrounded" (p. 38). Time rather than money is needed. Parents should spend time talking with their children, enjoying and sharing story books with them, and sharing and broadening their experiences. Children from low socioeconomic homes where parents pursue such activities have an excellent chance to become good readers.

Recently there has been much interest in cultural environment and its effect on a child's readiness. In our North American culture there are several subcultures (black, Mexican American, rural mountain, urban disadvantaged, Indian, and so on). These subcultures to some extent determine children's speech, their experiences and concepts, their attitudes, and their values (Mickelson and Galloway, 1973). Downing, Oliver, and Ollila (1975) for instance found Canadian native Indian kindergarten children significantly less able to recognize the function and acts of reading and writing. They were also less able to understand the technical terms of reading (e.g. "word", "letter"), and to recognize letters and hear various sounds in words. Some children from these subcultures are not ready for middle-class schools and their reading instruction. Reading and other intellectual activities are not highly valued in some subcultures (Deutsch, 1960). Stories may seem foreign to some children's previous experiences. Some of these children come from homes where a foreign language is spoken. Others speak variations of English which may be quite dissimilar to the English used in most schools. So teacher expectancies for behavior in school may seem alien to some children.

Language Abilities: Most school beginners will have the language readiness necessary to make good progress in reading. The richness of their vocabulary and complexity of their spoken sentences are likely to surpass the common words and simple sentences that they are taught in their beginning readers. Some children, however, have immature language development and faulty habits such as "baby talk." Some come from foreign speaking homes and are relatively unfamiliar with English. Others are members of culturally isolated groups where nonstandard English is spoken. Differences in grammar, language structures, and sounds may make these children's variations of English different from the English in the average reading program. These small groups will need some special accommodating instruction so they will not be handicapped in learning to read.

Social and Emotional Factors

Motivation   Motivation is a key factor in learning to read. It helps to explain why some children who are deficient in a number of readiness abilities make good progress in beginning reading, while other children with the same deficiencies are slow to read. Fortunately, most five- or six-year-olds are excited about going to school and want to learn how to read. Teachers should do everything in their power to sustain this enthusiasm and desire. However, some children would rather play games, climb, run, wrestle—anything but sit still and learn to read. Others would rather be read to by their parents or the teacher than have to read for themselves. The teacher must work hard to arouse these children's interest in learning to read. But there is little reason to delay reading simply because a child is not showing a desire to read. This motivation can and should be nurtured and encouraged during actual instruction.

Social and Emotional Maturity and Adjustment   A child's social and emotional adjustment and maturity may be a barrier or a help in learning to read. Harris (1961) emphasizes three aspects of emotional and social maturity—emotional stability, self-reliance, and ability to participate in groups—as particularly important for school or reading readiness.

A child should have a certain degree of emotional control. Boys and girls who have temper tantrums, cry and over-react when they cannot get their own way, or withdraw or sulk when they have trouble with a lesson will be less likely to make normal reading progress than children who do not.

Children need to be sufficiently self-reliant in a classroom. If the teacher hands out worksheets (suited to the child's ability level) and explains how to do them, each child should be able to continue working alone. Boys and girls who have grown too dependent may not be able to do independent activities by themselves and may make unreasonable demands on the teacher's attention. They may be less likely to make normal progress in reading than others.

As much of the instruction in the average classroom is done in groups, the ability to participate actively and cooperatively is important. Boys and girls should be able to listen well, pay attention to the teacher's explanation, and follow the teacher's directions. They should be able to take turns with the other group members and respect their rights. Children who cannot learn in group situations will be at a disadvantage in the average school.

Fortunately most children will come to school with personal and social adjustments sufficient for them to make normal progress in reading. A few children, however, may be emotionally and socially immature and show this immaturity in many ways. They may be relatively self-centered, inattentive, unwilling to cooperate with their teacher, and shy. Past preschool experiences may have given them marked feelings of insecurity, inferiority, or hostility that can inhibit learning. Sometimes their behavior disrupts not only their learning but that of their classmates. If the teacher suspects real emotional disturbance, the child should be referred to the school psychologist or other appropriate authority or agency.

On the other hand, immature behavior does not necessarily signal maladjustment. Time and familiarity with the teacher and classroom procedures are allies in working with immature children. One of the most important things a teacher can do is to help the child with social and emotional problems to achieve numerous successful experiences with reading.

Instructional Factors

So far we have focused on children—how experience and physical, emotional, social, and intellectual development influence their readiness for reading. We must now turn to the school's instructional program.

Kindergarten   Many studies stress the importance of kindergarten in helping children do well in first-grade reading programs. We would expect kindergartens which teach special readiness programs tailored to the needs of the children to be especially helpful. However, just the kindergarten experiences of becoming acquainted with the school, working with the teacher in groups and alone, and socializing with other children make school adjustment easier (Spache and Spache, 1977). Learning to listen and pay attention to the teacher, following directions to play games, even finding out how to use scissors, paste, and crayons all help develop a child's readiness for reading.

The Teacher: Researchers (Bond and Dykstra, 1967) continually point to the teacher as the key factor in the instructional program. The teacher influences the child's readiness in a number of subtle and direct ways. Teachers vary in their knowledge of beginning reading and their ability to organize and present such lessons. They may or may not have a warm learning atmosphere, a sincere interest in the children, and an enthusiastic approach to teaching. Some teachers are more effective than others. The good teachers will do a better job of teaching readiness skills. Also, the teachers' concepts of reading readiness and their expectancies will guide them in deciding who is ready and when reading should be begun. One teacher may decide who is ready to read by judging each individual child's maturity. Another teacher may decide that the children who have completed their readiness workbooks successfully are the ones ready for reading. A child labeled "ready to read" by one teacher may not be "ready to read" in another classroom.

The School's Beginning Reading Program: Many schools follow a set policy that prescribes a certain reading program or series. This reading program may influence the child's readiness to read. Some programs require more refined skills; a child may not be ready for such a program until age seven. Other programs may be modified and adapted so five-year-olds will be ready for them. Each teacher must know what skills and abilities are necessary for children to succeed in the adopted program.

Classroom Conditions Conditions such as class size and classroom resources and facilities may be factors in the teacher's readiness instruction. Teachers who have class loads of thirty to forty pupils will not be able to teach each child as effectively as those who have twenty to thirty children (Frymier, 1964). Some schools provide teacher aides (salaried or volunteer assistants for teachers in the classroom) or volunteer helpers. Such help allows the teacher to devote more time to individualizing instruction. Well-equipped classrooms, well-planned resource centers with varieties of audio-visual aids and books, and special services such as a psychometrist (a person in charge of school testing) and a reading coordinator are big assets in the teacher's instructional program.

DETERMINING READING READINESS AND INSTRUCTIONAL LEVEL

Although our teacher at Howard School has only known and worked with her group one week, she has already begun to evaluate and decide who is ready for reading and who needs further preparation. This is a *most important* step in good teaching and must be given the thought, time, and effort it deserves. A doctor does not prescribe treatment without a thorough diagnosis. Neither should a teacher.

A good evaluation answers two questions. First, it gives the teacher a global assessment. It tells who is ready to begin reading and who needs further preparation. Second, it points out fairly specifically what instruction is needed by each child. This is most important because children not only vary among themselves but within themselves. Not every child develops the various abilities that comprise reading readiness simultaneously. For instance, a child's oral language abilities may be well developed, but at the same time have trouble detecting likenesses and differences between words seen. Because of the varied abilities in each individual, one writer (Durkin, 1976) suggests that teachers talk in terms of child "readinesses" rather than the all-encompassing "readiness." Therefore the teacher asks specific questions such as: Can the child match letters? Can he participate well in group instruction? The teacher must also consider the beginning reading program that each child has to be ready to undertake. All this knowledge will provide the raw material for designing an effective and more individualized prereading and reading program.

Determining Where the Child Is Now

Techniques to determine the child's prereading strengths and capabilities include both formal tests and teacher judgments. The teacher will want to know if the child has any physical conditions that might hinder success in beginning reading. Ideally each child will have a physical check-up, including an eye and ear examination, prior to school entrance. The teacher should be liberal in referrals if anything is amiss. Readiness tests, valuable to many teachers, especially inexperienced ones, serve to support and reaffirm the teacher's judgments and provide a quick assessment. The subtests may also be a source of ideas for readiness training activities. Some teachers also use intelligence tests. However, there is a danger of too much reliance on formal tests. Their results may influence the teacher's expectations of a student.

Some factors, such as interest in reading, attention span, and social adjustment, cannot be easily measured by tests. These can be better measured informally. Teachers can use "homemade" tools such as check-lists, anecdotal records, and teacher-made specific skills tests. The first-grade teacher can tap the previous kindergarten teacher's knowledge about the child. The experience charts that are used to prepare children to read can also serve as a test of children's progress. Simply trying the child out on a sample of the beginning reading task may provide an excellent basis for evaluation. For instance, the teacher may print the vocabulary of the first preprimer on cards and have the children learn the words. The child that learns the words quickly is more apt to be ready for the task. Downing and Thackray (1975) report that this practice is used by many teachers in Great Britain for grouping beginning readers.

Teachers also can form judgments from observing children in and out of the classroom. Is the child interested in the stories that the teacher reads? Can the child work alone? The knowledge of each child's prereading strengths and weaknesses can be summed up on individual checklists. An example of a checklist is shown on pp. 248–249. Teachers may wish to modify this one or develop one of their own to suit their particular situation.

Determining What the Program Requires

Next the teacher will want to have a knowledge of the beginning reading program to be used. Both kindergarten and first-grade teachers should become acquainted with the method, materials, content, and principles of instruction used in the program. Teachers should ask themselves, "What skills does this particular child need to succeed in this program? Does this program stress any particular method of teaching reading?" We know that language-experience programs, phonic programs, and linguistic programs, to use some examples, may emphasize some prereading skills and place less importance on others. For instance, an individualized beginning reading program may put a greater premium on independent work habits and a lesser emphasis on group work.

Reading Readiness Checklist

Name of Child _____

Date _____

Write *yes* or *no* or other appropriate answer for each of the following questions:

Physical Considerations

What is the sex of the child?
Have the child's general health, vision, and hearing been examined?
If so, has any special restriction been imposed or has any special treatment been prescribed?
Are there any signs of visual, auditory, or speech problems?
Is the child's attendance in school regular?
Is the child alert and responsive to instruction?

Social and Emotional Adjustment in the Classroom

Does the child attend to the teacher's instruction in whole class situations?
Does the child attend to the teacher's instruction in small group situations?
Is the child overdependent on the teacher?
Does the child interact well with other members of the class?
Does the child adapt easily to new situations?
Can the child assume responsibility and work independently?
Does the child complete assigned tasks?
Does the child know when to talk and when to listen to the teacher?
Does the child participate well and take turns in group activities?
How well does the child cope with minor frustrations?

Desire to Read and Reading Concepts

Does the child enjoy hearing stories?
Can the child listen to a story with sustained interest for ten minutes?
Does the child voluntarily look at school books in the library?
Does the child seem to have established a sense of left-to-right, top-to-bottom orientation in experience chart activities?
Does the child show interest in words and messages in the classroom?
Does the child bring books from home to school?
Does the child handle books with reasonable care?
Can the child write his or her own name?
Does the child seem to understand that reading is talk written down?

Intellectual Factors

Has the child had an intelligence test? If so, what were the results?
Does the child seem to be mentally alert?
Does the child interpret pictures effectively, seem to contribute pertinent ideas to class discussions?
Does the child have a good memory for past experiences? Can he memorize simple rhymes or remember simple messages?

Does the child show originality in his ideas and classwork?
Does the child understand and follow directions with a minimum of assistance?
Does the child seem to reason well and pick up new learnings quickly?
Does the child show some ability in problem solving?

Background of Experience and Language Abilities

Is the child able to recite common nursery rhymes and is he acquainted with well-known fairy tales?
Has the child attended nursery school and/or kindergarten?
Does the child have knowledge about common concepts—food, family, house, animals, etc.? Are the child's concepts reasonably accurate?
Is English spoken in the child's home?
If not English, what language is spoken?
Can the child speak with reasonable fluency?
Does the child seem to have a reasonable vocabulary to communicate experiences?
Can the child use more complex language structures in addition to so-called simple sentences?
Does the child use and/or understand standard English?
Does the child use a nonstandard form of English?
Does the child understand the school's language of instruction?

Visual and Auditory Perception

Can the child see differences in pictures and geometric shapes?
Can the child recognize his own name?
Can the child match letters and discriminate words that have gross differences (*O* and *x*; *see* and *hello)?*
Can the child discriminate between words that have only minor detail differences (*wear, were)?*
Can the child recognize words that have been repeatedly presented to him?
Can the child rhyme words?
Can the child add to a list of words beginning with the same initial sounds?
Can the child discriminate between words that sound very similar (*watch* and *witch)?*
Does the child demonstrate knowledge of sound-letter relationships? (That is *d*. It makes the first sound in *dog.*)

PLANNING THE ASSESSMENT OF READING READINESS

Teaching reading readiness involves a commitment to instruction at the child's level. Therefore, the assessment of reading readiness should begin in the first weeks of kindergarten and first grade, or even with parent interviews prior to kindergarten. Assessment at this early stage involves informal measures. As children change rapidly in prereading skills and abilities, evaluation should be done continuously. Formal assessments—reading readiness tests—are usually conducted at the end of kindergarten and after the second or third week of first grade, and are often determined by school policy.

DEVELOPING READINESS SKILLS

Although children will learn some reading readiness skills incidently, readiness training should not be left to chance. Neither should it be concentrated entirely in isolated drills. A *reading* readiness program must go beyond teaching school readiness (social adjustment, lengthening attention span, etc.). It should emphasize and be directed toward tasks which prepare children to remember words (Samuels 1973), understand the communication purposes of reading, and motivate interest in beginning to read. A good training program is well organized and carefully thought out. Teachers should have a sense of where they are going—why they are doing a particular activity with a child. The diagnosis of each child's skills and abilities in relationship to the school's beginning reading program reveals the child's particular readiness needs. These needs determine the content and emphasis of the readiness program.

Evaluating the class at Howard School, Ms. Lane found that two children were reading at second-grade level. She also noticed that a few children scored very well on teacher-made and published texts of reading readiness. They seemed to have the maturity, intelligence, language abilities, and conceptual background needed for the beginning reading program. She decided to begin their formal reading as soon as was practical because they had no need for a readiness training period. After her best effort at assessment, the teacher was still not sure about three children's readiness to read, so she decided it was probably better to wait. Children who have been pushed into reading before they are ready are more likely to fail than ones who have been delayed a short period of time.

Most of the children in Ms. Lane's class would profit from readiness training. Some children in this group were strong in some readiness skills but needed training to bolster other skills. Her job was to strengthen the skills in which pupils had demonstrated weakness. A few children would require an extended time of training. They seemed to have deficits in almost every area. It is not uncommon to see one or two first graders from each class spend a half year in preparation. These very late starters are a real challenge to a teacher. She must try to keep the children from being discouraged as they see everyone else beginning to read. The teacher must also frequently contend with parents who come to school wondering, "Why isn't my child reading yet?"

ORGANIZING AND INDIVIDUALIZING A READINESS PROGRAM

There are a number of ways to organize and individualize a readiness program. Some schools have adopted unusual organizations, such as transition rooms, a sort of half step after kindergarten for those who are not ready for first grade. Some teachers in open area schools team teach, dividing their classes to arrive at groups of closer abilities. Some teachers have teacher aides. Most teachers, however, work in self-contained classrooms, and the readiness program must conform to this situation. Two useful aids in organizing readiness programs—flexible groupings and learning centers—are presented below. Other ideas for organization will be found in books listed at the end of this chapter.

Flexible Grouping Many teachers organize their classes into flexible groups, formed around special needs and interests, and later disbanded when they have served their purpose. These represent one method of individualiz-

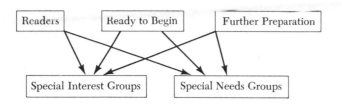

ing instruction. Ms. Lane established such groups on the basis of a global assessment of each child's present achievement. Her three basic groups were (1) readers, (2) children who were ready to read, and (3) children who needed further preparation before reading. She then went through each child's reading readiness inventory and placed individuals in special needs and interest groups. For instance, two children in the "ready to read" group needed further preparation in beginning consonant sounds, as did fourteen children in the "further preparation" group. Seven children had expressed an enthusiastic interest in trucks, so a special group was formed including both reader and nonreader members. A diagram of Ms. Lane's grouping appears above.

Notice that children in both "reading" and "ready to read" groups may also be involved in some readiness activities. This is because readiness and reading subtly blend into each other. Many of the readiness activities will probably be continued into initial reading, providing the child with added practice and review. There is no clear dividing line. The readiness program should provide a smooth transition between nonreading and reading.

Learning Centers   To facilitate all types of readiness experiences, learning centers can be established in the classroom. The centers consist of designated areas of the room in which children can do different readiness activities. Centers can be listed pictorially on a magnetic chalkboard. The children are given two or three name cards with which they can choose centers. Teachers can reserve two or three cards per child, and put them at the centers to which they wish to assign children, according to skill weaknesses. Children can remove the card as they complete the work at the center. Learning centers might include one or more of the following: a writing and word center, a book center, a play or game center, a story center, a phonics center, a building and block center, a printing center. There are many more. Types of centers are limited only by the creativity of the teacher and the special needs of the class.

The teacher introduces each center to the children and discusses the different activities that can be done in each. The activities or centers may be changed from time to time and each new addition discussed. Not all these centers will appeal to every prereader. However, many teachers have found learning stations effective in coping with individual differences and providing activities for free play or independent work periods.

The *writing and word center* is for children who want to learn a "special" word. There is a large pocket-chart in which each child has a pocket for storing words. The teacher prints the child's word on a card. On succeeding visits to the word center, the teacher may review the child's old words. No pressure should be applied. If the child does not remember the word after being told it several times, it should be unobtrusively destroyed. The center can also be used in writing captions for pictures. Other children may have a special message or story they want to have written down. For instance, children may draw a front cover for their mother's birthday card and dictate a message which the teacher copies on the inside of the card.

A *printing center* contains samples of letters that children can copy and practice.

A *book center* or library is set up in a corner of the room. This area can be made quite cozy and inviting with a *small area rug,* book shelves, some little chairs, or a small table with books displayed on it. Children may come here when they are through with their work or at playtime to look at the books. This book corner can contain a variety of books—both published children's books and class-made diaries or illustrated short stories dictated by members of the class to the teacher.

A *play or game center* provides a variety of individual and group readiness games. The games might include puzzles, flannel board story kits, lotto, a magnetic board with magnetic letters, picture or shape dominoes, sequence puzzles, and so on. The teacher should introduce each game to the children, showing them how each can be played.

ACTIVITIES TO IMPROVE READINESS SKILLS

There are vast numbers of activities that the teacher can use to prepare children for reading. The author has included a few examples for each skill. (The reader will notice that one activity may develop a number of readiness skills.) At the end of the chapter and in the section on the current readiness programs, sources for other activities are presented. Also, much of value can be learned through visits to different classrooms and schools in the area.

Teachers should choose activities that can be made interesting and meaningful. For example, the teacher should not say, "What words begin with the same sound as *moon?*" when there is a Mary in the class. The teacher should use Mary's name, which makes the lesson more interesting to the children.

Adjusting to Physical Deficiencies How can the teacher help a child with poor vision, speech, and hearing in the prereading period? There are a number of ways. The teacher may modify the prereading program to adapt to the child's deficiencies, keep a sharp eye out for signs of physical problems, and make referrals when necessary. Important, too, is a good cooperating relationship between teacher and parent. For instance, if the child comes to school each day looking tired, the teacher should feel free to suggest to the parents that perhaps the child may need more sleep.

Improving Personal and Social Adjustment to School It is very important for reading and other learning as well that a child's first experiences with the school be happy and successful ones. During the prereading period, the teacher should watch each child's personal and social adjustment carefully. Often, work in small groups, group games, praise, encouragement, and success in learning activities will help children who are having adjustment problems. Parents and teachers should feel free to discuss and enlist each other's aid in improving the child's emotional and social development. Many helpful suggestions may be found in books included at the end of this chapter.

Developing Background of Experience   Many children have a background of experiences which enables them to understand what they will read about in the beginning reading program. However, a small group of children, including those from culturally different or culturally disadvantaged backgrounds, may not. For all children a stimulating classroom environment, rich in firsthand experiences, is beneficial. However, with children of limited and meager concepts and experiences, this rich and varied background building program becomes even more important. Such a program must be carefully structured. Some ideas for building backgrounds are listed here.

1   Look at the beginning reading program. What are the stories about? The background of experience and concepts needed to understand the stories should be introduced in the prereading program as well as other concepts.
2   Active, firsthand experiences are very valuable. Children might plan and care for a school garden, care for classroom pets, prepare a rhythm band, and make a play store, house, or post office. Field trips are good for enlarging concepts and knowledge about the community. They can include excursions to places like the zoo, the neighborhood fire station, the post office, and a farm. Science experiments also are useful in providing firsthand experiences.
3   Audio and visual aids are useful. Records, motion pictures, models, pictures, television, photographs, and slides can be looked at, handled, or heard and then discussed with the teacher. Classroom discussion is very important. It broadens the child's understandings and provides the teacher with some feedback on the children's thinking. Mere exposure to the audio-visual aid is not enough.

Developing Attention and Persistence   Goals for improving attention and persistence should be included as a part of all other lessons in preparing a child for reading. Attention and persistence will improve if the teacher remembers to:

1   Capture the child's interest with the lesson. It should be meaningful. Children who have notoriously short attention spans in the classroom often sit and play with favorite toys or watch cartoons for lengthy periods at home.
2   Keep the room as free of distractions as possible.
3   Ensure that all children experience success. Then they are apt to be more interested. Their attention span and persistence with the lesson will increase.
4   For children who have extremely short attention spans, begin with brief activities. The length of the activities may be gradually extended. Seat these children close to the teacher. Then it will be easier for the teacher to direct each child's attention to the learning.

To develop persistence, the teacher should require the child to complete what he has begun. Children should be given classroom responsibilities such as taking care of the library or of outside play equipment (balls, jump rope) and feeding fish or gerbils. The teacher should consistently check to see that these are well done to encourage habits of persistence. If children have not completed an activity that is at their instructional level, they should be encouraged to finish it. A number of teachers also recommend behavior modification techniques as helpful in improving attention in their class.

Developing the Desire to Read An essential goal of the teacher during the readiness training program is to develop and maintain a desire to read. There are many ways of doing this. First, the child should feel that to learn to read is something important personally. The teacher can make reading meaningful for the child by:

1 Writing the schedule for the day on the chalkboard and reading it with the children. The class will be interested in what they are going to do, especially if something special is happening (someone has a birthday, a visitor is coming). The chalkboard can also be used to write shorter messages of interest to the children. For instance, some days the teacher may go to the board and say "Good morning" while writing it on the chalkboard. Other phrases such as "Happy Birthday, Sally," "John, pass out the papers," "Harry, put on your coat" can be used.
2 Having the children help compose experience charts about field trips they have taken, new people in the class, special messages for parents, and so on.
3 At story time frequently giving different children a chance to pick a story they like to hear. Teachers can let children bring stories from home for them to read. They can let them pick from three available stories. When reading a story, the teacher can let the children discuss some of the pictures.

The teacher's interest in books can be a model for the child. Children like to imitate their teacher. Many love to play school. By reading to the class, with expression and enthusiasm, a teacher is building a foundation for a lifetime love of reading in students. Visitors can be invited to read stories to the class. The school principal can also give valuable help in this way. Boys will be quite impressed also when an older fourth, fifth or sixth grade boy reads a story to them.

Teachers also influence a child's desire to read by the negative and positive comments they make during prereading instruction. Browne (1972) studied this teacher-pupil verbal interaction during first-grade reading periods. She found that the high achieving groups were able to respond more successfully to the reading tasks and were met with much praise from their teachers. On the other hand, children in the low achieving groups had much more difficulty with their reading tasks and received for their effort more corrective statements from their teachers. Browne also found that the teachers spent more time with the lower achieving children. Thus, the lower achieving children, who needed praise and encouragement, received a longer period of continuous negative comments.

Children need praise and success with the various prereading activities if they are to develop and maintain a desire to read. If a child is not succeeding in some prereading activity, the teacher should muster some encouraging words and lower the level of difficulty of the activity so that the child can succeed and receive positive reinforcement. Then learning can start from that level.

Developing Concepts about Reading We as adults have already learned to read. Having accomplished this task, we often take for granted certain basic concepts about reading that children may not know. These basic concepts and words should be presented clearly in the classroom. They include ideas such as "reading is talk written down" and the meanings of reading instruction words such as *letter, word,* and *sentence*. Teach the children how to handle books and read from top to bottom, left to right. Remember also to share with the children the ideas of reading as adventure, escape, mystery, and excitement. We not only want children to learn to read, but also to become lifelong readers.

A readiness program should be rich in experiences with words. Vocabulary skills and concepts can be emphasized indirectly and informally through experience charts, reading readiness books, and other meaningful and relevant activities with letters and words. Repeated informal mention of these concepts is helpful. Long, detailed explanations of words and letters will most likely be wasted effort. Vocabulary can be taught well by pointing out examples when the child shows interest or by using the right term at the right time.

**Developing Language Abilities—
Speaking and Listening**

Speaking and *listening* are two of the major building blocks for beginning reading. Armstrong (1967) explains the importance of oral language:

> Oral language is needed to relate the child's background to the story, to enlarge concepts necessary to an understanding of the story, to relate concepts to vocabulary, to build interest, to build familiarity with unfamiliar language structures, and to enhance the functioning of the higher mental processes used in reading. Discussion, skillfully guided, does these things (p. 57).

Most children will have a vocabulary and store of concepts that are more than adequate for getting meaning from the beginning readers. In many classrooms, then, the major emphasis will be on improving other language abilities. Some children may need to develop a greater range or fluency of oral expression. When the teacher asks a question, the child may answer only with gestures or monosyllables. At the other extreme are the children who reply with a long-winded answer plus a few extra bits of information that are not really needed.

Some children will also need help in developing more complex sentence structures—for example, "I like dogs when they let me pet them," rather than simply, "I like dogs." They need to be familiar with language patterns similar to those used in the stories so that they will read to get meaning from the stories. They also need to be familiar with the language of instruction used by the teacher. This similarity of language patterns can be developed by: (1) planning oral language training for children, (2) writing down the language for them to read as in the language-experience approach, and (3) helping children participate effectively in class and group activities. Some children need help in overcoming shyness in a group. Some children need to learn how to ask questions.

Language Training: A Part of All Activities   The majority of training in language is done indirectly outside the isolated "language training sessions." Language training involves the total time that the teacher is with the child in school. The first step is to provide many chances for self-expression. The child should talk to and listen to the teacher, talk to and listen to other children. The teacher can provide an atmosphere where children feel free and are encouraged to express themselves within classroom limits.

Communication skills can be developed during art, music, free play, science, and other times. Conversation is often easier for children with poorer language development when they are actively involved in an activity. The teacher should make a point of talking individually to each student. This is especially important with children who need extensive improvement. The teachers "model" their language for each child to copy.

Besides serving as a model for language development, the teacher must take time to listen to what the class has to say. Although this sounds very obvious, researchers have found that teachers do almost all of the talking in the class. Children spend far too much of their time sitting and listening. Improving language abilities requires that classroom communication be a two-way street.

Direct Language Training Activities   Although language training should be seen as a part of every school activity, there are a number of games and activities which develop language skills directly. They may be used with the whole class or smaller groups. Smaller groups are often more effective with timid and less verbal children. Several examples of "teacher tested" activities are listed below:

1   Take Polaroid pictures of a class field trip, classroom activities, free play, or lunchroom happenings. Ask children questions about them. Use a toy telephone or tin can telephone, puppets, child-made imaginary paper animals, and so on to stimulate conversation.
2   Having a "show and tell" period where children tell about objects, share interesting events, or tell a story they made up to the other children in the class. For a variation, try "choose and tell." In this activity the teacher provides various objects or pictures, and children pick one and talk about it.
3   Take advantage of children's imagination and love of make-believe. Children can take various roles in dramatic play. They can pretend to be a teacher, a mother, a father, a storekeeper, and so on.
4   Develop grammatical drills using models or miniatures. The children or teacher can move these around and make up sentences about them to develop proficiency in verb forms, comparative terms, prep-

ositions, and singular and plural forms. Example: The cow is eating grass. The cow is bigger than the chicken.

5 Ask the child to draw a picture and then give a verbal description of it. Draw some pictures yourself and have the children give verbal descriptions of them.

Listening Comprehension Children need training in listening comprehension skills—understanding what other people are saying. This type of training is the preliminary step in comprehending stories in the readers. It enables children to go beyond just parroting words in a book. Children need to understand what the words say so they can react to them. This includes both knowing the meaning of specific words such as *boy* and *bathtub* and comprehending sentences, paragraphs, and stories. Children also need skill in listening to benefit from reading instruction. They must listen to and understand what the teacher is teaching them. They must learn how to follow directions. Below are a few suggestions for developing listening comprehension:

1 To provide practice in understanding and recalling facts: Read a story to the children and ask them specific questions about it.

2 To provide practice in putting events in a sequence: Ask the children to draw pictures illustrating a story and then have them line up the pictures in the right order for showing on the class-made cardboard television set.

3 To provide practice in following directions: Demonstrate how to make a simple art project before the class. Then let each child do the project. Ask children who have trouble in following directions to explain what they did to make the project.

4 To provide practice in interpreting and evaluating ideas and stories: When discussing a story read to the children, go beyond asking factual questions and develop some of the following questions: "Could this story really happen?" "Why?" "Why did you think George was nice to his little sister?" "Why did you or why didn't you like this story?" "What do you think will happen next?" and "What would you do in this situation?"

Auditory Discrimination Children must be able to hear likenesses and differences in sounds in order to recognize words by a phonics method. Activities to develop this skill should follow in a sequence from gross to finer discriminations. They can be taught in games, in rhymes, and as drills. Most children will need very few lessons with the more basic discriminations, such as hearing the difference between the *moo* of a cow and the *quack* of a duck. For many children these basic lessons can be skipped altogether. Some children will need frequent practice in hearing sounds in words, so teachers often use commercial materials designed for this purpose. Types of training activities that develop skill in auditory discrimination include the following:

1 Ask the children to be silent for a moment. Then they can discuss the sounds they heard.

2 Play short records with different but familiar sounds. Children can identify each sound as it is played. Sometimes pictures of the objects making the sound are used. Children can take turns finding the right picture from a group on the bulletin board.

3 Have children guess the sources of sound as one child hides from view and does the following things: (a) claps hands softly; (b) shakes a rattle; (c) crumples a piece of paper; (d) bangs on a drum.

4 Introduce the concept that words are made up of sounds. Have children listen to different common long and short words. Pronounce the words slowly and see if the children can tell how many separate sounds they hear.

5 Recite or play records of nursery rhymes. Point out which words rhyme. Have children complete rhymes such as "I know a mouse. He lives in my _____." Have children pick out from a group of four words the one that does not rhyme. Ask children to say a word that rhymes with another word.

6 Introduce initial consonants in a word context. Say that *b* is the first sound of *balloon* rather than that *b* says "buh." Start with easy to learn and common consonants such as *m,b,f,* and *p* and then continue with others, *g,c,t,l,d,h,j,k,r,n,w,s,y,v,x,*and *z.* Vowels are frequently introduced later, although for a few basal programs the opposite is the case. It is a good idea to gear the auditory discrimination training program to what will be taught in the children's beginning reading program.

Some teachers like to introduce initial consonants with worksheets which include activities such as circling or coloring all the pictures that begin with a certain sound. Others prefer to use scrapbooks with pages to be filled with pictures of words starting with the various consonant sounds. Some teachers combine both formal and informal approaches. Games provide good practice. For instance, the teacher reads a list of words and requires each child to stand up or clap when a word beginning with a certain sound is said.

7 Teach initial consonants in a story context. Say, for example. "Charlie put ____ ____ on his hands so he could make snowballs." Explain that what he put on begins with the same sound as *Mary.*

Developing Visual Discrimination

In their research on dimensional dominance, May, Oliver, and Fernandez (1976) found that kindergarten children who attended more to color than shape did more poorly on a letter-word matching task. It seems, therefore, that children who do not make fine discriminations of letters and words will need additional practice. Training should start at the level of the child as determined by readiness and teacher-made tests. Children who recognize most letters but have difficulty in discriminating between *b,p,* and *d* should not have to begin their training with low-level activities such as matching pictures or geometric forms. For some children weakness in visual discrimination is a problem of short attention span or lack of interest in words. When these problems are solved, visual discrimination will improve. Frequently finer auditory and visual discrimination skills are taught together so that children will learn the sound-letter relationship in words.

Perception and Discrimination of Non-Letter Forms   Some children are not able to see differences in letters and words. With these children, visual discrimination training begins with activities stressing likenesses and differences in objects, pictures, and geometric forms. When the child shows some skill in these basic discriminations, the teacher should begin discrimination training with words and letters. The value of exercises with non-letter forms may be rather limited. Robinson (1972), in a review of research findings, says, "The research shows no conclusive answers to the question of the effectiveness of perceptual training to improve reading. While some programs appear to improve perceptual performance in the areas trained, the long-term effect on reading is uncertain" (p. 145). In general, the more visual discrimination training resembles reading tasks, the more effective it will be in developing reading readiness. Exercises with non-letter forms may, however, help some children who have short attention spans, have trouble following directions, and have no background of looking at words or books (Durrell, 1956). They are also fun for many children to do and can be made easy enough to give almost any child a successful prereading experience.

Activities to develop general perceptual skills are found in many basal readiness books, children's magazines, and commercially produced activities books. There are even whole commercial programs devoted to developing visual perception. As noted before, the value of using these *whole* programs in readiness training is questionable (Paradis, 1974). Some activities with non-letter forms include:

1   Matching of objects, pictures, and geometric forms. A child is given a miniature cow and then is asked to pick out an identical cow from a group of animals. Matching with pictures and geometric forms is done in the same manner. The activity can be made more difficult by increasing the alternative choices or making the alternative choices very similar.
2   Lotto and bingo type games with pictures and shapes. A child holds up the master picture and the other children cover the same picture on their individual card with the master picture or a marker. The first child to have all the pictures covered or, in bingo, a straight row marked, wins the game.
3   Toys and puzzles where children have to fit a certain shape in the right place may be useful.
4   Pictures containing hidden pictures can be found in some basal readiness books. The children have to find and color the hidden pictures. In other exercises the children must discover what is missing (picture of a dog minus one ear) and draw it in.

Visual Discrimination of Letters and Words   Activities for seeing likenesses and differences in letters and words start from gross discrimination of letters, such as telling *x* from *o*, and proceed to fine discrimination between words, such as *mat* and *met*. Much of the teaching in fine discrimination of words will be done during beginning reading instruction as sight vocabulary is introduced. Isolated drills and worksheets should not be overstressed, since children quickly lose interest in simply matching or copying words and letters. Suggested activities are listed below:

1   Worksheets using the following types of exercises may be developed by the teacher or ordered from commercial publishers. The difficulty of each worksheet can be increased by (a) increasing alternatives to choose from; (b) increasing the number of right answers; and (c) choosing alternatives that are very similar to one another.

   a   Circle the letter that is different.

o	w	o

   b   Underline the word in the big box that is the same as the one in the little box.

be	rain	to	be	see
wet	Mary	wet	see	here

   c   Underline the word in the big box that begins with the letter in the little box.

h	school	me	from	hunt
l	love	three	sun	peace

   d   Circle the two words that have the same beginning and ending letter.

went	wheat	where

   (Although children should be able to see likenesses and differences in all parts of words, the teacher should provide more exercises that stress differences in beginnings of words. This helps to develop the habit of looking at a word from left to right.)

2   Develop small group activities and games similar to the above worksheet exercises. As examples:

   a   Each child in the group is given three letters (words). The teacher prints one of three letters on the chalkboard and each child must hold up the same letter card.

   b   Lotto and bingo type games can be made with letters and words.

3   Have the children trace various words or letters. Variations of this activity include finger tracing of letters or words made from sandpaper, tracing words with a pencil or crayon, or forming letters and words from clay. Example:

4   Activities which develop writing skills can be useful in developing visual discrimination. As the children copy a short message to take

home, they must look very closely at each word so that they can reproduce it.

5 Develop discrimination in words and letters in other situations:

  a Point out various differences in words on experience charts by saying, "Can anyone find another word in the chart that is exactly the same as this one I've printed on this card? Look at this word. It's really long."

  b Say, "All boys whose names begin with the first letter of Bobby's name (already printed on the chalkboard with first letter underlined) may get their coats."

(This last exercise also develops skills in auditory discrimination.)

Learning the Alphabet and Recognizing Letter Names   Educators disagree about whether it is necessary for children to name letters and know them in alphabetical order prior to beginning reading. If letter names will be used during beginning reading instruction, they should be learned first. Below are suggestions for those teachers who wish to include this skill in their readiness program:

1 Either capital or lower case letters may be first. Some teachers teach both forms of each letter together. Durrell (1956) suggests an order for learning capitals from easiest to hardest:

O, X, A, B, T, C, L, R, I, S, P, N, F,
E, H, D, M, K, Z, J, Y, W, G, Q, U, V.

For lower case letters the order is:

o, x, s, c, i, p, t, m, k, z, e, w, r,
j, y, f, n, a, h, v, u, b, d, l, g, q.

2 Point to a letter and say, "This is b (B)." Then associate the b with a key word. (It is a good idea to have classroom alphabet cards with a picture for every letter; the word is used for that picture, such as b as in boy.) Teach the letter with its sound, explaining that the letter b is the first sound in boy.

3 Use ABC picture books and picture dictionaries to reinforce letter names and sounds.

4 Use worksheets in which children must match capital and lower case letters or trace over one letter and color a picture whose first sound is the sound of the letter.

5 Play letter recognition games.

Developing Left-to-Right Orientation   Children must acquire the habit of looking from left to right along a line of print and proceeding from the top of the page to the bottom. Marchbanks and Levin (1965) and Timko (1972) found that the first letter was the most important clue in recognizing words for first-grade children. Kindergarten children in Marchbank's study also used the first letter in recognizing words. However, kindergarten boys used the last letter almost as much as the first letter. Without proper training they could develop the habit of looking at words from right to left (ball). Habits of left-to-right and top-to-bottom orientation can be taught at various opportune times during the school day. Most children will gradually establish this orientation. Special practice can also be given to a few children who experience unusual difficulty with it. The teacher can:

1 Teach children the terms *left* and *right* not only in reference to their hands, but also in reference to the chalkboard, bulletin board, and pages in a story book. Singing games such as "Looby-Lou" and direction games like "Simon Says" will be more useful than formalized drills.

2 Constantly repeat the idea of left to right by moving the finger or a pointer along chalkboard messages, experience chart stories, and so on when reading the words.

3 Use readiness workbooks and other picture books for practice in working from left to right. Each child has a copy and follows along with the teacher. Careful teacher monitoring is needed in this exercise.

4 Cut apart a series of pictures and paste them on heavy cardboard. The pictures are mixed up and a child is asked to put them in the correct order from left to right.

5 Make or buy special practice worksheets in which the child must draw various straight or curvy lines from left to right. Example:

Developing Motor Skills The value of motor skill training in readiness programs is controversial. Although motor development has little relationship to success in reading, exercise in body coordination may prove helpful to normal but grossly uncoordinated children and to children with cerebral palsy or brain damage (Spache and Spache, 1977). To ensure developing prereading abilities, this author suggests connecting motor skill training as closely as possible to other prereading activities. The following suggested exercises are taken from a program developed by Peake (1972). They show how reading readiness can be fostered in other lessons besides reading.

1 Draw a square grid on a gym mat 4'3" by 8'7" and print a different letter of the alphabet in each square. Ask a child to jump to certain letters.

2 Write the following words on cards: *leap, backwards, forwards, slide, turn, skip, gallop, jump, stretch, shrink, run, walk, hop, crawl, kick, throw, catch, stop,* and *go.* Ask the children to react according to the action of the word shown. At first, show each word and read it aloud. Later the children can read it themselves.

3 To a drum beat children do any one of the following actions or a combination of several to form a sequence: sit and clap, stamp feet, clap and stamp feet (standing), step in time, jump in time, run in time, run (quick soft beat) followed by a step (loud drum beat), twirl around, crawl, skip.

4 After reading aloud a short story with no more than five actions involved, ask the child to interpret it through body movement.

5 Make cue cards with a picture of an animal and its first letter below. Hang the cue cards on the wall. Put the corresponding letter cards in a hat box. Each child, in turns, draws a card from the box and matches it with the cue card letter hanging on the wall. The children then act out that animal for several minutes until it is the next child's turn to select a card.

Fine eye-hand coordination can be taught through coloring, cutting, pasting, tracing, and copying activities. The teacher might provide some special training in how to hold scissors for cutting and a crayon or pencil for drawing and printing. However, these fine muscle activities can usually be taught together with another skill. For instance, the children can be given a worksheet in which they must visually match identical letters by drawing a circle around them. Encircling the letters gives practice in hand-eye coordination.

Using Experience Charts

Developing experience charts is one of the more widely used techniques for helping children make a smooth transition from prereading to reading. The charts are compositions based on meaningful shared experiences and produced cooperatively by children and their teacher. Class discussions about what to include in the charts can extend children's experiences and oral language. The children are not necessarily required to read the charts. The teacher points to what is being read so the children can follow along. At the same time, the pupil develops (1) directional orientation—left-to-right and top-to-bottom; (2) more refined visual discrimination skills; (3) concepts of words and sentences (the teacher may say, for example, "What should we say in our next sentence?" or "Who wants to read the sentence I've just pointed to?"), and (4) the idea that reading is meaningful and is talk written down. The charts can also provide the teacher with excellent opportunities to informally diagnose how the above readiness skills are progressing.

Using Commercial Programs

There is a vast array of commercially published materials that the teachers may use to supplement readiness programs. Below are listed three different types with examples of each type.

1 Colorful games, audio-visual aids, records, charts, and worksheets designed to provide practice in strengthening various readiness skills add variety to any readiness program. The following are representative examples:

Picture Readiness Game. Champaign, Illinois: Garrard Press. This is a lotto game consisting of six cards with pictures on them. Children are supposed to develop attention and perceptual skills by matching a picture to its duplicate on the card.

Continental Press Reading Readiness Program. Elizabethtown, Pennsylvania: Continental Press Incorporated. A series of twelve sets of worksheets that are sold in liquid duplicator form to be reproduced for classroom use. Rhyming, beginning sounds, visual motor skills, visual discrimination, thinking, and independent activities are stressed. Various levels of difficulty are provided for each skill.

2 Commercial programs have been developed to teach one particular skill. For example:

The First Talking Alphabet. Chicago: Scott, Foresman and Company, 1967. This program was developed to teach the phoneme-grapheme (sound-letter) relationship. The program includes records, worksheets, individual picture and letter cards for each child, and a teacher's manual. The children listen to the recorded instruction and follow along on their card by pointing to pictures and repeating and tracing the letters.

3 Some commercial programs provide training in a variety of skills. Most of the companies which publish basal reading series also have readiness programs to be used specifically with that series. However, these programs can often be adapted for use with other types of first grade instruction. An example of a readiness program used in connection with a basal series is:

Getting Ready to Read. Boston: Houghton Mifflin Company, 1976. The first level of the prereading series *Getting a Head Start* claims to develop language facility, broaden conceptual backgrounds and readiness for a decoding strategy. The second level *Getting Ready to Read* introduces word attack skills—distinguishing letter forms, using spoken context, listening for initial sounds in words, making letter-sound associations, using spoken context and first letter of a printed word, and matching end sounds and letter forms. The series is accompanied by teacher's guides, "Big Books" for large-group instruction, pupil workbooks, letter cards, letter form board, Letto cards and Word cover (bingo-like games), plastic objects and set of twenty-two boxes to practice discrimination between sounds and letters, picture and key cards, letter-picture solitaire, word cards (the prereading series presents fifteen words), and a pocket chart.

Commercial Programs— A Mixed Blessing

Reading educators often consider commercial readiness materials and programs a mixed blessing. Many have observed with dismay the abuses involving these programs in classrooms across the country. Commercial programs lend themselves neatly to an oversimplified approach to preparing children for reading. It is easy for teachers to say, "I teach reading readiness. Look, every morning between nine and ten o'clock I have my children take out their *ABC Easy Reading Readiness Workbooks* and we do three pages." Commercial materials should never be considered the entire readiness program. Neither should they dictate what skills are to be taught or the pace at which they should be learned.

Another oversimplified practice which is often linked with commercial programs is having all the children in the class go through all the steps of the program whether they need them or not. The teacher treats all pupils as though they were alike, insisting that even the one or two children who are reading books complete all the readiness activities. At the other extreme, there are children who are not ready to learn the readiness activities in the commercial program, but these too are forced to join in, although they cannot possibly benefit and may be harmed by being pressured through the program. Even though there may be only five children in the room who really need to use a particular activity, everyone is forced to waste time on it. Requiring a whole class or each group to go through the *entire* commercial program regardless of individual differences in skill needs, learning rates, and level of achievement is a waste of valuable learning time.

Frequently commercial materials are misused by being made into "busywork." This is especially true of the many master duplicator materials which are run off in tall stacks for classroom use. In some classrooms preparation for reading consists of a steady diet of these every day. Although some of these worksheets may provide good skill building activities, they must be used in moderation. They may be good activities to keep children busy and quiet, but all teachers should keep asking themselves, "Is the child learning something from this, or is it just busywork?" Learning time is too precious to be wasted on the latter.

Although commercial programs claim to teach a number of skills—visual perception, auditory discrimination, sound-letter relationship, and so on— several studies, such as Ollila (1970) and Jacobs (1968), have found that children were not necessarily better prepared in those skills because they used *one* particular program. In Ollila's study of three commercial readiness programs, no one training program was more effective in teaching the skills of visual perception and auditory discrimination than the other two. This result is of special interest considering that one program was designed specifically to develop visual perception and did not attempt to develop any auditory discrimination skills. Findings such as these should make the teacher look carefully at his commercial readiness program. Is it really doing the job it should be doing? Is it really helping to make each child more ready for reading?

Commercial materials must be chosen with an eye on the beginning reading program. Does the beginning program place a premium on any skill? If so, the teacher should choose readiness materials that provide lessons and practice in that skill. For instance, a beginning reading program with heavy doses of phonics can be supported by readiness materials emphasizing sound-letter relationships. It does not make much sense to use commercial materials to teach the traditional alphabet in kindergarten and then teach beginning reading with the initial teaching alphabet (i.t.a.) in first grade. Kindergarten and first-grade teachers should discuss their readiness and reading programs and coordinate their materials.

If commercial materials are used well, they can add valuable interest and variety to a readiness program. Readiness workbooks and books provide experiences in handling and caring for books and help in developing left-to-right orientation to reading. For the few children who may need a long extended period of readiness, these books and workbooks provide certain psychological advantages. As these children see their peers beginning to read books, they will want books, too, so they will feel that they are making progress.

Commercial readiness materials can also be sources of sequenced lessons and extra practice materials. Some teachers, especially beginning teachers, may not have the time, background, or experience to develop a large variety of sequential skill building lessons. While one child may learn a skill in one lesson, another child may need thirty practice sessions. Commercial materials can provide those thirty practice lessons, saving the teacher hours of preparation time. Even if teachers choose not to use commercial materials in a readiness program, they may want to develop a collection of them and occasionally scan them for ideas. They frequently provide reference lists of other materials and books as well.

If the teachers decide to use commercial programs, and according to most surveys the chances are good that they will, the materials should be adapted to fit the class. Remember, there is no rule that says the teacher must use the entire program as is. The more closely the materials are fitted to individuals in the class, the better the program will be.

PRE-SCHOOL AND KINDERGARTEN TRAINING PROGRAMS

Reading readiness instruction is an integral part of the average North American first-grade classroom. Many kindergarten teachers are also involved in teaching reading readiness skills. Ching (1970), in a survey of California kindergarten teachers, reported that 80 percent said they provided a "planned sequential reading readiness program" in their classrooms. Reaching down the ladder to three- and four-year-olds, readiness programs are now being experimented with in an increasing number of pre-schools. The following section explains how children are currently being prepared in nursery schools, kindergartens, and pre-schools for the culturally disadvantaged.

READING IN THE NURSERY SCHOOL

Nursery school teachers (those qualified with a background of reading courses) can help prepare children for reading in many of the ways used in the kindergarten. For instance, discussions between children and between teacher and child can help develop oral language abilities which are important to reading. Developing a rich background of experience, promoting healthy emotional and social growth, and encouraging children to think and to be curious about their environment will indirectly prepare children for reading. Nursery schools can have library corners available for those children who want to use them. Teachers can share story books with children who are interested. A number of further recommendations for improvement in pre-reading programs for young children has been listed in a joint statement written by various early education organizations and the International Reading Association (Strickland and others, 1977).

Other reading educators have suggested more direct instruction for children who are *interested*. Durkin (1973) recommends that "children's interests and reactions dictate materials and methods" (p. 6) used to help those children who *wish* to learn to read. She suggests experience charts and other homemade material, individual attention and small group work, and a combination of planned and on-the-spot teaching.

In contrast to the above proposals, several experimental, highly structured formal group approaches to teaching readiness and reading skills have been developed and shown to be of some benefit (Di Lorenzo and Salter, 1968). Characteristics of these programs include short blocks of time set aside daily for direct group teaching of skills like oral language and visual and auditory discrimination. The teacher presents the skills to the children and then directs their activity.

READING IN THE KINDERGARTEN

Readiness and formal reading are presented in kindergarten classrooms in a striking variety of ways. Organization, content, method, and materials differ widely from one class to another. This can be easily illustrated by the variety of answers given by kindergarten teachers when asked in recent surveys such as Ching's (1970) and LaConte's (1970) about the reading readiness programs in their classes. Some teachers said that all their children were included in readiness programs; others said that none were. A majority felt that most kindergartners would profit from training. Teachers disagreed on which readiness skills were most valuable for kindergarten and most deserving of instructional time. When asked about the type of program they thought was most effective, most teachers agreed that a combination of planned materials and workbooks plus informal activities and direct experiences was best; however, some teachers used one approach exclusively. Ching found that 25 percent of the teachers who taught readiness also taught reading to their kindergartners. Other surveys, such as LaConte (1970), have found even fewer kindergartens involved in direct reading instruction. Here again ways of teaching reading to kindergartners were as varied as any found in first-grade classrooms.

Kindergarten teachers today are seeing a widening gap in the knowledge of kindergarten beginners. With increased opportunities via television, records, and books to become acquainted with letters and words, a growing number of children already can, for instance, recognize certain alphabet letters and letter sounds on entering kindergarten. On the other hand, there are children at the other end of the spectrum who are obviously unprepared for reading. The kindergarten teacher must work toward individualizing instruction to help meet the needs of all the children in the class.

To what degree can the kindergarten teacher practically and effectively organize readiness and reading instruction that will meet the needs of each child? Downing and Thackray (1975), who report successful experiments with early readers in Great Britain, maintain that "the younger the pupils, the greater the need of an individual approach." In most current kindergartens, however, with their high pupil-teacher ratio, wide range of differences in readiness and experience, and limited class time, it is difficult to organize readiness programs that not only fit the situation but also fit the needs of the child. A common procedure in kindergartens is the mass instruction approach, in which all the kindergartners in the class are taught together in the same readiness or reading program. But it is highly unlikely that all children in any one kindergarten class will profit from the same early reading instruction given at the same pace. Many critics are skeptical of the way the concept of early reading has been translated into classroom practices. Hymes (1970) and Sheldon (1964) express deep concern over the serious, no-nonsense atmosphere, the silent, passive learning, the pencil-pushing activities, and the irrelevant materials which all too frequently creep into these programs. Critics also argue that some current kindergarten readiness and reading programs are actually poorly diluted copies of first-grade reading programs without adequate adjustments for kindergarten differences.

Probably the most realistic key to individualizing the kindergarten teacher's program is flexible grouping. In smaller group settings it is easier for the teacher to differentiate readiness and reading instruction. A number of school systems, recognizing the kindergarten teacher's need for providing both individual instruction and maintaining an active supervision of the whole class, have used "teacher aides" in the kindergarten. These classroom assistants can help oversee certain activities freeing the teacher to give more direct instruction to a few. Some school systems, as mentioned earlier, are exploring different classroom organizations to prepare children for reading. One example of this is the Transition Room. Suppose a child has completed kindergarten but is still judged quite unready for first grade. The child is not a slow learner and has an intelligence that is probably average or above. Yet this pupil will probably have trouble learning to read in an average first-grade classroom. So the child is put into a Transition Room—a step up from kindergarten, but not as advanced as first grade. Classes are small—many number around fifteen. Children get more individualized instruction. Towards the end of the year, many Transition Room children begin formal reading and have a better chance for success in beginning grade one.

USING PARENTS IN PRE-SCHOOLS AND KINDERGARTEN

One of the most promising trends in pre-reading education is for the schools to reach out and involve the parents and community in their children's education. The relationship between the parent and the child's reading and the reason why parents should be involved in reading activities is summed up in a position paper on the Right to Read (1972):

> Realistic programs to stimulate reading must have parental and community support. Most agree that the child's intellectual and cognitive capacity is largely established by age three, before most enter a classroom. Even then only 10.6 percent of a child's time is devoted to formal schooling. Parents, like it or not, have a role as educators; the only question is how well they educate. The home environment may stimulate the child's sense of self, his interest, his perception, his desire to experiment—or it may suppress these qualities. Parents may encourage the skills associated with reading and cognitive activity—or they may provide no inspiration, or even stifle incentive . . . While influence of parents on learning may be compared to that of teachers, most parents are completely untrained in supporting school learnings, and have no way to get training and understanding for their role if they want to (p. 9).

What can the school do to help parents prepare their children for reading? With the help of federal and local funds a number of programs have been planned and developed to involve parents in the education of their child (Quisenberry, Blakemore, and Warren, 1977). Special programs have been designed to teach parents how they may foster in their children the social, emotional, and intellectual growth necessary for learning to read. Many of these are directed at the culturally different or disadvantaged, though there are some pre-school programs for other children. These programs are extremely diverse—both in the type of parental activity and in the degree of parental involvement. This is partly because each school needs to develop a program for its particular parents and community setting, and partly because any new program requires constant experimentation. In many schools the parents are involved only in the school. In others, teachers and paraprofessionals are sent into the parents' homes.

Parent involvement, as interpreted by various schools, includes a variety of educational, observation, and participation programs.

Educational Programs: Parental involvement usually takes two forms: (1) educating parents in the ways and means of preparing children for reading; and (2) providing clear explanations of the school's prereading program. Many kindergarten programs provide booklets and other handouts on reading readiness for parents. Some school systems are beginning to move away from a complete reliance on handouts and formal teacher-talking-down-to-parents programs to a more informal and frequent exchange of ideas between parents and teachers (Vukelich 1978). Typically, these involve demonstrations and discussions of desirable ways to prepare children for reading and ways to avoid undesirable behavior, such as babytalk. These meetings may take place on a regular or infrequent basis in the school or parents' home. They may involve the teacher with one parent, or a small or large group. In several pre-school programs for the culturally disadvantaged, teachers and paraprofessionals visit each house on a regular basis (Palmer, 1972). Sometimes these visits are mainly for discussion; other times special educational toys and games are lent to families after the teacher demonstrates their use.

Although studies (Swift, 1970) have shown that these parent education programs are effective, they must be undertaken cautiously. Some parents get highly anxious and involved trying to teach their child to "do it right." Teachers should warn parents that this may happen and suggest that when they feel these anxieties and emotions rising they discontinue the lesson.

Observation and Participation: Schools encourage different degrees of parental involvement. Some schools specify a few days on which parents may come and observe. Other schools follow an open door policy. Some schools permit observation only, while others offer superficial participation—mothers may pour juice or put on coats and hats. In some schools parents participate by occasionally reading a story, leading the children in some game, or writing captions on children's pictures. In a few pre-schools parents are invited to relate as they wish with the children.

In a growing number of pre-schools, the parents help plan and develop the school's educational program. For instance, parents in some programs help in choosing educational experiences—suggesting field trips, class visitors (doctor, dentist, fireman), activities for various lessons—and help to set up and participate in volunteer aide programs.

Parents are also frequently involved in ordering, making, and selecting toys, games, books, and consumable materials (paint, paper, etc.) for the classroom. Sometimes parents are in charge of book and toy lending libraries connected with the school.

Many educators foresee good results from the trend toward more direct involvement for parents in school programs. Involved parents better understand how to help their children develop skills basic to reading. They tend to be more interested and sympathetic to the schools, and they can play an important role as part of the child's instructional team.

SUMMARY

There is no one best method or program for preparing all children for formal reading instruction. Some children will learn better with one program than with another; some teachers can teach one program quite well but have trouble obtaining the same success with another. Although there is no one best readiness program for all situations, there are certain features common to all good programs. Such programs start with a competent teacher who is thoroughly acquainted with both the school's reading program and the child's instructional level. From this base the teacher develops and organizes a readiness program geared to fit the needs of the children, keeping in mind general long range and specific daily objectives. In some readiness programs the children are exposed to skills that they already know, or skills that have no value as prerequisites to the skills needed in the initial reading task. It is important for teachers to assess what they are doing constantly, asking themselves, "Is this activity really helping this child become more ready for reading?"

A good readiness program gives children many opportunities to become acquainted with the act of reading and helps children to feel that reading is personally important to them. But the most crucial part of the program is the teacher, who, by giving the child praise, encouragement, and success, nurtures a positive attitude toward learning to read.

REFERENCES

Anderson, I. H.; Hughes, B. O.; and Dixon, W. R. "The Rate of Reading Development and Its Relation to Age of Learning to Read, Sex, and Intelligence." *Journal of Educational Research* 50 (1957): 481–494.

Armstrong, R. D. "Language: The Essence of Readiness." In *Education 6.* Toronto: W. J. Gage, 1964–1967, pp. 57–61.

Bereiter, C., and Engelmann, S. *Distar.* Chicago: Science Research Associates, 1969.

Blakeley, W. P., and Shadle, E. M. "A Study of Two Readiness-for-Reading Programs in Kindergarten." *Elementary English* 38 (1961): 502–505.

Bond, G. L., and Dykstra, R. *Final Report of the Coordinating Center for First-grade*

Instruction (USOE Project X-001). Minneapolis: University of Minnesota, 1967.

Browne, P. M. *An Exploratory Study of Teacher-Pupil Verbal Interaction in Primary Reading Groups.* Unpublished doctoral dissertation, University of Alberta, 1972.

Ching, D. *The Teaching of Reading in Kindergarten.* Paper presented at the International Reading Association Convention, Anaheim, California, 1970.

Davidson, H. P. "An Experimental Study of Bright, Average and Dull Children at the Four Year Mental Level." *Genetic Psychology Monograph* 9 (1931): 119–289.

Deutsch, M. "Minority Group and Class Status as Related to Social and Personality Factors in Scholastic Achievement." *Monographs of the Society for Applied Anthropology,* 1960, No. 2.

Di Lorenzo, L. J., and Salter, R. "An Evaluative Study of Prekindergarten Programs for Educationally Disadvantaged Children: Follow Up and Replication." *Exceptional Children* 35 (1968): 111–119.

Downing, J. "Children's Concepts of Language in Learning to Read." *Educational Research* 12 (1970): 106–112.

Downing, J.; Ollila, L.; and Oliver, P. "Cultural Differences in Children's Concepts of Reading and Writing." *British Journal of Educational Psychology* 45 (1975): 312–316.

Downing, J., and Thackray, D. V. *Reading Readiness.* London: University of London Press, 1975.

Durkin, D. "Children Who Learned to Read Before Grade 1: A Second Study." *Elementary School Journal,* 64 (1963): 143–148.

Durkin, D. *Teaching Young Children to Read.* Boston: Allyn and Bacon, 1976.

Durkin, D. *Teaching Them to Read.* Boston: Allyn and Bacon, 1978.

Durkin, D.; Butler, A.; Cole, E.; Nurss, J.; Smethurst, W.; and Sparrow, S. "Day Care and Reading." *The Reading Teacher* 26 (1973): 2–8.

Durrell, D. *Improving Reading Instruction.* New York: Harcourt, Brace and World, 1956.

Eames, T. H. "Physical Factors in Reading." *Reading Teacher* 15 (1962): 427–432.

Edwards, T. J. "Learning Problems in Cultural Deprivation." *Reading and Inquiry,* 10. Newark, Del.: International Reading Association Press, 1965, 256–261.

Evans, E. D. *Contemporary Influences in Early Childhood Education.* New York: Holt, Rinehart and Winston, 1971.

Frymier, J. R. "The Effect of Class Size Upon Reading Achievement in First Grade." *Reading Teacher* 18 (1964): 90–93.

Gates, A. I. "The Necessary Mental Age for Beginning Reading." *Elementary School Journal* 37 (1937): 497–508.

Getman, G. N. *How to Develop Your Child's Intelligence.* Luverne, Minnesota: Announcer Press, 1962: 18–19.

Harris, A. J. *How to Increase Reading Ability.* 4th ed. New York: David McKay Company, 1961.

High Points. "Reading Help for the Disadvantaged." 48 (March 1966): 51–54.

Hymes, J. L. *Teaching Reading to the Under-Six Age: A Child Development Point of View.* Paper presented at the Claremont Reading Conference, Claremont, California, 1970, p. 76.

Jacobs, N. N.; Wirthlin, L.; and Miller, C. "A Follow-up Evaluation of the Frostig Visual Perceptual Training Program." *Educational Leadership Research Supplement* 26 (1968): 169–175.

LaConte, C. "Reading in the Kindergarten: Fact or Fantasy?" *Elementary English* 47 (1970): 382–387.

McCarthy, J. "Changing Parent Attitudes and Improving Language and Intellectual Abilities of Culturally Disadvantaged Four-Year-Old Children Through Parent Involvement." *Contemporary Education* 40 (1969): 166–168.

Marchbanks, G., and Levin, H. "Cues by Which Children Recognize Words." *Journal of Educational Psychology* 56 (1965): 57–61.

May, R.; Oliver, P.; and Fernandez, D., "Dimensional Dominance Hierarchies and the Matching of Letters and Words," *Journal of Reading Behavior* 8 (1976): 321–333.

Mickelson, N. I., and Galloway, C. G. "Verbal Concepts of Indian and Non-Indian School Beginners." *Journal of Educational Research* 67 (1973): 55–56.

Mills, Queenie B. "The Preschool Disadvantaged Child." *Vistas in Reading,* Part 1, 1966 Convention Proceedings, pp. 345–349.

Morphett, M. V., and Washburne, C. "When Should Children Begin to Read?" *Elementary School Journal* 31 (1931): 496–503.

N.E.A. Journal. "How Teacher Aides Feel about Their Jobs." 56 (1967): 17–19.

N.E.A. Journal. "How the Profession Feels about Teacher Aides." 56 (1967): 16–17.

Ollila, L. The Effects of Three Contrasting Readiness Programs on the Readiness Skill of Kindergarten Boys and Girls. Ph.D. Thesis, University of Minnesota, 1970.

Ollila, L.; Johnson, T.; and Downing, J. "Adapting Russian Methods of Auditory Discrimination Training for English." Elementary English 51 (1974): 1138–1141, 1145.

Palmer, F. H. "Minimal Intervention at Age Two and Three and Subsequent Intellectual Changes." In The Preschool in Action, edited by R. K. Parker. Boston: Allyn and Bacon, 1972, pp. 437–465.

Paradis, E. E. "The Appropriateness of Visual Discrimination Exercises in Reading Readiness Materials." Journal of Educational Research 67 (1974): 276–278.

Peake, L. "Skills and Practices for the Primary Years." Handbook, University of Victoria, 1972.

Peters, H. B. "Screening with a Snellen Chart." American Journal of Optometry and Archives of American Academy of Optometry 38 (1961): 487–505.

Quisenberry, N. L.; Blakemore, C.; and Warren, C. A. "Involving Parents in Reading: An Annotated Bibliography." The Reading Teacher 31 (1977): 34–39.

Reid, J. F. "Learning to Think About Reading." Educational Research 9 (1966): 56–62.

Right to Read, Report of Forum 7. The Reading Teacher 25 (1972): 9.

Robinson, H. M. "Perceptual Training—Does It Result in Reading Improvement?" In Some Persistent Questions on Beginning Reading, edited by R. C. Aukerman. Newark, Del.: International Reading Association, 1972, p. 145.

Samuels, S. J. "Success and Failure in Learning to Read: A Critique of the Research."

Reading Research Quarterly, Vol. 8, No. 2 (Winter 1973): 200–239.

Sheldon, W. D. "A Modern Reading Program for Young Children." In Teaching Young Children to Read, edited by W. G. Cutts. Washington, D.C.: United States Department of Health, Education and Welfare, Office of Education Bulletin No. 19, 1964, pp. 31–37.

Spache, G. D.; Andres, M. C.; Curtis, H. A. et al. A Longitudinal First Grade Reading Readiness Program. Cooperative Research Project No. 2742, Florida State Department of Education, 1965.

Spache, G. D., and Spache, E. B. Reading in the Elementary School. 2nd ed. Boston: Allyn and Bacon, 1977.

Stanchfield, J. M. "Development of Prereading Skills in an Experimental Kindergarten Program." In Some Persistent Questions on Beginning Reading, edited by R. C. Aukerman. Newark, Del.: International Reading Association Press, 1972, pp. 20–32.

Strickland, D. and others. "Reading and Pre-First Grade." The Reading Teacher 30 (1977) 780–781.

Swift, M. S. "Training Poverty Mothers in Communication Skills." Reading Teacher 23 (1970): 360–367.

Timko, H. G. "Letter Position in Trigram Discrimination by Beginning Readers." Perceptual and Motor Skills 35 (1972): 153–154.

Vernon, M. D. "Specific Dyslexia." British Journal of Educational Psychology 32 (1962): 143–150.

Vukelich, C. "Parents are Teachers: A Beginning Reading Program." The Reading Teacher 31 (1978): 524–527.

Weber, E. Early Childhood Education Perspective on Change. Worthington, Ohio: Charles A. Jones Publishing Company, 1970.

Willmon, B. "Parent Participation as a Factor in the Effectiveness of Head Start Programs." Journal of Educational Research 62 (1969): 406–410.

PREVIEW

Discussion of coding *emphases versus* meaning *emphases in reading programs will eventually arrive at a point of fundamental agreement: you must know what the marks on a page signify before you can respond to them. Word recognition skills, therefore, are important in any reading program. In this chapter Arnold and Miller provide you with a thorough background of research evidence on this topic as well as offer a variety of teaching suggestions. They cover the development of meaning vocabulary, sight vocabulary, and word recognition skills, and discuss the necessity for a balance among these three areas. Some aspects of this subject are controversial. Arnold and Miller explain the different points of view, and at the same time state their own positions.*

Both Arnold and Miller have worked with pupils who have become successful readers and with pupils who have not. Their experience gives them a firm foundation for the viewpoint they express—that learning to read requires the mastery of a set of complex and interrelated skills. To help a pupil acquire these skills and become more sophisticated in their application is one of your most important tasks.

10 | Word Recognition Skills

Richard Arnold, Purdue University
John Miller, Wichita State University

OBJECTIVES

After you have read this chapter, you should be able to:

1. **Recognize the interrelationships among meaning vocabulary, sight vocabulary, and the various word recognition skills.**

2. **Outline a scope and sequence of word recognition skills such as the one listed in this chapter.**

3. **Define these word recognition skills: meaning clues, visual analysis, structural analysis, phonics, and dictionary skills.**

4. **Differentiate among these meaning clues: expectancy, picture, and context.**

5. **Differentiate among the structural analysis skills: derivatives, variants, and compounds.**

6. **Differentiate among phonics, phonetics, and phonemics.**

7. **Differentiate between synthetic and analytic phonics.**

8. **Recognize the importance of developing a balance among the word recognition skills.**

9. **Understand the importance of developing a flexible hypothesis-testing approach to decoding.**

On the first day of school, when teachers arrive in new classrooms, they will be confronted with many faces with which they cannot associate names. Some children's names will be learned in the first few hours of school, because of a child's striking physical features, or because of the unusual way a child reacts. Other names will be learned because a concerned effort is made to do so. Unfortunately, there will always be those names and faces that are not readily associated. Jimmy's and Jeff's names, which the teacher confused on the first day, may continue to be confused some time into the school year.

Eventually, however, all the names and faces are readily associated. In effect the name has become the face—recognition and association are instantaneous.

The way children learn and recognize words is somewhat analogous to the task described above. They must develop strategies for associating printed representations of words with pronunciations and meanings that they have stored. Initially a word may be remembered by some distinctive graphic feature, such as the tail on *monkey*. Some associations may be formed because of the environment in which the words are encountered. *Stop,* for example, may be recognized as the word on those red, eight-sided street signs near which mom and dad always stop the car. As reading instruction proceeds children will use word analysis skills to recognize words. As they continue to meet these words in a variety of settings, the analysis and memory devices fall by the side as association and recognition become automatic. The visual representation of the word automatically cues the language referent and meaning. The word becomes a part of the child's sight vocabulary. As with the teacher's confusion of Jimmy and Jeff, there will be "problem" words which the child will have difficulty in raising to the automatic sight recognition level. Efficient reading depends on having a vast store of words that are recognized at sight.

The ultimate goal of reading instruction is to develop efficient, mature readers, but beginning readers must learn how to study words. Four major long-term goals of word study are: (1) building a meaning vocabulary; (2) building a sight vocabulary; (3) developing a set of word recognition skills; and (4) establishing for each child a balance among these: meaning vocabulary, sight vocabulary, and word recognition skills.

BUILDING A MEANING VOCABULARY

Research indicates that many children enter school with extensive listening vocabularies (Shibles, 1959) and language structures (McCarthy, 1954; Templin, 1957). These abilities should enable children to understand, at the oral language level, most of the words and sentences contained in printed matter for young children. However, this does not assure the teacher that all children will know all the meanings for all the words to be taught in a lesson. So the development of word meanings becomes a vital segment of the reading lesson. It does little good for children to know how to decode a word if, after the word is decoded, they are unable to verify its existence in their meaning vocabularies.

As children mature they begin to use reading as a way to add to their meaning vocabularies. But the shift from learning to read to reading to learn does not usually occur until they have learned word recognition skills quite well, typically in third or fourth grade. Even then, teaching word meanings is important. The development of special and unique meanings for words goes on throughout the school day in all content areas.

Techniques of teaching word meanings, which are described in more detail in Chapter Eleven, should be considered highly relevant to the overall scheme of developing proficiency in word recognition.

To be an efficient reader one must learn to perceive many words and phrases quickly and effortlessly. Skilled readers decode automatically (Samuels and Dahl, 1973) and pay little attention to visual stimuli—letters, words, and phrases. They have committed thousands of words to their sight vocabularies and can recognize them instantly and with minimal visual cues.

Building a sight vocabulary is a major goal of reading instruction, and the teacher should actively pursue it early in the reading program. Nearly every new word, or common word part, to which children are introduced should be considered a candidate for their sight vocabularies. Each time a word is seen, it should become more familiar so that ultimately it will be recognized instantly. Many children commit words to their sight vocabulary very quickly with a minimum of effort. Others need more practice. The number of new words a child is asked to learn in a given period of time can be critical. Teaching too few new words may slow children's learning, but teaching too many new words too fast can also create problems. A child who is not learning new words to the point of instant recognition is likely to develop into a disabled reader. Children who have learned to analyze words but have little or no sight vocabularies are probably over-analytical as they read (Bond, Tinker, and Wasson, 1979). An over-analytical reader reads slowly and laboriously, "sounding out" nearly every word. Remedial teachers see many children who need a sight vocabulary component built into a corrective program.

The concept of sight vocabulary should be differentiated from that of common sight words (Groff, 1974). Lists of frequently occurring words, many of which do not lend themselves to analysis, have been developed. They often form the core of the sight vocabulary program in first and second grades. These words are very important. If they form the only word set to be instantly learned at sight, the concept of sight vocabulary is too narrowly conceived, and children can be held back because they aren't encouraged to learn almost every word at the level of instant recognition. The only words that should be considered exceptions are rare words and certain foreign words.

Teaching Sight Vocabulary

Learning to recognize words involves three phases. At first, the word is not known when it is encountered in graphic form. Later it is partially recognized but must be analyzed for the remaining graphic components which are not yet instantly perceived. Finally the word reaches the point of immediate recognition, and it is then part of the reader's sight vocabulary.

Repetition is a key concept in building sight vocabulary. The word recognition skills to be discussed later provide a good opportunity for this, under structured conditions. But probably the most natural and effective way to expose children to words repeatedly is through recreational reading of easy materials. After children study a word in a reading skills lesson, meeting it in the reader and in other books provides much of the repetition they need.

Continued exposure also helps children to distinguish each word's unique visual characteristics. Some words, such as *house* and *baby,* are relatively easy to discriminate. Others, such as *house* and *horse,* will take more practice. It is especially difficult to discriminate between words like *house* and *home,* which have similar visual characteristics and similar meanings.

Teachers can use many kinds of activities to develop sight words. Children can make or use picture dictionaries, illustrate word cards, trace and copy new words, and match or compare word cards. Hopkins and Moe (1978) list several excellent sources of game books available on the market. Two sources for activities to develop sight vocabulary and other word recognition skills are *Spice* by Platts (1973), and *Reading Activities for Child Involvement* by Evelyn Spache (1976). Lists of common sight words readily available are the Dolch (1953) list of 220 words, the longer Stone (1956) list of 679 words, and the list of high frequency words (Moe, 1972a, 1972b) based on a computer analysis of words in children's literature.

DEVELOPING WORD RECOGNITION SKILLS

The following is a list of word recognition skills which children should learn early in their reading careers. The skills are grouped into five major categories:

1. Meaning Clues
   a expectancy clues
   b picture clues
   c context clues
2. Visual Analysis
   a configuration
   b striking characteristics
3. Structural Analysis
   a variants
   b compounds
   c derivatives
4. Phonics
   a initial single consonants
   b short vowels
   c final consonants
   d long vowels and vowel combinations
   e consonant combinations—two- and three-letter blends and digraphs
   f *r*-controlled vowels
   g syllabication
   h auditory blending
5. Dictionary Skills
   a location skills
   b pronunciation skills

Authorities in the field of reading tend to agree that the above skills are important and should be taught. However, considerable difference of opinion exists about the labels applied to the skill categories and about the importance of each category. It is our opinion that all five categories listed are important, that none should be excluded from the word recognition skills program, and that the categories are quite clear, though some may wish to use other labels.

The skills have been ordered according to their usefulness. Meaning clues and visual characteristics are used through the years by mature readers as major techniques for word recognition—more so than structural analysis, for example, because they can probably use meaning-related skills most quickly and efficiently for minor corrections in analyzing unknown or misread words in context. Similarly, mature readers will probably resort to structural analysis more frequently than phonics in their efforts to analyze an obscure or misperceived word. Phonics is probably a "last resort" for able readers, though it is an important skill to have and use when needed. Using the dictionary is a special skill which usually involves learning the meaning of a new word; it is not considered a word recognition skill exclusively.

Sequencing Word Recognition Skills

The order in which word analysis skills should be taught has not been empirically established. Reading experts do not agree on this issue, but they do tend to sequence word analysis skills according to frequency of encounter and ease of learning. Reliance upon these two major ideas has produced many similar sequences. While a few programs start with the teaching of vowels (usually short first, then long), the majority of reading programs begin by teaching initial consonants.

It is important to recognize that most eclectic programs include the teaching of several skills at the same time. Often beginning consonants, limited spelling patterns, variant endings, picture clues, and the like are introduced simultaneously, so that children, even early in the first grade, are developing a variety of word analysis skills to help them.

Also important to remember is that word analysis skills—especially phonics skills—taught early in the reading program are often those that have the least value in terms of the mature, efficient reader. While no one can deny the importance of sound-symbol correspondence in initial decoding instruction, for a mature reader it is probably the most time-consuming method of approaching an unknown word.

Table 11 is a compendium of word analysis skills by grade level. Deviations will occur from one reading program to another but usually the general sequence is quite similar to the one below. *It is important for reading teachers to know the content of the reading skills program.* Not only should they be aware of the scope and sequence of the skills at the grade level they are teaching, but they should also have a general knowledge of the skills that precede and follow the level they teach. The publishers of reading programs often include scope and sequence charts; teachers should study these carefully to gain a broader perspective of the reading goals for the materials used in schools. Teachers using less structured reading approaches without a scope and sequence chart such as the Language Experience Approach may wish to incorporate their own word recognition skills program into them.

This scope and sequence chart does not contain a list of word recognition skills taught beyond third grade because few, if any, new decoding skills are introduced in the intermediate grades. When such skills are taught, it is usually as review and for reinforcement purposes. It is extremely important that teachers of older children recognize the need for skill review.

Table 11 WORD RECOGNITION SKILLS—SCOPE AND SEQUENCE CHART

Readiness
1. Learning letter names.
2. Developing awareness of sound-symbol relationships.
3. Hearing similarities and differences in initial phonemes.
4. Hearing rhyming sounds.
5. Developing left-to-right orientation.
6. Tracing, matching, and copying letters and words.
7. Developing sentence sense.
8. Developing listening comprehension.

First Grade (Pre-primer and Primer)
1. Grapheme-phoneme correspondence (consonant).
2. Begin consonant digraphs.
3. Begin consonant blends.
4. Begin short vowels.
5. Begin spelling patterns.
6. Begin using initial consonants with context.
7. Begin final consonants.
8. Begin initial and final consonant substitution.
9. Begin inflectional endings.
10. Picture dictionary.

First Grade (First Readers)
1. Continue grapheme-phoneme correspondence.
2. Continue consonant digraphs.
3. Continue consonant blends.
4. Continue short vowels.
5. Begin long vowels.
6. Continue spelling patterns.
7. Continue final consonants.
8. Initial and final consonants with context.
9. Initial and final consonant substitution.
10. Inflectional endings.
11. Begin suffixes.
12. Begin compound words.

Second Grade
1. Review and continue grapheme-phoneme correspondence.
2. Unusual consonants (c and g, silent t) and consonant digraphs.
3. Continue consonant blends, initial and final positions.
4. Unusual vowels (y).
5. Vowel digraphs and diphthongs.
6. Schwa.
7. r-controlled vowels.
8. Syllabication (correspondence between # of vowel sounds and # of syllables).
9. Compound words.
10. Suffixes.
11. Prefixes.
12. Spelling changes involved in suffixes and inflected endings.
13. Using phonic elements with context.

Third Grade
1. Review grapheme-phoneme correspondence.
2. Difficult consonant blends, including triple clusters.
3. Unusual and difficult vowels and vowel combinations.
4. Structural analysis, including roots and affixes, compounds, and larger word elements.
5. More complex spelling patterns.

6. Syllabication—two- and three-syllable words.
7. Learning important phonics rules and their application.
8. Verification of phonics through use of context.
9. Simple dictionary skills; begin diacritical markings and pronunciation spellings.

In a typical fourth-grade classroom, for instance, the majority of the students will progress nicely with a review of the skills provided. Some children, however, will be ready only for third-grade word recognition skills, and it is quite likely that two or three children will be working below third-grade level. These children need instruction in materials at their respective levels—they need corrective or remedial reading. This area is too complex to discuss here; the interested reader is referred to Karlsen, Chapter Six, and to the many texts (Harris and Sipay 1977, Bond, Tinker, and Wasson, 1979) and university course offerings for further study.

MEANING CLUES

The use of meaning clues is very important in word recognition. Such clues help readers to anticipate words that they will encounter in the reading selection. The efficient reader uses these clues regularly, in conjunction with the other word recognition skills. An insufficient use of meaning clues often results in a slow, careful analysis of many words that should have been read with a minimum of inspection.

Three major types of meaning clues have been identified: expectancy, picture, and context. Expectancy clues are related to a given topic. When people think about a general topic or concept they develop a "psychological set" for that topic. Certain ideas, and especially words, rise to the threshold of their consciousness ready to be used. This process is called *expectancy*. When children discover, for example, that they are going to read a story entitled "David's Airplane Ride," the title in itself should cause them to "expect" to run across such words as *airport, pilot, sky, clouds, takeoff, fly,* and so on. Words associated with airplane rides can be anticipated in this story more than in a story entitled "David's Trip to the Farm."

Picture clues may be considered a special class of expectancy clues (Artley, 1943; McCullough, 1943). The words and concepts included in the verbal discussion of the story, both before and during the reading lesson, can often be enhanced and augmented by pictures. A picture can clarify concepts and present information to children. Pictures may draw children's attention to objects and to the tone of the story, and they can make a simple story more interesting and vivid. For example, in the story "David's Airplane Ride," a picture could show whether David is riding on a commercial airliner or in a small aircraft at the county fair. Pictures should not be used to carry the story line, however, even in the pre-primer stages of reading.

A few authors of children's readers (Bloomfield and Barnhart, 1961) believe that children should not be allowed to use picture clues. They believe that pictures detract from the task of decoding. The authors of this chapter believe a child should not be denied any reasonable method for analyzing unknown words, including picture clues, although excessive use of pictures— especially those which carry the story—can be detrimental to learning word analysis skills (Samuels, 1967).

Another important purpose that pictures serve in reading materials is to help build concepts. It is much more efficient to show a picture of an aardvark than to describe one, particularly in print.

A context clue is much more specific to the material being read than an expectancy or a picture clue. The term context clue refers to the arrangement of words in a sentence (or paragraph) in such a manner that only one word is likely to fit into a particular slot in that sentence. Essentially it is a method of limiting alternatives. In a complete sentence, if a word is missing (or unknown) the choice of the missing word is limited by the words surrounding it. We encounter this phenomenon frequently in reading a section in the newspaper where the paper has been creased or torn and we supply the missing word. We guess at the word and then confirm its "fit" by rereading the sentence (or paragraph) to see if it makes sense.

This process is similar to the skill children need when they run into an unknown word. Consider, for example, this sentence:

David wants to _____ in an airplane.

If Kim knows all the words in the sentence except the one represented by the blank, she should be able to infer that the new word is probably *fly* or *ride*. The inference can be confirmed easily and quickly if the initial consonant *r* is used as an additional cue:

David wants to r_____ in an airplane.

Teaching Meaning Clues

Expectancy   The skillful teacher develops expectancy as a new story is introduced. Having in mind the new words to be learned by the pupils, the teacher introduces the topic and carefully elicits those words from the students. As the children relate their personal stories, the teacher writes the relevant words on the chalkboard, preferably underlined in phrases or sentences. To continue with the example of "David's Airplane Ride," the teacher might start the lesson as follows: "Boys and girls, I wonder what it is like to ride on an airplane?" Usually such a question is sufficient to begin a lively discussion. Through guided questioning, the teacher can lead the discussion through nearly all the content needed to introduce the new words. An additional bonus for the pupils is that many more words contained in the story are likely to be discussed, some of which the children may not know. Such a discussion prior to reading the story or section can be properly labelled reading readiness in the broader sense, because it is preparing the child to meet concepts covered in the reading selection.

Children will probably have trouble with expectancy clues if they are unable to anticipate what words might appear in a certain type of story. If, for example, the teacher asks Mark what words he thinks might be in a story about a lost letter and he cannot think of words such as *post office, mailbox,* and *stamp,* he probably is not going to be using expectancy clues too well and will need careful, direct instruction.

Many kinds of exercises can be designed to build expectancy clues through knowledge of a topic:

1 Circle the words below that are things you can expect to find in a kitchen:

pan	dress	stove
bed	dish	meat
tree	sink	pond

2 Put an x by the words you might expect to find in a newspaper story about a violent earthquake:

_____ Geiger counter	_____ typhoid fever
_____ Richter scale	_____ death and destruction
_____ gas lines	_____ troops on the border

Picture Clues   Most children need very little teaching to begin to use picture clues. Even before formal reading instruction, most of them have discovered the relationship between the words on the page and the characters in the illustrations. Television often introduces the concept of the interrelationship between auditory stimulus and visual stimulus. The child easily realizes that neither the words without the picture nor the picture without the words is a *complete* television program. Movies, magazines, and other mass communication media imprint the fact that pictures can enhance stories.

Informal observations will help the teacher identify those children who are over-reliant on picture clues. A child's head may bob back and forth from the printed page to the accompanying page of illustrations. Some children will invariably look at pictures before words as they turn pages. The child who "reads" the pictures first may be attempting to maintain a story line without using word analysis skills. Thus, the task of the teacher is to help the child develop a balance between using picture clues to anticipate new words and overusing picture clues to gain meaning without reading the selection.

Context   The use of context clues—that is, the use of surrounding words to determine an unknown word's pronunciation and meaning—is a most effective strategy. Context limits possible alternative word selections. Students should know that they can decode an unknown word more easily if they use context clues to limit the number of words that might fit into a specific language structure. Children should be taught to verify a freshly decoded word by insisting that the word "makes good sense" in the sentence. This training begins with the development of *sentence sense* at the oral language level in many readiness programs.

Taylor (1953) presented a technique known as the *cloze* procedure.[1] Cloze involves filling in blanks that have been created by the deletion of words

---

[1] Further discussion of cloze will be found in Chapter Eleven.

from a prose passage on some regular basis. The creative teacher can devise many logical methods to utilize the cloze technique as an aid to decoding through context. In fact, modified cloze procedures have been historically synonymous with exercises to teach the use of context clues.

In some instances the teacher will wish to center the student's attention on a specific language clue. Here a modification of the cloze technique may be used effectively.

1   Using context to verify a word ending, constrained by a word in a previous position in the sentence:

Yesterday, the man walk _ _ home.
The man is run _ _ _ _ home.
I saw two little dog _ .

2   Verbs constrained by subjects and prepositions:

The dog _ _ _ _ _ _ over the fence.
The bird _ _ _ _ over the fence.
The snake _ _ _ _ _ _ _ _ under the fence.

3   Initial consonant plus context:

Jim hit the b _ _ _ over the fence.
The old m _ _ became very tired.
When the b _ _ _ rings it is time for lunch.

4   Triple consonant cluster plus context:

Thr _ _ strikes and you are out!
We str _ _ _ _ _ _ the coiled spring.
We stretched the coiled spr _ _ _ _ .

The examples are only a small sample of many possible exercises. Teachers must be aware that they are teaching context clues informally when they draw upon the child's previous experiences with language. They are not teaching grammar.

Emans and Fisher (1967) listed the different kinds of deleted-word exercises in order of difficulty (from most to least difficult):

1   No clue give other than context.
2   Beginning letter given.
3   Length of word given.
4   Beginning and ending letter given.
5   Four word choice given.
6   Consonants given.

In addition to varying the specific skill to be focused on, the teacher may wish to vary the degree of complexity of the task through the amount of information supplied. Three of the many possible formats are:

1   Multiple choice: This requires the child to read and mark.

Circle the correct word:
In the _____the streets are icy.
A. summer   B. running   C. winter

2   Context only: This requires the child to write the word. Beginners will probably find this task more difficult because they have yet to develop proficiency in writing and spelling.

> Fill in the blank:
> In the _____ the streets are icy.

3   Initial consonant supplied: This exercise asks the child to verify initial consonant with context. Exercises of this type teach the child to use more than one skill to analyze unknown words.

> Fill in the blank:
> In the w_____ the streets are icy.

Teachers of young children should be careful to avoid selecting exercises which require an undue amount of writing. By varying both specific skills and the complexity of the task, teachers can develop a store of exercises that can be beneficial, on an individual basis, to all the children in the classroom (McKee, 1966; Rankin & Overholzer, 1969). Published materials such as Continental Press *Reading-Thinking Skills* (Maney, 1965–1970) and Barnell-Loft's *Specific Skills Series* (Boning, 1976) also provide a good source of cloze worksheets.

In addition to using cloze exercises the teacher should seek every opportunity to discuss the relationship between various language units with the students. Students need to be made aware that the strings of words (usually sentences) they decode while reading must make sense. One simple method of demonstrating that words have relationships with other words in a sentence is to isolate a certain verb and subject in the child's reading material. For example, consider this sentence:

> The boy *prayed* for help.

The verb pray requires a certain type of subject. The subject must be an animate being, and furthermore it must be human. The teacher may ask the students to make a list of things that pray (boy, girl, mother, and so on). During the course of the discussion certain things that do not pray may be mentioned. These items should be fitted into the simple sentence framework.

> The _____ prayed for help.
>   dog   car   mother

The teacher must acknowledge that there are exceptions to many of our language rules. It is quite possible that a bright child will point out to the class that a mantis prays but is not human. In this manner children can begin to formulate hypotheses about the relationships and constraints that exist among words, and they may begin to use these language clues to help them decode unknown words.

VISUAL ANALYSIS

The importance of vision to reading is obvious, but the need for a child to learn systematic visual analysis of new words is sometimes underestimated or overlooked. Visual study of words does not always need to be used in conjunction with other word analysis skills. This is particularly true for the more skilled reader. For example, if Judy encounters a word that she has not completely mastered, all she may need to do is inspect the word carefully without resorting to other more time-consuming processes of word analysis.

The major task is to visually identify word units in the unknown word which will help the reader crack the code. The units identified are often word parts—discussed later in the sections on structural analysis and phonics. Obviously, then, skill in using visual cues often operates in conjunction with other word analysis skills. Often the exercises that teach phonics and other skills fail to communicate to the child that words must be visually segmented into smaller units before they can be properly identified and analyzed. The teacher must help children develop the habit of careful, flexible visual inspection of the problem words, always seeking possible cues for identification.

Children need to look especially carefully at words when they are taught by spelling patterns (Bloomfield and Barnhart, 1961; Fries, 1963) or word families. Consider what might happen if careful visual study of the following patterns is not encouraged.

cap   gap   nap   rap   tap

sit   set   sat   sad   sod

Exercises that are first begun in reading readiness programs—often labelled visual discrimination exercises—form the beginnings of careful visual inspection of words. Teachers need to continue with this type of exercise that encourages careful visual examination of words.

Two of the most common visual analysis skills taught are general configuration (shape) and specific striking characteristics of words. Able readers read many words by their general shape, particularly if they know the word well. Also some words do not lend themselves well to the usual analytical techniques, and they must be learned from their general shape or specific characteristics. Children study these as sight words and learn them from repeated exposure to their graphic form. Common examples are *the, together,* and *who.* They are learned as single visual units and may need to be seen thirty to fifty times before they are learned, depending on the individual child (Huey, 1908).

Teaching Visual
Analysis Skills

The purpose of studying words visually is to develop two primary abilities: visual memory and discrimination. Memory requires the child to recall what particular words or word parts look like. Discrimination involves differentiating between units: letters, groups of letters, and words. Many reading experts feel that visual analysis skills are very important. The exercises advocated for teaching visual analysis, however, have yet to be shown truly effective in the development of word analysis skills. Consider exercises such as the following:

Draw a circle around the little words in these bigger words:

electricity   uncanny   sifter

Finding little words in big words may sometimes be helpful. But it may also be confusing, particularly in isolated words—for example, *father, earth,* and *pigeon.*

We know that people read from visual cues derived from the upper portion of words much more so than the lower portions (Huey, 1908),

Father is a big man

Sister is a little lady.

and that visual cues are much easier to distinguish when lower case letters are used rather than upper case (Patterson and Tinker, 1946).

SUE SAW THE CAR.

Tom broke the chair.

Yet the teaching of word shape or word configuration seems to have limited direct value in making children aware of the differences between words. For example:

Draw a box around these words:

season   happy   baby

Such an exercise draws a child's attention to the box (or configuration) rather than to the letters of the words themselves. Since there are nearly as many shapes of boxes as there are words, it is probably more profitable to learn the words.

A better technique to get children to attend to visual differences may be for the teacher to talk about how the new words look different. "Boys and girls, our words today are *bird* and *some*. Notice how flat the word *some* looks" (teacher draws a line above and below the letters of *some*), "and the word *bird* has two tall letters—*b* and *d*" (teacher draws a line over *b, i, r,* and *d* to emphasize the difference in the way the two words look). This focuses attention on the difference in the visual characteristics of the words rather than the shapes of boxes.

Words that are "look-alikes" require special study. "We have a couple of tough ones today, kids. You know why?" (Teacher writes *when* and *then, quite* and *quiet*.) "Yes! Because they look so much alike. We need to be very careful when we read these words because they are easy to get mixed up." (Continue class discussion, pointing out the parts that look alike and the parts that are different.) Considerable practice with look-alikes will probably be needed before some students can recognize the differences with a minimum of effort.

Learning words on the basis of striking characteristics is also of questionable value. The child may learn that *monkey* has a tail on the end; but so do *money* and *donkey*. The fact that the word *Ohio* is round on both ends and *hi* in the middle is of limited usefulness.

Perhaps the greatest strength of this teaching procedure is that it helps children be aware that almost every word in our written language has its individual, idiosyncratic graphic representation. And perhaps the greatest problem in learning words from this technique is that what is learned about a particular word is not conducive to generalization to other unknown words. With other word analysis skills, children find certain characteristics in words that they may apply usefully to decoding other new words. In learning words on the basis of striking characteristics, the opposite is probably true.

Locational Errors

Some children develop faulty habits in their visual study of words. Certain error patterns become apparent. These error patterns are often called locational errors. That is, a child will make frequent errors in the initial, medial, or final positions of words. The teacher then must choose or design special exercises which require children to focus on the part of the word where they are consistently making errors.

When a child is observed erring in word beginnings, the teacher should prescribe exercises that draw attention to the initial elements of words. For example:

Circle the correct word:
We hear the little pig _____ .
heal   meal   squeal

Draw a line around the words that begin like *break*:

bring   train   bread   bash

Exercises in alphabetizing and simple dictionary work also help students focus on word beginnings. Many workbooks from basal reading series (Fay et al., 1978; Clymer et al., 1976) contain exercises of this type.

Other children may be having difficulty with the middles of words. Often these children observe the initial and final word sections but tend to hurry over the midsection—especially with longer words. Exercises should be designed to focus on the medial position of words. For example:

He's the new sixth grade _____ .
teamster   teacher   temper

Sometimes children regularly make errors in the medial position of words because they are having trouble differentiating vowels. Exercises should focus attention on vowels in the middle of words. For example:

Here is Mom's shopping _____ .
list   last   lost

Children sometimes have trouble with word endings. Qualitatively speaking, ending errors are not usually as serious as initial or medial word errors. Good readers tend to make more errors in the final position than in the initial or medial positions. Nevertheless, when needed, exercises requiring the child to attend to word endings are recommended. For example:

Draw a circle around the words that end with *elt:*
melt   sail   felt   tame   belt

The teacher should be cautious in the use of exercises emphasizing word endings; they may confuse some children's left-to-right orientation.

Breaking a large word into smaller units is often a useful way to analyze it. There are two major categories of skills that deal with analysis of smaller word units: structural analysis and phonics. Structural analysis deals with those word parts that carry some element of meaning. The smallest meaning units in English are morphemes. For example, the word *walked* is made up of two morphemes. One meaning unit refers to the act of locomotion, the other to the fact that walking took place in the past. Similarly, *ran* is also made up of two morphemes, although the *ed* is not present in the irregular form. Morphemes may be combined into new, larger meaning units frequently referred to as derivatives, variants, and compounds.

Derivatives

In analyzing a derivative or affix the student looks for a meaning-bearing unit affixed to the beginning or end of a root that also has meaning. The emphasis on meaning is essential when considering such examples as:

uneven   under   uncover

Which word or words have a prefix? The student must examine the root for meaning to determine that *under* is one morpheme, or meaning unit, while *un* + *even* and *un* + *cover* are derivatives containing two morphemes. *Un* can either be a morpheme or a phonogram (as in *under* or *run*), a unit which is discussed in the section on phonics. For decoding purposes, it makes little difference whether the unit is properly labelled a morpheme or a phonogram. What is important is that the *un* unit is familiar and therefore more easily decodable. In the study of word meanings, however, it is very important that the child recognize that the morpheme *un* has a meaning roughly equivalent to *not*.

Variants

Variants are words which contain a root and a variant or inflectional ending. The terms *variant* and *inflectional* are interchangeable, and for the purpose of early instruction in word recognition skills will be defined as words ending in *s, es, ed, ing, er,* and *est*. Variant endings perform a largely grammatical function. They change the root to allow it to conform to its grammatical environment. The following are examples:

Verb—time agreement

talk	talks, talked, talking
cry	cries, cried, crying

Nouns—number agreement

book	books
glass	glasses

Adverbs—degree

slow	slower, slowest
high	higher, highest

Adjectives—comparison

funny   funnier, funniest
small   smaller, smallest

In actual reading, knowledge of roots and variants will help children analyze words. Visual study is important here, to identify the root and variant. This takes place prior to the actual analysis of the word structure, although frequently these processes are so rapid that their sequence is not evident.

Compounds

Compound words require perhaps the closest combination of visual and structural analysis skills. A compound word is one in which two morphemes, both of which could stand as root words, are combined to form one new word. The new word may be very similar in meaning to the sum of its two roots, as in *police + man = policeman,* or the relationship may be obscure to the child, as in *turn + pike = turnpike,* or perhaps not evident at all, as in *dog, + wood = dogwood.* In what appears to be the vast majority of compound words the meaning is similar to the sum of the roots; so in the majority of encounters with compounds, structural analysis for meaning will make the reader more efficient. The initial visual clues, however, cannot be overlooked. Children must find just the right place to segment *dogwood.* Otherwise they may never get to the two roots. If they attempt to segment the word *backstop* into *backs + top* they may become confused.

Teaching Structural Analysis Skills

Derivatives   Mere listings of common suffixes and prefixes to be memorized will not improve students' structural analysis skills in dealing with derivative words. Children must be interested—they must encounter these words in the spirit of a "word detective." Then they can figure out meanings through structural analysis, as well as build new words by adding affixes to roots.

The teacher may be wise to begin to introduce affixes with suffixes rather than prefixes. In normal left-to-right progression the child will encounter the root word before a suffix (*care + less*). Initially, seeing the familiar root before the affix may facilitate meaningful structural analysis.

Three suffixes that are generally consistent in meaning are *less, ful,* and *ness.* These suffixes afford the teacher an adequate starting point. The teacher may seize the opportunity to discuss the fact that Phil was *shoeless* on the playground, or that Adrienne had been *careful* with the paints in art class. Examples such as "Brian's new dog has brought his family great *happiness*" should be avoided initially because of the spelling change from *y* to *i* in *happiness.* The discussion should proceed on the basis of meaning, looking at the differences the suffixes have caused in the total meaning of the derivative word.

shoe   care
shoeless   careful

It is not necessary, of course, that all suffixes be mastered before any prefixes are introduced. The prefixes *un, dis,* and *re* will provide adequate regularity for initial introduction to prefixes. This introduction can proceed in much the same manner as the introduction of suffixes. The teacher should choose concrete examples of the derivative words to be discussed, then point up the meaning changes while simultaneously displaying the graphic difference between the root alone and the root with prefix.

Goodman (1965) explained that children increase their ability to use context clues as they progress through the primary grades. Ramanaskas (1972) has demonstrated that these context clues operate between sentences as well as within them. Providing children with meaningful context is an immeasurable aid in helping them use acquired structural analysis skills.

> Tom struck out three times in the baseball game.
> This made him *unhappy.*

As the student becomes more proficient in analyzing roots with one affix, the more complex task of analyzing roots with multiple affixes may be attempted. These derivatives may take the form of a root with one prefix and one suffix.

> *happy*
> *un + happy*
> *un + happ(i) + ness*

The derivative with multiple affixes may also be a root and two suffixes.

> *care*
> *care + less*
> *care + less + ly*

The major difficulty with this type of structural analysis resides in the multiple meaning changes the root may undergo. The following is a four-step checklist which may help students in their structural analysis of derivative words:

1 Find the meaning of the root word.
2 Find the prefix and the resultant meaning change.
3 Find any and all suffixes and consider their meaning changes.
4 Test the derivative word in context.

The ways of constructing structural analysis activities are numerous. Make a word that means the opposite of its root by adding a prefix:

> un   _____comfort
> ir   _____happy
> dis   _____regular

Make a word that means the same as the word the root is paired with by adding a prefix:

> sad   = _____ happy
> bumpy   = __ __even
> raw   = _____cooked

The teacher can construct word wheels or word strips with common roots and affixes. In addition to these lists there are many published games, activities, and workbook pages to reinforce the teacher's explanation of derivative words. The study of structural analysis is an excellent example of how language study can be successfully combined with the development of word recognition skills. It further reinforces the intimate relationship of language arts and reading.

Variants   Variant forms of common roots are in the speaking vocabularies of the great majority of beginning readers. Children are familiar, for example, with the oral-aural representations of plurals. The instruction they need is in recognizing the graphic form of the word and connecting it with the already familiar pronunciation and meaning. Hanson (1966) found variant endings (*s, ing, ed, er*) successfully taught in pre-primers, primers, and first readers.

The variant endings *s* and *es* are used to change root words in two ways: (1) the conversion of a singular noun to its plural form (*dog* to *dogs* or *dish* to *dishes*), and (2) the conversion of a verb to third person singular (I walk, you walk, he walks, or I fly, you fly, she fli*es*). There are certain phonetic principles concerning the pronunciations of *s* as [s], [z], or [ez]; since the vast majority of children have incorporated these "rules" into their speech patterns long before entering school, that need not be of concern here. It is important, however, to make the child aware of the parallel uses of *s* and *es*.

The teaching of variant endings need not be difficult. The teacher should be certain to select roots the students can already read and then explain what adding the plural or third person does. This can be clearly exemplified by requiring the student to make comparisons with his oral language. Initially, the teacher may employ cloze exercises at the oral level.

"I have one dog, but Mary has two _____ ."

After students have had a brief encounter with the oral representations of these, they should progress to the important graphic recognition level. For example:

Fill in the missing endings:
She like____ the ten little pup _____ .

The teacher should begin with nouns that are clearly defined by context as being plural, as in the above sample.

The past tense of regular verbs is formed by adding *ed*. As with *s*, there is a variation in pronunciation with *ed*—[t] as in *asked*, [d] as in *pulled*, and [əd] as in *dusted*. If teachers concentrate instruction on recognizing the visual form, the children's incorporated language rules should give them the pronunciation.

The student also needs to be introduced to *ing*. This variant, when added to a verb root, forms a word that can either be used in the noun or verb position in a sentence. It may be wise to use it in the verb position in contrast to the *ed* past tense form. Exercises designed in this manner exemplify the uses of the two forms.

Lincoln began to walk.
He walk*ed* all day.
He was walk*ing* to his new home.

The teaching of the variant endings *ing* and *ed* is much the same as with *s* and *es.* The teacher should be sure that the root word is in the reading vocabulary of the student. The meaning of the variant ending should be discussed, and the instructional time should be balanced between recognizing visual forms and oral discussion.

The *er* ending is added to modifying words (adjectives or adverbs) and to nouns. In either case the student must once again be careful to analyze the root for meaning. In the following example *moth* is not a root.

faster mother hunter

A purely visual analysis of each of the above words would yield these patterns: *cvcc + er* (consonant, vowel, consonant, consonant + *er*). In fact when the *er* is removed all three words do contain a meaningful root—*fast, moth,* and *hunt;* however, a final check in meaningful context reveals that *mother* is, indeed, a single morpheme. Such an example, a sight word ending in *er* is when the *er* is not used as a variant ending, may help the child recognize the necessity for using meaningful units in structural analysis. It is also an excellent example of an exception to a rule.

The variant ending *est* may be added to adjectives such as *tall.* This *est* form may well be introduced in conjunction with *er.* Numerous games can be constructed with a deck of adjective roots and a deck of *er* and *est* endings. If a root card can be paired (and named) with an *er* and *est* ending then the "book" may be played. The games may follow the rules of the card games "Rummy" and "Go Fish."

Variants may be introduced and taught in much the same manner as derivatives with a root and suffix. The fact that variants usually clue only the grammatical function of the root makes them easily discernible if the child is reminded to test their use in context.

Compounds Recognizing compound words can be relatively easy for the student if the teacher begins instruction with two simple known words that may be combined to form a compound. Initially this may be easiest with monosyllabic words.

into sunset gunman outside

This skill should not be associated with the practice of looking for small words in larger ones. The concern must be with finding two meaningful units that combine to form a unit unit with a similar meaning. If this is not stressed, the child may begin to view some words inappropriately—*together* as *to* + *get* + *her,* for example.

After some of the simpler compounds have been introduced the sequence may progress to those compounds in which either or both of the roots have more complex spelling patterns.

stagecoach windshield corkscrew

Finally, the more difficult compounds, those in which the combined meaning of the two roots is obscured or totally different from the compound word, may be introduced.

broadcast tadpole wholesale

These words depend more on visual analysis than any other category of words discussed in structural analysis skills, because meaning units may not be evident. When a child encounters an unknown compound he will not know it is a compound until, through visual inspection, he discovers one or both of the smaller roots.

Numerous card and board games can be constructed for teaching compounds, variants, and derivatives. Published materials and workbook exercises are also plentiful and enumerated in such sources as Ekwall (1977).

Structural analysis is among the most important word analysis skills. To be an efficient reader, one must learn to use this set of skills in combination with other word analysis skills, especially context, in decoding unknown words.

PHONICS

Phonics instruction can be defined as a system in which the student learns the relationships between graphic symbols (letters and letter combinations) and the speech sounds they represent. Many teachers of reading confuse or misuse the terms *phonics, phonetics,* and *phonemics.* Smith (1971) draws the following distinctions:

> Phonics is not phonetics, which is the scientific study of the sounds of a language, and which has nothing at all to do with writing . . . phonetics is to phonics what brain surgery is to cutting-and-pasting.

> Phonics is not phonemics, which is the study of the classes of sound that do constitute significant differences in a language. In English there are about 46 phonemes (pp. 159–160).

The discussion here will pertain only to phonics—that is, symbol-sound correspondences, particularly as they relate to the process of learning to read.

In addition to confusion over the terminology of phonics, there are numerous misconceptions about what phonics can or cannot do, what should or should not be taught in phonics instruction, and so on. Wardhaugh (1969b) attempts to dispel some of the misconceptions:

1 Letters do not have sounds. . . . Letters are letters, and sounds are sounds; they must not be confused with each other.
2 Statements are often made about syllabication which only hold true for word-breaking in writing, but not for pronunciation.
3 Statements are often incorrectly made about children mispronouncing words, when in reality the pronunciations are acceptable as a part of their dialect.
4 Long and short vowel sounds have nothing to do with the duration of pronunciation.
5 Lessons in articulation are not a part of phonics instruction. Phonics is not a matter of teaching children the sounds of their language (p. 82).

In order to achieve efficiency in reading, the student needs to establish independence in word recognition skills. Phonics, or more appropriately phonics in conjunction with other word recognition skills, is an invaluable tool in achieving a degree of independence. Phonics is by no means a cure-all; nevertheless, it has an extremely important function in decoding words.

Analytic and Synthetic Phonics

Unfortunately, authors disagree as to how phonics should be taught. Presently, there are at least two quite different approaches to phonics instruction. Frequently they are characterized as synthetic and analytic phonics.

Synthetic phonics is concerned with the teaching of isolated symbol-sound correspondences. First the student learns the names of each letter, then the sound each letter represents. Once these two skills are mastered the student is expected to be able to sound out and blend an unknown word. Three variations of synthetic phonics are:

1 Sounding and blending of each letter (Brunner, 1968):

c-a-t
kuh-a-tuh

2 Sounding the initial consonant and vowel together, then blending the final consonant sound (Cordts, 1953; Gillingham and Stillman, 1956):

ca-t
ka-tuh

3 Sounding the initial consonant, then sounding the vowel and final consonants together (Wylie and Durrell, 1970):

c-at
kuh-at

One of the most common problems associated with synthetic phonics is that the child often produces extraneous sounds which tend to distort the pronunciation of the word. This problem is most apparent in words containing unvoiced consonants:

p-u -m-p
puh- uh- m- puh

Synthetic phonics involves the synthesis of small units, letters, into larger units, words. Analytic phonics, on the other hand, starts with words and proceeds to smaller units, letters.

Gates (1947) was one of the early proponents of analytic phonics. This is the position that is most often represented in present basal reading programs. It also is the approach taken most frequently in schools today. Although analytic phonics has many ramifications, it can be explained broadly as making use of the sounds of known units or words to unlock the pronunciation of an unknown unit or word. For example, if the new word is *cat*, children may recognize that the word begins with the same letter, and possibly the same sound, as another word they know—*can*. Furthermore, they may recognize that the ending is the same as the ending of *bat*. So cat may be analyzed as:

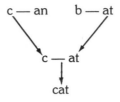

To analyze words in this manner, the student must have some known words to serve as referents.

In this chapter, we will discuss primarily the analytic approach to phonics instruction, since this is the direction of current trends.

Various generalizations about the sound-symbol correspondences have been formulated over the years. The work of such authors as Emans (1967), Clymer (1963); Bailey (1967), and Burmeister (1968a, 1968b) have revealed that a few of these generalizations have a great deal of utility while others have very little. The teacher must be careful to select examples which conform to the more useful generalizations.

Generally, basal reading programs and phonics workbook materials strive for vocabulary control, at least in part, by means of phonic regularity. Essentially this means that as a phonic generalization is introduced, the reading assignments will emphasize words which conform to the generalization. For example, the student may be introduced to the "silent *e* generalization." Essentially this rule refers to instances in one-syllable words where two vowels are separated by a consonant. The second vowel is an *e* which is not sounded and the first vowel is given the long sound.[2] At this point the reading material will emphasize new words such as *late* rather than *love,* which is obviously an exception to the rule. The teacher must also maintain this kind of control in phonics exercises.

After the child has learned to identify the letters of the alphabet rapidly, phonics instruction generally begins. Learning the sounds represented by initial consonants in readiness activities is usually the beginning of the program, and it extends through advanced concepts such as *r*-controlled vowels and triple consonant clusters. In between, final consonants, short and long vowels, consonant blends and digraphs, diphthongs, and vowel combinations are learned. Essentially, the child is instructed in a method of analyzing word elements for sound, blending these sounds together, and reaching an approximate pronunciation of the unknown word which should in turn cue a meaning association. Extensive practice is necessary for learning each phonic element to a level of instant recognition.

Teaching Phonics Skills

Beginning Single Consonants   Many basal readers and initial reading programs contain activities that present several pictures of objects, the names of which all begin with the same consonant. It is suggested that the program begin with the consonants *b, d, h, j, m, n, p, t.* For various reasons that will be

---

[2] Some linguists prefer to use the terms *glided* and *unglided* or *checked* and *unchecked* instead of *long* and *short.* These terms are also being used in some current reading systems.

presently discussed, these consonant sounds produce less confusion than the others. Pairing the beginning consonant with pictures is wise because it avoids the confusion in blending that may arise from learning letter sounds in isolation. The concept that *b* is the letter that represents the beginning sound in *baby, book, ball,* and *bell* may cause less difficulty later than learning that *b* represents the sound *buh.*

After the letters and sounds have been discussed, the teacher should progress to pairing them in a printed word which begins with the consonant in question, in this case *b.* The words used to illustrate may well be children's names in the class—Beth, Bill, or Bernie. The word might also be one of the initial sight words that the children have already learned as a whole word by configuration or picture association. In either case the teacher should list these words that begin with *b* on the chalkboard. The child's attention should be focused first on the visual similarity of the words—they all begin with the same letter. Then the teacher should focus on the auditory similarity—they all begin with the same sound.

The consonants *c* and *g* were not included in the beginning list because they vary in pronunciation according to the environment they are in: [c]-*cat* [c]-*city* and [g]-*gum* or [g]-*gem.* The consonants *f, l, r,* and *s* were not among those first introduced because they are often more difficult for children to pronounce correctly. *K* and *q* were omitted from the initial list because in many environments they have quite similar pronunciations, as in *queen* and *keen.* This problem is just the opposite of *c* and *g,* where there is one symbol with two pronunciations. *W* and *y,* because they may be sounded as semi-vowels as well as consonants, are also confusing. Finally, *v, x, y,* and *z* can be very confusing; their pronunciation varies greatly with the environment. The letter *x,* for example, represents several pronunciations ([*xylophone*], [*exam*], [*box*]).

Short Vowels   In this section, the terms *short* and *long* will be used because the reader is probably most familiar with these terms. The authors are aware, however, that some linguists (Wardhaugh, 1969a) think these terms are unscientific and confusing.

When the students have grasped the concept of symbol-sound relationships with some of the initial consonants, they may be introduced to short vowels, which are more consistent in their pronunciation than long vowel sounds. The short sound of *a* is commonly introduced first.

Once again the words selected to illustrate short *a* should be listed on the chalkboard, the visual similarities noted, and the sound similarities noted. The list might include:

cap   lap   bat   am   Sam   Pat   tan

Picture associations may often be useful. The pictorial form, the graphic form, and the auditory form of the word may all be presented at the same time.

Final Consonants   After students have attained some degree of mastery over initial consonants and short vowels, they may be introduced to consonants in the final position, which will enable them to use phonic attack to decode monosyllabic, closed syllable (cvc) words. Although many children may generalize the sounds of consonants from the initial to the final position, consonants in this position can cause difficulty for poor readers (Harris and Sipay, 1977).

At first it may be prudent to select words in which the initial consonant is repeated in the final position:

dàd   tot   nan   bib

As soon as these words have been illustrated, the introduction may proceed to those closed syllable words that are formed from initial consonants, short vowels, and familiar ending consonants which are different from the initial consonant:

Dan   top   nap   bit

Once the child has learned these sound-symbol correspondences, numerous methods of instruction in phonic attack can be employed. The child has attained enough phonic decoding skill to begin to isolate elementary generalizations. These may well take the form of looking at words in terms of families (also called phonograms or spelling patterns).

at	ap	it	ot	am
cat	lap	pit	lot	ham
fat	cap	sit	cot	jam
sat	sap	hit	got	dam
hat	tap	lit	not	Pam
rat	rap	fit	tot	ram
bat	map	bit	dot	Sam

This gives the child practice with a consistent ending phonogram and also with the initial consonants that have been substituted in the pattern. Word wheels prove very useful in reinforcing this decoding skill. The outer portion of the wheel contains various consonants, while the inner wheel contains phonograms. The child may choose one initial consonant and rotate the phonograms to form different words. Various other strips or wheels may be constructed in which the medial vowel or the ending consonant changes. Although at this point the closed syllable, cvc spelling pattern is the only one directly and completely decodable by phonic attack alone, students will be able to build from this unit when they have learned other symbol-sound correspondences and syllabication. By the time children have reached this level of knowledge in phonics, they will probably have attained some proficiency in using context for word analysis. Conjointly, context and phonics skills are powerful decoding tools.

Long Vowels and Vowel Combinations   Long vowels vary far more in pronunciation and are less stable than short vowels. Emans (1967) found that a vowel in the initial or medial position of a closed monosyllabic word represented the short sound 80 percent of the time. The exceptions occurred largely in words containing i or o followed by double consonants (for example, *right, thigh, blind, cold, toll, hold*). Because long vowels and vowel combinations are much less regular, the child must learn to try various sounds to see if they complete a word that he has stored in his meaning vocabulary.

For example, *ea* has the sound of [e]-*beak* approximately one-third of the time, but it is also pronounced as [a]-*great,* [e]-*dead,* and in other ways (*wear, earn, hear*).

The vowels which do not represent a sound but rather change the sound of another vowel in the word (silent vowels) serve to further confuse the issue. Although the silent *e* in monosyllabic, *cvcȩ* spelling pattern words is highly consistent (*hope, like, cake,* etc.), combinations with silent vowels such as *ea* are sometimes long *e,* silent *a (neat);* they are also often short *e,* silent *a (bread).*[3]

The difference between single-letter long vowel sounds and vowel combinations is apparent visually, but diphthongs need to be distinguished from other vowel combinations. A diphthong is a combination of sounds that is perceived as very nearly one sound. This sound is graphically represented by two letters. The most regular are: *au (caught), aw (law), oi (boil),* and *oy (toy).* The numerous other vowel combinations are less regular than the highly consistent diphthongs.

The teaching of long vowels and vowel combinations must account for irregularity of pronunciation. "Rules" may often be of little value when their validity is constantly challenged. If "rules" are encompassing enough to be useful they are in many cases too complex to be learned and applied. It is better for the child to be willing to forward reasonable guesses, using all available language clues.

Burmeister (1968b) points out that phonemes for vowel pairs tend to fall into these categories:

1. The first vowel may do the talking as in *ai, ay, ea, ee, oa,* or *ow* and say its name. *Ea* may be long *e* or short *e; ow* may be long *o* or *ow.*
2. The two vowels may blend as in *au, aw, oi, oy, oo; oo* may sound as in *lagoon* or *wood.*
3. The two vowels may represent a new sound; *ei, ow, ey, ew.*
4. Vowel pairs may separate (p. 449).

As the student meets new words in which the similarity or difference in the pronunciation of a given spelling pattern is exemplified, and as he learns some guidelines (such as those cited by Burmeister), he will begin to internalize some pronunciation generalizations of his own. If this internalization and experimentation with symbol-sound relationships is encouraged by the teacher, the child's proficiency with long vowels and vowel combinations will undoubtedly increase.

Consonant Combinations Consonants are combined in words in four main ways: (1) two-consonant blends, (2) two-consonant digraphs, (3) three-consonant blends, (4) three-consonant trigraphs. A consonant blend is formed by two or three letters that are combined together but maintain the distinction of their individual sounds in the blend (for example, [bl]-*blend,* or

---

[3] Terms such as *often, highly regular, irregular,* and so on are used in conjunction with phonic generalizations because various studies have reported somewhat different percentages of utility. Long *a* and long *i* are sometimes considered diphthongs by linguists. The reason will be evident if you say these in a prolonged fashion.

[*str*]-*strong*). Digraphs, on the other hand, are formed when two or more letters are combined to represent a single phoneme or speech sound that is different from the sound either letter typically represents (for example, [*wh*]-*when*, or [*ght*]-*bought*). Some consonant letter combinations are highly regular, such as *ng*. It is pronounced as in *ring* and occurs only in the ending position of a syllable or word. *Ch* is far more irregular. It stands for four different sounds [*ch, j, sh, k*] and occurs in the beginning of words or syllables as well as the middle and ending positions.

Two-letter consonant blends should be introduced in the initial position. Essentially they have the same characteristics as the beginning single consonant in monosyllabic words. The teacher may use pairs of *cvc* or *ccvc* words to demonstrate the use of blends.

fat–flat   pan–plan   lot–blot

As with initial consonants the visual as well as auditory differences should be pointed out. The entire presentation can be very similar to that of initial consonants. Many of the same teaching materials are also applicable. The outside wheel of the word wheel containing single consonants may now be replaced with one containing blends.

The consonant blends occurring in the final positions should also be introduced in monosyllabic words. The techniques are the same as for beginning blends.

Children will learn the consonant blends *sch, scr, shr, spl, spr, str,* and *thr* more easily if they are familiar with the concept of two-consonant blends. Then they can proceed to the concept of learning the visual representation of the three corresponding sounds.

Learning digraphs requires quite a different concept. The child must recognize that two or more consonants may combine to form one speech sound. The problem is complicated by the fact that certain digraphs have different sounds depending on their environment. *Gh* may be pronounced as in [*ghost*] in the initial position, or as in [*enough*] in the final position, or it may be silent as in [*bough*].

Teachers should present only words which conform to one pronunciation of the digraph at a time. Then the child may learn the environments in which second and third pronunciations occur. The teacher will be wise to check reading materials being used to determine which pronunciation is most common and teach that generalization first.

Triple-consonant combinations, or trigraphs, are rare; *ght* is the most common. It may be learned as pronounced in [*right*] or [*bought*].

R-Controlled Vowels Vowels that are followed by the letter *r* often are represented by a sound that is different from the sound the same vowel would make in a different environment. Two generalizations concerning the principle of *r* controls are regular enough to be useful to the child:

1   *a* followed by an *r* and the final *e* represents the sound heard in *dare*. Some words conforming to this generalization are *care, hare, mare,* and so on. A word such as *are* is an exception. Bailey, Clymer, and

Emans all found the utility of this generalization to be 90 percent or greater.

2   *r* gives the preceding vowel a sound that is not the normal short or long sound. Some words representing this generalization are *born, worn, darn, bar,* and so on. A word such as *tire* is an exception. Bailey, Clymer, and Emans found this generalization to have a utility ranging from 78 to 96 percent.

Vowels followed by the letter *l* are influenced in a manner similar to the *r*-controlled words. Teaching strategies used for *r*-controlled vowels can also be employed with *l*-controlled vowels.

Children need not be concerned with committing these generalizations to memory; but they should know that when they encounter a vowel followed by an *r*, the vowel may have a sound different from that which might normally be expected. Children should be encouraged to adopt a flexible attitude toward decoding. As they must be encouraged to make hypotheses regarding words in order to use context clues, they must also be encouraged to formulate hypotheses about the sounds that certain graphic symbols represent. Once they begin to develop a willingness to take a chance on various symbol-sound correspondences, they need to be reminded to search for sound combinations that form words they have in their listening vocabularies.

SYLLABICATION

A syllable is a group of sounds pronounced as a single unit. It always contains a minimum of one vowel and can contain a combination of vowels and consonants, but syllables must be pronounced in a single "chest pulse." In written form a syllable can be a single letter *(i, a)* or a combination of consonants and vowels *(aye, me, bout).* It is important for teachers to differentiate between spoken syllables and written syllables, as they do between letters and sounds they represent.

Knowledge of syllables is probably most important in two nonreading areas of the language arts—spelling and writing. Many spelling programs stress syllabication practice to help children divide long words into more manageable units. In spelling, the word is known, in terms of reading it, and it is pronounced quietly by the child to aid him in sequencing and writing the letters in known syllabic utterances. In writing, syllabication helps a child tell how to divide a word correctly at the end of a line. In writing, the word is already known in the child's listening, speaking, and reading vocabularies, but the restrictive conventions of the written language, the end of line dividing point, is unknown.

When decoding new words in reading, the child may use syllabication to segment longer words into smaller, more manageable (pronounceable) units, then decode the smaller units (syllables) and, finally, blend them together to approximate the pronunciation of the word.

The value of syllabication for decoding has been questioned (Glass, 1965), however, because it seems that students use the sounds represented in the words to determine the number of syllables, rather than vice versa. If this is the case, syllabication used as a word analysis tool is of little value. Another criticism of syllabication as used in word recognition (Wardhaugh, 1966) is that there is very little value in syllabicating words because the dividing point between syllables often is not at all clear. For example, the word *rabbit* appears in many dictionaries with the syllables divided between the *bb,* when in fact the word is probably spoken as [*rabb/it*] (or do you say [*ra/bbit*]?).

Nevertheless, there seems to be some pragmatic value in teaching syllabication as a word recognition tool, though probably the point of the instruction should be to help students approximate reasonable breaking points in polysyllabic words. Segmenting unknown words as described above may be argued to be part of visual analysis, since the student breaks words apart on the basis of visual inspection, looking for clues such as double consonants.

In recent years considerable effort has been made to reduce the number of syllabication rules from many and questionable to a few that are widely generalizable.

George and Evelyn Spache (1977), for example, suggest children should be taught seven concepts relevant to syllabication, but the concepts are far from the traditional rules suggested by many experts in the past.

Four syllabication generalizations seem dependable enough to be considered for direct teaching purposes:

1 Compounds usually are divided between the two smaller words.
2 Affixes usually form a syllable.
3 Double consonants usually mark the division point between syllables . . .
4 Except for certain clusters such as *sh, ch, th, ph,* and *ck.*

It is important to stress flexibility in teaching syllabication. The pupil must be encouraged to try different ways of breaking a word apart. With the word *rabbit,* for example, it matters little whether the word is divided between the *ab, bb,* or the *bi.* If the children divide it so as to come up with *rabbit,* they have used syllabication effectively (McFeely, 1974).

Auditory Blending

When pupils are asked to analyze a long, polysyllabic word they do not know, they must first separate the word into smaller units, such as syllables, affixes, and roots; they must then attempt to pronounce these units; and finally they must blend these units together to orally reconstruct the word which triggers a meaningful response. This blending of word parts is a necessary skill for successful decoding. Without the ability to blend sounds together, phonics skills in general are of little value because isolated word parts are meaningless unless they can be synthesized. Blending is even more critical in synthetic phonics since isolated sounds are stressed.

Many children have no trouble blending sounds. However, those who seem to be learning symbol-sound correspondences and still have trouble with phonics in general may well be experiencing auditory blending difficulties. The word parts can be said, but cannot be synthesized.

The teacher can identify this problem by asking the child to pronounce isolated parts of words. When it is clear that the child knows the individual parts, the teacher asks that these parts be blended to make a word.

Initially, this can be done by presenting a written word, broken into parts, to be pronounced.

oc   to   pus

au   to   mo   bile

After the child has pronounced the individual parts correctly the word without separation is shown, and the child is asked to say the whole word.

octopus

automobile

If the child fails on this task the teacher should proceed to the oral language level, pronouncing the word slowly, part by part, and asking the child to say what the whole word is.

Teacher: ad   van   tage

Child: advantage

If the child cannot do this, it is fairly clear that auditory blending problems are present, and children with these problems will experience difficulty with what is typically assumed to be part of phonics instruction. Some children with this problem will benefit from training in blending. Others may have difficulties so severe that phonics instruction may be far less profitable than instruction in other word analysis skills, such as context and visual analysis.

Exercises for beginners should expose children to word parts they already know and that form a familiar word.

in   to   into
a   way   away

Working with known words and word parts will help the child understand the usefulness of blending. After this has been understood, the child may begin to work with blending word parts into unfamiliar words.

se   cret   secret
le   ver   age   leverage

The most difficult form of auditory blending is with nonsense or unknown words. But this is the "acid test" of auditory blending and phonics in general. If a child is able to break a large unknown "word" into small parts, pronounce those parts, and then blend them together to arrive at an acceptable pronunciation—even with a nonsense word—it can be assumed this child has command of blending skills.

The teacher can make the real value of auditory blending clear to children by using words that are in most oral vocabularies but not yet in written vocabularies. Arranging the unknown word in context (usually a sentence), so that all words but the target word are known, also helps the child recognize the importance of blending.

DICTIONARY SKILLS

The more children read, the more unfamiliar, undecodable words they will encounter. These words may be irregular and therefore difficult to deduce. Other words may be decodable for sound but they are not in the child's meaning vocabulary. When children have exhausted their decoding skills and still don't know the word, an outside reference is needed. Since the goal in word recognition is developing efficient, mature, independent readers, this source must be one which the child uses independently.

The dictionary meets these requirements. However, dictionary usage slows the reading process significantly and must be viewed as a final alternative in decoding unknown words.

Teaching Dictionary Skills

Formal training in dictionary use may begin as early as third grade, but selected experiences with the dictionary may begin earlier. Many basal readers provide a glossary of "new" words that may also prove to be a beneficial tool prior to the third-grade level. Numerous publishers produce picture dictionaries that provide initial experiences.

In order to use the dictionary as a word recognition tool students must become familiar with two skill areas, *location* and *pronunciation skills*. Children must be able to find the word they cannot decode, and they must be able to pronounce the word to determine if they have already learned its meaning.

When children use the dictionary as a word recognition tool, they have encountered the unknown word in its written form. Therefore, there is no question as to how the word is spelled. Children must know the alphabetical organization of the dictionary and how to use this organization to find the word. Then they are ready to use pronunciation skills.

Pupils may have difficulty using diacritical marks to determine the pronunciation of a word for two reasons. First, different dictionaries and glossaries use different diacritical markings. Teachers must teach those markings used in the instructional materials being worked with. Second, knowledge of diacritical marks alone will not ensure that children can read the word. They still have to use regular phonics on those units not diacritically marked. Children must learn that the unknown word, as written in traditional orthography, is one representation of a set of given sounds and the phonetic spelling in the dictionary is merely another orthographic representation of the same word. The phonetic spelling may also be a useful method of writing the word, because it may lead to the correct pronunciation when the traditional orthography may not. In this case the phonetic spelling cues the meaning response. If it does not, the problem is one of word meaning as well as word recognition.

ESTABLISHING BALANCES IN WORD RECOGNITION SKILLS

We have discussed various strategies for decoding unknown words. While all of these strategies are important for efficient, mature, independent reading, they can and must not develop in isolation. Consideration must be given to relationships that exist among the various skills. Bond, Tinker, and Wasson (1979) state five important balances in word recognition:

1. *Balance between the establishment of word recognition techniques and the development of meaning vocabulary.* In order to decode a word for sound, the child need not know its meaning. However, because the sound alone is without meaning, the child who does not know a word's meaning may

not realize that the pronunciation is correct. Teaching solely analytical techniques with no development of meaning vocabulary may well reach a point of diminishing returns. The result may be what is termed a "word caller." Similarly, if meaning is emphasized and word analysis skills are neglected (Schell, 1967), children may not be able to decode words.

2. *Balance between sight vocabulary and word recognition skills.* Although it is extremely important to be able to analyze words, continued practice with these words is necessary to elevate them to the sight recognition level. Children who have adequate analysis skills but limited sight vocabularies are often slow, laborious readers. They lack the ability to read fluently and concentrate on gaining meaning, because they must continuously devote attention to word analysis. Some children, on the other hand, commit all words to their sight vocabulary and fail to develop skills in context, visual, structural, and phonic analysis. The more words the child commits to sight vocabulary, the fewer there are that need to be analyzed.

3. *Balance between meaning clues and analytical aids.* Proper decoding requires the use of clues within words as well as clues between words. The child who is over-reliant on context may deviate from the printed text, and, as the deviations mount up, stray from the meaning intended by the author. The child who depends too greatly on analytical aids and fails to use context as a check for meaning, however, may have poor comprehension of what has been read. Overinvolvement with decoding can result in loss of meaning.

4. *Balance among the analytical techniques.* Some words are more readily decoded by one technique of word analysis than another. The student needs to have mastered several techniques in order to be most efficient. Sometimes context clues provide enough information to determine the pronunciation and meaning of an unknown word; however, a phonic clue in addition to context will often be far more useful. Children need to develop all the decoding skills and use them in combination, not independently of each other.

5. *Balance between emphasis placed on knowledge of word parts and the orderly inspection of words along the line of print from left to right and from the beginning of the word to the end.* Prolonged, concentrated effort on isolated word parts may cause the child to look for familiar parts rather than inspect the word in an organized sequence from left to right. For example, if continued stress has been placed on word endings, the child may begin to analyze words from their ends, rather than their beginnings. Such an emphasis could cause serious reversal errors or other unfortunate habits.

The resourceful football coach knows that the most valuable players are those who have mastered running, passing, and kicking. Those with only one or two of these skills may or may not be successful players, and those who have not mastered any of them probably will sit on the bench. The same is true of word analysis skills. The efficient reader uses all of them together.

SUMMARY

Word recognition skills should always be taught along with meaning and sight vocabularies. If children are to learn new words in the reading lessons they must know those words at the oral language level. Otherwise they have no practical method of checking the decoded word in context to verify its accuracy. Many children have reading problems because they learn how to decode words and word parts, but they do not learn the words they decode to the level of instant recognition. These students spend a great deal of time and effort continually decoding instead of reading to gain information. Overemphasis on word analysis skills in the reading program can produce this result.

Students will decode most effectively if they develop a large set of word analysis skills. No one skill should be taught to the exclusion of others; they are all important and should be developed more or less simultaneously so the child has a combination of techniques to attack unknown words. The skills should be balanced, and the child should use them flexibly, viewing the task of word analysis as a form of hypothesis testing. If a word as it is decoded does not make sense in context that effort should be accepted as a possible error and a different analytical approach should be tried.

A skill program to develop word recognition techniques is a critical part of every reading program. These skills are not an end in themselves. They are means to very important goals—reading for information and enjoyment.

REFERENCES

Ames, W. S. "The Development of a Classification Scheme for Contextual Aids." *Reading Research Quarterly* 2 (1966): 57–82.

Artley, A. S. "Teaching Word Meanings through Context." *Elementary English Review* 20 (1943): 68–74.

Bailey, M. H. "The Utility of Phonic Generalizations in Grades One through Six." *The Reading Teacher* (Feb. 1967): 413–418.

Bloomfield, L., and Barnhart, C. L. *Let's Read: A Linguistic Approach.* Detroit: Wayne State University Press, 1961.

Bond, G. L., Tinker, M. A., and Wasson, B. B. *Reading Difficulties: Their Diagnosis and Correction.* Englewood Cliffs, N.J.: Prentice-Hall, 1979.

Boning, R. *Specific Skills Series.* New York: Barnell-Loft, 1976.

Brunner, E. C. "The DISTAR Reading Program." *Proceedings,* College Reading Association, Fall 1968, p. 9.

Burmeister, L. E. "Usefulness of Phonic Generalizations." *The Reading Teacher* (Jan. 1968a): 21.

Burmeister, L. E. "Vowel Pairs." *The Reading Teacher* (Feb. 1968b): 5.

Clymer, T. "The Utility of Phonic Generalizations in the Primary Grades." *The Reading Teacher* (Jan. 1963): 252–258.

Clymer, T. *et al. The Ginn Reading 720 Program,* Ginn and Co. Lexington, Mass. 1976.

Cordts, A. D. *Readiness for Power in Reading.* Chicago: Berkeley-Cardy, 1953.

Dolch, E. *Dolch Basic Sight Vocabulary.* Champaign, Ill.: Garrard Publishing Company, 1953.

Ekwall, Eldon K. *Locating and Correcting Reading Difficulties,* Second edition. Columbus, Ohio: Charles Merrill Publishing Co., 1977.

Emans, R. "The Usefulness of Phonic Generalizations above the Primary Grades." *The Reading Teacher* (Feb. 1967): 419–425.

Emans, R., and Fisher, G. M. "Teaching the Use of Context Clues." *Elementary English* 44 (1967): 243–246.

Fay, L.; Ross, R.; and LaPray, M. *The Young American Basic Reading Program.* Chicago: Rand McNally, 1978.

Fries, C. C. *Linguistics and Reading.* New York: Holt, Rinehart and Winston, 1963.

Gates, A. I. *The Improvement of Reading.* New York: Macmillan, 1947.

Gillingham, A., and Stillman, B. *Remedial Training for Children with Specific Disability in Reading, Spelling and Penmanship.* New York: Author, 1956.

Glass, G. G. "The Teaching of Word Analysis through Perceptual Conditioning." *Reading and Inquiry,* IRA Proceedings, 1965, p. 10.

Goodman, K. S. "A Linguistic Study of Cues and Miscues in Reading." *Elementary English* (1965): 42.

Gray, W. S. *On Their Own in Reading.* Glenview, Ill.: Scott, Foresman, 1960.

Groff, P. "The Topsy-turvey World of 'Sight' Words." *The Reading Teacher* 27 (March 1974) 572–578.

Hanson, I. W. "First Grade Children Work with Variant Endings." *The Reading Teacher* 19 (April 1966): 505–507.

Harris, A., and Sipay, E. R *How to Increase Reading Ability.* New York: David McKay, 1977.

Hester, K. B. *Teaching Every Child to Read.* New York: Harper and Row, 1964.

Hopkins, C. J. and Moe, A. J. "Gamebooks for Reading Instruction" *Reading Horizons* 19 (Fall, 1978): 75–77.

Huey, E. B. *The Psychology and Pedagogy of Reading.* Boston: Massachusetts Institute of Technology Press, 1908 and 1969.

McCarthy, D. "Language Development in Children." *Manual of Child Psychology.* New York: John Wiley, 1954.

McCullough, C. M. "Learning to Use Context Clues." *Elementary English Review* 20 (1943): 140–143.

McFeely, D. C. "Syllabication Usefulness in a Basal and Social Studies Vocabulary." *The Reading Teacher* 27 (1974): 809–814.

McKee, P. *Reading: A Program of Instruction for the Elementary School.* Boston: Houghton Mifflin, 1966.

Maney, E. *Reading-Thinking Skills.* Elizabethtown, Pa.: The Continental Press, 1965–1970.

Moe, A. J. *High Frequency Words.* St. Paul, Minn.: Ambassador Publishing Co., 1972 (a).

Moe, A. J. *High Frequency Nouns.* St. Paul, Minn.: Ambassador Publishing Co., 1972 (b).

Patterson, D. G., and Tinker, M. A. "Readability of Newspaper Headlines Printed in Capitals and in Lower Case." *Journal of Applied Psychology* 30 (1946): 161–168.

Platts, M. E. *Spice.* Stevensville, Mich.: Educational Services, Inc., 1973.

Ramanaskas, S. "The Responsiveness of Cloze Readability Measures to Linguistic Variables Operating over Segments of Text Longer than a Sentence." *Reading Research Quarterly* (Fall 1972): 7.

Rankin, E. F. and Overholzer, B. "Reaction of Intermediate Grade Children to Contextual Clues." *Journal of Reading Behavior* 1 (Summer 1969): 50–73.

Samuels, S. J. "Attentional Processes in Reading: The Effect of Pictures in the Acquisition of Reading Responses." *Journal of Educational Psychology* 58 (1967): 337–342.

Samuels, S. J., and Dahl, P. "Automaticity, Reading and Mental Retardation." U.S. Office of Education, Bureau of Education for the Handicapped, Occasional Paper No. 17, Project No. 332189, 1973.

Schell, L. M. "Teaching Structural Analysis." *The Reading Teacher* 21 (Nov. 1967): 133–137.

Schubert, D. G., and Torgerson, T. L. *Improving the Reading Program.* Dubuque, Iowa: William C. Brown, 1968.

Shibles, B. H. "How Many Words Does a First Grade Child Know?" *Elementary English* 41 (1959): 42–47.

Smith, F. *Understanding Reading.* New York: Holt, Rinehart and Winston, 1971.

Spache, E. B. *Reading Activities for Child Involvement.* Boston: Allyn and Bacon, 1976.

Spache, G., and Spache, E. *Reading in the Elementary School.* Boston: Allyn and Bacon, 1977.

Stone, C. R. "Measuring Difficulty of Primary Reading Material: A Constructive Criticism of Spache's Measure." *Elementary School Journal* 51 (1956): 36–41.

Taylor, W. L. "Cloze Procedures: A New Tool for Measuring Readability." *Journalism Quarterly* 30 (Fall 1953): 360–368.

Templin, M. "Certain Language Skills in Children, Their Development and Relationship." University of Minnesota, Institute of Child Welfare, Monograph Series No. 26, 1957.

Wardhaugh, R. "Syl-lab-i-ca-tion." *Elementary English* 63 (Nov. 1966): 785–788.

Wardhaugh, R. *Reading: A Linguistic Perspective.* New York: Harcourt, Brace and World, 1969 (a).

Wardhaugh, R. "The Teaching of Phonics and Comprehension: A Linguistic Evaluation." In *Psycholinguistics and the Teaching of Reading,* edited by K. S. Goodman and J. T. Fleming. Newark, Del.: International Reading Association, 1969 (b), pp. 79–90.

Wylie, R. E., and Durrell, D. D. "Teaching Vowels through Phonograms." *Elementary English* 47 (1970): 787–791.

PREVIEW

Few will deny the importance of comprehension in reading. Without it, reading has no value. However, considerable controversy exists concerning what comprehension is and how it should be taught.

Guszak and Hoffman define comprehension and consider several theoretical models and taxonomies related to both the process of comprehension and its products. They describe problems in detail, and discuss the reasons for these problems. The importance of teachers' questioning techniques is emphasized. Attention is given to defining your role as a teacher in setting purposes, stimulating various levels of comprehension, and controlling pupil responses.

Methods of planning the comprehension program and strategies for teaching comprehension skills are discussed, and in a way which is directly applicable in the classroom. Guzak and Hoffman show how varied reading-thinking skills, skills management, and critical reading skills may be developed.

The chapter presents a synthesis of new ideas about comprehension in a contemporary, creative, and practical manner.

11 | Comprehension Skills

Frank J. Guszak, University of Texas at Austin
James V. Hoffman, University of Texas at Austin

OBJECTIVES:

After you have read this chapter, you should be able to:

1. Describe and differentiate between process and product views of reading comprehension.

2. Specify steps in the planning of a reading comprehension program including: creating varied practice formats, securing positive models for proficiency, and providing for direct instruction.

3. List and discuss the specific stages for developing a direct instruction program in reading comprehension including the following: establishing realistic goals, building a management system for following pupil skills growth, acquiring needed subsystems, and scheduling direct teaching and pupil-managed learning components.

4. Describe effective means for teacher questioning, using cloze techniques, stimulating critical reading, and socializing experiences in literature.

The teaching of reading comprehension has been topical since William S. Gray called for a "new" emphasis in reading instruction in "intelligent silent reading" (1924). Gray introduced the term largely in reaction to what was perceived as an overemphasis on oral reading in schools. He felt that reading could not occur without some degree of comprehension (Smith, 1963). Thorndike, at an even earlier date (1917), put reading in its proper perspective with the simple statement, "Reading is Thinking." Evidently, the reading process is intimately linked to cognition. These connections will have direct implications for those who are charged with responsibility for moving students toward increasing levels of reading proficiency.

A good place to start in understanding the nature of reading comprehension is to recognize that reading is one manifestation of a more generic comprehension activity—one which is free from specific processing features. At a minimum there is at least one other member of this language processing class and that is listening comprehension. The major difference between reading and listening comprehension is the nature of the incoming coded signal. The encoding processes of writing and speaking parallel and complement their receptive counterparts. These multiple and interactive aspects of language use provide the basic communication channel with the real world across which information is both transmitted and received. Language, in other words, provides a medium through which we actively relate what we know to what we experience. Sticht, et al. (1974) label this activity *languaging*. Reading comprehension is related to both in the way this knowledge is organized as well as the manner in which such structures interact with our experiences during thought. A discussion of reading comprehension skills, therefore, must examine both the nature of thinking and its application to the reading act. Basic definitions of thinking, reading comprehension, and interrelated terms provide the background for this section. Only then can we move on to consider the pragmatics—how to plan reading comprehension programs and strategies for developing comprehension skills.

DEFINITIONS OF TERMS

Thinking is the inferred mental activity that happens when a person senses and makes discriminations among people, objects, places, and ideas in any given environment. Thinking can progress through varying levels of difficulty such as cognition, memory, divergent thinking, convergent thinking, and evaluation.

Reading is thinking in response to selective graphic cues. As Goodman (in Harris and Smith, 1972) states, it involves the partial use of available minimal language cues selected from perceptual input on the basis of reader expectation.

Cognition means the discovery or rediscovery of something.

Memory is the retention for some period of time (long-term or short-term memory) of that which is cognized (discovered or rediscovered).

Intelligence is often defined as a person's innate capacity for generating thought.

Comprehension refers to the process of generating thought. As pointed out in the definition of reading, that process is stimulated in reading by the response to selective graphic cues.

THE STRUCTURE OF KNOWLEDGE

Piaget (1952, 1963, 1969) describes intellectual development in terms of two basic human tendencies: organization and adaptation. Organization refers to the tendency to arrange processes into coherent systems. Adaptation refers to the tendency to change or refine such systems in response to novel interactions with the environment. The complementary processes of assimilation and accommodation acting on experiences provide the basis by which this adaptive cycle moves an individual toward a more sophisticated internal representation of *reality*. Piaget refers to this internal representation as cognitive structure. The child moving through rapid stages of intellectual growth is portrayed in an active role in this developmental process; that is, one who seeks out and uses experiences to reinforce existing structures as well as build new ones.

Smith (1975) explains these same cognitive structures in terms of a child's "theory of the world in the head." He identifies three aspects of how these structures are organized. First, we distinguish between categories or classes of objects. These categories form the basic building blocks of our knowledge and may have direct, tangible referents in the real world, for example paper, a spoon, and so on. Others are more abstract or generic in nature such as relatives, love, and space. The second aspect of identifying cognitive structure is the rules for allocating objects into categories. These rules are stated in terms of *distinctive features*, that is, those critical characteristics or attributes which allow us to differentiate one category in our memory store from another. Every category in our knowledge store must be different from every other item with respect to at least one distinctive feature. Smith describes the third aspect of cognitive structure as a network of interrelations among the categories themselves. All categories within the system are connected in some fashion, either directly or indirectly. It is this network or system of interrelations which is at the core of our cognitive structure.

Cognitive psychologists have increasingly come to refer to this structure of knowledge as *schemata*. The introduction of the term to modern psychology is most often credited to Bartlett (1932). A schema (singular) defines the network of interrelations among the constituents of a given concept (Rumelhart and Ortony, 1977). Schemata exist at all levels, from concrete to abstract (Adams, et al., 1977). For instance, we have a schema for each of the letters of the alphabet as well as for the alphabet itself. We have a schema for each word in our lexicon which most likely specifies connotations and denotations as well as co-occurrence relationships, grammatical constraints, and auditory and visual distinctive features. The schemata we have developed are, simultaneously, a record of what we have experienced in the past and a framework for how we will organize, interpret and comprehend future experiences.

COMPREHENSION: A PROCESS PERSPECTIVE

Comprehension is said to occur when an individual can successfully call upon an existing schematic structure to account for (explain) an experience. In this sense comprehension is neither a passive nor a totally receptive process; rather, it relies on the active participation of the individual. Smith (1975) suggests that our normal psychological condition is one of comprehension—so unnoticed that we only pay attention to it when it doesn't work. In a Piagetian sense, we can conceive of the relationship between a developing cognitive structure and an expanding world of experiences as an interactive one in which our goal is to achieve a state of equilibrium—that is, the stage at which our cognitive structures can satisfactorily account for, explain, and/or reduce the uncertainty surrounding the reality we encounter. It is in this search for equilibrium that learning occurs through the process of adaptation. Schemata undergo change by gradual extension, articulation, and refinement (Anderson, 1977).

Readers interacting with a text encounter a form of reality. In the process they call up schemata from their knowledge store which provides the basis for interpreting the author's message. Ausubel (1963, 1968) has proposed that cognitive structures provide the *ideational scaffolding* for the information presented in a text. The reader activates certain structures based on a general examination of the context or cues presented in the text and these schemata provide the structures for comprehending the discourse. As a very simple illustration, anyone reading an Agatha Christie novel brings a certain framework to bear which allows them to anticipate or not to anticipate certain situations, characters, and outcomes. This illustrates the effects of a very general orienting form of schemata that could just as well be examined at the sentence or word level.

Pearson and Johnson (1978) have developed a guide to teaching reading comprehension which attempts to build on these and similar conceptual notions implicit in schema theory. They identify certain *inside the head* factors (e.g., linguistic knowledge, semantic knowledge, interest, and motivation) as well as *outside the head* factors (e.g., vocabulary difficulty, sentence complexity, and story structure) which can influence reading comprehension. They then proceed to explain in depth how each of these factors operates to affect comprehension. They also speculate on ways in which these factors might be directly manipulated in an instructional setting.

COMPREHENSION: A PRODUCT PERSPECTIVE

The result of the interaction of thinking operations upon contents (text materials) produces thought products. While the ideas presented so far are helpful in understanding cognition and the process of comprehension, it is equally important from an educator's perspective to examine comprehension as a product or an outcome of efficient reading. Since comprehension is more readily measured as an outcome, rather than a process, the research literature in reading tends to be dominated by this product perspective. As we shall see in the following discussion of selected theories, thought products can be described in varied ways.

Bloom—Taxonomy of Educational Objectives: Cognitive Domain

The *Taxonomy of Educational Objectives: Cognitive Domain* (Bloom, 1956) grew from the efforts of examiners to standardize the various types of examinations that were being written to evaluate pupil understandings. In order to deal with the widely different types of thinking necessary to perform certain tasks, the group worked out a model of a taxonomy of thinking behaviors that could be built upon indefinitely.

Now an educational landmark, the Bloom Taxonomy serves as a guide to thousands of educators. They describe their educational goals in terms of the following progression of thinking skills:

1 *Knowledge:* The knowledge category is broken down in terms of increasingly difficult types of knowledge—for example, knowledge of specifics and knowledge of ways and means of dealing with specifics.

2 *Comprehension:* Comprehension is the ability to understand or generate logical thoughts about one's knowledge. The taxonomy differentiates between increasingly difficult comprehension tasks: translation, interpolation, and extrapolation.

3 *Application:* Application suggests that the individual can actually apply the knowledge and understandings to a simulated or real situation— for example, rebuilding a car engine or writing a short story.

4 *Analysis:* Analysis is the ability to analyze elements, relationships, and organizational principles.

5 *Synthesis:* Synthesis is the ability to take the elements of analysis and synthesize them into a unique communication—for example, a critique of a play; a plan, or a set of abstract relations—a novel mathematical formula, a working design of an invention.

6 *Evaluation:* Evaluation is the ability to place value on some thing or idea by judging it according to internal logic (logic within it) or by comparing it with other elements of the same type (external evaluation).

Sanders—Taxonomy of Questions

In his book *Classroom Questions: What Kinds?* Sanders (1966) has developed a most valuable group of suggestions on questioning pupils for the various levels of thinking. For the teacher seeking further detail, such a reference is quite valuable.

While Bloom and his associates focused upon a classification of objectives, Sanders looked more closely at teachers' questions. The results of Sanders' viewpoint are seen in the following revised categories of the original Bloom taxonomy.

1 *Memory:* Memory is the process called for by teacher questions that require the recognition or recall of information—for example, "In what year did the American Revolution begin?"

2 *Translation:* Translation is the ability to change information into different symbolic forms or language called for in a question such as, "Would you summarize the events that led up to the American Revolution?"

3 *Application:* This is "the ability to solve a lifelike problem that requires the identification of the issue and the selection and use of appropriate generalizations and skills." A student might apply the lessons learned in a study of revolutionary history to potential causes of current revolutions in the world. For example—what major forces in the French and Russian revolutions can be seen in the Iranian revolution?

4 *Analysis:* Analysis is the ability to solve problems by examining the elements of the problem and using logical forms of thinking—for example, "Can you analyze the specific causes that are creating tension in the Middle East? Can you detail the historical tensions between Arabs and Jews?"

5 *Synthesis:* Synthesis is the ability to solve a problem that requires "original, creative thinking"—for example, "What kind of peace agreement might be negotiated in the Middle East which would satisfy the major combatants?"

6 *Evaluation:* The student evaluates something as good or bad, right or wrong in accordance with some standards that have been developed —for example, a judgement is made about the relative merits of the political party platforms in the election—or, indicate what you feel to be the correct position with regard to the "right to work" stances of the two parties.

Barrett—Taxonomy of Cognitive and Affective Dimensions of Reading Comprehension

After analyzing and synthesizing the ideas of Bloom, Sanders and others, Barrett (in Clymer's chapter, *1968 National Society for the Study of Education Yearbook, Part II*) developed a taxonomic structure that would describe the specific outcomes of reading. His taxonomy also attempted to describe the affective dimensions of reading. Consequently, the structure might permit the measurement of both understandings and feelings about various types of reading.

The Barrett taxonomy has been recently (1978) revised to order reading outcomes as follows:

1 *Literal Recognition or Recall:* Literal comprehension focuses upon those elements explicitly stated in the selection. It involves, for example, recognizing a piece of information or remembering a story character's name. Literal comprehension tasks include recognition or recall of details, main ideas, sequence, comparisons, cause and effect relationships, and character traits.

2 *Inference:* Inferential comprehension involves the inferences that students make using a synthesis of the literal content of a selection, personal knowledge, intuition and imagination. Such inferences might be either convergent or divergent thoughts that go beyond the statements on the pages. The arrangement of inferential comprehension skills is: inferring supporting details, inferring the main idea, inferring sequence, inferring comparisons, inferring cause and effect relationships, inferring character traits, predicting outcomes, and inferring about figurative language.

3 *Evaluation:* Barrett's evaluation category is substantially the same as Sanders'. The reader must make evaluative judgments on the basis of either external criteria (comparisons with other sources) or internal criteria (comparisons within, such as internal logic or consistency). Evaluative thinking includes the following: judgments of reality or fantasy, judgments of fact or opinion, judgments of adequacy and validity, judgments of appropriateness, judgments of worth, desirability, and acceptability.

4 *Appreciation:* Appreciation, according to Barrett, involves all the previously described cognitive dimensions because it deals with the aesthetic impact on the reader of what is being read. A reader may be deeply touched by a beautiful description at one moment, angered by a slanted argument at another moment, and delighted by a whimsical bit in the next paragraph. Many feelings are aroused when reading including the purpose for reading—emotional response to the content, identification with characters or incidents, and reactions to authors' use of language and imagery.

Obviously, it is not necessary to hold every dimension of Barrett's Taxonomy in mind in order to develop written and oral comprehension tasks for children. A teacher needs to be aware of the various major groupings and provide reading-thinking situations in each one.

A popular misconception is that "literal comprehension" questions are unimportant. This is nonsense! Literal comprehension forms the basis for higher level comprehension skills and the Bloom, Sanders, and Barrett taxonomies do not support the elimination of literal comprehension. They emphasize a need for the recognition and development of varied types of thinking.

Synthesis of Product Models

Each of the models presented provides a useful means for discussing the products of reading comprehension. Some are more useful than others because of their explicit attention to the end result that we call reading. The Bloom and Sanders descriptions seem to lack the substance of the kinds of observable behaviors that we might want to measure after our pupils read something. The Barrett classifications give us the clearest set of descriptors of this group.

PLANNING A COMPREHENSION PROGRAM

Sometimes in the minds of most educators preparing to instruct there is a secret, compulsive desire to break down the content into subclasses, levels, and/or schematic representations of that which is to be learned. Their goal is certainly understandable: to pave the student's road to proficiency with nice easy steps; and to provide teachers with some concrete, measurable objectives around which they can focus instructional efforts. Such a perspective for teaching is as popular today in reading as in any other curricular area.

Many introductory methods texts, for example, will tell you that developmental reading instruction divides neatly into word recognition and comprehension skills. Such texts then proceed to delineate assorted configurations of subskills under these two headings which, taken as a whole, define the scope of an instructional program. This structure is further expanded to include a sequence which both specifies the levels at which particular skills are taught under each subcategory as well as how instruction across levels is coordinated between the various skill areas. It is not surprising that when programming with materials which bring this scope and sequence to an explicit, operational level, teachers sometimes lose sight of the forest for the sake of the trees—that is, they have a plan but no design. This appears to be the case, particularly with respect to the place of comprehension skills in reading instruction. Can we focus teaching in certain aspects, levels, or *skills* associated with comprehension process without destroying the process itself? The answer to this question is most assuredly *yes*—if the teacher has a firm grasp of the kinds of process and product perspectives for comprehension that were previously outlined. Such perspectives allow for the teacher to both construct and manipulate a reading environment which is conducive to successful comprehension as well as permit the observation of changes in student behavior relative to the adjustments that have been made.

Olson (1977) has observed that knowledge may be acquired through a variety of means: private experience, observation of a model, or explicit instruction. He labels these respectively muddling, modeling, and meddling. Though the primary focus for the remainder of this chapter is on methods for explicit instruction, it would be inappropriate to conclude that the first two means of acquisition should be ignored in developing a reading comprehension program. Quite the opposite is the case. The first two methods provide the foundation and framework for successful programming in the third.

Private Experience — or
Muddling in Books

Learning by doing is a recurrent theme in modern instructional programs. It is presumed that children involved in a reading program should do a lot of reading if they are to develop an adequate repertoire of comprehension skills. Unfortunately, this assumption appears to be far from what the reality is in many schools across our country (Allington, 1977). A recent study of the actual amount of time first-grade students spend in connected independent reading from books, in the typical instructional day, revealed that an average of less than three minutes per child per day was devoted to such activity (Paulissen, 1978). These findings may be more representative of common instructional practices than we would like to think.

A first step in organizing a program that is conducive to the development of reading comprehension is to create *multiple* opportunities for students to actually practice reading. Typically, teachers respond to this suggestion or similar suggestions by noting that there isn't enough time in the day to read with each child every day. True enough! There are alternate formats though for practice which do not require direct teacher involvement as well as adaptations to traditional guided reading procedures which permit a more judicious allocation of teacher time. Some examples follow:

1 *Instructional reading* in the classroom (as evidenced in most basal designs) generally carries with it two conditions: (1) material at the student's instructional level; and (2) teacher guidance. Practice in this format has as its goal promotion of maximum growth in word recognition and comprehension skills. Teacher guidance should include: questions to set the stage for reading—for example, assist the child in looking for certain important elements of what is to be read; questions

inserted at different sections, paragraphs, pages—to alert and monitor student understanding of key points; and, finally, questions or comprehension tasks following reading which take on forms such as inferring motivations or evaluating content.

2   *Independent reading* also carries with it two conditions: (1) reading material at the student's independent level; and (2) no direct teacher assistance. This format provides practice that is designed to develop rate and fluency. One of the problems with reading programs which rely exclusively on instructional practice is that students are seldom given the chance to get "too good" with the material they are reading. For the student, being "too good" means it's time to move up to the next level of difficulty. Independent reading promotes synthesis of new skills to an automatic level of processing (Biemiller, 1978).

3   *Recreational reading* carries with it a single condition: self-selection of materials. No controls are placed over the level of difficulty of the materials in relation to student ability. The primary purpose of this format is to develop a positive attitude toward reading by building on a student's own interests and experiences. Recreational reading provides for broad experiences in materials which vary not only in difficulty level but also content and style of writing.

There are, of course, other formats for practice; but these three provide the basic triad around which a balanced program can be initiated.

Learning by Observation — Modeling

There are numerous positive and negative models available to students which can and do affect the development of reading proficiency. Parents, peers and teachers all exert varying degrees of influence on what and how students learn by the example they set. While parental behavior is quite often beyond a teacher's control, there are numerous ways in which teachers can provide positive models of proficient reading behavior within the school setting. Two such procedures are to be found in Uninterrupted Sustained Silent Reading (USSR) programs and oral literature.

USSR Programs have been recognized in their many formats as one of the most powerful and dramatic means to build on positive reading models (Hunt, 1970; McCracken, 1971). Programs are generally organized around the following four elements:

1   a regular time set aside for silent reading as a group.
2   everyone (including the teacher) reading from material they have selected for themselves.
3   sustained silent reading until there is a disruption, at which time USSR is concluded for that day
4   no formal evaluation of individual student performance.

USSR time is a refreshing addition to most reading programs. It provides both positive peer and teacher models as well as sustained practice in a wide variety of materials.

A systematic program in oral literature is another excellent way to provide students with positive models. Teachers in the classroom, like parents at home, have been reading literature out loud to children for years. Seldom, however, has the importance of this activity been given proper recognition or priority status in the reading curriculum. Too often oral literature is relegated to early primary classroom levels and included only when there are a few *extra* minutes before recess or dismissal. A well planned oral literature program, on the other hand, can be a tremendous asset to a reading comprehension program:

1   by providing students with experiences in literature which are appropriate in topic, content, and interest to their age level, but which they are unable to process independently.
2   by providing students with a background in traditional literature which will be helpful in comprehending what they read on their own.
3   by providing the teacher with an opportunity to instruct students in basic characteristics of literature (such as plot, character, theme, and literary type) so that the students bring these concepts with them to assist in their own reading experiences.
4   most importantly—by providing the student with a model of good reading.

These modeling effects which accompany oral literature programs range across many levels, from the fluency and rhythm of interpretive reading to the kinds of questions the teacher uses to elicit student response and participation.

USSR and oral literature are just two examples of how teachers can provide their students with frequent, positive models of proficient reading.

**Explicit Instruction in
Reading Comprehension
Skills—Meddling**

Durkin (1978) has recently published the results of an extensive observational study into classroom reading comprehension instruction. The findings are staggering. After analyzing the data from almost 300 hours of direct observation of both reading and social studies classes, she reports:

1   Practically no comprehension instruction was seen. Comprehension assessment, carried on for the most part through interrogation, was common. Whether children's answers were right or wrong was the big concern.
2   Other kinds of reading instruction were not seen with any frequency either. It cannot be said, therefore, that the teachers neglected comprehension because they were too busy teaching phonics, structural analysis, or word meanings.
3   In addition to being interrogators, teachers also turned out to be assignment-givers. As a result, time spent on giving, completing, and checking assignments consumed a large part of the observed periods. Sizeable amounts of time also went to activities categorized as "Transition" and "Noninstruction."

4 None of the observed teachers saw the social studies period as a time to improve children's comprehension abilities. Instead, all were concerned about covering content and with having children master facts. (p. 47)

Like so many things, good reading comprehension programs do not "just happen." They are the result of careful planning and execution. This is particularly true with respect to explicit instruction in reading comprehension skills. Because program execution in this area is so dependent on sound planning, this portion of the chapter examines some crucial planning decisions. These decisions concern:

1 Establishing realistic goals.
2 Building a tracking system.
3 Acquiring needed subsystems.
4 Scheduling direct teacher and pupil-managed components.

Establishing Realistic Goals

Comprehension goals are sometimes difficult to decide on. Different authors use different labels and list varying numbers of skills. The ultimate recipient of the confusing goals is the teacher who sees the following:

Basal Program's Goals

Identifying meaning of:
    word
    phrase
    sentence
Identifying story problem
Making and checking inferences
Grasping implied meanings
Anticipating actions
Perceiving relationships
    analogous
    cause-effect
    general-specific
    sequence
Forming sensory images
Sensing emotional reactions
Evaluating actions
Following plot
Comparing and contrasting

Teacher Goals

Literal
Inferential

Some teachers prefer to rely on intuition rather than on a list of specific goals. Inadvertently, they often neglect to develop many basic comprehension skills—locating information in reference texts, for example. Others may fail to develop some skills for the opposite reason—they are fearful of departing from the basal manual and rely too little on their own judgment Obviously, neither extreme is satisfactory for the teacher who wants to develop the full range of comprehension skills.

Realistic comprehension goals must be those which the teacher internalizes and understands. The teacher should ask:

1 Can the behaviors be described easily (so they can be recognized)?
2 Can the behaviors be measured with relative ease?
3 Are such behaviors developed in the available reading materials?

The Barrett Taxonomy provides the most usable set of reading behaviors in terms of outcomes that can be described and measured. Teachers can work first from the major skills: literal comprehension, reorganization, inference, evaluation and appreciation. Then they can determine how parts of reading programs might contribute to the development of each skill. A first-grade teacher might choose to focus upon a few basic skills of inference and literal comprehension. A fifth- or sixth-grade teacher might look into the various categories for more sophisticated skills—inferring main ideas, appreciating certain types of rhyme, and so on.

Since the behaviors are described rather precisely in the Barrett Taxonomy, they can easily be measured. Teachers must decide how the measurement should be done. They might use the following methods, for example:

1 Literal comprehension: Ask pupils to mark a specific sentence, tell what happened, or put cut-out sentences in order (as determined by story read previously).
2 Inference: Ask students to predict from pictures or sentences, fill in details in outline story, or create visual representations of next event (after hearing preceding events).
3 Evaluation: Ask students to draw lines between inconsistencies in story, detect fallacious reasoning, mark unsupported claims.
4 Appreciation: Ask students to describe feelings for character, action, plot, description, and so on.

Often there are teacher questions listed in the basal manual, specific workbook pages, and other supplemental comprehension skills materials that can be used to test and develop the desired skills.

Building a Management System[1]

Once a teacher establishes a set of realistic goals and writes them down, then what? The next step is to make a plan for tracking the various pupil needs and developments of the various skills. With so many children, skills, and materials, it seems improbable that any teacher can keep an accurate *mental* account of each child's needs and developments. Management systems such as the *Reading Skills Checklist* provide the teacher with means for noting increasingly complex skills.

Listed on the fourth level of the *Reading Checklist* are five major comprehension skills: predicting/extending, locating information, remembering,

---

[1] Guszak's term "tracking system" is similar to what Johnson and Moe, in Chapter Eight, term "management system."

organizing, and evaluating critically. Each of these large skill areas is broken down into sub-skills.

By testing pupils for the specific skills on the checklist, the teacher can make appropriate entries on an individual pupil's *Comprehension Check-sheet.* Figure 11.2 indicates that John needs to work on locating stories in the table of contents and remembering the sequence of the story.

As John masters the various comprehension skills, the teacher will put a plus (+) sign by each one. More skilled readers can note their own progress and needs on the checksheet.

Figure 11.3 reveals a more sophisticated set of comprehension skills.

The teacher has noted that Mary has specific needs in four of the five comprehension areas. First of all, she needs to sharpen her closure skills. Consequently, cloze tasks employing an every-fifth-word cloze pattern are prescribed. Presumably, such tasks might be needed because Mary is not inferring well enough to read efficiently.

Mary apparently needs work in locating words in the dictionary that involve going to the third letter for identification, work in rapid location in a phone directory, as well as location work using the legends of a topographic map.

The notation "Loft D" under *Remembering* suggests that Mary might profit by doing remembering tasks in a commercial specific skills series. Mary will read a brief selection and then answer questions about it.

Organizing needs indicated for Mary on the checksheet include the outlining of a story in sentences. She might outline a chapter in her geography book. Frequently, outlining will be preceded by comprehension tasks that involve the selection of the main events, ideas, or components.

Such tracking systems as the *Reading Checklist* and *Checksheet* cannot ensure that pupils will receive proper instruction. They can, however, assist the teacher in making a systematic needs assessment. Identifying these needs can help the teacher determine the skills materials which must be purchased, borrowed, or constructed.

Once the materials are acquired they need to be made operable. When many different children are working in a variety of materials (as they should), the teacher does not have time to personally select the needed materials for each pupil on a daily basis. Rather, the effective teacher must: (1) organize the materials into a system whereby pupils can readily find what they have to do, and (2) establish checking systems that permit pupils to get immediate feedback as to their success or failure.

Usually the range of skills within a given classroom will be so great that the teacher will need to set up a wide range of materials (from readiness tasks to involved evaluations). This requires that space be made available and organizer boxes arranged, and that the system be readily accessible to all the pupils. Consequently, the teacher may wish to build a series of boxes to house graded levels of difficulty, as shown below.

Figure 11.1
*Reading Skills Checklist:
Comprehension.*

Predicting/Extending	Locating Information	Remembering	Organizing	Evaluating Critically
Predicts convergent outcomes from: pictures picture and title title oral description story situations	Locates specifics within written materials phrase (s) sentence (s) paragraph (s) page numbers parts of a story (beginning, middle, end, etc.)	Remembering simple sentence content Remembering the content of two or more simple sentences in sequence	Retells: sentence sentence set paragraph story	Makes judgments about the desirability of a: character situation
Predicts divergent outcomes	Locating information with book parts titles stories table of contents	Remembering the factual content of complete and complex sentences and sentence sets	Outlines orally the sequence of the story	Makes judgments about the validity of a: story description argument, etc. by making both **external** and **internal** comparison
Explain story character actions		Remembering paragraph content	Reorganizes a communication into a: cartoon picture picture sequence	Making judgments about whether stories are fictional or non-fictional by noting: reality fantasy exaggeration
Explain gadget operations Generalizes from sets of information in story(ies) (Include task of identifying an unstated **main idea**).	Locating information with reference aids picture dictionaries maps (political) encyclopedias atlases globes telephone books newspapers	Remembering story content		
Restores omitted words in context				Making judgments about whether the author is trying to amuse, bias, etc. the reader.
Labels feelings of characters, i.e. sad—glad				Detects in reading materials the following propaganda techniques: —bad names, e.g. wallflower —glad names, e.g. superstar
Explains why story characters hold certain viewpoints				

4 COMPREHENSION

Source: Reading Skills Checklist, Services in Education, 300 E. Huntland Dr., Austin, Texas 78752. Copyright © 1972.

Predicting/Extending	Locating Information	Remembering	Organizing	Evaluating Critically
	Loc. stories in contents	Remember sequence of story events.		

COMPREHENSION CHECKSHEET

Figure 11.2
*Comprehension
Checksheet: John*

Figure 11.3
*Comprehension
Checksheet: Mary.*

Predicting/Extending	Locating Information	Remembering	Organizing	Evaluating Critically
Restore every omitted word in <u>Zany Times</u> (5ᵗʰ word closure)	Locate: - words in dict. (through 3rd letter) - phone nos. in phone dir. - topographic info. on map	Details in <u>Loft D</u>	Outline story in sentence outline Outline events in chapter	

COMPREHENSION CHECKSHEET

Through the use of individual contracts such as the following, the teacher might easily send pupils to the various boxes to do tasks unique to their needs.

```
Monday

P-6

R-5
```

This would mean that the students would be expected to go to the *Predicting* box, pull out P–6, perform the skill task, look up the answer(s) on the self-checking answer key, and then write down some description of their task accuracy in a manner similar to that suggested in the diagram below.

```
Monday

P-6    6/8

R-5    4/4
```

The notations 6/8 and 4/4 would indicate that the pupil got 6 of 8 items correct on P–6 and 4 of 4 correct on R–5.

Acquiring Needed Subsystems

Tracking systems can have little value if the pupils do not have access to suitable tasks for developing the various types of comprehension skills they need. Many teachers lack the necessary materials; others may have such materials but lack the organization necessary to make them usable.

Some teachers are eager to make their own comprehension materials. While the attitude is admirable, the logistics frequently make such a task very

Major Skill Area	Specific Materials	Publishers
Predicting	*Specific Skills Series* (Using the Context, Drawing Conclusions)	Barnell-Loft, Ltd.
	Kaleidoscope Readers	Field Educational Publications
	Reading-Thinking Skills	The Continental Press
Locating	*Specific Skills Series* (Locating Information)	Barnell-Loft, Ltd.
	Study Skills Labs (Reference FFF)	Educational Development Laboratory

Major Skill Area	Specific Materials	Publishers
Remembering	*Specific Skills Series* (Getting the Facts)	Barnell-Loft, Ltd.
	New Reading Skilltexts	Merrill
	Reading for Meaning	J. B. Lippincott
	Reading Laboratories	SRA
Organizing	*Reading Skills Laboratory*	Houghton Mifflin
	Reading-Thinking Skills	Continental Press
	Reading for Meaning	J. B. Lippincott
Evaluating	*Reading-Thinking Skills*	The Continental Press

difficult. Consequently, the emphasis here is upon the acquisition of commercially prepared materials which may prove less costly in the long run.

While such materials can be helpful, they can also accumulate on shelves if not organized into a working system. Such systems are not built over a weekend but require careful, deliberate planning. It is well to plan to work on one element at a time.

Scheduling Direct Teacher and Pupil-Managed Components

Teachers often put too much time into comprehension tasks that have a low yield—certain guided reading tasks, for example. Since teachers have limited amounts of time, they need to use that time wisely.

One efficient method or organization is to program all children onto completely individualized contracts (which include comprehension tasks). This means that each child has a written contract or guide that can be readily understood. The contract directs them toward certain types of tasks to perform during the reading period (or larger contract period). It is their responsibility to perform the tasks called for on the contract, to check the correct answers from an answer key, and to record scores on the contract.

If the teacher has arranged the room with subsystems and all pupils are taking care of their own needs, then the teacher can plan the *direct teaching role* in terms of the following:

1 Direct teaching of small groups with common skills needs (or individuals with a particular need).
2 Determining the appropriateness of contract tasks.

Few teachers will be able to program their time so well that no direct teaching of small groups is necessary. Rather, the teacher's concern is to pull small groups together on the basis of need, quickly teach the needed skill element, and immediately send the group back to its individual contracts. Thus, small group meetings with the teacher might last five, ten, or fifteen minutes, seldom longer.

Daily planning by the teacher is crucial in order to meet a wide array of needs. The following schedule shows what a single day's schedule might entail:

Teacher Actions	Pupil Actions

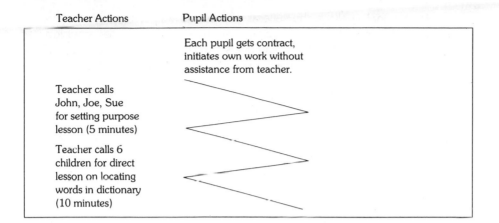

Teacher calls John, Joe, Sue for setting purpose lesson (5 minutes)

Teacher calls 6 children for direct lesson on locating words in dictionary (10 minutes)

Each pupil gets contract, initiates own work without assistance from teacher.

The teacher might pull six or seven such groups during this day's reading period and the following day pull some of the same groups as well as other groups. Some groups might meet as few as one or two times a week with the teacher for direct teaching instruction. These latter pupils can learn as easily or more easily without direct teacher intervention, so they are contracted to do so.

The teacher must also plan the time to *determine the appropriateness of every pupil's contract* and their work on it. Essentially, this means that their teachers must build some so-called "float time" into their schedule—time during which they are free from direct teaching to move among the pupils as they perform their contract tasks. The following outline schedule shows both *direct teaching* and *determining* functions.

	Teacher Actions	Pupil Actions
8:30		Each pupil gets contract, initiates own work without assistance from teacher.
8:40	Teacher works with John, Joe, Sue on setting purposes.	
8:45	Teacher works with 6 students on dictionary.	
8:55	Teacher works with 5 students on main idea.	
9:05	Teacher floats.	
9:10	Teacher works with Tom & Henry on task.	

Using this schedule, the teacher can pull small groups daily, biweekly, or weekly for direct teaching of skills that are not as easily taught through pupil-managed tasks.

In the final analysis, the success of a comprehension program depends on the quality of the teacher's decisions about individual needs, provisions for meeting those needs (including materials and decisions about direct teaching tasks) and provisions for feedback to children about their accuracy and progress.

STRATEGIES FOR DEVELOPING COMPREHENSION SKILLS

While there must be a myriad of strategies for developing reading comprehension skills, the following were chosen because they are adaptable to most instruction settings:

1 Measuring reading comprehension
2 Cloze techniques
3 Critical thinking
4 Socializing experiences in literature

Measuring Reading Comprehension

Teacher questioning usually involves the literal, interpretative, and evaluative dimensions. In the section which follows, we discuss each of these dimensions, asking, "How *do* we measure it?" and "How *should* we measure it?"

How Do We Measure Literal Comprehension?   Literal comprehension is measured through the student's ability to recognize or recall some literal element of reading.

Typically, basal reader programs include recognition questions designed to guide the pupil's understanding of the stories. Frequently referred to as the "guided reading strategy," this technique places the teacher in the role of a guide, asking leading questions in advance of a page or story. As the students respond to the task by searching out the element, the teacher can observe those who are succeeding as well as those who are not. The teacher asks questions to check out their observations. The whole task goes something like this:

Teacher: Find the name of the story.
Child: "The Trip."
Teacher: Right! Now read the first page and find out when the Parks were taking a trip and where they were going. (Silence as pupils read.)
Child: On June first.
Teacher: Good, and where were they going?
Child: To the mountains.

Such questions guide pupils to the primary elements of the story and help them learn how to identify these elements themselves in a variety of reading materials and tasks.

This approach will be most valuable if:

1 The questions direct the pupils to the most important elements.
2 The directing questions are appropriate because they direct only when necessary.
3 A majority of the pupils provide their share of the answers.

Guidelines for recall-type questions are similar to those listed above. Teachers should be careful not to program children to look for insignificant information or to remember insignificant facts to the neglect of basic considerations.

How Should We Measure Literal Comprehension? Before questioning pupils, teachers should assess the reading content as to its most basic concepts and its sequence of events (and their relative importance). Such an assessment can indicate how many questions should be asked, and which are the most pertinent questions. Nothing is more defeating than to squeeze a multitude of questions out of something that has relatively little significance or meaning to the readers or, conversely, to miss many basic points in something of particular interest or importance. The first step to better assessment is to know the content, the backgrounds of the students, and the interrelationships of the two.

In oral questioning of the recognition type it is a good idea to *spot different tasks* by saying:

John, please find out why they were taking this trip.
Mary, find out where they were going and how long they were going to stay.
Sue, see if you can find things that tell how each of them feels about the trip.
Bob, I'm hoping that you can find out . . .

Because students may complete these assignments very quickly, it is useful to *set purposes in advance* by writing them on the chalkboard and ask the students to *use a marker technique* (such as a paper clip) to mark the specific elements as they find them in their reading. This way the rapid readers can complete the assignment and go on to something else while the slowest readers have time to finish. A variation of this has the children jot down the page, paragraph, and sentence number of certain elements.

For purposes of measuring recall, group response instruments such as a color wheel can permit the teacher to find out precisely which students know the answers to specific fact questions. Each child holds a color wheel, and the teacher asks a question which may be answered by one of three colors.

Teacher: The real winner of the game was Tom, Bill, or Joe. Show blue for Tom, red for Bill, and white for Joe.
Pupils: (The pupils flash the color on signal to the teacher, who notes the responses.)

How Do We Measure Reorganization? Research and observation by the author suggest that we do not measure reorganization skill often enough. A study of the questions asked by certain second, fourth, and sixth-grade teachers (Guszak, 1967) showed that less than one percent of the questions were of the reorganization type.

In all fairness to the teachers, we must acknowledge that it is difficult to measure reorganization skills by means of the oral techniques that characterize reading group discussions. Such tasks take time; when a single student is asked to summarize a story, for example, there is little left for the other group members to do but to make some additions or corrections.

How Should We Measure Reorganization?   Silent strategies such as the following are good ways to measure reorganization:

1   *Sequence tasks:* Students are given pictures, sentences, or paragraphs and are asked to order them by their occurrence in the story. Teachers can construct the sequence sets themselves or use the ones that appear in basal workbooks.
2   *Synopsis, summary tasks:* When writing skills are fairly well developed, the pupils can go beyond the ordering of pictures and sentences and do their own summaries.

Reorganization is an important skill. It develops the student's ability to produce precise (short and accurate) reorganizations essential to effective communication.

How Do We Measure Inferential Comprehension?   Before allowing the children to turn to the next page, the teacher asks, "Well, what do you think Jack's going to do?" Instantly the children respond: "He's going to swing from the rope." Inferential training is certainly useful; we can think and read more ably when we can accurately anticipate what is coming. By constantly anticipating and seeking verifications of our anticipations we can increase both the speed and accuracy of our reading.

Unfortunately, though, most teacher-pupil exchanges of the sort described above do not test inference but rather whether or not the students have (1) listened to another reading group encountering the same bit, (2) flipped ahead to see the picture, (3) read the next page. Consequently, much of the value of the exercise is lost. This will happen unless we rigidly hold every child to the same reading selection and page-turning pace.

How Should We Measure Inferential Comprehension?   Teachers can guide pupils to make inferences on the basis of the smallest of clues, beginning with the title of a story, or a picture. After pupils make their inferences, they test them by reading. Upon verification, they make further predictions and set about further verification.

The following conditions are essential to carrying out this strategy:

1   The availability of multiple sets of readers, so that the fastest readers will not always preview the stories for the slower readers (multiple adoptions will allow for this).
2   The choice by the teacher or group leader of a significant organizer for inference—for example, a suggestive title or clue.
3   The sampling of a wide variety of conjectures so as to increase children's interest and sense of participation.
4   The accurate verification of the most precise conjecture.

Pupils will learn to sense when to apply convergent conjectures or divergent conjectures. At times, they will realize that they totally missed the significant cues that might guide their anticipations. Still, the exercise will refine the processes of anticipation that are capable of making us either strong or weak readers.

How Do We Measure Evaluation?   Have you ever heard or used any of these questions?

Well, how did you like that story (ending, character, etc.)?
Would you like to be in a situation like that?
What kind of boy do you think Bill was?
Which story did you like best in this unit?

If you have, then you have surely heard the droning "yes" and "no" answers, as well as the "goods," "bads," and other judgment terms.

How Should We Measure Evaluation?   There's nothing wrong in asking for evaluations if we ask for support for the evaluative statements. All too often, according to the author's research and that of others, we fail to plug in the "why" follow-up questions, such as:

Why did (or did not) you like the story?
Why would (or would not) you like to be in a situation like that?
Why do you think Bill was that kind of boy (whatever kind was indicated)?
Why did you like that story best?

Cloze Techniques

The cloze technique not only provides teachers with a valuable means of assessment, it provides them with a useful teaching tool.

When a pupil is tested with the cloze technique, the task is to effect closure in a selection such as the following:

It was the last ＿＿ game of the year. ＿＿ boys wanted to make ＿＿ good showing before the ＿＿ town crowd. Everybody would be in ＿＿ stadium at the eight ＿＿ kickoff time.

Tom laced up his ＿＿ while Bill adjusted his ＿＿ pads so they wouldn't ＿＿ blisters. Most of the team ＿＿ already dressed and were ＿＿ up and down so ＿＿ wouldn't feel so tense. A few boys were ＿＿ the ball back and ＿＿ across the dressing room.

The following are the steps involved in the preparation, administration, scoring, and judging of a cloze test.

Preparation

Step 1. Select a relatively free-standing selection of at least 275 words (55 cloze blanks) from the portion of the book you plan to use for instruction. (Free-standing means the beginning of a section, chapter—material that does not depend too much on previous information).

Step 2. Delete every fifth word.

Step 3. Type up the cloze test, being sure to allow the same number of spaces for every deleted word. The spaces should be large enough for the students to write in the longest words.

Administering, Scoring, and Judging

Step 1. Hand tests to the students and ask them to write in the blank spaces the words they think should be there. Indicate that you realize the task is difficult and that it will probably be necessary for them to erase and change words as they work on the problem. Encourage the students to complete every blank. *Do not provide a time limit, as this is a power test.*

Step 2. When the tests are completed, mark every word that is not exactly the same as the deleted word from the story. Total up the number of correct responses (unmarked) and place that score at the bottom of the paper.

Step 3. Determine the difficulty level of each pupil's effort on the following scale (established by Rankin and Culhane, 1969):

Independent level—the student correctly replaces 61 percent or more of the deleted words. (Thirty-three words or more correct.)

Instruction level—the student correctly replaces 41 percent or more of the deleted words. (Twenty-two words or more correct.)

Frustrational level—the student correctly replaces 40 percent or less of the deleted words. (Less than twenty-two words correct.) *Note:* Bormuth (1967) recommends other percentage criteria for making such determinations.

Although the preceding testing may seem complex, it is actually rather easy from the standpoint of the examiner, who only has to make a deleted word selection, administer it, and then compute the scores. The technique seems most appropriate for upper-grade teachers in assessing the readability of a multitude of instructional materials such as *My Weekly Reader* and content area texts (geography, science, English), as well as the assigned reading materials. In addition to the advantages of wide content sampling, cloze testing is rather simple in terms of administration and scoring. Among the disadvantages are the frustrating nature of the task (especially to children below fourth-grade level) and test score variation that appears more akin to topic content than vocabulary and sentence difficulty.

Teaching tasks which have been found to be successful are the following:

1 Prereading pupils can be taught to listen and insert the next word. For example:

> Familiar rhyme: Jack be nimble, Jack be _____ .
> Sequence: One, two, _____ , here we go.
> Expected: It became dark and the wind began to blow very
> _____ .

2 *Cloze words* are those words that are covered on the pocket chart as the teacher seeks to get good "guesses" from pupils as to the missing words. For example:

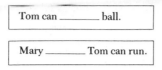

Tom can _____ ball.

Mary _____ Tom can run.

3   *Cloze readers* are any pupil readers where flip tabs are placed over strategic words. The pupils are asked to read the readers and guess the covered words. Then they are to look and verify their guesses (presuming that they know the covered words).

4   *Cloze transparencies* can be made, in which every fifth word or so is omitted and a square of the word left in its place. The teacher can have children read aloud together or independently to provide closure words. Someone (probably the teacher) can write in the words suggested and change the words as pupils see a better word subsequently.

CRITICAL READING

If there is one thing all experts would agree upon, it is that we should teach our children to read critically. However, if we were to ask what "reading critically" means we might hear several different explanations, such as: (1) detecting propaganda devices in printed material, (2) differentiating fact from fiction, (3) measuring the validity of statements, or (4) evaluating what is read.

Wolfe, King, and Ellinger (1967) define critical reading as an analytical and evaluative process which requires the reader to make rational judgments about both the content and style of writing based upon valid criteria. Readers vary the criteria in accordance with the type of material and their purpose for reading it. For instance, if you were to read a sworn statement against you by another party, you would sift each statement carefully against the evidence that you had first hand. Thus, you would apply tests (criteria) of the accuracy of the statements. This definition of critical reading comes under "evaluative reading" in the Barrett Taxonomy. We could represent it in a formula as follows:

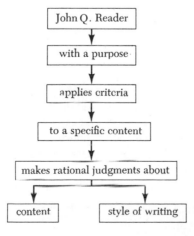

Suppose that John Q. Reader has received an advertising offer to buy a waterfront lot at the bargain price of $600. Because he would like to own such a lot, John reads carefully in order to determine whether the offer is legitimate or not. His purpose is to find out the following things:

Is a specific lot offered?
Are there hidden costs that are not represented in the brochure?
Is a valid title of ownership provided?
Is the lot actually above water, usable, etc.?
Is this strictly a come-on to get a prospective purchaser?

He will apply many criteria. He will, for instance, check the validity of the offering firm through the Better Business Bureau. He will check the wording of the brochure to determine what is specifically offered. He may check the offer out with his attorney to determine its legal basis. All these things will help him determine the *internal* as well as *external* validity of the offer.

On the basis of his findings, John will make a rational judgment as to whether the offer is good or bad. In this instance his judgment will primarily concern the content of the brochure, although the style of writing may influence him as well.

Two of the most important teaching applications of critical thinking or critical reading are set forth in the studies of Taba (1965) and Wolfe et al. (1967). We will discuss each briefly.

Taba   Taba sought to design teaching strategies that would affect cognitive development. Two groups of teaching functions were identified: (1) teacher questions or statements which are managerial, and (2) teacher questions or statements which give direction to discussions and are related to the logic of the content and of the cognitive operations sought. This latter group included focusing questions, extending through on the same level, lifting the level of thought, and controlling thought. Taba gives examples of teachers managing the thinking levels in various kinds of discussions. In order to be effective, the teacher strategy had to be carefully managed so as to allow for variation in the pacing of each step, determining how long to continue on the plateau of each step, and deciding when to make a transition to the next one. Because all of this was done in class discussions, it is difficult to see how Taba assessed the impact of the program on the individuals in the class.

Wolfe et al.   Wolfe and her associates did the most extensive study of critical reading undertaken to date. Their research involved the teaching of critical reading strategies to children in the first six grades.

Initially, the researchers determined that the primary forms of content were (1) informational and persuasive materials and (2) literary materials. Obviously, different criteria had to be applied to the different types of material, so the authors determined the following criteria:

I   Informational and Persuasive Material
   A   Semantics in Writing

1 Distinguishing between vague and precise words.
2 Recognizing the difference between connotative and denotative meanings of words.
3 Recognizing the persuasive use of words through such devices as name calling, glittering generalities, and plain folks. (Note: These are the commonly mentioned propaganda techniques used to brand rival politicians, show why one soap is the best, etc.)
4 Evaluating the effectiveness of the use of words according to the author's purpose.

B Logic in Writing
1 Recognizing and evaluating the validity of writing (examining validity of an argument, classifying into groups and subgroups, determining appropriate use of all, some, and none statements, discovering unstated premise and conclusions).
2 Recognizing and evaluating the reliability of printed materials (testing the reliability of information, determining soundness of premises and conclusions, detecting material fallacies such as hasty generalizations and false analogies, recognizing illogical reasoning in persuasive writing such as testimonial, band wagon, and card stacking, distinguishing between objective and subjective evidence, judging the reliability of information).

C Authenticity in Writing
1 Recognizing adequacy of information or the necessity of suspending judgment.
2 Comparing relevant information from multiple sources to recognize agreement or contradiction.
3 Recognizing authoritative sources and evaluating them according to established criteria.
4 Evaluating the qualifications of an author.
5 Recognizing the publisher and sponsor's commitments.

II Literary Materials
A Literary Forms
1 Recognizing characteristics of various genres of fiction, such as: fantasy, realistic fiction, historical fiction, and biography.
2 Distinguishing among variants of a particular form of fiction, e.g. fantasy, forms of make believe, fairy tales, etc.
3 Developing criteria for evaluating each type of fiction.
4 Recognizing the characteristic forms of poetry, e.g. narrative, lyric, haiku.
5 Developing criteria for evaluating poetry.

B Components of Literature
1 Identifying and evaluating characterization.
2 Identifying and evaluating plot structure.
3 Identifying and evaluating setting.
4 Identifying and evaluating theme.

C Literary Devices
1 Identifying and evaluating author's use of language.

2 Identifying and evaluating mood of writing.
3 Identifying and evaluating point of view.

Wolfe and her associates applied the preceding elements in a program and found that elementary school children (grades one through six) could be taught to read critically through the application of logical reasoning skills. While grade level did have a bearing upon the development of different types of skills, it was apparent that even the youngest children were capable of certain critical skills. Furthermore, the researchers concluded that instruction in critical reading had no apparent ill effect upon the children's growth in other reading skills.

SOCIALIZING EXPERIENCES IN LITERATURE

Piaget tells us that there are at least two critical ingredients in learning: (1) the experience; and, (2) the socializing of the experience. The potential for learning from an interaction with a text is fulfilled only when the reader has an opportunity to socialize that experience. Socialization can take many forms from artistic expression to group discussion—all of which share the common goal of communicating personal understandings and reactions to others.

While the facilitating effects on comprehension of such socializing activity have been demonstrated in many different ways and formats (see, for example, Zajonc's summary of research in social facilitation) for many teachers, these kinds of actions are seen as a luxury rather than a necessity. It is our contention that varied opportunities to socialize reading experiences should become a high priority concern in a program designed to improve reading comprehension skills.

Roach van Allen (1976) offers a functional scheme for organizing diverse activities which share a common goal of socialization, including:

1 Sharing of ideas orally
2 Visually portraying experiences
3 Dramatizing experiences
4 Responding rhythmically
5 Discussing and conversing
6 Exploring writing
7 Writing individual books

These activities, of course, are only a beginning in providing students an opportunity to respond to literary experiences in personal ways.

SUMMARY

Our definition of reading comprehension has a major influence on our classroom comprehension program. It is on the basis of this definition that we begin to make important decisions as to what we should or should not include in our program. We have examined reading comprehension from two broad perspectives: as a process, we have described theories related to both the structure of knowledge as well as how this knowledge store interacts with experiences to generate thinking; as a product, we have described theories related to comprehension in terms of outcomes of proficient reading. These two facets of comprehension (process and product) form the basis on which a sound instructional program can be organized.

The three broad categories of activity to be included in a well-rounded instructional program to develop reading comprehension are: (1) direct experience, (2) observation of models, and (3) explicit instruction in skills.

To plan an explicit comprehension skills program, teachers must establish realistic goals; build management systems whereby they and the students can gauge student progress through a program of increasingly difficult skills; acquire the necessary types of reading comprehension skill materials; and finally develop a plan that will make the best use of the teacher's direct teaching actions and the pupil's independent efforts. Teachers may use many strategies for developing skills. They may use questioning strategies that develop varied reading-thinking skills, cloze teaching techniques, methods of reading skills stimulation, and they may provide students with ample opportunities to communicate their reactions in print with others.

REFERENCES

Adams, Marilyn J. and Collins, A. Bolt Beranek and Newman Inc. A schematheoretic view of reading. University of Illinois at Urbana-Champaign: Center for the Study of Reading, Technical Report No. 32, 1977.

Allen, Roach Van. *Language Experiences in Communication*. Boston: Houghton Mifflin Co., 1976.

Allington, R. If they don't read much, how they ever gonna get good. *Journal of Reading*, 21 (1) 57–60, 1977.

Anderson, R. C. The notion of schemata and the educational enterprise. In R. C. Anderson, R. J. Spiro, and W. E. Montague (Eds.), *Schooling and the Acquisition of Knowledge*. Hillsdale, N.J.: Laurence Erlbaum Associates Inc., 1977.

Ausubel, D. P. *The psychology of meaningful verbal learning: An introduction to school learning*. New York: Grune and Stratton, 1963.

Ausubel, D. P. *Educational psychology: A cognitive view*. New York: Holt, Rinehart and Winston, 1968.

Barrett, T. *Innovation and Change in Reading Instruction*, edited by H. Robinson. National Society of the Study of Education Yearbook, Part II. Chicago: University of Chicago Press, 1968, pp. 19–23.

Barrett, Thomas C. A taxonomy of reading comprehension. Mimeograph. University of Wisconsin, 1978.

Bartlett, F. C. *Remembering*. London: Cambridge University Press, 1932.

Biemiller, Andrew. Relationships between oral reading rates for letters, words and simple text in the development of reading achievement. *Reading Research Quarterly*, Vol. XIII, No. 2, 1977–78, pp. 223–253.

Bloom, B. S. *Taxonomy of Educational Objectives: Handbook 1, Cognitive Domain*. New York: David McKay, 1956.

Bormuth, J. "Comparable Cloze and Multiple Choice Comprehension Test Scores." *Journal of Reading* 10 (1967): 291–299.

Durkin, Dolores. What classroom observations reveal about reading comprehension instruction. University of Illinois at Urbana-Champaign: Center for the Study of Reading, Technical Report No. 106, 1978.

Gray, William S. The Importance of Intelligent Silent Reading, *Elementary School Journal*, Vol. XXIV, Jan. 1924.

Guszak, F. *Reading Skills Checklist*. Austin, Texas: Educational Program Development, 1971.

Guszak, F. "Teachers' Questions and Levels of Reading Comprehension." In *The Evaluation of Children's Reading Achievement, Perspectives in Reading No. 8*, edited by T. Barrett. Newark, Del.: International Reading Association, 1967, pp. 97–110.

Harris, L. and Smith, C. *Reading Instruction*

through Diagnostic Teaching. New York: Holt, Rinehart, and Winston, 1972.

Hunt, L. The effect of self-selection, interest, and motivation upon independent, instructional and frustration levels. *The Reading Teacher,* Vol. 24 (1970), pp. 146–151.

McCracken, R. A. Initiating sustained silent reading. *Journal of Reading,* Vol. 14 (1971), pp. 521–524.

Olson, David R. The language of instruction: the literate bias of schooling. In R. C. Anderson, R. J. Spiro, and W. E. Montague (Eds.) *Schooling and the Acquisition of Knowledge.* Hillsdale, N.J.: Lawrence Erlbaum Associations, 1977.

Paulissen, Margaret E. An observational study of the use of time during the designated reading period in first-grade classrooms. Unpublished doctoral dissertation. University of Texas at Austin, 1978.

Pearson, P. David and Johnson, Dale E. *Teaching Reading Comprehension.* New York: Holt, Rinehart and Winston, 1978.

Piaget, Jean. *The Language and Thought of the Child.* London: Routledge and Kegan Paul, 1951.

Piaget, Jean. *Origins of Intelligence in Children.* New York: Norton, 1963.

Piaget, Jean and Inhelder, B. *The Psychology of the Child.* New York: Basic Books, 1969.

Rankin, E. and Culhane, J. Comparable cloze and multiple choice comprehension test

scores. *Journal of Reading, 13,* 1969, 193–198.

Rumelhart, D. E. and Ortony, A. The representation of knowledge in memory. In R. C. Anderson, R. J. Spiro, and W. E. Montague (Eds.), *Schooling and the Acquisition of Knowledge.* Hillsdale, N.J.: Lawrence Erlbaum Associates, 1977.

Sanders, N. *Classroom Questions: What Kinds?* New York: Harper and Row, 1966.

Smith, Nila Banton. *American Reading Instruction.* Newark, Delaware: International Reading Association, 1966.

Smith, Frank. *Comprehension and Learning.* New York: Holt, Rinehart and Winston, 1975.

Sticht, Thomas, G.; Beck, Laurence J.; Hauke, Robert N.; Kleinman, Glenn M.; and James, James H. *Auding and Reading.* Alexandria, Virginia: Human Resources Research Organization (HumRRO), 1974.

Taba, H. The teaching of thinking. *Elementary English, 42,* 1965, 534–542.

Thorndike, E. Reading as reasoning: a study of mistakes in paragraph reading. *Journal of Educational Research,* 1917, 323–332.

Wolfe, W. et al. *Critical Reading Ability of Elementary School Children.* Project No. 5–1040, U.S. Office of Education, 1967.

Zajonc, R. B. Social facilitation. *Science,* 1965, *49,* 269–274.

PREVIEW

Smith and Smith begin this important chapter with a definition of content area reading and indicate its significance with particular reference to older pupils. They note that children enter the middle grades already possessing many of the skills needed for successful content area reading. Smith and Smith reject the belief that pupils learn to read in the primary grades and read to learn thereafter. Throughout this chapter, they stress the importance of your guidance. Effective content area reading by itself is not the result of incidental learning. Smith and Smith include many valuable suggestions that will help children acquire specialized vocabularies and see the different contents which may give words different meanings.

There is an extensive treatment of critical reading and suggestions for teaching the skills involved. You should find the study skills checklist especially helpful, but should also be aware of the role played by informal teacher observation. Reading rate and skimming and scanning are discussed in a thorough and practical manner. The chapter concludes with a list of teaching principles that make it clear that Smith and Smith consider content area reading a constructive and interactive process in which you should assume a major role.

12

Study Skills in Content Areas

Carl Smith, Indiana University
Sharon L. Smith, Indiana University

OBJECTIVES

After you have read this chapter, you should be able to:

1. **Relate content reading to a range of reading experiences.**

2. **Identify skills that elementary children need in order to find and organize information for specific purposes.**

3. **Construct various aids and plan projects that will give children a variety of experiences using reference tools and informational materials.**

4. **Guide children in the development of effective study strategies, vocabulary development, and reading flexibility.**

5. **Understand the basis for promoting children's growth in critical reading and thinking in content subjects.**

READING FOR LEARNING

In spite of the growing influence of electronic media in our culture, we remain a print-oriented society. For accessibility, completeness and variety of information, there is no rival to the written word. To test the truth of this statement, pose this question to yourself: If you wanted to find out how to do something, or learn about a particular subject, which of the following would you do—turn on the television set, or go to the library?

Obviously, if you are seeking information for your purposes, you cannot wait for someone else to decide to treat your topic and beam it across the airwaves. You may learn a lot from the programs that others plan; but to follow through on your own questions, you need the ability to make use of the resources that exist in a form you can seek out for yourself.

Because reading is so important as a vehicle of learning throughout the school years and after, the relationship that children develop with books and other printed materials is an important part of elementary education. The early experiences that children have in reading for a variety of purposes, and in a variety of kinds of materials, are often crucial in the later development of their attitudes toward and competencies in learning. From the beginning, education is, largely, a process of learning to learn, and facility in using printed language is surely the most essential skill that a child can acquire. Starting in kindergarten, for example, children see the need for following written directions in order to do a number of things that they like, such as making cookies. This chapter, then, is about helping children develop the general and specialized skills they will need in reading for content and other information.

A word about what is meant by *skill* in this context is in order. This term is often used to designate specific abilities that an individual can develop through practice. We speak of swimming skills, cooking skills, social skills, and reading skills. *Skill* is also used in a more global sense, however, to indicate excellence and reliability of performance. Consequently, we speak of a skilled craftsman not simply as a person who knows how to use certain tools, but, more significantly, as a person whom we can trust with a certain kind of task. That is, we can tell the craftsman *what* we want done but do not have to explain *how* to do it.

When it comes to learning, the second concept of skill is central to all that we do in the classroom. We want children to develop into skilled learners in the sense that they are able to use the tools of the classroom trade competently and on their own. This means, of course, the steady development of the ability to use books and other printed materials as media for learning. For this development to occur, children must have the kinds of experiences with books that help them grow toward independence.

Content Reading—The Umbrella

The phrase *content reading* is an umbrella term that covers just about any reading that is connected with a specific knowledge subject taught in school. The term also implies that this reading is done not for its own sake but in order to promote the growth of knowledge and thinking powers of the reader. This is the kind of growth that we associate with learning. Therefore, content reading might also be called "reading to learn."

Looking at content reading in this way helps us to realize the close connection between subject-related materials and the kind of informational reading that people do in every day life. In both instances, the readers are hoping to gain something from the reading that will help them perform more effectively in some important area of living. In school, learning is central, and so content reading plays a role in the child's life similar to that of newspapers, magazines, informational books and other such material in the adult's.

Because children in our culture grow up in an environment in which it is commonplace to consult printed sources for information, they may actually know a great deal about content-related reading when they first enter school. Children will be delighted to share what they already know and to discover, in the process, how knowledgeable they really are. In the earliest grades the teacher can stimulate further awareness by having children talk about the books they have read, the kinds of books they like to read, and other things they read or like to read. Most of them will have received letters or birthday cards from people who live at a distance, and discussing these will help them realize how written words help people talk to each other across barriers of time and distance. This may seem to be a simple and obvious concept, but consider how important it is as a foundation for accepting the printed page as a source of information from a person who is remote in time and space, if not both.

Developing Content Reading
Through Daily Activities

Using books in the classroom, the teacher can find out more about what children know or can readily discover what they know about the nature of information books. This exploration activity can be organized around questions that direct children to the different contents and formats of books in their room. This activity will, of course, be more successful if the teacher has made sure, in advance, that there are a variety of kinds of materials available.

As children progress through the elementary school years, they should be guided in the ways to discover information and ideas for themselves. In this pursuit they learn to use many special types of printed media: periodical publications such as newspapers and magazines; textbooks and other subject matter materials; encyclopedias, dictionaries, and other reference books; library collections; paperbacks; and even books or magazines that they create themselves. All of these help children experience the versatility and range of the written word.

In the middle grades, and even earlier, teachers can devise learning centers that give children practice in using common informational materials. Jill Frankel (1975) has described successful learning centers which use familiar reference sources such as store catalogs, the yellow pages of the telephone book, and television guides for finding and evaluating information. These give children practical experience in using topical indexes, alphabetical order, and chronological order as aids in getting information. They can also be used in problem-solving activities which simulate daily life tasks such as finding someone to do a repair job or deciding on which item to purchase. Another idea would be to use food packages in an activity geared toward fostering awareness of nutrition and comparison shopping for groceries.

Through these activities, children will gain experience in attending to and handling different kinds of printed materials, and they will be reminded of many things that they already know. Then they can begin to look more closely at books for learning provided in the classroom and the school library.

The classroom is a good place to begin, because there the teacher can set the stage for more independent work in the library. Except for the procedures that are specific to using the cataloging and arrangement systems in the library, students can learn most of the skills they need, particularly those relating to locating and recording information, working with the books in their own classroom.

Transferring Skills to Content Reading

Middle-grade students, especially, need to realize that they already have used many skills to read content texts. Responses that they have learned in their earlier reading experiences—the sense of order, holding events and ideas in chronological or logical sequence, and following a series of ideas to a conclusion—are applicable to content reading just as they are to the reading of narrative material. Many students fail to realize that over the years they have developed a considerable body of skills and habits that serve them well in a variety of books and magazines. Sometimes all it takes is to have the teacher remind them that their earlier learned reading skills are also valuable tools for understanding textbooks and other subject matter materials, and reassure them that the skills involved in more specific content reading will be learned gradually, just as the general skills for reading were acquired with practice.

By the time they reach the fourth grade, most children have already had experience with a variety of prose forms other than narrative or story structures. For example, one reading readiness book gives instructions for making monster hand puppets out of socks. The brief verbal instructions are accompanied by photographs that clearly illustrate each step of the process. This format enables even very young readers to relate verbal and graphic information, a very important strategy at all levels of content reading.

Another useful device frequently found in primary reading materials are questions directed from the page to the reader. A first-grade book, for example, invites the child to respond personally to photographed scenes that a bus rider might observe. Again, the content is primarily pictorial but no less informational. This approach encourages children to impose their own verbal structures upon the information given in the pictures and to supplement it with their own knowledge. Later in the same series—still at the first grade level—informational content becomes predominantly verbal and other conventions of content prose, such as captions under pictures, are introduced. A good illustration of early content reading is a piece called "Animal Friends" by Alma Whitney, intended for advanced first graders. Following is a sample of the text:

> Here are two animals that live in the water.
> They don't look very much like each other, do they?
> But they are friends.
> The little one is called shrimp.
> The big one is an eel.
> This eel is not a friend to other fish.
> Sometimes he likes to eat them.

But he will not eat this shrimp.

This shrimp takes tiny animals off the eel.

The eel gets cleaned up and the shrimp gets his lunch!

Source: Smith and Wardhaugh, Macmillan *Series R,* Level 10, pp. 72–73.

This pattern of information is repeated in descriptions of other odd pairs of animals so that the young reader is led to develop the concept of symbiosis long before he is exposed to the term. By providing parallel examples the writer is encouraging inferential thinking. This particular text is accompanied by professional wildlife photographs like those found in upper level science books and children's nature magazines. Also like these publications, the pictures have printed-in typography that is different from that of the text. This teaches the young reader to look for information in places other than the main text and encourages flexibility.

These examples are illustrative of the resources that most early readers have for teaching study reading skills. Williams (1959) examined ten series of basic readers and found suggestions for teaching 33 skills applicable to critical and content reading. Since textbook publishers have become more alert to this aspect of reading during the past two decades, an even greater array of possibilities now exists.

Children's Expectations of
the Text

From early reading experiences such as these, children are able to construct their own set of text expectations. Foremost among these is the expectation that the material will be organized in some sensible way, and that they will find it coherent and appropriate to the setting in which they read it (Halliday, 1976). To bring this expectation more to the surface, where it is accessible as a conscious strategy, teachers can help students identify the increasingly complex organizational schemes in middle-grade materials.

One of the most common and useful organizational schemes is chronological order. This order is quite natural for children to grasp as most stories, and indeed their own experiences, proceed in this fashion. Besides narratives, chronological order is characteristic of many social science and science materials. Even simple directions are ordered in time. The concept of sequence is the basic organizing factor for describing any process, whether historical, cultural, scientific or imaginary. Thus it is not surprising that the majority of materials at the fourth- and fifth-grade level have a chronological basis for organization.

The sense of sequence that stems from awareness of events ordered in time provides a framework for recognizing other logical patterns of organization. In one reading text designed for fifth graders, a number of patterns and formats departing from narrative-like presentation are used. One selection uses chronological order to organize an explanation of how the passenger pigeon became extinct. While this selection is ordered primarily as a sequence of events spanning a century, the article also focuses on strictly contemporary concerns about species survival. As readers mature, they must become accustomed to the fact that patterns will change. The same book presents a number of charts showing different logical relationships. For example, one shows how different animals contributed to the economy of American Indians during an early period of history. Another combines space and time as organizing factors by showing a geographical summary of the development of the ancient horse. Also included is an actual magazine article on the current condition of wild horses in America. Throughout the book, the role of pictorial information ranges from being purely decorative to carrying the primary burden of the content. The book also contains an author's preface, introductory notes to some selections, explanatory footnotes, word histories and a glossary. In one reader there is enough variety of informational formats and organizational patterns to provide a solid foundation for instruction in several study-reading techniques.

Transferring Analytical Skills

Besides learning to make use of a variety of organizational and format cues, students need analytical skills in order to structure information in their own terms as they read. These analytical skills include the ability to identify main ideas and supporting information, to spot key terms and concepts, to use context to augment understanding of word meanings, and to find information for specific purposes, such as answering questions. These can all be taught directly by the teacher through experiences in and practice with books in the classroom. Hill (1962) suggests having children compare books on specific aspects, for example, comparing the work of illustrators. In middle grades students can compare different books on the same topics; biographies are especially good for this approach. These can be used for distinguishing between fact, legend and fiction. Kermoian (1961) describes a classroom activity in which first-grade children compared a statement in a book with other sources of information, including direct observation, information in other books, and statements by experts, in order to resolve discrepancies about the number of toes their pet turtle had. The greater the variety of kinds of books and other sources of information to which students learn to apply their skills, the better prepared they will be for the broad range of content reading in upper level classes.

Besides using their existing skills, students need to know that the teacher will help them sort out the intricacies of reading in new subjects, that is, work out the additional complexities that the subject poses. To accomplish that, they may have to learn additional vocabulary and expand their word analysis repertoire, think about the organization of information in the subject, be more selective in setting purposes for reading, and organize their study to facilitate learning. Also as children progress through the upper elementary grades, they will be asked to evaluate information more and more. Thus, they will need to learn strategies and techniques specific to content reading.

PRACTICING WITH BOOKS

Content texts ordinarily are read to find information. Either a teacher makes an assignment and directs the student to find information, or students read in preparation for a test, or they are trying to improve their knowledge or follow directions in working out a problem. In other words, there are, typically, specialized searches associated with reading content books. For that reason, any discussion of content reading has to focus on those practical skills that enable students to find information, to study and organize information, and of cousre to be flexible in their approach to reading.

In order for these skills to develop, students need opportunities to use them. Consequently, to learn how to find things on a map, or to locate the answers to specific questions in a large body of text, or to scan the materials to find specific answers, students need directed practice. As is the case with any habit, it is not sufficient for a teacher to say only once, "here is how it is done," and then expect a student to have mastered that skill. Repeated practice is a necessary component of becoming an effective reader.

Study Guides

The study guide is a highly regarded and versatile device for assuring adequate practice after specific skills have been taught as well as an aid in teaching content (Herber, 1978). A study guide is a set of questions and/or directions keyed to a reading assignment that is designed to be used by the student in conjunction with reading. Tutolo (1977) has identified two basic kinds of study guides, one focusing on level of understanding (for example, literal versus application) and the other focusing on the internal structure of a paragraph or longer passage to be read. Of course there can be any number of approaches and therefore types of study guides depending on the purpose that the teacher has set. Other themes or major purposes might be to help students expand understanding of particular words and concepts, to have them practice summary writing, or to guide them in outlining.

An illustration of how a study guide can be used to teach outlining is shown below:

OUTLINING PROCEDURES

Provide children with an outline that is complete through the first three levels. Their task at this stage is to compare the outline with the text, noting form and the relation among elements of the chapter.

Chapter 4 Pollution Problems

I. Air Pollution
    A. Automobiles cause most of air pollution
        1. Poisonous gases go into air
        2. Unleaded gasoline is required
    B. Power plants and industry contribute to pollution
        1. Smoke carries chemicals
        2. Filters can be applied

II. Water Pollution
    A. Cities dump sewage
        1. Sewage plants dump wastes in lakes and streams
        2. People dump trash
    B. Factories dump chemicals
        1 Factory wastes kill fish
        2. Oil and acids "choke" the water

The second step in this procedure is to provide children with an outline that contains labels for major sections and a list of the number of points to be found under each label. Children must provide the information that is missing from the outline.

Chapter 5   Rivers and Lakes

I. Rivers Provide Water and Transportation
    A. Water for Drinking
        1.
        2.
        3.
        4.
    B. The River as a Road
        1.
        2.
        3.
  II. The Food Supply in Water
    A. Rivers
        1.
        2.
    B. Lakes
        1.
        2.

The third step is to provide children with an outline that contains only a list for major sections and subsections. The child must complete the information that has been omitted.

Chapter 6   Farming and Irrigation

I. Rainfall aids some farmers
    A. 1.
        2.
    B. 1.
        2.
II. Western farmers need irrigation
    A.
        1.
        2.
    B.
        1.
        2.
        3.

Next the children can supply all of the labels for an outline. Only the form of the outline is given, with the number of points in each section indicated.

Chapter 7   Food for Your Table

I.
    A.
        1.
        2.
        3.
    B.
        1.
        2.
        3.
II.

Locating Information

Giving a sense of the overall organization of a book helps the student locate specific information. It may seem strange to say that locating information is a skill. But when you consider that student readers are asked to use a wide variety of books in order to find answers to questions, it becomes apparent that they can use help in that skill. Gaus (1940) in a study of the ability of fourth, fifth and sixth graders to select information for particular purposes, found three relevant variables: reading ability, selection-rejection patterns, and a type of delayed recall. It is the selection-rejection techniques that lend themselves most readily to direct instruction.

Various kinds of textbooks and reference books have different information capabilities, for example:

> textbooks
> tradebooks
> dictionaries
> encyclopedias

If the above list isn't enough to demonstrate the variety of knowledge that a person has to have, and to show the need for learning different search techniques for the information contained in those books, consider a single book and the different categories of information contained in a book:

> table of contents
> indexes
> glossaries
> bibliographies

In order to use these resources, a student needs to know how to alphabetize, to use a multiple classification system, to use pronunciation keys, to use subheads in the text, and to use specialized charts and graphs, including maps.

One of the ways that an elementary teacher can help students with these kinds of skills is to demonstrate their use with specific periodical articles or specific books. When the occasion arises to use a reference book or to use an information search technique in a textbook, the teacher could say to the class: "We are going to have to find a different kind of information in this textbook and I want to list three or four questions on the board and show you how I would go about finding that information in the textbook." With that kind of introduction, the teacher then demonstrates the techniques for finding information and follows up by posing a couple of sample questions to give the students practice in using the same technique. As the assignment is made, the teacher can remind the students that finding information in the textbook or in the reference book cited is not a matter of reading every page but is a matter of locating the desired information and recording it. Students ought to realize, too, that the search for information in a textbook does not mean that they no longer try to find the main idea and some of the important details in the textbook. The teacher's demonstration of locating information could include a demonstration of how the main idea of a passage or of a chapter can be obtained by using subheads and an initial sentence or two under the subhead.

Practice in these skills can be given with textbooks by using the table of contents, the index, the glossary, subheads, pictures, graphs, charts, and maps. An occasional group practice session and a reminder to use the kinds of skills that the teacher demonstrated will reinforce the students' use of skills that will help them become more efficient in reading. The teacher may even want to encourage the students to set up problems for themselves after they have looked through the chapter to see what its main idea is. There is good reason for them to use the subheads or to use an idea or two they picked up as a search question to see if they can find the answer to something specific or to exchange their questions with another child and thus create an added sense of competition. And the teacher as well can promote the use of those new location skills by giving them problems that would require the use of different kinds of resources, such as encyclopedias or bibliographies of authors.

LEARNING NEW CONCEPTS AND NEW WORDS

Because a major part of teaching is to help students use what they already know, the teacher must persistently remind, explain, and demonstrate how the skills that students have picked up do in fact apply to reading materials in health, science, and the other subjects. Reading content books is a continuation of learning to read just as it is a continuation of many other experiences and knowledge that students have acquired over the years. Most of the words in content texts, for example, are going to be the same words used in other books. And previously learned word analysis skills will serve students well in pronouncing the new words that appear in the content books. Certainly the teacher must help students work with technical terms and other difficult words that are used to explain the processes or to describe the events portrayed in the books. But one of the most beneficial things a teacher can do is to show students that new ideas and new vocabulary are picked up every day. Even in elementary grades, children are hearing about and responding to an astonishing range of world events. Matilla (1962) describes ways that critical reading can be taught through the use of current science topics, using materials drawn from advertisements, news articles and television programs. The launching of a space satellite, the collapse of a government, or the economic crisis of a country will all be reported in the newspaper and can be brought in for discussion and learning. New terms, new ideas, and broadening concepts appear all around them.

By relating the learning of new vocabulary and concepts to events outside the classroom as well as to the prose contexts in which the word is encountered, the teacher helps the child to realize that everything reported in print is a reflection of happenings in the real world—past, present or future. Even the imaginary events in fiction reflect the reality of a human imagination. Difficulties with reading begin to develop when it seems to have no connection with the three-dimensional world. By using all kinds of opportunities the teacher shows students that with energetic practice they will be able to manage the text and the newspaper as well as the adults around them. Students do need regular reminders to use context, to apply the sound-spelling patterns they know, and to visualize ideas and place them in order for recall.

Vocabulary: Its Content-Specific Nature

Vocabulary and related word identification problems cannot be brushed off with a statement like, "clarify those things for the student." The teacher, with all his or her background, may tend to gloss over the difficulties that students have. The word *run,* for example, seems common enough. After all, it is one of the first words introduced in many beginning reading programs. But does anyone ever stop learning new meanings for this word, to which a full column and a half is devoted in the American Heritage Dictionary? The word may be used in history and in economics, for example, to describe the withdrawal of money during a panic, that is, a "run on a bank," in which *run* has a quite complex meaning. In that instance, none of its common uses helps the student decipher what *run* means in this context. And do you know its application in golf, in music, or in steel production? Oftentimes teachers misjudge the difficulty of a word because students can pronounce it or because they have encountered it in other contexts. Often we seem to think that a word pronounced is a word known. This thought, of course, is not true.

In approaching this topic from another angle, a teacher will find word awareness is an effective way of keeping children alert to the subtleties of language in their texts. Archer (1960) describes a project in which fourth graders compiled a list of words that could be used instead of *said,* the word they selected as the most frequently overused. Using both their own experience and reference books to find substitutes that conveyed more precise meanings, they came up with a list of 104 words, thus defeating a fifth-grade class with whom they were in competition. At the children's own suggestion, the list was mimeographed so that each child could have a copy.

The variety of meanings that a word can have makes it difficult for the adult teacher to simply preview a reading selection and decide which are the problem words. The teacher will usually have to ask questions of the students— questions about single words, and questions calling for a restatement of certain sentences in which important ideas (words) occur. Story problems in mathematics offer a good illustration of the ambiguity in words. *Is, more, less, times,* and *greater* are computational signals and stand as indicators of relations between quantities. If the concepts of these words are not understood, the teacher may have to make direct and explicit definitions and descriptions of their use. Other ways of calling attention to the technical use of those terms in mathematics is to write equations and ask students to write sentences that match the equations. Thus $3 \times 8 = 24$ is written: *Three times eight is twenty-four.* Another device is to tell the students that the equation is a headline for a story. They are to write a paragraph which tells the story behind this headline: $18 \div 3 = 6$. That reverses the translation process and causes students to think through the terms that stand for the numerical symbols they use.

Vocabulary and conceptual clarity develop across all grade levels. For some, a simple explanation is enough; for others, experiences with varying degrees of concreteness are required. *Sound waves* may not be understood by some until they see them related to the ripple effect of dropping an object into a pool of water. Dictionaries and glossaries are useful tools for developing vocabulary. There are continuing references for new words and for refreshing the meaning of an old word whose subtleties have slipped away from the memory. Repeated encounters with words are often necessary to fix them in memory. Until the word becomes permanent, the dictionary and the glossary should be used. An alternative to using the dictionary is to conduct word and definition matching exercises. If words and definitions are on separate cards, the exercise could be turned into a game. Students try to see how many they can match without looking up the definition, or they compete against other students to see if they can get more matches.

The teacher of content, then, considers word identification and word meaning as regular parts of examining the concepts in the subject. As effective teachers do, they then search for new ways to make the study of words and new concepts as interesting and as useful as possible—for example, by providing first-hand experiences where the terms are used, dramatizing a situation, having exhibits with appropriate labels, showing films and filmstrips, encouraging students to use context clues, and then dictionaries and glossaries when context does not provide satisfactory results.

RECALLING INFORMATION

It is true that middle-grade students have practiced recalling information, but much of that time was spent on trying to remember the details of a narrative. Almost everyone has a built-in narrative outline in his mind (Stein, 1978). As the result of hearing (and seeing on television) hundred of stories, we all know that a story involves a kind of real-life situation in which some characters are faced with a problem they have to work out. Because that narrative outline is in our minds, most of us have very little difficulty recalling the important events or details that take place in a short story. But do we have the same facility with other prose?

To demonstrate the point, give yourself a brief test. Read the following selection quickly and then answer the questions that follow:

> Political theorists teach that sovereignty cannot be divided. A single person or institution must make and enforce the rules—for example, a king. When there is more than one sovereign, the political game quickly degenerates into a free-for-all.
>
> Our Founding Fathers defied this traditional philosophy. In our Constitution they divided sovereignty along two dimensions: geographically, into a federation of states and a central government; and functionally, into a rule-making assembly and a captain. They also added a high court, the third entity in the political power game.
>
> The Fathers believed that through a three-part division, freedom could be better served than under a single sovereign. They trusted the broad moral and religious as well as political consensus of the citizens to hold the parts together.
>
> Was the traditional philosophy right? A division of sovereignty might be possible in practice, but each of the sectors seems to have an inherent drive toward unitary power. Each sovereign in its own way, would strive

for exclusive power. Our political history shows each moving in cyclical pattern up and down the scale toward exclusive sovereignty. In our own lifetime, we have seen books which proclaim the truth of that claim: *The Imperial Presidency, The Warren Court,* and why not soon *The Imperial Congress.* We rely on the pendulum to right itself, hoping that the Founding Fathers' insight was correct.

Stop.

Now answer these questions without looking back at the text.

1 Who said that sovereignty should not be divided?
2 Along what two dimensions did the Founding Fathers divide our sovereignty?
3 What was supposed to hold the three separate but equal parts of our sovereignty together?
4 What evidence is there that each part of our government tries to hold all the sovereignty for itself?
5 What is the main idea of this passage?

Source: *The National Review Bulletin* 30 (August 25, 1978).

Those five questions are reasonable requests for some of the information contained in the passage. Naturally, the main interest centers on the readers' ability to answer the last question, the one that determines whether or not they got the idea that the passage was trying to communicate. Your ability to answer the questions correctly depended on your understanding of the word *sovereignty,* the metaphor of a game, and the concept of cyclical activity in a political power struggle. Unless those concepts are part of your background, there can be little hope that you would recall and analyze correctly in answering the five questions. Some of those concepts might be labeled technical (sovereign) and some of them (game and cyclical) are part of the general background expected of the reader. Therefore, depending on your background, the passage was directly understandable, confusing, or completely hopeless. And please note that it was not written for advanced graduates of the department of political science, but for any reasonably well educated reader.

Background for the Child

If all that background and preparation are necessary for a skilled adult reader, much more care is needed in guiding the child's recalling of information—especially when it is outside the narrative framework as was this article on political sovereignty. Children's concepts develop over time, and teachers must be sensitive to their evolving ideas of a concept. People cannot recall a concept in a manner any clearer than is seen in their own mind. For that reason the teacher works constantly at clarifying concepts. If, for example, the word *sovereign* seems to be only another word for king, a student would not grasp the abstract idea of undivided power in governmental affairs as it is used in the passage above. A teacher may then use local examples to help the students see the meaning. Perhaps the decision-making authority of two parents sharing the "sovereignty" of the family would be a way of making the concept clear. Only then can the student proceed to work with the original text.

CRITICAL READING

The basis of most important learning is the ability to think critically—to suspend judgment and evaluate evidence before reaching a conclusion. In one of the best known analyses of critical thinking, Ennis (1962) identified three dimensions: (1) the logical dimension, or judging the relationships between statements; (2) the critical dimension, or judging the ideas presented; and (3) the pragmatic dimension, or judging whether material is suitable for the purpose at hand. DeBoer (1946) identified three necessary conditions for critical reading: (1) an active rather than a passive approach to the printed page, (2) the ability to distinguish relevant from irrelevant data, and (3) an abiding skepticism, which leads to the careful evaluation of evidence and conclusions. Artley (1959) has also associated critical reading with reader judgment.

Frequently teachers associate these thinking skills with junior high and secondary level learning; but critical reading can—and should—begin with the child's early reading activities. Indeed, critical thinking is an integral part of all thinking processes (Ziller, 1964). Stauffer (1960) has shown that as early as the first grade children can learn to read and think critically about matters that are within their experience, providing that (1) these experiences are examined, (2) pertinent facts are noted, (3) relationships are noted, and (4) generalizations are reached. For example, a story in one first grade reader is about a man who rescues a stray kitten and then tries to find a home for it. After repeated failure, he takes the kitten to the pound, but once there has a change of heart and decides to keep it. Through discussion and questioning, children can be helped to examine the experience of this character (and of the kitten) in terms of their own experience. The story suggests a great deal regarding attitudes toward and care of small animals, and children should be encouraged to respond to what the story is trying to tell them at various levels.

Analytic and Judgmental Skills

Most teachers are not interested in students simply memorizing ideas and terms. Ordinarily they want students to read in order to analyze and to make judgments about what they are reading. They want the students to examine the relevancy, the value, and the accuracy of the information, and the opinions that are expressed in the book. The question is, how does the teacher transform the expectation of analysis and evaluation into a reality in students? Since content reading often contains a heavy conceptual load, and the material is presented in an organizational pattern which is different from the patterns the students are used to reading in short stories, both the analysis of that material and the evaluation of the ideas need explanation and aid from the teacher. Students do not have in their experience and repertoire of skills a ready reference to handle many of the analytic and evaluation tasks and questions that the teacher wants them to accomplish. In other words, students have to be taught how to do these tasks and to perform these mental operations.

Literal Meaning Base

In moving into what has to be considered a more complex comprehension of material, the teacher helps the student draw out the literal meaning. This can be done by asking questions that get at elements such as the main idea, factual support for the main idea, sequence of events and acts, questions about the organization of the material, and the author's purpose or point of view; and evidence of the validity or veracity of the information can be asked for.

In other words, if the teacher used a questioning pattern that started with a search for basic information, then moved toward analysis for the main idea while categorizing, making judgments, and extending the information, the thinking process is more likely to carry students across the necessary information base into the more complex analyses of that information as indicated by the answers to the judgment and application questions.

To help students develop those comprehension skills for content reading, the teacher can use typical activities of analysis and evaluation, such as:

—relating past knowledge to the present situation;
—distinguishing similarities and differences, fact from fantasy;
—making predictions about what will happen or what will occur;
—drawing conclusions or inferences;
—organizing material to suit the purposes for reading;
—judging the relevancy, adequacy, and authenticity of the information.

These activities do not produce mutually exclusive answers. They all presuppose the ability to isolate facts, to discriminate, to categorize, and to make any judgment which requires the establishment of some standard or criterion against which that judgmental decision will be made.

Because students are not likely to transfer automatically the thinking skills that they developed in other places to a new subject or to a different subject, the teacher must make a constant effort to test students in the kinds of thinking needed to accomplish the task. When they are unable to respond in a manner which is appropriate, then they must be provided with an explanation and a demonstration of that kind of thinking operation in the subject in question. All of this will help the teacher demonstrate how people in particular fields—that is, scientists, social scientists, health experts—mentally organize and think about the information of their fields. Once the thinking characteristics for the subject matter are established, then it is easier to ask students to apply their general reading skills and some of the new reading skills that the teacher is demonstrating on the current subject.

The process can be aided considerably if teachers will think about the following kinds of questions concerning the material and what they want done with it:

1 What is the structure of the content of the subject matter material in this chapter or selection? What concepts does the author assume the reader knows and what is the style of presentation? How does the

author organize the material and what assumptions are made about the background knowledge that a person need to understand it?

2   For what purpose are we going to read this material? Do I expect my students to be able to do something special when they are reading or when they are finished? Do I have to help them set up some purposes for reading and give them certain concepts or certain guidelines as they proceed?

3   Does the reader have the experience to grasp the vocabulary and the concepts presented by the author?

4   Under what conditions will the material be read? Is there adequate time in school? Are distractions minimized? How long will it be between the time students read the selection and the time they have to give back the information? Therefore, what directions or guidelines do the students need to try to hold the information that they will have to use?

Harris (1963) has pointed out that critical skills operate in three kinds of reading: developmental, functional, and recreational. Critical reading, or the habit of exercising judgment while reading, is significant in all reading situations. Most current reading theorists believe that the active mental operations of the reader create the meaning of a text. Smith (1975) has defined comprehension as "the condition of having cognitive questions answered" and learning as "the revision of a theory that does not work." Finally, he defines teaching as "an effort to make print comprehensible." These principles apply at all levels. Children must be encouraged to let their own processes and knowledge interact with the content of what they read. At the same time, as Macklin (1978) has said, teachers cannot assume that children will automatically assimilate new information into prior experience. They need guidance in making connections and synthesizing. He suggests discussing the basic concepts underlying specific content first, for example the concept "change," and then proceed to the text itself.

Virtually all of the teaching strategies discussed in this chapter entail critical thinking. As children are taught to select information for specific purposes, to compare sources of information, to respond personally to verbal and pictorial content, and to make use of library resources, they are being guided towards critical reading.

Along these same lines, children will observe, as they are exposed to information from various sources, that different writers say different things that readers must put together in their own minds. This is why leading them into an ever broadening field of materials is so important. As they are weighing and synthesizing, and sometimes deciding among conflicting information, children are engaged in inferential thinking. Clements (1964) has made this distinction between facts and inferences: facts can be seen or felt; they are experienced directly. Inferences, on the other hand, are thoughts, opinions or conjectures. In this framework, all reading involves inference in that it creates thought. All reading should be the basis for extending thinking, or, in the words of Bruner (1973) "going beyond the information given." Charles (1965) suggests that we stop confusing facts with immutable truth. Man's knowledge is always changing and so is the child's. Facts, then, are transitory; it is the thought processes that they set in motion that endure.

When children take on the task of learning information for a class or for some project, they want to do it in the most efficient and the most powerful way possible. What many young people don't understand is that there is an orderly way to proceed. The teacher knows that study can become much more effective if it is approached in an orderly manner, by using a few guidelines to help the reading, and the study of the assigned sections or of the material.

An orderly approach to study requires a) a setting conducive to reading, thinking and writing; b) the selection of a means to obtain and hold the information sought; and c) taking notes and summarizing the information so that it can be used and reviewed efficiently. In order to accomplish those ends, students need to discipline themselves. With all of the distractions in school and at home, with television and phone calls and the typical restlessness associated with students in classrooms, it takes a determined effort to carve out a place where a pupil can study and get the job done. That can probably be accomplished with the help of the teacher. Suppose that teachers ask their pupils to think of a place where they could study and not be distracted. They should search their minds for a place like that and imagine that they are in that place so they can tackle the next assignment in science reading. By asking them to create that image the teacher not only helps them to search their minds for a place to study in school and a place to study at home, but also establishes the need for using a place that will not create considerable distraction for them.

Study Technique

Once a place of study is decided upon, students can use any of the typical study techniques to guide their approach to a book. Students are first asked to *review* the selection to determine in advance the purpose for study (often times that purpose is established by the teacher). With that purpose in mind, the student looks at the book, usually using the topics and the subheads, and determines what specific *questions* need to be answered. Oftentimes it is helpful for students to write those questions out and to keep them at hand as they proceed to read the chapter or the assigned section. *Reading* with a specific purpose and with specific questions in mind holds the reader's attention and provides a specific focus. It also enables the student to take notes that will be beneficial. And, finally, the student has to *recall, review,* or summarize what has been read in order to hold it, or to relate it to the purpose for reading the selection. The summary stage at the end tells the reader whether it is necessary to go back and reread certain passages or certain sections or to rethink certain parts in order to get a better sense of content. In some instances, students won't have to reread because their purposes have been achieved with one reading.

In other words, a study technique for elementary school students is a four-step process:

1 Set a purpose for reading. (Purpose)
2 Ask questions or establish questions in advance of reading. (Ask)
3 Read with purpose and questions in mind. (Read)

4 Summarize with the purpose and the questions answered in the summary. (Summarize)

The checklist below on Work Study Skills could be used by the teacher to collect information and to provide instruction as needed. The checklist could also be distributed to students as a means of self-examination.

STUDENT'S NAME WORK STUDY SKILLS	Has great difficulty	Making progress	Grasps essential elements	Completely independent
I. Organization Can the student do the following?				
a. Take notes				
b. Determine relationship between paragraphs				
c. Follow time sequences				
d. Outline single paragraphs				
e. Outline sections of a chapter				
f. Summarize single paragraphs				
g. Summarize larger units of material				
h. Make generalizations				
i. Draw conclusions				
j. Derive "drift" of unit from table of contents, topical headings, topic sentences, and so on				
II. Knowledge and use of reference materials Can the child do the following?				
a. Place words in alphabetical order				
b. Easily locate words in dictionary				
c. Use table of contents				
d. Use indexes of books easily and efficiently				
e. Apply the above skills in the use of encyclopedia				
f. Use library card catalogue				
g. Use the telephone directory				
h. Understand the purpose of footnotes and bibliographies				
i. Utilize the following sources to locate materials				
1. Atlas				
2. World Almanac				
3. Glossary				
4. Appendix				
5. Newspapers				
III. Following directions Can the student do the following?				
a. Follow one-step directions				
b. Follow steps in sequence				
c. See the relation between purposes and directions				
IV. Specialized skills Can the student demonstrate the following graph and table skills?				
a. Understand how to use the calendar				

	Has great difficulty	Making progress	Grasps essential elements	Completely independent
b. Interpret a table by reading across and down from given points				
c. Understand the purpose of lines and bars in graph measurement				
Can the student demonstrate the following map and globe skills?				
a. Understand and interpret simple street or "landmark" type of maps				
b. Make practical use of a road map "key"				
c. Use an air map; understand such symbols as railroads, boundaries, rivers, mountains, and lakes				
d. Have the knowledge and ability to measure distance, area, and evaluation, and locate certain points				
e. Indicate ability to interpret the following:				
1. Outline map				
2. Population map				
3. Crops map				
4. Elevation map				
5. Mineral production map				
6. Rainfall map				
V. Other specialized skills				
Can the student do the following?				
a. Understand the significance of pictorial aids				
b. Observe and infer from picture representations				
c. Read and interpret charts				
d. Read and interpret cartoons				
e. Read and interpret diagrams				
f. Read and interpret scales				
g. Read critically in content material				

Another source of information on pupil progress is teacher observation. An alert teacher can gain insight into the skills and deficiencies of students by observing their behavior in the library. For example, self-directed youngsters who consult the card catalogue for books concerning their personal interests contrast with those who must ask the teacher, librarian, or a friend where to look. Children who know which reference volume meets their need for information may be observed in the process of answering a question or solving a problem. The teacher can also gain valuable information about a youngster's progress when special projects are assigned in one of the content areas. Self-directed students may be observed going about the job of completing their assignments; those with skill deficiencies will need special assistance.

Developing Concentration

How often have you faced a task that required solitude and concentration but, instead of quietly settling down to work, found yourself moving about and distracting yourself in every conceivable way? Suddenly your pencil needs sharpening, your coffee cup needs filling, some notation for your calendar pops into your mind, and you remember something important that you must tell a friend or colleague. And when you do settle down, the "noise" in your mind keeps you from thinking the thoughts you hoped would materialize.

If this has been your experience as a mature and seasoned adult, consider the internal distractions that children must deal with when they sit down to read a textbook. Elementary school pupils are full of energy, interested in interacting with others, and are easily stimulated by the attractions of a full environment. Yet they must begin to develop both the art and discipline of solitary concentration as part of their intellectual maturation.

The classroom provides the setting for practicing periods of sustained concentration within a group in an atmosphere of serious involvement that supports the individual student's effort to keep attention focused. During these periods of sustained silent activity, children should try to monitor their own concentration by keeping track of times when distracting thoughts take attention away from the object of study. With practice and feedback from their own notes, they should see the number of distractions per page diminish. One way to monitor distractions is to have students make a pencil mark in the margin each time their mind starts to drift away. Through daily practice students try to reduce the number of pencil marks from that of the previous day. This simple technique, through self-awareness, leads students to change their habits of concentration.

Creating Interaction

Sustained silent activity should be followed by small group work in which students discuss what they learned from their period of individual study. This group follow-up serves at least two important purposes: (1) it sets a goal beyond the reading of the assignment itself, so that students are conscious of preparing for a specific task as they read; and (2) it provides a social reward for the effort of independent study.

A good way for channeling physical energy that might otherwise be lost in random displacement activities (the shuffling, searching and moving about that often substitute for actual work to be done) is to learn to work with paper and pencil in hand. Writing along with reading sets up a dialogue situation in which young readers can experience their own active participation. At the same time the student can learn the skill of notemaking, that is, converting information into a set of cues that can later be used for retrieval and reconstruction of information. This kind of notemaking, in which the student tries to construct an abbreviated form of the information given, is considered to be an important learning activity. Because the student is actively involved in a problem-like task, it also improves concentration and involvement.

Notemaking

Younger students will have some difficulty learning to restate, rather than simply copy, what the author has written. Indeed, this difficulty remains through the college years for many students if they are not guided in techniques of notemaking. The teacher should understand that it is the technique and not the amount of material covered that is important for students who are beginning to learn notetaking. It is probably wise to start with relatively short passages to summarize. Students can begin by distinguishing between main ideas and details. For this purpose, a notebook might be set up with pages divided as follows, with approximately two thirds of the page to the right of the division:

Main Topic	Supporting Information

With this format students can begin to make distinctions by using subheadings as main topics and then listing, in abbreviated form, details that constitute the information under that topic. This may seem to be an arduous process at first because finding an abbreviated form involves transforming the information, and students are actually trying to manipulate meanings through altering symbolic representation. Given time, and with practice, this process should become almost automatic; but to the beginning notemaker, short passages are essential for becoming familiar with the technique. A single paragraph may be quite appropriate as a beginning.

Notemaking as an aid to independent study logically precedes efforts to teach the more refined techniques of outlining, which requires greater analysis of material. Notemaking requires only a two-step breakdown. Outlining can extend to almost any level of analysis of material. While outlining can eventually develop into an effective method of notemaking, it is probably best taught separately as a strategy for bringing out the primary structure of a piece of writing, an activity most appropriate for upper elementary and secondary students.

Reading Flexibly

With all the emphasis on speed reading that television advertising suggests, some of the American population may begin to believe that there is an ultimate speed to achieve. The ads talk about people who read 2,000 and 4,000 or 8,000 words a minute. And of course people who time themselves realize that their reading speeds are considerably lower than that. The reading speed of the average middle-grade student is probably closer to 225 words a minute than it is to 1,000 words a minute (Harris and Smith, 1976). An elementary school student can probably double that 225 word average with a little direction and practice. But the question of reading speed ought to be looked on as a matter of learning how to be flexible, that is, being able to adjust the speed of reading to accomplish the kind of reading that a person is engaged in. Shores (1961), basing his conclusions on studies done with sixth-grade students and adults, found that purposes set in advance are what determine speed. Flexibility is characteristic of effective adult readers; but rereading and reorganizing what has been read is part of "word and study" reading and often is not related to speed or rate of reading.

To draw an analogy, consider running and runners. There are runners who are trying to keep fit and they enjoy running as a fitness activity. These people may jog along at a fairly slow pace. In fact, some of them jog and talk to one another at the same time; or they may jog and use the time to think over the day or think through their lives or establish a kind of meditative state. To these people the speed at which they are going is not a factor. They are trying to enjoy this fitness activity as they are experiencing it and are not trying to rush to some destination. On the other hand, someone who is running to catch a train or someone who is in a race or someone who is trying to break the four-minute mile is clearly running with speed in mind. Still another example is someone who is running on dry ground using a technique different from that of someone else who is running on snow or ice. Each of those runners uses a different technique and a different speed because of the purpose to be accomplished. The same thing is true as far as speed in reading is concerned. Readers learn to adjust to the way that they read (and therefore the speed as well) depending upon the purpose for reading or the kind of information that has to be sought out.

Skimming and Scanning

A reader who wants to be able to read quickly has to practice and maintain good condition, just as the runner does who wants to run fast. Fast readers need to have many words stored in automatic memory. They have to be able to respond instantly to a large group of words that are found in the material being read. Otherwise very fast reading is not possible. In addition to that, a person who wants to read very quickly has to realize that it is not possible to read every single word, that is, their eyes will not fix on every word and the vocal mechanism will not pronounce every word; rather, a page will be skimmed for major ideas, scanned to locate a specific detail, thoughts organized by using the title and subheads, and the reader will in general learn to move across the page at a regular and determined pace.

A reader can learn to use some specific techniques—like tracing a finger across the page in a zigzag fashion in order to get the ideas without trying to focus on every word on the page. The more practice a reader has in a technique like the zigzag tracing pattern, the more likely it is that the pace will increase and the z-shaped zigzag will become an even larger sweep that includes more lines in each of those sweeps. The diagrams below are illustrations of the gradual stages through the zigzag technique that a teacher can lead students. Understandably it must be adjusted to the age of the students. As students become more proficient in using the technique, they learn to grasp more text on both the forward and backward sweep of their eyes. Instead of trying to read words they are learning to use words to construct a message in their heads.

The Zigzag Technique

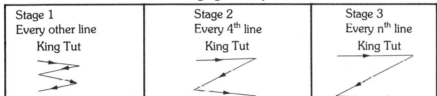

Stage 1 Every other line King Tut	Stage 2 Every 4th line King Tut	Stage 3 Every nth line King Tut

Using the Library

The effective use of the library, a major resource for every content subject, constitutes an important work and study skill. Learning to use it is a gradual developmental experience that takes place through repeated activities in a school library or media center.

Corliss (1961) has suggested an outline of cumulative library skill development for grades K through 6. Teachers might encourage their colleagues to include these suggestions in the curriculum. During kindergarten there should be a sharing of a variety of pleasurable interactions with books including listening to stories, looking at pictures, handling books, retelling stories, and visiting libraries. First graders continue their interactions with books because of more experience with special reading places, such as book corners in the classroom and in the library. Children should now be learning appropriate behaviors for using book collections, for example, "What am I" books and the grading system that identifies picture books and first-grade books. In the second grade, there should be a growing awareness of books as sources of information and of different kinds of writing, for example, poetry and humor as well as content subject matter. Second graders need to see and understand the division in their section of the library between fiction and information books.

Third graders should increase their range of reading interests, including fables and folklore. In the library they should receive training in finding books grouped according to special interests and in finding the desired book. Since fourth graders often need to search for specific subject matter facts, they could benefit from an introduction to the use of encyclopedias, using index and guide words. At this age they need practice in locating books in the school library and in taking advantage of the public library.

Fifth graders should receive continued emphasis on nonfiction categories, especially biography and history. They should develop facility in using the table of contents, index, and card catalog. In the sixth grade, children should receive continued development of all previously initiated skills and the ability to use the Dewey Decimal system or a local system of book cataloging. By the end of the sixth grade, chlidren should be able to use the library with confidence because they have used its main resources several times over a six or seven year period.

Planning Library Activities

Many activities in the classroom have already prepared children for library experiences by developing general reference skills such as using alphabetical order, using key words in an index, and locating specific information in a book. Dallman (1958) suggests having students prepare a title and author catalog for books in their classroom, using the reference cards in the library to establish a format. Older children can group classroom books by subject matter, and also create a subject matter catalog. When each book has two or three reference cards, these can be used to teach the concept of cross-referencing.

Once children are prepared to use the library for finding information, it is important to organize projects carefully from beginning to end. Miller (1961) describes the following procedure which helped the young researchers in her fifth grade remain organized through several steps of a complex process.

1 Determine a purpose for the research: in this class, the students were to make a booklet on a topic that could be read by other children in the class.
2 Post topics chosen so the children can help each other.
3 After helping children narrow down the focus of their topics, help them decide on subtopics that should be covered.
4 Provide each child with a large envelope or folder in which to keep information (notes, pictures, etc.) as they are collected.
5 Prepare children for notetaking by providing them with a set of sheets stapled together, with a subtopic written at the top of each.
6 Provide a common box to which children can contribute pictures, poems, and other "decorative" materials that might be useful to others.
7 Help establish priorities, such as having children do their information collecting and notetaking *before* they get involved in artwork and the construction of their booklets.
8 Hold a reading party at which books are shared and perhaps outside guests (local authors or illustrators of children's books) are invited to discuss a topic.
9 As a summary activity, have children compose lists of the different steps they went through in the process of constructing their informational booklets.

This activity can be adapted to individual or small group participation. In either case, children have been working cooperatively in some areas and at the same time have completed a number of projects independently. In the process, they have learned a great deal about the purpose and organization of the library and how they can use it.

By way of contrast, consider what happens when children are not well prepared for a library project and are sent to the library at a scheduled time, perhaps without the help of the teacher who made the topical assignment. The teacher passes out a question or topic to be pursued along with a list of references. The students are then dismissed from the classroom and sent to the library. The first few students to get through the library doors grab off the shelves whatever books are on the list (assuming that the teacher has checked to make sure that these books are actually in the library). The books vanish before the last students have arrived. As a result, some students have a collection of books that were taken for no reason other than they were "on the list," while other students have nothing. Both groups are likely to be frustrated; one because the students don't have materials to work with, the other because they don't know what to do with their prizes now that they have them.

Some of the brighter students in the "have none" group may seek out other relevant references in the school library, while others will try their luck at another library. Most students will give in to the frustration of the situation. Even for those with books the choice has been essentially arbitrary, and all efforts that the teacher might have made to learn something about reading abilities and interests of students cannot be used. The result is likely to be that well-known artifact of school library assignments; a pastiche of copied-out passages from two or three reference books, if not just one.

Library Assignments

To avoid this type of outcome, the teacher must plan carefully for library assignments, keeping in mind that skills will develop as students become involved in projects that mean something to them—tasks that engage them at a problem-solving level.

The first step, planning the assignment, starts in the teacher's mind but once the idea begins to take shape, the teacher begins collaboration with the librarian regarding the materials available for students to be using in this task. Teacher and librarian, working with the class's background in mind, discuss what students can use to solve the problem the teacher will pose. Many questions will need to be considered.

Will the materials now available in the library suffice, or should other resources be brought in? Will special or additional materials from the library be needed for poor readers? Will materials be available to challenge the brighter students? Are filmstrips or slides available as alternatives to printed information? Will the class have to use any special tools that will be new to them, such as tables, an index or an atlas? If so, teacher and/or librarian should prepare the students for using these tools. Students should be encour-

Source: Ideas presented in this section were suggested by Evelyn Mason of Indianapolis Public Schools.

aged to help with this stage of the planning. In this way, they learn to pose their own questions concerning what they need from a library.

Once questions concerning materials have been settled, teacher, librarian and students should work out a fair method of distribution (for example, reserve or limited circulation). Also, the decision should be made regarding how to give the assignments so that students can find the materials they need to solve the problem. Ideally, the assignment will include steps for solving the problem and a bibliography with annotations, not only of what the materials cover but also with such key words as *readable, popular treatment, scholarly,* and *highly technical* to help students find appropriate references. Needless to say, they should also be taught the concepts underlying these terms.

Now is the time for the librarian to review whatever skills the student may need for attacking the problem to be solved, for example, using the *Reader's Guide* or checking cross references in the card catalog. This assumes that the librarian is thoroughly familiar with the assignment in progress and knows exactly what kind of help students will need.

This approach to using the library is based on a very important premise: that the teacher/librarian team cannot teach reference skills in an abstract sense but will teach those skills needed for a specific assignment. As an example, one teacher tried to teach the use of the *Reader's Guide* as a lesson without a project. Some students learned how to use it, but most didn't. When their social science teacher required them to use periodicals for a report on contemporary problems, however, almost all the students used the guide without difficulty. The trick, obviously, is to plan assignments that will get students involved in a variety of library experiences.

As new skills in library use and information collecting are introduced, it is important to make sure that children are actually acquiring the competencies they need. Some children will need additional practice while others are ready to move ahead. To keep track of individual child progress, the teacher may wish to keep an informal inventory of skills for each student, using daily work as diagnostic data. See the checklist of work study skills earlier in this chapter as an example of an inventory that could be made for each student.

Another important source of information is immediate observation of children's behavior in the library. Some children will find their way among various reference aids with confidence while others will need considerable help from others. Children with a sure grasp of library procedures will be seen helping others; the teacher can intervene effectively by encouraging independent and cooperative work and helping those who still have questions. The library setting is also an excellent setting for observing general reading and book-handling competencies.

Jerome Bruner (1973), writing about the role of discovery in learning, stresses the importance of what he calls inquiry in education, whether in kindergarten or in graduate school. The spirit of inquiry, or looking for answers to one's own questions, depends upon certain assumptions. One is that there is information to be discovered. That is, the child must be "armed with the expectancy that there are things to be found out." Second, there must be methods for finding answers: places to look, procedures to follow in making the search, and ways of organizing the information once it has been found. The library is essential to that process.

What has been said about library skills and the organization of subject matter reading suggests certain principles that a teacher will want to keep in mind. These principles underlie teaching effective reading in content subjects. They include the following:

Teachers should know the structure of the subject matter.

Teachers should understand the level of abstraction of the concepts in a selection and present them at the level of abstraction of their students.

Teachers should adapt learning activities to the nature of the material in the text and the ability of the students in the class.

Teachers should associate experiences in the class with concepts in the text.

Teachers should stress reading as a vehicle for learning, the most effective long-term medium for continuing learning in the subject matter.

Teachers should provide practice and application to develop competence in desired reading skills or mental operations.

Teachers should determine what special characteristics a text has and help students to understand them.

In addition to the above principles (general statements of good teaching), each subject matter area contains specific problems and reading needs. To be effective each teacher needs to analyze the subject and determine the peculiar or unique reading problems contained in the types of material in a subject area. For example, every subject has its own unique vocabulary, and it is a problem that must be overcome in helping students read in that subject area. What content teachers often forget is that the terms that they sometimes take for granted are unfamiliar or vague to the student. In mathematics, for example, the terms *sum, plus, minus, difference, product,* and *divided by* may not be clearly understood by the students in the class.

The same is true of all kinds of typographical cues. Different typographical arrangements are often used to set off specific kinds of material and to indicate how the material is organized. Even though charts and graphs are used in several subject matter areas, they have different characteristics in the math text, in the science text, and in the history text. Within the running text there are typographical cues that enable the student to zero in on a problem. In math, for example, the use of the question mark often shows what the student has to search for. In other texts, such as history and social studies and science texts, summaries at the end of the chapters are often set off in italics or in boxes.

Illustrations are other aids that seem so commonplace that teachers often forget to point them out. Many student readers admit to ignoring the illustrations in the text, even though the text can be understood only in conjunction with the illustrations. Diagrams, charts and maps are examples of those very important illustrative materials, and students have to be taught how to use them.

Students frequently need guidance in the different kinds of reading that they have to do in a subject. For example, should they skim for the purpose of the passage? Should they read only to answer specific questions? Should they locate key words and phrases in order to understand the organization of the chapter? Should they be searching for certain operational terms, such as computations in math or certain processes in science? These are typical questions which direct content teachers in their service to children as they read and study subject matter books.

A list of the more common features for various subject areas is presented in the Table below: "Subject Matter Reading Features."

Table 12

SUBJECT MATTER READING FEATURES

Students must be taught how to read content subject books. It is helpful to alert them to specific reading features for each subject matter. Samples are given below.

Mathematics

1. *Vocabulary Features*
   Essential key words or phrases help to determine operation or operations to be utilized e.g.:

   Addition: Total, sum, add, add to, in all, altogether, plus
   Subtraction: Difference, left over, minus, subtract
   Multiplication: Total times, how many times, product
   Division: How many times more, divided by, how many would

2. *Typographical Features*
   a. Question mark (gives clue to the question's location)
   b. Charts, and graphs (give essential information for problem on page—usually located in another area of the page)
   c. Signs (percent, decimal point, computation signs)

3. *Kinds of Reading—Read to:*
   a. Skim for the purpose and overall comprehension
   b. Answer a question
   c. Find key words or phrases
   d. Find operation or operations to be utilized
   e. Write equation
   f. Reread problems to justify equations—redo if necessary
   g. Solve problem

4. *Special Considerations*
   a. The same term is not always used to indicate the same operation (e.g.: and, added to, and plus are interchangeable)
   b. The same term can indicate different operations (e.g.: altogether could indicate either addition or multiplication)
   c. Several technical terms have different meanings in general conversation (e.g.: square, mean, product, etc.)
   d. Mathematics involves the understanding of the many terms which must be learned by memorization or by structural analysis (e.g.: Multiplier, divisor, radius, diameter, circumference)

5. *Problem Organization*
   a. A situation is given
   b. Numerical question is asked
   c. Equation must be formulated

Science

1. *Vocabulary Features*
   a. There are certain words that all pupils should know in order to read almost any science material above the primary level.
      1. Things "in common", "characteristics", "various", "classified", "similarities".
      2. Common Latin or Greek or other derivations:
         a. "hydro"
         b. "electro"
         c. "photo"
         d. "un"
         e. "bi"
   b. Every new science lesson requires the teaching of terms pertinent to that selection.

2. *Typographical features*
   a. In most science textbooks selections there are subtitles and chapter headings to use.
   b. Often there are summaries at the end of chapters.

3. *Kinds of Readings*
   a. Surveying the material
      1. Attention to pictures
      2. How many main parts, names of the subheadings
      3. Read the first paragraph, perhaps orally, and the summary if given
      4. Formulate questions for reading
   b. Reading to find answers to questions
      1. Appreciation of facts and objective data
      2. Critical reading
   c. Reviewing the material read
      1. The discussion and evaluation of the reading is probably the most important part of the lesson
      2. Pupils should be urged to report what they have read
         a. "*Most* kinds of bats are useful to mankind, because they eat harmful insects."
         b. "*Some* scientists believe there is life on Mars."

4. *Special Considerations*
   a. Ability to read symbols
   b. Ability to follow diagrams
      ex: A student must understand the idea of completeness, as in an electrical circuit, or a chemical equation

5. *Organizational Guides*
   Various organizational approaches typical of science selections are:
   a. Generalizations are given first, then the examples and data (Deductive)
      1. All mammals have hair, bear young alive, etc.
      2. The different kinds of mammals are listed.
   b. Examples and supporting data
      1. Information on different mammals—their size, speed . . .
      2. In other selections—phenomena about light, heat . . .
   c. Classification of data
      1. Different classes of mammals, stars, etc.
      2. Differences and similarities among the classes
   d. Often the data is given first, then the generalization (Inductive).

Geography

1. *Vocabulary Features*
   a. Extend concept of a previously known word (e.g., range—mountain range)
   b. Homonyms (e.g., plain—plane)

    c. Refer to glossary

    d. Develop vocabulary in context (e.g., Bananas are a *tropical* fruit)

2. *Typographical Features*

    a. Chapter headings, main headings, and subheadings are given.

    b. The format of the book includes illustrations, glossary, appendix, and index.

    c. The book is often set up with two columns to make reading easier and to facilitate scanning.

3. *Kinds of Readings*

    a. Survey for overview

    b. Read to answer specific questions

    c. Skim to find specific answers and make generalizations (e.g., What are the natural resources of Manitoba? How does this affect the industries of Manitoba?)

    d. Detailed reading of charts, graphs, maps, etc.

4. *Special Considerations*

    a. Statistical reading: This type of reading is developed through repeated use of statistics (e.g., Present statistical data and provide an exercise for using the data such as comparing the area in square miles of several given countries)

    b. Symbolic language of maps (e.g., develop a child's use of the map legend)

    c. Recognize that a map is a ground plan drawn to scale

    d. Interpret different kinds of maps (e.g., population, political, rainfall, topographical)

    e. Reading graphs (e.g., the reader learns to interpret data of various types of graphs—circle, line, bar, and pictorial)

    f. Authenticating facts (e.g., the reader must verify the date of statistical information such as the population of a given area)

5. *Organizational Guides*

The material in a geography book is generally organized in one of two ways:

    a. A specific area is given and all geographical aspects are examined. (e.g., The New England states would be thoroughly discussed as to topography, climate, population, industries, etc.)

    b. A geographical feature is considered as it is found throughout the world.

Social Studies

1. *Vocabulary Features*

    a. Pronunciation skills

        1. Multisyllabic words (i.e.: as–tro–labe)

        2. Foreign words (i.e.: apartheid)

    b. Meaning skills

        1. Technical words (latitude)

        2. Abstract words (democratic)

        3. Concepts—an abstraction (tolerance)

        4. General Terms (elevator, grain, or passenger)

2. *Typographical Features*

    a. Develop the ability to utilize headings and subheadings for survey and response to questions

    b. Acquire the ability to use the parts of the book

    c. Relate text and graphic content such as maps, graphs, and cartoons to corresponding text material

3. *Kinds of Readings*

    a. Main idea and supporting details

    b. Use of key words, concepts, and literal facts

    c. Read critically

        1. Appraisals

        2. Conclusions and inferences

        3. Propaganda

4. Current events
d. Organize ideas to recognize relationships, sequence of events, and identify central issues

4. *Organizational Guides*
General organization of the content:
Material in the social studies area is usually organized by the initial statement of a selection (i.e.: the current voter age limit), a practice (i.e.: selection of the president by an electoral college), an event (i.e.: passage of the 18th Amendment), or a method (i.e.: representative democracy) and an exposition to explain, support or discredit the topic. Often, a point of view is presented, usually subtly (i.e.: private enterprise is best for the country), in some cases, overtly (i.e.: dictatorships are bad). A relationship often presented is one of conditions surrounding an effect: condition-effect relationship.

SUMMARY

In this discussion a number of aspects of content area reading have been considered, some theoretical and some practical. Approaches to the subject are based on one premise: that learning is a constructive activity. In a school books and thinking are basic ingredients of that constructive process.

Elsewhere, the authors have coined the term *bookthinking* to represent the readers' constructive interactions with the printed message toward the end of their own intellectual growth. This process is defined as the ability to think through and interact with written discourse, which is the literate person's basic skill in advancing both personal development and the development of society. It is also the young learner's basic academic skill and key to independent growth. Content area reading can be a help or a hindrance to the development of the bookthinking process. Which one it will be depends largely on the kind of guidance that the classroom teacher provides.

In summary, it can be said that a main principle in content teaching is that the teacher has to show children how to read in the specific content area and how to use the particular book concerned.

REFERENCES

Archer, M. P. "Building a Vocabulary with a Fourth Grade Class." *Elementary English, 37* (1960): 447–448.

Artley, A. S. "Critical Reading in the Content Areas." *Elementary English,* 37 (1959): 122–130.

Bruner, J. *Beyond the Information Given,* edited by J. Anglin, New York: Norton Press, 1973.

Bruner, J. "The Skill of Relevance or the Relevance of Skills." *Saturday Review* 53 (1970): 66–68, 78–79.

Charles, C. M. "Teaching About Facts." *The Instructor* (February 1965): 48–54.

Clements, H. M. "Inferences and Reading Instruction." *Claremont Reading Conference Yearbook* 28, (1964): 144–156.

Corliss, W. "Elementary School Libraries." *Elementary English* 38 (November 1961): 494–496, 505.

Dallman, M. "The Development of Locational Skills." *Grade Teacher* 75 (January 1958): 56–57.

DeBoer, J. J. "Teaching Critical Reading."

The Elementary English Review 23 (October 1946): 251–254.

Ennis, R. "A Concept of Critical Thinking." *Harvard Educational Review* 32 (Winter 1962): 81–111.

Frankel, J. C. "Learning Centers for Reading in Junior High." *Journal of Reading* 19 (December, 1975): 243–246.

Gaus, R. *A Study of Critical Reading Comprehension in the Intermediate Grades,* New York: Bureau of Publications, Columbia University Teachers College, 1940.

Halliday, M. A. K. and Hassan, R. *Cohesion in English,* London: Longman Group, Ltd., 1976.

Harris, A. L. "Three Kinds of Reading." *NEA Journal* 52 (January, 1963): 42–43.

Harris, L. A. and Smith, C. B. *Diagnostic Teaching in the Classroom,* New York: Holt, Rinehart and Winston, 1976.

Herber, H. *Teaching Reading in the Content Areas.* 2nd ed. Englewood Cliffs, N.J.: Prentice-Hall, 1978.

Hill, J. "Teaching Critical Reading in the Middle Grades." *Elementary English* 39 (March 1962): 239–243.

Kermoian, S. "Cactus Pete." *NEA Journal* 50 (September 1961): 29.

Macklin, M. D. "Content Area Reading Is a Process for Finding Personal Meaning." *Journal of Reading* 22 (December 1978): 212–215.

Matilla, R. H. "Accent on Thinking Through Reading at the Intermediate and Upper Grade Levels." *Science Education* 46 (March 1962): 174–176.

Miller, E. "Stimulate Reading with Individual Research Projects." *Grade Teacher* 89 (December 1961): 28–29, 84–85.

Shores, J. Harlan. "Are Fast Readers the Best Readers? A Second Report." *Elementary English* 38 (April 1961): 236–245.

Smith, C. B., Smith, S. L., and Mikulecky, L. *Teaching Reading in Secondary School Content Subjects.* New York: Holt, Rinehart and Winston, 1978.

Smith, F. *Comprehension and Learning.* New York: Holt, Rinehart and Winston, 1975.

Stauffer, R. G. "Children Can Read and Think Critically." *Education* 80 (May 1960): 522–525.

Stein, N. L. *How Children Understand Stories: A Developmental Analysis.* Center for the Study of Reading Technical Report No. 68. Urbana Champaign: University of Illinois, (March 1978).

Tutolo, D. J. "The Study Guide—Types, Purposes and Value." *Journal of Reading* 20 (March 1977): 503–507.

Williams, G. "Provisions for Critical Reading in Basic Readers." *Elementary English* 36 (May 1959): 323–331.

Ziller, R. C. "The Origins of Critical Thinking." *Dimensions of Critical Reading,* compiled by R. G. Stauffer, Newark: University of Delaware, 1964, pp. 13–19.

PREVIEW

This chapter will inspire as well as inform you. Strickler and Eller focus on a fundamental point: children should learn that reading is a joyful process, and learning to read should be fun. As teachers we often lose sight of this in our eagerness to instruct. We forget that reading skills are not ends in themselves.

Strickler and Eller begin by presenting a list of objectives for the affective component of reading, and by describing the reading habits of adults, adolescents, and children. They discuss reading interests and what determines them. They explain how you may develop positive attitudes toward reading in your students.

In the next section of the chapter the authors deal with interest inventories and other ways of assessing attitudes and interests. They stress the importance of literature as a vehicle for stimulating and maintaining pupils' interest in reading.

Finally, Strickler and Eller give suggestions on how to create a classroom climate that is conducive to developing and sustaining lifelong interest in reading. This is the basic goal of all of the contributors to this text, and it should be your goal as a teacher.

13

Attitudes and Interests

Darryl Strickler, Indiana University
William Eller, State University of New York at Buffalo

OBJECTIVES

After you have read this chapter, you should be able to

1. Discuss the importance of placing a major emphasis within the elementary school reading program upon children's affective development in relation to reading.

2. Explain how reading interests, attitudes toward reading, reading habits, and interest in reading are interrelated.

3. List the major research findings on children's reading interests and preferences.

4. Identify factors within the home and school environment that have the greatest influence on the development of reading attitudes and interest in reading.

5. Describe numerous strategies that can be used in the elementary school setting to increase children's interest in reading.

6. Construct and administer an interest inventory appropriate for a specific individual or group of elementary school children.

7. Develop a classroom library containing a wide range of reading material appropriate for a given elementary school grade.

8. For a given elementary school grade, design and implement a component of a language arts program that deals with the development of reading interests and positive attitudes toward reading.

INTRODUCTION

American schools have sometimes been accused of producing generations of people who can read, but choose not to. Huck (1974) used the term "illiterate literates" to describe such people—they are able to read but lack the interest and desire to do so. If the teaching of reading is directed solely to the development of reading skills, and no attempt is made to influence children's reading attitudes and interests, our efforts may well result in still another generation of illiterate literates.

The fact that schools have in the past failed to accept responsibility for developing reading habits is evidenced by a number of studies which have shown that a large percentage of the adult population seldom reads either for information or enjoyment (Ennis, 1965; Trisman, 1972; Bamberger, 1975). A recent Gallup Poll, for example, indicated that only 26 percent of the adults surveyed had read in a book during the thirty days prior to the survey (Gallup, 1973). Perhaps this is because too many of these adults completed elementary school with the idea that reading was a "subject" they had studied for six or seven years and, as such, had little relevance to their lives. Or perhaps it is because they were "turned off" by too much reading instruction and not enough reading. Whatever the reason, children who leave school knowing how to read, but do not know why to read, what to read, and when to read, cannot make full use of their skill in reading. In short, they will not have learned that reading can make a valuable contribution to the continual process of learning and personal growth that must take place throughout their lives.

Although the development of children's reading skill is unquestionably one of the teacher's major responsibilities, an equally important responsibility is the development of positive attitudes toward reading and a lifelong interest in reading. If children are to develop attitudes toward reading that result in an interest in reading and in personally constructive reading habits, they need other reading-related experiences in addition to direct instruction in reading skill. They must experience the excitement and personal fulfillment, as well as the practical value, of learning through reading.

A balanced reading program must, therefore, include an *affective component* which provides for the development of children's interests, attitudes, and personal values in relation to reading for enjoyment and information. It is suggested that the major goal of the reading instructional program—whether a school-wide program or an individual teacher's program—should be to help each child develop purposeful and personally constructive reading habits. In other words, the kind of reading habits that serve some purpose the reader has established—either informational or recreational—and which contribute to personal growth and understanding.

OBJECTIVES FOR THE AFFECTIVE COMPONENT

The following objectives for the affective component of the reading program are directly related to the major goal of helping children develop purposeful and personally constructive reading habits (Strickler, 1977).

1 *Awareness.* Students will:
be aware of the various purposes that reading can serve.
They will:
—be aware of the information-gathering potential of reading
—be aware of the enjoyment which can be derived through the reading of literature
—be aware of the opportunities for personal growth which reading provides

2 *Interest.* Students will:
demonstrate an active interest in reading as a source of enjoyment and information.
They will:
—consider using books and other printed media as a source of information
—actively attend to, and derive enjoyment from, literature being read to or by them
—actively seek out and examine books and other printed matter to explore their potential for fulfillment of personal needs

3 *Attitude.* Students will:
demonstrate a positive attitude toward reading and reading instruction.
They will:
—frequently engage in recreational reading when faced with a number of equally attractive alternatives for use of leisure time
—frequently use reading as a means of gathering information, deriving knowledge, and seeking understanding
—actively participate in learning activities designed to increase their reading skill

4 *Value.* Students will:
incorporate reading into their personal value system.
They will:
—develop their own purposes for reading in relation to their personal value system
—identify and read specific literature which is related to their personal value system
—effectively use various resources to locate literature and other printed media related to their enjoyment and information needs

In order to reflect the developmental nature of reading habits, the objectives listed above have been arranged in a four-stage hierarchy, or taxonomy. The arrangement of the sub-objectives in a taxonomy suggests that before children can achieve the major goal of developing purposeful and personally constructive reading habits, they go through various stages of affective development in relation to reading and literature. For example, children must first be aware of the informational and recreational purposes which reading can serve (*Awareness*). As their awareness of the purposes of reading develops, their interest in reading and attitude toward reading begin to form (*Interest* and *Attitude*). It is at the interest and attitude levels in children's affective development in reading that the elementary school reading program can exert the greatest influence. Obviously, the influence of the reading program can be in a positive or a negative direction! If the influence is in a positive direction, it is more likely that children will incorporate reading and literature into their personal system of values *(Value)*, and ultimately achieve the major goal of developing purposeful and personally constructive reading habits.

Although the above description of the taxonomy serves as a simplified example of children's affective development in reading, in reality the development of reading habits is a long and complicated process involving many interrelated variables.

FORMATION OF READING HABITS

Current evidence suggests that the reading habits children develop while they are in elementary school set the pattern for their reading habits as adults. Over the past several decades literally hundreds of studies have been conducted in an attempt to identify the reading interests and preferences of children. The results of many of these studies have been summarized by Weintraub (1969), King (1972), and more recently by Cook and Nolan (1976). Careful analysis of the studies of reading interests and preferences indicates that most were apparently motivated by the assumption—although it is seldom stated explicitly—that if we could discover what content is of greatest interest to children, we would then have only to place such *interesting* reading materials before them and they would become *interested in reading*. Although the results of these studies have yielded somewhat useful, if overly-generalized, information, the assumption on which they are based appears to be unacceptable in light of our growing knowledge of the complexities of reading habit and attitude formation.

Our understanding of the development of reading habits has been aided in recent years by the work of such researchers as Purves and Beach (1972), Hansen (1969, 1973), Bamberger (1975), and others who have attempted with some success to identify specific factors which influence reading habits. For example, several investigators have studied what Hansen (1969, 1973) referred to as *home literary environment,* and have found that such variables as the number of books and magazines in a child's home; the amount of time spent in reading aloud to the child; and, the presence of significant people in the home who serve as *models* of reading habits, all appear to influence the child's formation of reading habits. Bamberger's (1975) UNESCO-funded studies of the *reading situation* around the world indicate that in countries such as Sweden and Japan, where there is a permeating *value on reading* within the culture and where books are readily available, readership is more in evidence.

Although the effects of television viewing on reading habits have not been systematically studied to date, several potentially contradictory hypotheses seem feasible. First, in terms of the average amount of time children spend viewing (approximately 6 hours per day; 18,000 hours by the time they reach the age of 18), it is probable that time spent on viewing detracts from time that might be spent on reading. Second, it is possible that television viewing could contribute to the development of reading habits if direct attempts were made to capitalize on its informational and educational potential. Third, it is possible that television is a self-perpetuating medium, for example, viewing leads to more viewing rather than more reading. While all of these hypotheses are open to speculation, and require further study, there is little doubt that television does affect reading habits.

In addition to the sociocultural and home-rooted influences on reading habits, several studies have yielded information pertaining to school-related factors. For example, Lamme (1976) conducted a three-year longitudinal study of intermediate grade (4–6) students in which she examined the relationship between reading habits and reading abilities. Among her conclusions was the fact that better readers tend to read more books. Whether advanced reading ability is a cause or an effect of reading more books is, of course, not a question that can be answered from Lamme's research. Although it was not her purpose to study the formation for reading habits directly, Lamme's research does suggest that several of the variables she studied correlate positively with reading ability, and, by inference, with reading habits. These include the number of books subjects borrowed from their friends; the number of books recommended by their friends; and the number of books written by a given author whose other book(s) had been read previously. Lamme's findings suggest that for older children, peers have an important influence on their reading habits.

The influence of peers on children's reading habits was also verified in a comprehensive study of reading habits conducted by Strickler and Gaither (1978). In their study, a group of sixth-grade students who had developed *positive attitudes toward reading* was compared with a group who had *negative attitudes toward reading*. It was found that students whose attitudes were positive tended to have one or more close friends who frequently read for enjoyment. This was not true for students with negative attitudes.

The research by Strickler and Gaither also underscored the importance of such factors as book ownership, the role of parents as models of reading behavior, and the importance of being read to. Students with positive attitudes toward reading had been read to more frequently; owned more books; had visited a library more often; had more frequently observed their parents reading in the home; and had received more encouragement to read specific materials than had students in the negative attitude group. Somewhat surprisingly, Strickler and Gaither found no significant difference between the positive and negative attitude groups in the average amount of television they watched per week—approximately 15 to 16 hours.

The body of research literature, as represented by the studies reviewed above, leads to several conclusions related to the status of our knowledge about how reading habits are formed. First, it is clear that the literature yields a number of variables which appear to have a potential influence on reading habits (for example, home literary environment, social-cultural context variables, availability of reading materials, peer pressure variables, media utilization variables, instruction-related variables). Second, it is equally evident that these variables warrant further consideration and must, therefore, be operationalized and their effects validated through subsequent research. Finally— and perhaps of greatest importance—it is apparent that reading habits can be, and are, influenced by the reading-related activities which take place within the school setting.

The School's Influence on Reading Habits

When children begin school they bring with them a wide variety of reading-related concepts, interests, attitudes and values which might be viewed as the *raw material* from which reading habits develop. Although schools may have little control over the concepts, interests, attitudes, and values children have when they begin school, they play a major role in influencing the kind of reading habits children will take with them when they leave school.

Within the school setting, teachers can plan and conduct numerous activities for children that will contribute to the formation of positive reading habits. In order to do this, the teacher must be aware of the more subtle, and often unplanned, occurrences within the classroom that can negatively influence children's attitudes toward reading and their reading habits.

In their desire to develop children's reading skill, well-intentioned teachers have sometimes overlooked the necessity for developing reading attitudes. In classrooms where there is an overemphasis on skill development and little attention to attitudes, children often feel that it is the acquisition of reading skill per se that is valued and not the application of the skill for deriving information or enjoyment through print. Children might easily get such a message in a classroom where they spend many hours per week engaged in activities designed to develop and refine their skill in reading, but are provided little time within the school day to use their reading skill to pursue their own interests and purposes. It is well to remember that what is *caught* is often as important, and in some cases more important, than what is taught.

Children's exposure to *formal reading instruction,* which typically occurs at the end of kindergarten or the beginning of first grade, often alters their attitudes toward reading. If one were to ask a group of kindergarten children near the beginning of the school year how many of them would like to learn to read, the chances are good that a large percentage would enthusiastically respond in the affirmative. After children have been introduced to reading instruction in the first grade their response to such a question may be quite different. Fewer are likely to respond as enthusiastically.

Both the amount of difference and the specific factors that account for the difference between the attitudes of kindergarten and first-grade children toward reading vary greatly from one school situation to another. It is probable, however, that kindergarten children perceive the question of learning to read in relation to their previous experiences with reading and books. Most kindergarten children want to learn to create for themselves the kind of positive experiences they have gained from being read to by parents and teachers. The first-grade children, on the other hand, having been exposed to reading instruction, would more likely respond to the question on the basis of how they perceived that instruction. The fact that children's attitude toward reading often appears to change after they are introduced to *formal reading instruction* points to the necessity of developing reading attitudes concurrently with reading skill.

The reading instructional program, or system, used can also influence children's reading attitudes. More important than the program itself, however, is the way in which the teacher uses the program and materials. With few exceptions, authors and publishers of basal reading instructional systems recommend that teachers judiciously select and adapt appropriate activities from the variety of teaching suggestions provided in teacher's manuals. Yet, in practice, some teachers apparently feel compelled to use many of the suggestions provided without adapting them to the specific children with whom they are working. Perhaps this is due to a lack of self-confidence, or an inability or unwillingness to make necessary adjustments. Whatever the reason, slavish adherence to teacher's manuals often results in instruction that is inappropriate for a specific group of children.

One outstanding example of inappropriate reading instruction is instruction on skills that children have previously mastered. When this occurs too frequently, children are likely to lose interest. The danger here is not only that they may become bored with reading instructional activities, but that they may generalize their dislike for reading instruction and develop negative attitudes toward reading as a process of gaining information and enjoyment. Anyone who has heard the statement made by children that they "hate reading" cannot help wondering whether children are referring to the instruction they receive in school, or to the process of learning, discovering, and experiencing through the medium of print. In most cases they are probably referring to the former and have, unfortunately, been provided with very little assistance in truly discovering the latter.

Another significant influence on reading attitudes is the readability, or reading difficulty, of instructional materials provided for children. If children are to learn to enjoy reading—or the process of gaining new insights and experiences through reading—the readability of textbooks and other printed materials they are expected to use must be appropriate for them. Few people enjoy activities that are too difficult; yet too often children are expected to use instructional materials that require reading skill beyond their present competence. When children experience continual difficulty due to material containing vocabulary and concepts far beyond their levels of understanding, obviously they are not likely to develop positive attitudes toward reading.

The use children are permitted to make of classroom and school libraries and the amount of time they are permitted to read self-selected books can also influence their reading attitudes. If, for example, a teacher regularly schedules his class to use the school library for selecting books for voluntary reading, he should also use some of the valuable time within the school day to allow children to read and discuss the books they have selected. Despite the pressure many teachers feel to "cover" the essential elements of the curriculum, time used by children for reading and discussing self-selected books is time well spent. Children derive clues to what is valued within the school setting by the amount of time and attention devoted to a given activity or area of instruction. If books are merely made available, and no specific time is allotted for reading and sharing them, children are not as likely to view books and reading as being worthy of their attention.

Depending upon the degree to which children respond to or are affected by peer pressure, their reading attitudes may be altered by a peer reference group. Since the elementary school is one of the primary settings for peer interaction, the teacher must be particularly aware of the ways in which children influence each other's perceptions and attitudes toward reading.

Such an awareness can be gained through attitude questionnaires and informal observation techniques (which are discussed later in this chapter), and through sociograms, which indicate the peer interaction and friendship patterns of children in the classroom. After such data are gathered the teacher can regroup children within the classroom for reading-related activities that involve interaction among children with varying attitudes toward reading. If, for example, teachers find that several children appear to view reading, or reading instruction, rather negatively, they should make a concerted effort to structure situations that will allow these children to interact with other children in the class who have developed more positive attitudes. In this way, the teacher can affect reading attitudes through peer influence, which, for some children, is a stronger influence than the teacher's.

Teachers often provide subtle clues to their own attitude toward reading, which over a period of time can greatly influence their students' views of reading. For example, a teacher might tell pupils that after they finish their "work" they may read whatever they wish. Here children may get the message that the work is important and the reading is merely something to do to occupy time. Furthermore, it is usually the more able pupils who finish their work first and have more time for reading.

Finally, and perhaps most important, is the matter of children's interest in the specific content of what is to be read. If children are to discover the value of reading, both as an information-gathering process and as a process of self-fulfillment, they must be provided with reading materials and reading-related activities in which they are interested. Of equal importance is the teacher's ability to stimulate children's interest in specific topics or reading materials through readiness and motivational-building activities. It may not always be possible to provide for every child's interests in every classroom activity. Nor is it always possible to develop the interest where it is lacking. However, a teacher can, through his knowledge of the interests of each child, structure follow-up and enrichment activities geared to individual interests. The degree to which this is done will have considerable influence on children's attitude toward reading and, in turn, their reading habits.

Strategies for Developing
Reading Attitudes and
Interests

The attitudes and interests an individual develops in relation to reading exert a significant influence upon his reading habits. Further, there is considerable evidence that the reading habits students develop while in elementary school will set the pattern for reading habits in adulthood. For this reason, developing children's attitudes and interests within the elementary school is a primary means of affecting their lifelong reading habits. Specific strategies that can be used to develop children's reading attitudes and interests and, in turn, their reading habits are described below.

Before considering these strategies, however, it is necessary to examine some of the assumptions upon which they are based. The efficacy of the strategies described will depend on the acceptance—at least in principle—of the following assumptions:

1   Children's reading habits can be influenced by providing them with appropriate reading and literature-related activities and experiences within the elementary school setting.

2   A primary means of affecting interest in reading (and, consequently, constructive reading habits) is by determining an individual's interests so that reading instructional materials and reading literature-related experiences can be provided which are aligned to those interests.

3   The interests, attitudes, and personal values students have in relation to reading exert a significant influence on their reading habits.

4   The degree to which children discover personal relevance and value in what they read will to a large extent influence their attitude toward reading and, in turn, their reading habits.

Although not all of the above assumptions can be tested directly through experience or research, the literature on reading habits, interests, and attitudes that was reviewed in the preceding part of this chapter seems to adequately justify their acceptance.

Keeping in mind the long-range goal of developing purposeful and personally constructive reading habits, the basic question the teacher faces is "how to turn kids on to reading." Just as there is no single approach to teaching children *how* to read that has been found to be consistently more effective than another approach, there is also no single most effective approach to developing children's attitudes and interests. For this reason, many approaches and strategies are detailed in the following sections.

The following general guidelines are suggested for teachers who wish to build their students' interest in reading. Some of the guidelines refer to aspects of the reading/language arts program, some refer to the classroom climate for reading, and others imply teacher behaviors that encourage children to read independently.

1   *Get to know each of your students well. Use children's interests in planning instruction.* Determine what interests each child has and provide reading and literature-related activities and materials which are aligned to these interests.

2   *Assure that children develop efficient meaning-getting strategies.* Help each child develop comprehending strategies that will allow them to gain meaning from print in an efficient and effective manner. Make learning how to read enjoyable. Show children that their listening and speaking skills help improve their reading and writing skills.

3   *Read to children often.* Set aside time in the schedule to read to children on a regular basis. Expose them to creative and colorful use of language in poetry and narrative. Introduce them to the sounds and rhythms of language. Select what you read to children with the same care you exercise in choosing your own reading material.

4. *Carefully select books for your literature program.* Become familiar with the best in children's literature. Use your knowledge of children's books to select books for your classroom library and to recommend specific books to your students. Use children's literature to supplement learning of, and interest in, content areas of the curriculum, for example, social studies and science.

5 *Be an enthusiastic model of reading habits.* Share your enthusiasm for reading and books with children. Be caught "read handed" in the act of reading for your own enjoyment.

6. *Fill the bookshelves in your classroom.* Provide a great quantity and variety of books and other printed matter within your classroom—especially paperback books. Beg, buy, borrow, or make books; but by all means make them available and accessible to children.

7 *Encourage children to read and share what they have read.* Set up "sharing" and "celebrating" activities through which children can stimulate the interests of their classmates. Have pupils compile lists of their "best books" or "favorite books."

8 *Provide time for independent reading.* Allow time within your schedule for sustained silent reading of student-selected reading materials.

9 *Help children discover their own purposes for reading.* Show them that reading is not a "subject" in the school curriculum, but a valuable tool for expanding and clarifying their experiences. Help them learn why, when, and what to read, as well as how to read.

Within the guidelines listed above are many specific strategies that can be effectively applied in an elementary school reading/language arts program. In the following sections of this chapter these guidelines are expanded to include suggested activities and strategies.

Assessing Children's Reading Interests and Attitudes

A major means of building the kind of interest in reading that helps form constructive reading habits is to provide children with reading materials and reading-related activities that interest them. The degree to which this can be done successfully depends, of course, upon the teacher's knowledge of each child's interests. Unquestionably, the best way of determining what interests a child is by getting to know the child well. Although this may seem like an over-simplification, the importance of knowing each child personally cannot be emphasized too strongly.

The most useful information about interests and attitudes is that which is gathered by the teacher daily. Within every school day there are countless opportunities for determining children's interests and attitudes, and the teacher who employs diagnostic teaching techniques can capitalize upon them. Conversations between children, products of their creative activities, class projects, trips to the library, group sharing activities, and a variety of other situations in which children are involved in self-initiated activities provide rich sources of information about their interests and attitudes toward reading. The teacher who is aware of the opportunities that all of these situations provide will not only make a concerted effort to observe and interact with children in a variety of learning situations, but will also spend as much time as possible talking informally with individual children. Time spent with one child looking through and discussing various books in the school or classroom library can not only provide the teacher with greater insight into the child's interests and attitude toward reading, but can also communicate to the child the teacher's genuine concern and interest in that child as a person.

Determining Reading Interests and Preferences   While there is no real substitute for first-hand knowledge about the child that is gathered through informal observation and interaction, there are various techniques and instruments the teacher can use to discover children's interests. Interest inventories, questionnaires, structured and informal interviews, autobiographies, circulation records from school or classroom libraries, and records of books the child has read provide valuable clues to reading interests and preferences.

Included under the general category of interest inventories are a wide variety of specific instruments. Basically, interest inventories consist of a series of questions or incomplete sentences, which are designed to elicit responses from the child about experiences, likes and dislikes, hobbies, and use of free time. Most interest inventories are not copyrighted. Sample copies of such inventories can usually be obtained from school district language arts coordinators, from reading clinic personnel, or from college and university teacher education program faculty.

An interest inventory may be administered orally or used as an outline for an interview conducted by the teacher, or it can be duplicated so that children may read it by themselves and record their own responses. Whichever method of administration is used, it is usually desirable to have children respond as spontaneously as possible so that they do not spend undue time and energy speculating on what response the teacher would *like* them to give. If the child is asked to respond rapidly, this so-called "halo effect" will, hopefully, be reduced. Since the usefulness of children's responses will be determined by their candidness in answering the questions, it is also important the inventory be administered in such a way that the child feels free to respond frankly.

In addition to the *Interest Inventory* (*Table 13,* p. 386), an incomplete sentence, or open-ended, inventory may prove to be very useful to the teacher. Following are several examples of items which might be included in an incomplete sentence interest inventory:

I like ....

It's fun to ....

After school ....

Reading ....

TV ....

I think that school ....

I would read more often if ....

Again, this type of inventory may be administered orally, or read and completed by the child. As with the question-type inventory, it is important to have the child respond as spontaneously as possible.

Whatever the format or method of administration, the most valuable interest inventory is the one the teacher himself constructs to use with a particular individual or group. Such an inventory can be related to a specific purpose the teacher has, and the vocabulary used in the items can be adjusted for the particular children who will use the inventory. Items to be included in a teacher-made inventory should be selected carefully to avoid embarrassing particular individuals.

Table 13

┌─ INTEREST INVENTORY ──────────────────────────────

Name: _____ Age: _____ Date: _____

Grade: _____ Teacher: _____ School: _____

(Check One): Read to child: _____ Read by child: _____

General Interests

1. What do you like to do in your free time?
2. What do you usually do after school?
3. What are your favorite TV shows?
4. Do you have any hobbies?
5. Do you collect anything? What?
6. What things do you like to make?
7. Do you belong to any clubs or scout groups?
8. What games or sports do you like best?
9. What kind of places do you like to visit?
10. Have you taken any trips with your family? Where?
11. Do you have any pets at home? What kind?
12. What kind of work do you want to do after you finish school?

Reading Habits and Interests

13. Do you go to the public library (or bookmobile)? How often?
14. Do you have any books of your own? About how many?
15. Does someone read to you (or with you) at home? Who?
16. What things do you like to read about?
17. What is the title of the best book you ever read?
18. Do you read comic books? Which ones?
19. Do you read magazines? Which ones?
20. If you were to write your own book what might it be about?

To make the best use of an interest inventory, the teacher should review and summarize the child's responses, listing several topics or even specific reading materials or books in which the child may be interested. This summary can then be recorded on a file card so that it can be readily referred to for planning instructional strategies, or for helping the child select reading materials.

The teacher can also find valuable clues to children's interests in library circulation records and records of books the children have read—kept either by the teacher or the children themselves.

Discussions with parents about the interests of their child are another important source of information. Informal contacts with parents as well as questionnaires and parent-teacher conferences provide opportunities for the teacher to learn a great deal about the child that could not be learned in the school setting.

The above strategies for determining individual children's interests will provide useful information in most cases. However, within any given classroom there are likely to be some children who appear to have no well-defined interests that can be capitalized upon for building interest in reading. While it is certainly true that some children lack the desire to read—or at least are not interested in those things that teachers think they should be—it is equally apparent that every child is interested in something. No matter how difficult it may be for the teacher to determine what that something is, the effort is well worth expending since it is often the case that those children who appear to lack well-defined interests also require the most assistance in discovering the personal value of reading.

Interests, like attitudes, are constantly subject to change as a result of new experiences. The teacher must not just survey children's interests at the beginning of the year, and then assign, or ascribe, areas of interest to a given child. Certainly a major aspect of the teacher's role includes helping children to expand their present areas of interest and providing experiences that help them to develop new interests.

Assessing Attitude toward Reading The extent to which children discover the personal benefits of reading will affect, and be affected by, their attitudes toward reading. That is, a child who has developed a negative attitude toward reading and/or reading instruction may also develop an "avoidance reaction" that could preclude development of constructive reading habits.

The first step in positively influencing a child's attitude toward reading is the collection of relevant data. The primary means of gathering data about a child's reading attitude is by observing responses to reading in a variety of instructional and noninstructional situations. Rowell (1972) developed an observation instrument that can serve as an aid to the teacher in gathering attitudinal data related to reading.

Other means of assessing reading attitudes are also available. Numerous questionnaires have been developed that are intended to "measure" children's attitudes toward reading. Although the results of some of these questionnaires are generally no more valid than data derived from continued observations by an experienced teacher, questionnaires can provide potentially useful information about children's attitudes toward reading.

An example of an attitude questionnaire that has been widely used is the *San Diego County Inventory of Reading Attitude* (San Diego County Department of Education, 1961). It consists of twenty-five "Do you like to . . .?" items in a written format. The child's *yes* or *no* responses to the items yield a stanine score that is supposedly indicative of his attitude toward reading.

Another attitude questionnaire, *The Estes Attitude Scale: Elementary Form* (Estes, 1975), contains fourteen statements related to reading; children indicate their agreement or disagreement with each item on a three-point scale.

Fiddler (1973) constructed and standardized an instrument for assessing sixth-grade students' attitudes toward reading which differs markedly from other attitude questionnaires because of the way in which it is administered. Of the 100 items in the questionnaire, only twenty are directly related to reading attitude. These twenty items are based upon Fiddler's adaptation of Krathwohl's (1964) taxonomy of the affective domain. Because the purpose of the Fiddler questionnaire is disguised by the eighty "distracting" items, the probability of a "halo effect" is greatly reduced. Therefore this questionnaire is likely to yield a more accurate indication of a child's attitude toward reading.

In the research by Strickler and Gaither (1978) cited previously, *The Fiddler Reading Attitude Test* (FRAT) was found to be a very good predictor of leisure reading, for example, students who achieved a high score on the FRAT also spent considerable time on nonassigned reading out of school. In fact, in this study the FRAT was a better predictor of leisure reading than was teacher perception. This is possibly the result of the fact that some teachers seem to equate attitude toward reading, in general, with attitude toward reading instruction. Certainly there are a few students in almost every classroom who appear to have negative attitudes toward reading instruction, but have well-developed leisure-time reading habits.

The data gathered through informal observation or attitude questionnaires must be used to plan reading-related activities if it is to affect children's reading habits. If, for example, you have some children in your class who appear to view reading quite positively, but who lack the basic reading skills, it will be necessary to spend additional time diagnosing and correcting their specific reading deficiencies so that their positive attitudes can be maintained. If, on the other hand, you find that several children in your class appear to view reading and/or reading instruction rather negatively, it will probably be more beneficial for these children if you place greater emphasis on developing their attitudes toward reading. This can be done through informal counseling or group therapy where reading attitudes and habits are the focus of the discussion, and through the use of the various strategies in this chapter that are designed to develop children's interest in reading.

Assure Early and Continued
Success in Learning to Read

Most children enter school eager to learn to read. In fact, for some children, starting school and learning to read appear to be synonymous. At the same time, it is often difficult for children to understand that the ability to read cannot be mastered instantly. The fact that the children want to be able to read on the first or second day of school presents the kindergarten or first-grade teacher with the difficulty of maintaining children's enthusiasm for learning to read while developing initial reading skills. The way a teacher deals with this dilemma will have considerable impact on pupils' attitude toward reading.

Children need to experience some degree of success with reading even before they are able to employ meaning-getting strategies independently. No matter what approach or specific instructional materials are to be used for initial reading instruction, early success with reading can be provided by developing "experience charts" that contain stories or experiences that are dictated by the children and recorded by the teacher on the chalkboard or chart paper. Similarly, children can dictate captions or brief stories related to their creative artwork. The experience charts or captions are then "read" either by individuals, or chorally by the group. Through such activities children can develop a number of important concepts and prereading skills while experiencing the visual and mental processing skills involved in reading. As children recall the words they have dictated, they begin to understand that their speech can be represented by printed symbols that are graphically produced and visually processed in a left-to-right sequence. In addition to exposing children to such conventions of English orthography as capitalization and punctuation, experience charts also help children make associations between printed symbols and the concepts and objects those symbols represent.

The labelling of items in the classroom such as chairs, tables, and windows can also help children associate words with concrete objects. Such labels also help children establish sound-symbol correspondences and sight recognition of the visual form of words.

While the above strategies are often associated with what is known as the *whole-word* or *sight-word* approach to beginning reading, we do not suggest that such an approach be used exclusively. The above *language-experience* strategies can be used in conjunction with virtually any method or approach to beginning reading instruction. By using experience charts, writing captions to pictures, and labelling classroom objects, children can experience some degree of early success with reading even before they can actually employ a decoding strategy. Perhaps too often teachers have dutifully begun teaching decoding skills and have apparently overlooked the importance of providing experiences and activities for children that sustain their interest in learning to read.

Beginning readers should also have many opportunities to experience books in various ways. For example, they can listen to recordings of a book while following the pictures in a copy of the book. Through repeated experiences of this kind, many children are able to "read" the books, although they may not actually attend to individual words that appear on the pages. Nonetheless, the feeling of success this kind of activity can provide is very important to the young reader's attitude.

Books that have a "predictable pattern" should also be read to children frequently during the initial stages of reading instruction. Such books allow children to anticipate, or predict, what will come next because the language patterns used are "predictable," or because there are ample cues that can be used to anticipate what will happen in the story. Current theories of the reading process stress the importance of readers' ability to make accurate predictions about what they are reading. The use of "predictable books" can greatly assist children in their ability to read independently. *Three Billy Goats Gruff, The Three Little Pigs, Where the Wild Things Are, The Great Big Enormous Turnip, Too Many Lollipops,* and *Rosie's Walk* are a few examples of the many predictable books available.

The many excellent "wordless picture books" currently available should also be used frequently with beginning readers—and with older readers who are experiencing difficulties. Because these books have no words, the child is not intimidated by a lack of reading skills, but relies, instead, on picture cues to follow the story line of the book. Wordless picture books can do a great deal to maintain children's interest in reading while they are improving their ability to gain meaning from books.

Maintaining children's interest in learning to read and in improving their skill in reading is, of course, not only important during the initial stages of reading acquisition, but throughout all grade levels. As has been noted previously, the way children are taught how to read—that is, the way reading instruction is managed in the classroom—can have a major effect upon their attitudes toward reading.

Obviously, it is important that children experience success and enjoyment in learning to read. They must experience the same degree of success that all of us need to continue in demanding tasks. Children cannot reasonably be expected to develop positive attitudes and interest in reading if they continually experience difficulty gaining meaning from print.

The teacher should be aware not only of each child's need to develop strategies for gaining meaning, but also of the need for developing the reading attitudes and interests that contribute to constructive reading habits. Some teachers seem to feel that *reading skills* should be developed first and that interest in reading will follow naturally. As well as being unrealistic from a child's point of view, such a perception is both limiting and short-sighted. Reading programs based on this position—whether by design or by practice—fail to capitalize on the motivation generated when children are helped to uncover the many and varied uses they can make of their reading skill. When they are engaged in reading that is aligned to an existing interest, or generates a new interest, children are far more likely to see the usefulness of reading.

Reading to Children

Perhaps the best way of inspiring a young child with a desire of learning to read is, to read to him, with proper intervals, some interesting story, perfectly intelligible, yet as full of suggestion as communication; for the pleasure of discovering is always greater than that of perceiving.

(Horace Mann, 1838)

Horace Mann's advice is as cogent and timely for children of the electronic age as it was for the children of Massachusetts in 1838. Although he referred to building children's desire to learn to read, his advice is equally applicable to sustaining and building interest in reading.

Most teachers and parents would agree that reading to primary grade children can provide them with many benefits that they cannot derive for themselves because of their lack of reading skill. Yet for many reasons—not the least of which is lack of time—the practice of reading to children seems to decline rapidly when children reach the upper primary and intermediate grades. Children of all grade levels can profit from and enjoy being read to.

Reading to children serves many purposes. In addition to the more obvious purposes of modeling good oral reading habits and building children's listening skills, reading to children allows them to experience literature which they might not be able to read or be inclined to read for themselves. Oral reading to children can also whet their appetite to read more on their own. For example, an exciting chapter of a book that is read aloud can often stimulate children to read the entire book themselves. In addition to providing exposure to specific books, reading to children can also introduce them to creative and colorful use of language in prose and poetry, introduce new vocabulary and concepts, and acquaint children with the variety of language patterns found in written and oral communication.

For the individual children, being read to and reading to themselves are very different. Because they are freed from the visual processing aspects of reading, and because they can think much faster than the reader can read orally, the children can devote greater attention to the images evoked by the story or poem being read to them. They can, for example, imagine that they are living the part of one of the characters in the selection; or they can see, smell, hear, taste, or feel what the author describes.

Much of the message of reading orally to children is communicated by the medium itself. For this reason, how a selection is read is often as important as what is read. When you read to children, let your own enthusiasm for the material show. Your voice inflection, intonation, and facial expressions will not only add interest and meaning to the selection, but will also convey your own attitudes toward reading and books.

Certainly you can do a great deal to add interest to a story that is to be read to children by prereading it to practice the mechanics of reading it orally. It is doubtful, however, that mechanical perfection alone will achieve the purpose for which such reading is intended. If you yourself do not have a genuine interest in the selection you read to children you are less likely to secure their interest. For this reason it is obviously very important to select books to read aloud that you find especially appealing. With the variety and quality of children's books available this should not be difficult.

Before you begin reading to children, it is helpful to spend a few minutes building their readiness for the selection. This might be done by leading children into a discussion of prior experiences pertinent to the selection, or by giving them some basic information such as the title and asking them to speculate upon what the story might be about. Interesting biographical information about the author might also be used. In other cases the use of "realia" (tangible objects) or pictures and illustrations might be helpful. Readiness activities should be brief and should build interest while introducing or reviewing concepts contained in the selection to be read.

If the main objective of reading to children is to build their interest in reading, any discussion of the selection that follows the reading should reflect this purpose. Few adults would enjoy being closely questioned about what they have read, yet some teachers have an inclination to interrogate children after reading a story to them or to fractionate a story by interrupting with questions. And, while the use of effective questioning strategies can do a great deal to build comprehension skills, it is possible to "beat a story to death" by asking too many of the wrong types of questions. It is better to ask a few well-selected questions that serve as a stimulus for discussion of the major concepts developed or implied in the selection. In addition to reviewing some of the major aspects of the selection, such questions should also focus upon the feelings and emotions the selection evoked, as well as some of the elements of form or theme that make the story or poem especially appealing. A discussion of E. B. White's *Charlotte's Web* could, for example, focus primarily upon the concepts of "true friendship" and "the cycle of life." And, while it is true that the events in the story are essential for the development of these concepts, the children's feelings about the events are of greater importance.

Exposing children to literature through reading aloud need not be limited to the situation where the teacher or librarian reads to the entire class. Many excellent cassette tapes, phonograph records, films, and correlated filmstrip and tape recordings of children's books are commercially available and can be used independently by children. For example, a cassette recording of Sendak's *Where the Wild Things Are* (Weston Woods)—as well as other recordings—could be placed in the classroom reading corner or language arts center along with several copies of the book and a tape recorder. An individual child or a small group of children using a listening station with jacks for multiple head sets, could then listen to the recording while reading along in the books. This type of activity can generate a great deal of interest in a variety of selections while providing another medium through which children can experience literature.

The current state of school finance should not keep the resourceful teacher from providing activities of this type for children. It is not necessary to achieve the studio quality of commercially prepared tapes. Teachers can make homemade tapes, either of an entire selection or just enough to stimulate children to finish reading it on their own. A recording made by a child who is reasonably fluent in oral reading can also be used to stimulate other children's interest in a book.

Having children read to other children in a "live" situation can also build interest in reading. While this can be done within the classroom among classmates, it is often mutually beneficial to have older children read to younger children. This not only provides the older children with an eager audience for whom to refine and use their skill in oral reading, but it also widens the younger children's experience with literature and allows them to see older children modeling reading behaviors they can emulate.

Whether or not you can recall the specific *content* of stories or poems which were read to you in the elementary grades by a parent, teacher, or librarian, you can no doubt remember such experiences. For the most part, the recollections of these experiences evoke positive feelings. Perhaps this is because people who frequently read to children seem to do so because they are convinced that children can benefit by experiencing literature in this manner. The positive feelings you remember are also likely to be partly the result of the skill and enthusiasm with which the selection was read, and partly the result of the person having carefully selected what was read to you.

BECOMING FAMILIAR WITH CHILDREN'S BOOKS

Literally thousands of children's books are published each year. Current estimates of the number published annually place the figure at more than 3000. While this figure may be somewhat misleading since some of these are reprints of books published in previous years, the responsibility of teachers to familiarize themselves with children's books is none the less formidable. The sheer number of children's books on the market might be somewhat intimidating, since a teacher cannot reasonably hope to read all of them. Because the time required to read children's books and the availability of the books are important constraints that teachers face in familiarizing themselves with children's literature, the numerous sources of book reviews and other compilations of children's books are very helpful. Most periodicals pertaining to elementary education include reviews of children's books. Reviews can be found, for example, in *Language Arts, The Reading Teacher, Childhood Education, The Instructor, Grade Teacher, Early Years,* and *Learning.* In addition there are several periodicals devoted almost exclusively to children's literature. The *Horn Book Magazine, Bookbird, Bulletin of the Center for Children's Books, Booklist,* and the *School Library Journal* include current reviews as well as recommended, and in some cases non-recommended, titles. Reviews of children's books can also be found in the *New York Times,* the *Chicago Tribune,* and in *Saturday Review.* The *New York Times* also publishes an annual supplement devoted to children's literature.

In addition to these book review sources, numerous reference publications contain annotated lists of recommended children's books. Some of these publications that the teacher will want to consult are listed at the end of the chapter. (See "Aids for Selecting Children's Books.")

Another useful source in selecting children's books is a listing of Newbery and Caldecott award winners. The John Newbery Award is presented annually to the author whose book is most highly evaluated on the basis of literary merit, while excellence in illustration is the criterion used in awarding the annual Randolph Caldecott Medal. Generally speaking, many of the Newbery Award books are most appropriate for independent reading by children in the intermediate grades, but could be read to younger children. Many Caldecott Medal books, on the other hand, are geared to the interests and preferences of preschool and primary grade children, since they contain numerous illustrations of a very high quality.

In addition to the Newbery and Caldecott awards, several other awards for outstanding children's books are presented on a regular basis. Information about these awards is contained in the Children's Book Council publication entitled *Children's Books: Awards and Prizes.* While most of these awards are determined by committees of adults, the Young Reader's Choice Award, which is presented annually by the Pacific Northwest Library Association, is based upon the preferences of children in the northwestern United States and British Columbia.

Finally, teachers who are skeptical of book reviewers and children's book award committees, and who subscribe to the "best seller" method of determining which children's books are read most frequently, will want to consult Kujoth's *Best-Selling Children's Books* (1973). Although this publication is very useful, it should be kept in mind that most children's books are probably purchased by adults.

Reading book reviews and reference lists will unquestionably conserve a great deal of time and energy which might otherwise be spent searching through the stacks of a library. Consulting a school librarian or the children's librarian of a university or public library will also be quite helpful. However, these references and resource persons are only a starting point. If you want to become truly familiar with children's books, you will have to read them.

Reading Children's Books   Before you embark on a continuing regimen of reading children's literature, stop for a moment to consider why you need to be familiar with books for children. How, for example, can you hope to interest children in books which you have not read yourself? How can you select the "right" books to read to your students if you are not aware of the many exciting possibilities? How can you refer individual children to specific books that could help them gain insight into a particular problem they have if you are not aware of the bibliotherapeutic qualities inherent in many children's books? Finally, how can you decide which books contain the "stuff of which childhood is made" if you have not sampled many of these books yourself?

Once you have convinced yourself of the importance of being familiar with children's literature and have developed a basic reading list, the next step is, of course, to begin reading. Read as many books as you have the time and interest to read. Visit an elementary school library and the children's book room of a university or public library. Check out books, and read them. Start your own file on children's books by selecting those books that you feel are the best. Briefly summarize the plot of the book on an index card; list some of the major concepts the book develops; and, where appropriate, list any bibliotherapeutic value you think the book might have for specific children. Make your book notes as detailed or as brief as you like so long as they help you to select books you want to read to children or help you recommend a specific book to a specific child.

In considering which are the best books to include in your classroom program, take into account the various aspects of literature normally used in literary analysis—style, theme, characterization, and plot. Most importantly, however, try to evaluate a book from a child's point of view. Ask yourself whether the book seems to be relevant to the lives of children in your classroom; whether it is likely to have some impact upon them; whether it meets some basic psychological need—including the need to laugh; and, equally important, whether it is simply fun to read.

CREATING A CLASSROOM CLIMATE FOR READING

The teacher's familiarity with children's literature is one of the basic ingredients of any program that succeeds in developing children's interest in reading. In addition, there are several other significant classroom influences upon children's reading attitudes and interests and, in turn, their reading habits. These include the attitude toward reading and books which the teacher demonstrates daily; the availability and accessibility of a wide variety of reading materials within the classroom; and multiple opportunities for children to read and share the pleasure they derive from books they read. The sum total of these factors is the primary indicator of what might be called the "classroom climate for reading." More broadly conceived, the climate for reading can extend far beyond the walls of the classroom.

Modeling Reading Habits   As a teacher your own attitude toward reading will be one of the most significant factors in determining the classroom reading climate. And while you might be able to pretend to be interested in books and reading by affecting enthusiasm, you will probably not be able to fool many children for very long. Children are quick to detect insincerity, whatever form it takes. Regardless of what you say about reading in general or about specific books, your own personal behavior in relation to reading will speak loudest. So let your actions do the talking; let children see that reading is an important part of your personal life as well as a necessity in your profession. Bring your own reading to school to fill your spare moments—be they ever so few. Instead of going to the teachers' lounge during your free period, relax with a book in a comfortable chair in your own classroom reading corner. (And don't be afraid to be "caught" there when your class returns from their gym period.) Share your enthusiasm for reading with children. Catch up on some personal reading while children are reading; share what you have read with them. Let them know what reading has meant to you, how you feel about what you have read, and what difference it has made in your life. In short, be a model of the kind of reading habits children will want to emulate.

Making Books Available   If children are expected to develop purposeful and personally constructive reading habits they must have a sufficient quantity and quality of books at their fingertips. Ideally, every elementary school classroom should contain its own collection of books suitable to the range of interests and preferences of each child in the class. A useful rule of thumb is to have at least fifteen books in the classroom collection for each member of the class. The fact that many elementary schools have adequate school library facilities and provisions for regularly scheduled visits by individual classes does not reduce the necessity for creating classroom libraries where books and other reading materials are invitingly displayed.

One way of starting a classroom library is to borrow a basic collection of books from the school library or the public library. Many public libraries have provisions for lending collections of children's books to schools. Such collections should be rotated frequently enough to provide a continually fresh supply throughout the year.

Paperback books are a particularly good source of supply for classroom libraries. The number of high quality, inexpensive paperbacks on today's market allows for the addition of many volumes to the classroom library with only a moderate investment. Many titles by such children's authors as Judith Viorst, E. B. White, Ezra Jack Keats, Laura Ingalls Wilder, Maurice Sendak, and Judy Blume are currently available in paperback at prices well below the original hardcover editions. Many classroom teachers have discovered that paperback books appear to be less formidable to many children than hardbound books and therefore seem to have greater appeal. Whether this is because paperbacks seem more manageable or because hardbound books remind children of "school books," the special appeal of paperbacks should be capitalized upon to encourage independent reading. Fader et al., (1976) have described a successful reading program for reluctant readers built around the use of paperback books.

Children's book clubs that offer inexpensive paperback books provide another source of supply for classroom libraries. Many of these book clubs offer "dividend books" when a class orders a given number of books. These dividend books can be donated by the class to the permanent collection in the classroom. In addition, children are often willing to share their own books by donating or lending their personal copies of books to the classroom library so that other children can read them. Although it is probably wise to check with parents first, the practice of donating books can be encouraged by having

children autograph the inside cover accordingly: "Donated by _____";
or, "On loan from the private library of _____."

In times of tight school budgets many teachers have purchased books for
their classroom libraries at their own expense. In addition to being a good
investment in "tools of the trade," such expenditures are usually tax deducti-
ble. The teacher who is fortunate enough to be given responsibility for allocating a portion of the school's materials budget to purchase items for his own
classroom should seriously consider spending part of the allocation to augment the classroom library. Money that might be spent to purchase the latest
"skills kit" or a new set of workbooks could be used to far greater advantage if
it were allotted to the purchase of many inexpensive paperback books. Furthermore, such an investment will probably pay far greater dividends in the long
run.

So far we have suggested that teachers beg, buy, or borrow books for
the classroom collection. We have not recommended stealing books, but
there is a fourth alternative—make them. Books written and illustrated by
members of the class are often the hottest items on the shelves. Furthermore,
there is usually no communication gap between the author and the reader of
such books. It is fair to assume that children know what other children would
like to read about, so there is no problem of a credibility gap either. If a child
wants to know why a story written by a classmate turned out as it did, the child
can simply ask.

Class bookmaking projects not only provide a creative outlet for budding
authors, they also serve as a springboard for getting children into a whole
range of related topics such as plot, theme, characterization, and illustration.
The books produced in such projects can range from the first grader's collection of language-experience stories stapled between two sheets of construction paper to a fourth grader's elaborately bound "first edition," produced in the
classroom from remnants of sewing fabric, cardboard, dry mount tissue and
construction paper. Student-made books can be shared with other classes
and grades.

Allowing children to borrow books from the classroom library to take
home is often a good idea, since this encourages more independent reading.
A simple check-out system can be instituted by having the children sign their
names on a file card or in a notebook kept in the classroom library. Some
teachers have found that they can successfully use an "honor system" for
lending books. Whatever system is used, it is a good idea to keep the loan
policy flexible enough so that children will not be discouraged from borrowing
books. You need not be too alarmed, for example, if the best books in your
classroom library appear to be missing most of the time. In fact, if a book is not
an expensive one and has been borrowed for an extended period of time by a
child who was previously a reluctant reader, you might consider replacing the
book with a new copy. While being too lenient may result in the loss of many
of your books, it is equally probable that being too rigid may discourage
independent reading. The question really becomes one of deciding where a
given book might do the most good—in the hands of children who do not
have any books of their own, or in the classroom library.

Children need not start their own personal libraries at the expense of the
classroom collection, however. Book ownership can be promoted through

paperback book clubs, through school-wide "book fairs" where children can trade, buy, or sell used paperbacks, or through a program such as the Smithsonian Institution's Reading Is Fundamental Program which provides children with books either free of charge or at a substantially reduced cost. The experience of many teachers and the success of various Reading Is Fundamental projects throughout the country have adequately demonstrated that children's motivation to read can be substantially increased by emphasizing the pleasure of reading through personal ownership of books.

When stocking your classroom library do not overlook other sources of printed media such as pamphlets, magazines, and newspapers. Although comic books are still controversial, they can sometimes be used to attract the attention of reluctant readers. Paperback books containing cartoons, such as Schulz's "Peanuts" series, can often serve a similar purpose. Once children begin the habit of reading, they can be encouraged to undertake more substantive reading. The classroom library might also contain periodicals such as *Children's Digest, Highlights for Children, Jack and Jill, Boy's Life, National Geographic World, Cricket, Kids,* and *Child Life,* as well as copies of the daily newspaper.

It is also important to create an attractive physical environment in the classroom that encourages the development of reading habits. The classroom library collection should be housed in a prominent location in the "reading corner" or "language arts center." A carpet, some plants, a few lamps, and comfortable seating can make the classroom library more inviting to children. Furnishing the reading corner can be a real adventure. If no permanent shelving is available in the classroom, shelves can be made from bricks and boards, or from sturdy cardboard boxes covered with contact paper (such as liquor cartons). Revolving book racks of the type drugstores often use to display paperback books are particularly useful and can sometimes be obtained free of charge if you are willing to haul them away. Teachers who are particularly skillful at "scrounging" materials for their classrooms have found that an old bathtub filled with pillows, a refrigerator carton with one side cut out, or an industrial-type cardboard drum with a hole cut in its side will attract children to the reading corner. If extra tables and chairs are needed for the reading corner, they can be secured free of charge. Large telephone cable spools make particularly sturdy tables, while seating can be made from large potato chip cans padded on top and attractively painted. Also, do not overlook the local Salvation Army, Goodwill Industries, and used furniture stores as a source of low-cost furnishings.

Providing Time to Read and Share Books   While the physical environment is important, even an attractively designed language arts center and a wide variety of reading material in the classroom will not accomplish the purpose of developing reading habits if there is no time for children to read and to share books with one another. Opportunities for sustained silent reading of self-selected materials must be built into the classroom schedule so that reading does not become merely something for children to do when they have finished their "work." At least as much time should be devoted to applying reading skills through independent reading as is devoted to the development of those skills through direct instruction. Regardless of what specific instructional program or approach is used to develop reading skills, independent reading within the classroom serves as a necessary and logical application of those skills.

Many of the features of the so-called "individualized approach" to reading instruction can be incorporated into any classroom reading program. In fact, many skillful teachers have successfully built their entire reading instructional program around self-selection of reading materials and sustained silent reading—both of which are associated with the individualized approach. This approach is based on the assumption that children's motivation to read, and their motivation to improve their skill in reading, can be increased if they select their own reading material.[1] In theory, the operation of an individualized reading program is rather straightforward, although in practice the successful operation of such a program requires considerable professional expertise as well as a working knowledge of the developmental aspects of the reading process.

As many variations of the individualized approach exist as there are teachers using it. Basically, however, many teachers who use this approach schedule most of the reading instructional period for children to read self-selected materials silently. If children appear to need guidance or if they ask for specific suggestions of what to read, the teacher helps them select a book. While children are reading silently the teacher is free to hold individual conferences or conduct ad hoc skill development sessions with a small group of children as the need arises. Frequently in such programs children maintain their own "word banks," which contain new words they have selected from their reading. These individual word banks also serve as a basis for vocabulary development and word analysis exercises, which are conducted on an individual basis or with a small group.

Another significant feature of an individualized reading program—and one that should also be included in every elementary school reading program—is the "sharing" or "celebrating" which children engage in after they finish reading a book. Although such activities often carry the somewhat negative connotation of "book reports," there is no reason why the sharing of books should be limited to the standard oral or written reports. There are many creative ways in which children can share the books they have read. For example, they can make puppets; use flannel board figures to dramatize a story; create a colorful mural, collage, or mobile; make a poster or write a television commercial to advertise a book; produce a play based on the book; write book reviews for the school newspaper; or construct a diorama.

Other interesting means of sharing books include films, filmstrips, and videotapes. Scenes from a book, for example, can be dramatized or reconstructed using animation techniques, then recorded by children on "Super 8" film or videotape for later viewing. Filmstrips can be produced by drawing directly on exposed 35 mm film with felt pens, or they can be produced photographically with a half-frame 35mm camera by shooting all frames horizontally and having the film developed as a continuous roll. "U-make-it" kits are also commercially available for producing filmstrips. Such multi-media methods of sharing are not always prohibitively expensive; it is surprising how

---

[1]For a more detailed description of individualized reading programs see: Veatch, 1978; Duker, 1969; Hunt, 1967; and Aukerman, 1971. See also Chapter 8 in this text.

inexpensively filmstrips, films, and videotapes can be produced and how much enthusiasm they generate among children.

In addition to the suggestions listed above, Jensen (1956) and Williams (1969) have listed many other creative means of sharing books.

To help children decide upon the best means to interest other children in the books they have read, the teacher may suggest several possible ways and discuss with them how and when each might be used. Several different means might be suggested during one period of time, and other means suggested later. As children gain experience with various methods, they can devise their own techniques to generate interest in the books they have read. They need only be reminded that their mission is to "sell" the book to their classmates.

Time must be scheduled not only for reading books, but for sharing books as well. Ideally, much of this sharing will be spontaneous and ongoing, although it is sometimes necessary to set aside specific time periods for sharing activities. The teacher who is able to make reading and sharing of books a naturally occurring part of classroom activities will find that time spent in this way pays off in the development of reading attitudes and interests.

Encouraging Children to Read   The best advice for teachers who want to foster the development of children's reading habits is to direct their professional efforts toward *inspiring* rather than requiring. Although requiring students to read a given number of books may seem justifiable, there is considerable evidence that coercing children to "read for enjoyment" may actually be detrimental to their development of purposeful and personally constructive reading habits.

Certainly teachers can and should provide children with much external motivation to read by employing the strategies described in this chapter. Modeling good reading habits, exposing children to a variety of literature, making a wide range of reading matter available within the classroom, and providing time within the school day to read and share books are highly recommended practices. If creatively applied by the teacher, all of these strategies can be used successfully to encourage and inspire children to read independently. The use of competition among students to encourage independent reading is not, however, recommended.

Teachers have sometimes attempted to use competition among individuals as a form of external motivation. While competition may serve a useful function in some classroom activities, its use to encourage independent reading is of questionable long-range value. Because some children have been conditioned by prior experiences to compete fiercely with their peers, they may be inclined to try to read more books than other children in order to gain recognition. This is especially true if such competition continues to be encouraged by the teacher.

The teacher should discourage competition if he discovers that children are merely going through the motions of reading a large number of books for competition's sake alone. For example, rather than placing stars on a chart to indicate the number of books each child has read, it is preferable to focus upon the reading accomplishments of the entire class. This could be done by making a chart entitled *Books We Have Read,* or by making the head of a "bookworm" which is placed on a colorful bulletin board under the caption

Help Me Grow by Reading. The children add body segments to the bookworm on which are printed the titles and authors of books they have read.

Care must be taken to see that independent reading and sharing activities within the classroom do not stress quantity over quality. Keep in mind that there is nothing sacred about a child completing a book he has begun to read. It is surprising how many adults are inclined to insist that children finish a book they have started, when they themselves have often begun reading a book, and, after reading a few chapters, have put it aside because it failed to hold their interest. Certainly children should be afforded this same privilege. They should also be allowed to reread the same book several times if they wish, particularly if the book is one that might provide new insights with each subsequent reading.

HELPING CHILDREN LEARN WHY TO READ

Within the context of the elementary school, teachers can provide much external motivation to encourage children to read independently. However, only by replacing such external motivation with internal motivation—that is, by helping children learn why to read—can teachers develop purposeful and personally constructive reading habits in their students.

Learning why to read is primarily a matter of discovering for one's self the many purposes of reading in relation to one's own personal needs and value system. Helping children make this discovery is, of course, not something which can be accomplished in three easy steps; nor can it be accomplished by simply telling children why other people read. Each child must make this personal discovery independently.

For a child, learning the varied purposes of reading begins early in life with the first exposure to the medium of print. Gradually, the preschool child who is exposed to printed media by being read to, or through television programs such as "Sesame Street" and "Electric Company," realizes that books and other printed media contain meaning-bearing symbols that represent speech and that are arranged in an order that conveys information and/or enjoyment. In addition, most children see persons significant to them engaged in the act of reading. Whether that person is reading a newspaper, a magazine, a book, a recipe, or the *TV Guide,* through observation the child begins to form concepts of why people read. For this reason, it is extremely important for children to be exposed to adults and peers who read in a variety of situations.

Children who have not seen people read, or whom no one has read to, may be totally unaware of the many purposes and applications for reading. Opportunities should be provided throughout the elementary grades for them to develop their own purposes for reading. This can be done partially through discussions with individual children or small groups where the content of the discussion focuses directly on the various purposes for reading. Such discussions might center around the pleasurable aspects of reading as a potentially rewarding use of leisure time and the applications of reading for the acquisition of new knowledge and understanding.

In order for discussions of the purposes of reading to be most productive, they must be related to the circumstances of the children's lives. Teachers sometimes tend to refer rather abstractly to future applications of reading such as, "When you grow up you will need to read because . . ." Although such references are undoubtedly made with good intentions, they are often difficult for young children to appreciate fully. Future oriented statements of this type also tend to convey the message that adulthood is the only time in one's life when reading is important. While education is viewed by some as *preparation for life,* it must be remembered that children are living *now* and that they have a whole range of personal needs and interests to which reading can be related. Children who are fortunate enough to have teachers who help them discover the ways in which their reading skill can be applied to fulfill their current needs and interests are much more likely to learn why to read.

In addition to promoting discussions of the purposes of reading, the teacher must structure classroom activities in which children will turn naturally to reading as a source of information and enjoyment. The teacher's assumption of the role of a "stimulator for reading" and the accessibility of reading material within the classroom are particularly significant factors in building the kind of classroom climate in which children turn spontaneously to reading.

When the teacher assumes this role and when reading materials are readily available, many opportunities can be found within the school day to get children interested in reading and thereby help them discover for themselves why to read. Teachers who effectively stimulate children to read tend to make frequent and spontaneous references to reading such as the following: "Hey! Speaking of that, did you read that new book we just got in our classroom library?" or "Have you checked some of the reference books we have to find some information that would help you with your project?" or, "Here's a book you might be interested in reading. Why don't you take a look at it and see if you think it might be helpful."

When children continually meet the right book at the right time, they usually have no difficulty discovering the relevance of reading to their lives— that is, learning why to read. Helping to arrange such meetings through the creative application of the strategies suggested in this chapter is what the teacher's role as a stimulator of interest in reading is all about.

Suggested Activities

1 Design an interest inventory for a specific individual or group of elementary school children. Administer the inventory and summarize the results. Where possible, suggest specific selections to be read to the group and list specific books that you think may be interesting to specific individuals.

2 Design an attitudes survey that takes into account the child's experience with reading and books, factors within his home environment, and his television viewing habits.

3 Design a reading corner or language arts center for an elementary school classroom. List the title and author of books you would like to include in the classroom library; list other reading and writing materials; describe how you will organize your classroom schedule to encourage use of the center; and draw a sketch or floor plan that illustrates the physical arrangement of the center.

4 Outline a language-arts program component that is designed to develop reading attitudes, interests, and habits. Include descriptions of specific

activities as well as statements pertaining to the structuring of the "classroom climate for reading."

5 Arrange to read a story or poem to a group of elementary school children. With the aid of the teacher, decide upon an appropriate selection and plan and conduct an introductory and follow-up discussion of the selection with the children.

6 Visit the children's room of the local public library. Examine circulation records or consult with the children's librarian to develop a list of the most frequently read titles.

7 Examine some of the sources listed under *Aids for Selecting Children's Books*. Make a tentative list of books that you feel would be appropriate to be read to or by children at a given grade level.

8 Read a number of children's books with which you would like to become familiar. Write a brief summary of the books including title, author, illustrator, publisher, estimated reading level, plot summary, suggested uses for content area instruction, concepts developed, and a statement about possible bibliotherapeutic value of the book. Type the summaries (one-half page each) on duplicating masters so that multiple copies can be reproduced and shared with other class members.

9 Begin a file of poems for special occasions such as holidays, rainy days, the first snowfall, and seasons. A good sourcebook is *Poetry for Holidays,* edited by Nancy Larrick (Champaign, Ill.: Garrard Publishing Co., 1966).

10 Write to the Reading Is Fundamental Program (c/o Smithsonian Institution, Washington, D.C. 20560) to request program guides and book lists. Investigate the procedures for initiating a RIF project in your local area.

SUMMARY

The information and enjoyment derived through reading can make a valuable contribution to the continual process of learning and personal growth which takes place throughout an individual's lifetime. Reading can help people learn more about themselves and their world, and can help them enlarge and clarify their own experiences. Whether people use the reading skill they have developed to the fullest extent in this learning and growth process will depend upon the degree to which they have discovered the value of reading. One of the primary responsibilities of a teacher is to help children make this discovery.

If we expect children to become "readers"—people who can read and *do* read because they have discovered the value of reading—we must begin when they are in elementary school to help them understand what reading can do for them. This cannot be accomplished simply by teaching children how to read. Thousands of adults know how to read but seldom do so for other than routine, functional purposes. What is needed is to place the development of reading habits in its proper perspective as the most important goal for reading instruction. We must abandon any reading instructional practices that do not lead toward this goal, and we must adopt new practices that will help us attain the goal more effectively for all the children we teach. The benefits to society and to individuals of achieving this goal are numerous; the consequences of failing to attain it are nothing short of tragic.

Aids for Selecting Children's Books*

American Library Association. *Books for Children 1971–1972*. Chicago: The American Library Association, 1973. (Original edition 1960–1965; annual supplements published yearly.)

Arbuthnot, May Hill. *Children and Books*. 4th ed. Chicago: Scott Foresman, 1972.

Baker, Augusta. *The Black Experience in Children's Books*. New York: The New York Public Library, 1971.

Bauer, Caroline Feller. *Handbook for Storytellers*. Chicago: American Library Association, 1977.

Best Books for Children. New York: R. R. Bowker (annual publication).

Bowles, Catherine, ed. *Good and Inexpensive Books for Children*. Washington, D.C.: Association for Childhood Education International, 1972.

Catterson, Jane, ed. *Children and Literature*. Newark, Del.: International Reading Association, 1970.

Chambers, Aidan. *Introducing Books to Children*. London: Heinemann Educational Books, 1977.

Childhood Study Association of America. *Books of the Year for Children*. New York: Childhood Study Association of America (annual publication).

Children's Book Council, *Children's Books: Awards and Prizes*. New York: Children's Book Council, 1973.

Dreyer, Sharon Spredemann. *The Bookfinder. A Guide to Children's Literature About the Needs and Problems of Youth Aged 2–15*. Circle Pines, Minnesota: American Guidance Service, Ind., 1977.

Eastland, Patricia Ann. "Read-Aloud Stories in the Primary Literature Program." In *Individualizing Reading Instruction, A Reader*, edited by Larry Harris and Carl B. Smith. Chicago: Holt, Rinehart and Winston, 1972.

Favat, Andre F. *Child and Tale: The Origins of Interest*. No. 19 in a series of research reports sponsored by the NCTE Committee on Research. Urbana, Illinois, National Council of Teachers of English, 1977.

Feaver, William. *When We Were Young*. New York: Holt, Rinehart, and Winston, 1977.

Gillespie, John T., and Lembo, Diana L. *Introducing Books: A Guide for the Middle Grades*. New York: R. R. Bowker Co., 1970.

Gillespie, Margaret C. and Conner, John W. *Creative Growth Through Literature for Children and Adolescents*. Columbus, Ohio, Charles E. Merrill Publishing Co., 1975.

Griffin, Louise. *Multi-Ethnic Books for Young Children*. Washington, D.C.: ERIC-NAEYC Publication in Early Childhood Education, National Association for the Education of Young Children, 1970.

Haviland, Virginia. *Children's Books*. Washington, D.C.: Library of Congress, 1973.

Hays, Ruth M. *The Black Experience: Books for Young Children*. Boston: Boston Public Library, 1971.

Hemsig, Esther D. *Good and Inexpensive Books for Children*. Washington, D.C.: Association for Childhood Education International, 1972.

Howell, Lillian. *A Book of Children's Literature*. New York: Holt, Rinehart, and Winston, Inc., Third Edition, 1966.

Huck, Charlotte S., *Children's Literature in the Elementary School*. New York: Holt, Rinehart, and Winston, 1976.

Kujoth, Jean Spealman. *Best Selling Children's Books*. Metuchen, N.J.: The Scarecrow Press, 1973.

Ladley, Winifred C. *Sources of Good Books and Magazines for Children*. Newark, Del.: International Reading Association, 1970 (annotated bibliography).

Lukens, Rebecca J. *A Critical Handbook of Children's Literature*. Glenview, Illinois: Scott Foresman and Company, 1976.

Martignoni, Margaret E. *The Illustrated Treasury of Children's Literature*. New York: Grosset and Dunlop, 1955.

---

*Updated and compiled by Robert Cowan.

McDonough, Irma. *Canadian Books for Children (Livres Canadiens pour Enfants).* Toronto: University of Toronto Press, 1976.

Perkins, Flossie L. *Book and Non-Book Media: Annotated Guide to Selection Aids for Educational Materials.* Urbana, Ill.: National Council of Teachers of English, 1972.

Riggs, Corrine W., comp. *Bibliotherapy.* Newark, Del.: International Reading Association, 1971 (annotated bibliography).

Rollins, Charlemae, ed. *We Build Together: A Reader's Guide to Negro Life and Literature for Elementary and High School Use.* Champaign, Ill.: National Council of Teachers of English, 1967.

Root, Sheldon L., Jr., ed. *Adventuring with Books.* 2nd ed. New York: Scholastic Magazines, Citation Press, 1973.

Rudmann, Masha Kabakow. *Children's Literature, An Issues Approach.* Lexington, Massachusetts: D. C. Heath and Co., 1976.

Sadker, Myra Pollack, and Sadker, David Miller. *Now Upon a Time. A Contemporary View of Children's Literature.* New York: Harper and Row, 1977.

Shor, Rachel, and Fidel, Estelle A., eds. *Children's Catalog.* 11th ed. New York: H. W. Wilson Co., 1966 (annual supplements, 1967–1974).

Simmons, Beatrice, Ed. *Paperback Books for Children.* New York: American Association of School Librarians, Citation Press, 1972.

Smithsonian Institution. *Reading Is FUN-damental Booklist.* Washington, D.C.: Smithsonian Institution, 1973.

Smithsonian Institution. *RIF's Guide to Book Selection.* Washington, D.C.: Smithsonian Institution, 1971 (ERIC: ED 062095).

Smollar, Eleanor, ed. *Guide to Book Selection.* Washington, D.C.: Reading Is Fundamental Program, 1970.

Spache, George D., *Good Reading for Poor Readers.* Champaign, Ill.: Garrard Publishing Co., 1974.

Stensland, Anna Lee. *Literature by and about the American Indian—An Annotated Bibliography for Junior and Senior High School Students.* Urbana, Ill.: National Council of Teachers of English, 1973.

Sunderlin, Sylvia, ed. *Bibliography of Books for Children.* 1970 Edition. Washington, D.C.: Association for Childhood Education International, 1971.

Sutherland, Zena and Arbuthnot, May Hill. *Children and Books.* Fifth Edition. Chicago: Scott Foresman and Company, 1977.

Sutherland, Zena, ed. *The Best in Children's Books: The University of Chicago Guide to Children's Literature, 1966–1972.* Chicago: University of Chicago Press, 1973.

Tanyzer, Harold, and Karl, Jean. *Reading, Children's Books and Our Pluralistic Society.* Newark, Del.: International Reading Association, 1972.

Whitehead, Robert. *Children's Literature: Strategies of Teaching.* Englewood Cliffs, New Jersey: Prentice Hall, Inc., 1968.

Williams, Frank E. "Media Resource Book—A Total Creativity Program for Individualizing and Humanizing the Learning Process." Vol. 4, April 1973. (ERIC: ED 070 244).

REFERENCES

Aukerman, Robert C. "The Individualized Reading Approach." In *Approaches to Beginning Reading.* New York: John Wiley and Sons, 1971, pp. 383–389.

Bamberger, R. *Promoting the Reading Habit.* Paris, France: UNESCO Press, 1975.

Beta Upsilon Chapter of Pi Lambda Theta. "Children's Reading Interests Classified by Age Levels." *The Reading Teacher* 27 (April 1974): 694–700.

Bloom, Benjamin S. *Stability and Change in Human Characteristics.* New York: John Wiley and Sons, 1964.

Campbell, Laurence R. "Teenagers' Media Habits." ERIC: ED 033 955, September 1969.

Cook, V. J., and J. D. Nolan. *Children's Interests and Preferences in Reading Materials.* University of Nebraska and Columbia University. Unpublished manuscript, 1976.

Dejardins, Mary. "Reading and Viewing: A Survey." *School Libraries* 21 (Spring 1972): 26–30.

Duker, Sam, ed. *Individualized Reading: Readings.* Metuchen, N.J.: Scarecrow Press, 1969.

Dulin, Kenneth L., and Chester, Robert D. "A Validation Study of the Estes Attitude Scale." *Journal of Reading* 18 (October 1974): 56–59.

Durkin, Dolores. "Children Who Read Before

Grade 1: A Second Study." *The Elementary School Journal* 64 (December 1962): 143–148.

Ennis, Philip A. "Adult Book Reading in the U.S." National Opinion Research Center, University of Chicago, 1965 (ERIC: ED 010 754).

Ennis, Philip A. "Book Reading Audiences and the Mass Society." Paper delivered to American Sociological Assoc., Miami, Florida, August 1966 (ERIC: ED 014 402).

Estes, Thomas H. "Assessing Attitudes Toward Reading." Paper presented at International Reading Association Convention, Detroit, May 1972 (ERIC: ED 063 007).

Estes, Thomas H. "A Scale to Measure Attitudes Toward Reading." *Journal of Reading* 15 (November 1971): 135–138.

Estes, Thomas H., et. al. *Estes Attitude Scales: Elementary Form* (Experimental Version). Charlottesville, Virginia: Virginia Research Associates, Ltd., 1975.

Fader, Daniel N., et. al. *The New Hooked on Books* (Tenth Anniversary Edition). New York: Berkeley Medallion Books, 1976.

Feeley, Joan T. *Interest Patterns and Media Preferences of Boys and Girls in Grades Four and Five.* Unpublished doctoral dissertation, New York University, 1972.

Feeley, Joan T. "Television and Children's Reading." *Elementary English* 50 (January 1973): 141–148.

Fiddler, Jerry R. *The Standardization of a Questionnaire to Ascertain the Attitude Toward Reading of Sixth-Grade Pupils.* Unpublished doctoral dissertation, The State University of New York at Buffalo, 1973.

Hansen, Harlan S. "The Impact of the Home Literary Environment on Reading Attitudes." *Elementary English* 46 (January 1969): 17–24.

Hansen, Harlan S. "The Home Literary Environment—A Follow-Up Report." *Elementary English* 50 (January 1973): 97–98, 122.

Huck, Charlotte S. "Strategies for Improving Interest and Appreciation in Literature." In *Reaching Children and Young People Through Literature,* edited by Helen W. Painter. Newark, Del.: International Reading Association, 1971, pp. 37–45.

Huck, Charlotte S. "Strategies for Improving Interest and Appreciation in Literature." In A. Beery, T. C. Barrett, W. R. Powell (Eds.), *Elementary Reading Instruction: Selected Materials,* 2nd ed., Boston: Allyn & Bacon, 1974.

Hunt, Lyman C., ed. *The Individualized Reading Program.* Proceedings of the 11th Annual Convention, Vol. 2, pt. 3. Newark, Del.: International Reading Association, 1967.

Huus, Helen. "Interpreting Research in Children's Literature." In *Children, Books and Reading,* edited by Mildred Dawson. Perspectives in Reading No. 2. Newark, Del.: International Reading Association, 1964.

Jensen, Amy E. "Attracting Children to Books." *Elementary English* 33 (October 1956): 332–339.

Jung, Raymond. "Leisure in Three Cultures." *Elementary School Journal* 67 (March 1967): 285–295.

King, Ethel M. "Critical Appraisal of Research on Children's Reading Interests." In *Language Arts Concepts for Elementary School Teachers,* edited by Paul C. Burns et al. Itasca, Ill.: F. E. Peacock, 1972, pp. 258–271.

Krathwohl, David R. et al. *Taxonomy of Educational Objectives, Handbook II: The Affective Domain.* New York: David McKay Co., 1964.

Kujoth, Jean Spealman. *Best-Selling Children's Books.* Metuchen, N.J.: The Scarecrow Press, 1973.

Lamme, L. L. "Are Reading Habits and Abilities Related?" *Reading Teacher,* 30, 1976, 21–27.

Long, Barbara H., and Henderson, Edmund H. "Children's Use of Time: Some Personal and Social Correlations." 1970 (ERIC: ED 054 475).

Nelson, Richard C. "Children's Poetry Preferences." *Elementary English* 43 (March 1966): 247–251.

Peltola, Bette J. *A Study of the Indicated Literary Choices and Measured Literary Knowledge of Fourth and Sixth Grade Boys and Girls.* Unpublished doctoral dissertation, University of Minnesota, 1965.

Plessas, Gus, and Oakes, Clifton. "Pre-Reading Experiences of Selected Early Readers." *Reading Teacher* 17 (January 1964): 241–245.

Purves, Alan C., and Beach, Richard. *Literature and the Reader: Research in Response to Literature, Reading Interests, and the Teaching of Literature.* Urbana, Ill.: National Council of Teachers of English, 1972.

Rowell, C. G. "An Attitude Scale for

Reading." *The Reading Teacher* 25 (February 1972): 442–447.

San Diego County Department of Education. "An Inventory of Reading Attitude." In *Improving Reading Instruction, Monograph 4.* San Diego, California: San Diego County Department of Education, November 1961 (ERIC: ED 028 893).

Sharon, Amiel T. "Reading Activities of American Adults." Paper presented at meeting of American Educational Research Association, Chicago, Illinois, April 1972 (ERIC: ED 061 013).

Smithsonian Institution. *RIF's Guide to Developing a Program.* Washington, D.C.: Smithsonian Institution, 1972 (ERIC: ED 062 094).

Strickler, Darryl J. "Affective Considerations in Reading." *School Psychology Digest* (Winter 1978).

Strickler, Darryl J. "The Affective Component." In *Classroom Practice in Reading,* edited by Richard A. Earle. Newark, Del.: International Reading Association, 1977.

Strickler, Darryl J., and Gaither, Penny. "Reading Habits of Sixth Grade Students." Paper presented at annual meeting of Great Lakes Regional Council of the International Reading Association, Cincinnati, Ohio, (October 1978).

Sutton, M. "Readiness for Reading at Kindergarten." *Reading Teacher* 17 (January 1964): 234–240.

Trisman, Donald A. "Adult Readers: Activities and Goals." Paper presented at meeting of American Educational Research Association, Chicago, Illinois, April 1972 (ERIC: ED 061 024).

van der Brink, R. E. M. *Book Reading, Borrowing, and Buying Habits.* Eighteenth Congress, International Publishers Assoc., Amsterdam, The Netherlands, 1968 (ERIC: ED 059 736).

Veatch, Jeannette. *Reading in the Elementary School.* New York: The Ronald Press, 1978.

Weintraub, Samuel. "Children's Reading Interests." *Reading Teacher* 22 (April 1969): 655, 657, 659.

Williams, Lois E. *Independent Learning in the Elementary School Classroom.* Washington, D.C.: American Association of Elementary-Kindergarten-Nursery Educators, 1969.

Witty, Paul. "Studies of the Mass Media—1949–1965." *Science Education* 50 (1966): 119–126.

Witty, Paul, and Melis, Lloyd. "A 1964 Study of TV: Comparisons and Comments." *Elementary English* 42 (February 1965): 134–141.

Zimet, Sara F. "Children's Interest and Story Preferences: A Critical Review of the Literature." *Elementary School Journal* 67 (December 1966): 122–130.

INDEX